# Order within Anarchy

*Order within Anarchy* focuses on how the laws of war create strategic expectations about how states and their soldiers will act during war, which can help produce restraint. International law as a political institution helps to create such expectations by specifying how violence should be limited and clarifying which actors should comply with those limits. The success of the laws of war depends on three related factors: compliance between warring states, compliance between soldiers on the battlefield, and control of soldiers by their militaries. A statistical study of compliance of the laws of war during the twentieth century shows that joint ratification strengthens both compliance and reciprocity, that compliance varies across issues with the scope for individual violations, and that violations occur early in war. Close study of the treatment of prisoners of war during World Wars I and II demonstrates the difficulties posed by states' varied willingness to limit violence, a lack of clarity about what restraint means, and the practical problems of restraint on the battlefield.

James D. Morrow is A. F. K. Organski Collegiate Professor of World Politics and Research Professor at the Center for Political Studies, University of Michigan. He previously taught at the Graduate Institute of International Studies, Stanford University, the University of Rochester, and Michigan State University. He is the author of *Game Theory for Political Scientists*, co-author of *The Logic of Political Survival*, and author of more than sixty articles in refereed journals and other publications. He was president of the Peace Science Society (International) in 2008–2009. Morrow received the Karl Deutsch Award from the International Studies Association in 1994 and has been a National Fellow at the Hoover Institution and an Advanced Research Fellow in Foreign Policy Studies for the Social Science Research Council.

# Order within Anarchy

## The Laws of War as an International Institution

**JAMES D. MORROW**
*University of Michigan*

CAMBRIDGE
UNIVERSITY PRESS

# CAMBRIDGE
## UNIVERSITY PRESS

32 Avenue of the Americas, New York, NY 10013-2473, USA

Cambridge University Press is part of the University of Cambridge.

It furthers the University's mission by disseminating knowledge in the pursuit of education, learning, and research at the highest international levels of excellence.

www.cambridge.org
Information on this title: www.cambridge.org/9781107626775

© James D. Morrow 2014

First published 2014

Printed in the United States of America

*A catalog record for this publication is available from the British Library.*

*Library of Congress Cataloging in Publication data*
Morrow, James D., 1957– author.
Order within anarchy : the laws of war as an international
institution / James D. Morrow, University of Michigan.
    pages   cm
Includes bibliographical references and index.
ISBN 978-1-107-04896-6 (hardback) – ISBN 978-1-107-62677-5 (paperback)
1. War (International law)   I. Title.
KZ6385.M67   2014
341.6–dc23       2013048952

ISBN 978-1-107-04896-6 Hardback
ISBN 978-1-107-62677-5 Paperback

# Contents

# Tables

# Figures

# Acknowledgments

Like whales, elephants, and asses, this book has had a long gestation period. I began thinking about the laws of war in the summer of 1995, triggered by the fortieth anniversary of the atomic bombings of Japan. Since that time, I have read and worked on and off on the project that led to this book. I hope the reader will find that the long gestation has made this book a whale of a book, rather than elephantine or asinine.

I have been generously supported by four great institutions while I worked on this project. I began work on it at the Hoover Institution where I was a Senior Research Fellow. John Raisian, the Director of the Hoover Institution, provided me with both a supportive environment and resources to begin this project. He also gave me the opportunity to return during summer fellowships after I left Hoover to become a professor at the University of Michigan; I used these months of splendid isolation at Hoover to write several draft chapters of this book. After arriving at Michigan, the Center for Political Studies has been my research home. The support of the Center staff was invaluable in securing funding to support the data collection used in Chapter 4. The National Science Foundation supported data collection and analysis and the formal model under grant SES-0111787. The Graduate Institute of International Studies in Geneva provided me with a home during my sabbatical leave when I completed the first full draft of most chapters. None of these institutions bears any responsibility for the arguments I make here.

This project has been helped greatly by the many talks I have given from it over its long period of gestation. I would like to thank conference and seminar participants at the University of Arizona, Boalt Law School at the University of California at Berkeley, the University of California at Davis, the University of California at Los Angeles, the University of California at San Diego, the University of Chicago Law School, the PIPES seminar at the University of Chicago, Emory University, George Washington University, the Graduate

Institute of International Studies, the Harvard Law School, the Hoover Institution, the University of Konstanz, the University of Michigan, University of Michigan Law School, New York University, New York University Law School, Northwestern University, the University of Pennsylvania, Princeton University, Rice University, the University of Sao Paolo, the Center for International Security and Cooperation and the Department of Political Science at Stanford University, the University of Virginia, and the Center for Comparative and International Studies in Zurich for their many incisive and helpful comments. All errors that remain are mine alone.

Many colleagues have also been generous with their comments as I worked on this project. Hyeran Jo provided valuable comments on the draft manuscript. Beth Simmons at Harvard and Allan Dafoe at Yale both taught the manuscript in their graduate seminars during the winter of 2013, and I thank them and their students for their comments and reactions. The students in my graduate seminar on war in the same semester also read and commented on the manuscript. Anna Gryzmala-Busse organized a book workshop including Jenna Bednar, Skip Lupia, and George Tsebelis; their comments and advice immensely improved the book. Jenna was also kind enough to provide detailed comments on the manuscript. Hyeran Jo also gave me useful comments on the project at the final rewriting.

Data collection is not a solitary job. A number of research assistants at the University of Michigan aided the process. Through the Undergraduate Research Opportunity Program at Michigan, Alex Geralds, Fenlene Hsu, Jim Huyhn, Heath Ranger, and Mike Wakeley all contributed to the collection of information used in the coding. Graduate students Sarah Croco, Tom Flores, Jiyun Kim, Shanna Kirschner, Rich Maher, and Dominick Wright helped complete the collection and develop the coding rules from the treaties. Hyeran Jo and I did the coding together from the collected information, and I thank her for keeping me honest with her attention to detail and consistency in that thankless task.

I would like to thank my editor at Cambridge, Robert Dreesen. Robert immediately saw the impact of the project and pursued it.

I dedicate this book to my wife Karen McKinney for her love and support over the years. Fortunately for us, we need no laws of love.

# 1

# Introduction

During the night of June 19, 1945, aircraft from the U.S. Eighth Air Force conducted an incendiary bombing raid on the city of Fukuoka, Japan. The bombing destroyed 22 percent of the buildings in the city of 323,000.

At noon on August 15, 1945, Emperor Hirohito of Japan broadcast to his
nation that Japan would surrender to the combined forces of the Allied Powers.
After listening to the broadcast, a group of Japanese officers at Fukuoka led
by Colonel Yoshinao Sato, Chief of the Intelligence and Air Defense Sections
of the Western Army headquarters, took seventeen captured U.S. airmen to
Aburayama outside of the city. There they executed the airmen with blows to the
airmen's necks using their samurai swords. First Lieutenant Hiroji Nakayama,
who was accompanied by a young lady from the Intelligence Section, made
certain that he and the other Japanese did not decapitate their victims as such
was considered insulting to the victims in Japanese tradition. They acted under
the provisions of Japan's Enemy Airmen Act of 1942, which classified air raids
on Japan as violations of international law punishable by the death penalty or
prison terms of at least ten years. This Act sought "to prevent further [air] raids
[on Japan] by giving stern disposition to enemy airmen, thereby inculcating
fear in American mothers and possibly resulting in an anti-war movement in
the United States (Francis 1997, 480)."

On December 29, 1948, Colonel Sato and twenty-four other Japanese officers were found guilty of the murder of these prisoners of war and others; seven
other defendants were acquitted. Sato and eight other officers were sentenced
to death by the Commission. Upon review, General Douglas MacArthur com-
muted the death sentences on July 9, 1950, instead sentencing Sato to "hard
labor for the term of his natural life."[1]

---

[1] Francis (1997) discusses this case and related executions in detail. I have also drawn on the trial
summaries available at the U.S. Archives.

1

Atrocities breed outrage, charges of war crimes, and revenge. How can
outrage at wartime atrocities be directed into a system of law that controls
such actions? During the twentieth century, states developed international
humanitarian law to regulate conduct during wartime. The record of success of such treaties is mixed. The chemical weapons treaties have generally been followed, limitations on targeting civilians have often failed, and
regulations for the handling of prisoners of war has worked in some cases
but not others. Why have some of the laws of war succeeded and others
failed?

This question leads directly to the more general question of how international law operates. States have created a large body of international law to
regulate their interactions. This legalization of international affairs is a distinctive property of the international system in the twentieth century. As this body
of law expands, understanding how it operates is critical for understanding
international politics in the contemporary world.

These questions of international law also address one of the great questions of international relations: does the normative structure of the international system matter? Principles of right and wrong have always been applied
to international politics. The existence of such standards, however, does
not mean that they have any real impact on behavior. Scholars of international relations have debated this question throughout the twentieth century,
with implications for the international politics of their times. The realists
and idealists faced off during the interwar period (Carr 1946); the British
School (e.g., Bull 1977) challenged the dominance of American realism
(e.g., Morgenthau 1978) after the Second World War; now the constructivists (e.g., Wendt 1999) oppose the neorealists (e.g., Waltz 1979). The pro-
liferation of "isms" in international relations theory demonstrates the lack
of consensus on the role and effect of normative standards. If these norms
matter, the world can be changed through moral force; if not, the law of the
jungle rules.

In the broadest scope, I also address a profound question about politics.
International law works only to the extent that the parties can enforce its provisions and procedures on themselves. Political institutions, including international law, must be self-enforcing. Successful political institutions are machines
that run on their own. If effective political institutions are necessary to protect
the values we hold most dear, how can such institutions induce the parties to
protect those values?

This is an ambitious list of questions, and I do not purport to give final
answers to any of them. I do hope, however, that this book will help the reader
understand better why the laws of war have restrained violence during war in
some situations but not in others, how international law works, what the role
of norms in international politics is, and how political institutions are self-
enforcing.

## LAW FOSTERS STRATEGIC EXPECTATIONS

For the law of war to limit violence during war, states and their soldiers must follow its prescripts. Consider two stories from World War II, one of law limiting violence and the other not:

> [A] member of a patrol along the river Roer was wounded and left lying helpless on the bank in advance of American lines. "Pulling on his Red Cross bib, Doc stood in the open to make sure the Germans spotted him. He then walked slowly toward the river." The medic, while able to bandage the soldier's wound and ease his pain with morphine, realized that he would be unable to carry him to safety, so he returned alone, retrieved a wheelbarrow, and started back. "Men yelled across the river to the Germans, 'Okay, hold it, hold it,' and the Germans hollered back, 'Okay.'..." Though the rescue "proceeded in agonizingly slow motion" and one German rifleman continued to fire, Doc was finally able to propel his makeshift ambulance the quarter of a mile to safety. "As he finally pushed the wheelbarrow into an alley behind a ruined house ... a cheer went up from every man in K Company"(Linderman 1997, 103).

> Marine officer Frank Hough described the Japanese soldier in the South Pacific as one who "would as soon kill a chaplain administering the last rites to the dying as he would an active enemy. Nothing delighted him more than killing our wounded lying helpless between the lines, unless it was killing the doctors and hospital corpsmen who went out to attend them." That medics were not armed – "not at the beginning, anyway" – was important, thought Hough, because it *drew* the Japanese to attack them. Aidman Robert Thobaben, when accompanying patrols on Peleliu, carried a carbine: "I never did have a red cross painted on my helmet. I thought ... that ... was insane. It ... was only a target"(Linderman 1997, 149, italics in original).

In the first story, Doc is willing to advance out from cover because he expected that the Germans would not shoot at him once they recognized he was a medic seeking to treat a wounded man. In the second story, Aidman Thobaben did not seek the protection of the symbol of the Red Cross because he expected that the Japanese would not respect the legal protections of the latter and so needed to arm himself in violation of the law of war. War creates the grim logic of kill-or-be-killed; restraining that logic requires expectations that others will observe the law. When soldiers believe that grim logic will not be restrained, they will take measures to preserve themselves, including committing their own violations as Aidman Thobaben did.

Strategic expectations – what state leaders and soldiers think the other side will do – are key to producing a restrained battlefield. These expectations determine whether soldiers believe they will receive the protection of the law and so take the risk of acting in accord with the law themselves. They determine whether state leaders adopt policies that support or breach the law. Social life is structured by such strategic expectations, even under the chaotic conditions of war.

Creating and sustaining expectations of restraint requires meeting six challenges. First, soldiers on both sides need to recognize which people and sites receive protection under the law. In the cases quoted earlier, medics are supposed to be inviolate because of their roles in aiding the wounded, and the Red Cross serves as the symbol so that both sides know which people and sites receive that protection. Without the public sign of the Red Cross and the shared understanding that people and sites displaying it should not be attacked, medics would find their job of tending to the wounded on the battlefield much harder, as was the case in the second example.

Second, warring states and their soldiers need to understand exactly how war will be limited, because many systems of limits are possible. The law of war obligates medics to treat enemy wounded as well as their own. German medics during World War II sometimes killed their own wounded to end the suffering of a dying man (Linderman 1997, 108). How would U.S. soldiers, whose medics did not practice mercy killing, view German medics killing a wounded U.S. soldier in their care? In the absence of agreement on what limits apply, one side could believe the other has violated limits on violence when the latter thought it was observing those limits.

Third, novel situations may arise, and the parties need to be able to work through what restraint means in those situations. Failure to do so can lead to escalation to unrestricted violence by both sides. During World War I, Germany launched the first major attack using chemical weapons by releasing them from cylinders, in part because that means of delivery was not explicitly banned in the Hague Conventions as "projectiles the sole object of which is the diffusion of asphyxiating or deleterious gases" were (Roberts and Guelff 2000, 60). Within eighteen months, Germany, Britain, and France were all using gas shells – a clear violation.

Fourth, some states do not wish for violence to be limited during war. In the second story quoted earlier, Japanese treatment of medics and the wounded resulted from training in the Japanese military that saw the wounded as an impediment to fighting and so not worthy of protection. Expectations among U.S. servicemen changed with their experience of fighting the Japanese.

Fifth, not all soldiers will follow the law even if their military wants them to. One German continued to fire his rifle during the spontaneous cease-fire for Doc to evacuate the wounded soldier. These violations by individuals can corrode expectations of restraint and force soldiers to abandon their legal responsibilities to protect themselves.

Sixth, these expectations need to be shared across both states and their armies. All need to know what the rules are and when they apply. They also need to know that they are expected to follow them and that they can expect the other side to follow them as well. Finally, they need to know that both militaries will try to discipline those soldiers that commit violations on their own.

International law fosters and sustains these strategic expectations by addressing the six challenges. Treaties specify how violence during war should be restrained by creating protected classes of people and sites, how they should be identified, and what protections they receive. Principles of restraint undergird treaty law, which allows the parties to address novel situations. Public acceptance of treaties through ratification screens out those parties that will not respect limits on violence during war. Military training instructs soldiers in their rights and responsibilities under the law; military discipline enforces those responsibilities.

Expectations of restraint are difficult both to form and to sustain in the face of the violence of war. Although Doc expected the Germans not to fire on him, he made sure they recognized what he was doing, and both sides confirmed that they would not fire while he evacuated the wounded man. Even with those reassurances, one German continued to fire. Some soldiers in even the best disciplined armies violate the laws of war, and those violations can corrode expectations of restraint. Uncertainty about whether the other side is committed to restraint opens room for suspicion of their intent. International law helps to restrain violence by fostering expectations, but it does not guarantee that everyone will follow its precepts in every situation.

## SELF-ENFORCING INSTITUTIONS AND INTERNATIONAL LAW

For international law to succeed at creating shared expectations of restraint during war, it must be self-enforcing. International law is a political institution and, as such, must meet the same conditions that allow political actors to enforce institutions on one another, thereby bringing order to political life. Political institutions serve as the "rules of the game" for political actors (North 1990). They embody the collection of considerations beyond the control of an individual – norms, organizations, and formal processes and rules – that impinge on his or her choice of action. Political action depends both on what an actor wants to accomplish and the institutional setting that he or she faces. Institutions describe the rules that actors are to follow and the roles that the actors fill, and prescribe the consequences if an actor fails to follow the rules. Although this view of institutions has primarily been applied to domestic politics, it also holds true for international institutions.

Political institutions are designed to make political life and economic exchange regular and predictable (North 1990). Actors may wish that one another will act in a particular way when they create an institution, but they will act in accord with the incentives that the institution produces. Because the actors themselves fill the roles in the institution, only they can make the institution work. The initial question faced by institutions is: Given that each actor will pursue his or her best interest within the incentives that the institution creates and the actions of others, what stable collections of behavior do those incentives produce? Successful institutions induce stable behavior and incentives that support that behavior. Unsuccessful institutions fail to provide the incentives needed to check defections from the prescribed order. Institutions do not directly cause outcomes or force actors to behave in accord with the order they prescribe; they influence how actors understand and pursue their interests, and so affect outcomes by changing how actors behave.

The value of institutions lies in their persistence. Actors, however, are free to change institutions at any time. Because institutions affect outcomes, some actors may always wish to change institutions. A successful institution must ward off these demands for change. Actors opposed to a change must have the ability to defend existing institutions for those institutions to persist. The second question faced by institutions is "Why do institutions persist given the demands to change them?"[2]

Drawing on game theory, we can think about political institutions as equilibria of some game (Schotter 1981; Shepsle 1986; Calvert 1994, 1995; Greif 2006). An equilibrium in game theory is a configuration of behavior in which no actor wishes to change his or her behavior given the actions of the other actors. Equilibria are patterns of behavior that can persist, making the concept of equilibrium a useful way to think about how political institutions persist and operate. Institutionalized behavior must be an equilibrium of the game underlying the social situation.

An equilibrium in game theory requires two things. First, the actors' behaviors are *mutual best replies*. No actor believes he can improve his position by changing his plan of action. Second, the actors share a *common conjecture* that one another will play according to the equilibrium. The shared understanding of a common conjecture is necessary for the players to understand that their equilibrium strategies are indeed the best actions for themselves. Because the outcomes of social situations depend on the possible choices of more than one actor, each needs some stable expectations about each other's actions to understand how to act in her own interest. Common conjectures assure that the actors form accurate expectations about what others will do. Political institutions require a shared understanding to allow the actors to anticipate one another's actions and then act within that institution. Without such an understanding, there is no reason to believe that the behavior will persist.

I elaborate this view by defining an institution to be *a constellation of equilibria that address related strategic problems* rather than an individual equilibrium.[3] The different but related strategic problems must all be addressed to create a stable institution. Each equilibrium depends on the others because each problem in isolation assumes an answer to the other problems. Different sets of actors play in each of these different but related games and so must take

---

[2] These two questions are those of institutional equilibrium and equilibrium institutions (Shepsle 1986).

[3] Tsebelis (1990) considers the similar idea of nested games, but his emphasis is on how the linked games change the payoffs of the players across them, leading them to make strategic choices that seem surprising within the context of any one game in isolation.

those other equilibria as given in the strategic settings they face. For example, an effective trial system of criminal law requires – at a minimum – addressing the related problems of conducting a trial as a contest between the prosecuting and defense attorneys, a political issue of disciplining prosecutors so they pursue only appropriate cases, the relationship between the defendant and his attorney to ensure proper representation, and the issue of providing judges with incentives and training to act on behalf of the law as opposed to other interests. Because each actor plays in only some of these games, he or she takes the equilibrium behavior in the others for granted. All the equilibria depend on one another; in some systems, trying to bribe the judge is the best defense strategy, whereas in others it would only hurt the interests of the defendant.

Abstract principles knit together the common conjectures of the equilibria within an institution. In the earlier example of criminal law, the abstract principles center on judging cases on the evidence using the appropriate laws. All of the problems concern ways in which a case might fail to be judged on its merits, such as if the defense attorney fails to mount a cogent defense of the accused. These principles explain why the actors should expect that others will act in accordance with the institution in the games in which they do not play. Will the judge rule on principle instead of prejudice? These principles, like the common conjectures, must also be shared across all actors. Additionally, they also aid the players in modifying the institution as conditions change.

International law helps actors develop the strategic expectations that parallel the common conjecture and establish the abstract principles that coordinate different equilibria underlying certain institutionalized behaviors in world politics. Although such a shared understanding can arise simply through a history of interactions, public negotiation and agreement on the principles of that shared understanding could help confirm both what the understanding is and who holds it. International law embodied in multilateral treaties negotiated as public documents and formally ratified by states helps to create shared expectations of how states and their agents will act. Treaty law aids states by helping them anticipate one another's behavior more fully.

A shared understanding alone is insufficient to ensure that the parties will comply with the principles embodied in that understanding. Actors still have to be willing to act in accordance with those principles. Here mutual best replies reenter the picture. Those shared understandings that do not produce a self-enforcing pattern of behavior will fail in practice. Not only do we need to know the legal specifics of international law, we also need to understand the motivations and incentives of the parties under that law. Law could fail under two conditions: (1) when a party explicitly rejects that law, signaling that it does not intend to comply with the law; or (2) when the law fails to induce the parties to comply with its provisions. Legal principles must be married to practical politics for international law to succeed.

The laws of war are the most dramatic example of this argument about political institutions and equilibrium. Because the parties are already at war, they have no recourse to a higher sanction to enforce legal obligations on one another. Laws of war can be effective in limiting violence during wartime when the warring states understand what the limits are and act to live within those limits. Additionally, the laws of war create obligations and rights for individual soldiers as well as states, because these laws address the related strategic problems of violence on the battlefield, the strategic competition between states at war, and how states control their soldiers as their agents. As discussed later, *when* states comply is a complicated question. The combination of shared understanding and restraint through self-interest can fail in many ways. This book seeks to illuminate those difficulties by examining the strategic logic of the laws of war and the historical record of their successes and failures in the wars of the twentieth century.

## INSTITUTIONS AND NORMS IN INTERNATIONAL RELATIONS THEORY AND INTERNATIONAL LAW

As mentioned earlier, scholars of international relations have long argued whether standards of right and wrong play a role in world politics. The current version of this long-running debate matches the neorealists and the constructivists. Both camps agree that international politics is an anarchy; actors cannot appeal to a higher authority to enforce agreements and resolve their conflicts. Neorealists argue that anarchy forces states to distrust one another and rely on their own capabilities to defend their interests. Calculations of power and interest trump principles of right and wrong. Constructivists contend that shared understandings shape international politics and allow states to transcend the effects of anarchy. In the memorable epigram of Alexander Wendt (1992), "anarchy is what states make of it."

Neorealists believe that the necessities of international competition compel states to act in the ways they do. The anarchic system means that a state's power alone is the ultimate guarantor of its continued existence. In some cases, threatened states may be aided by others who benefit by providing that aid, most commonly through defeating the power that threatens them as well. The balance of power does not work automatically, however, and states cannot assume that others will come to their aid when they are threatened by an aggressor. Consequently, some states seek to increase their power, even through war if necessary, creating a threat to the security of other states. In all these decisions, states choose on the basis of a calculation of power and interest. Neorealists place no value on normative commitments to defend others, as in a system of collective security. If one state fights to save another, it does so because it is in its interest to do so. To quote John Mearsheimer, "[r]ealists ... believe that institutions [defined by Mearsheimer as 'a set of rules that stipulate the ways in which states should cooperate and compete with each other'] cannot get states to stop behaving as short-term power maximizers" (Mearsheimer [1995b, 82], quoting Mearsheimer [1995a, 8]).[4]

Constructivists believe that norms and identities shape international politics to the extent that they constitute power and determine interests. They link the two concepts of norm and identity; norms are "collective expectations for the proper behavior for a given identity" (Jepperson, Wendt, and Katzenstein 1996, 54), whereas identities are "images of individuality and distinctiveness held and projected by an actor and formed through relations with 'significant others'" (Jepperson, Wendt, and Katzenstein 1996, 59). I focus here on identity as a social role because that concept of identity naturally links to norms and is more widely used by constructivists in international relations.[5] Social roles prescribe norms of conduct for the given role, and actors share an understanding of what role each holds in a given situation. The shared understanding of which role is active in a given situation is essential because actors have multiple identities. A simple illustration may help. I hold several identities; one is the father of my children, another is a university professor who teaches undergraduate students. Both of these social roles prescribe norms of acceptable and unacceptable behaviors, and I and others know which role I am supposed to fill and so what conduct is appropriate and what is inappropriate by the current social setting. Acts that are appropriate for one identity, say, inviting my children to sit in my lap while we talk, are completely inappropriate for the other. Returning to international relations, constructivists describe how the identities of states and the norms attached to them have changed over time. Wendt (1999) criticizes the realists as assuming that the role of states as suspicious competitors cannot be changed; he argues that states under anarchy could hold identities as enemies, rivals, or friends, all of which entail different norms of international relations. These identities trump the nature of anarchy to determine what they expect from one another and how they behave toward one another.

Scholars of international law separate along parallel lines on whether legal obligation to that law restrains states. Realists, such as Jack Goldsmith and Eric Posner, argue that international law and compliance with that law by states is a product of their interests. "It [international law] is not a check on

---

[4] Realists do not agree completely on the corrosive effects of anarchy. Mearsheimer (2001) argues for offensive realism in which all states must pursue power in the short term; whereas Glaser (2010) contends that states may be able to resolve some of the insecurity of anarchy under the right conditions. Even for Glaser, structural factors, such as the offense-defense balance, rather than ideational factors, such as a shared commitment to defend the peace and sovereignty of other states, are the key to overcoming anarchy.

[5] I do not consider intrinsic identities of individual actors if they are not recognized to entail norms of behavior. I also collapse Wendt's four types of identities – personal or corporate, type, role, and collective (1999, 224–233) – into one because they all share the two key elements I discuss: norms linked to each identity and a shared understanding of which actor has what identity in what situation.

state self-interest; it is a product of state self-interest" (Goldsmith and Posner 2005, 13). Their position is not that international law is ineffectual, but that the beneficial effects of international law lie in clarifying state positions and aiding states in reaching mutually beneficial agreements. Law exists because states see it as a way to advance their interests, and so it exerts no independent pull toward compliance. Most scholars of international law believe, however, that international law creates obligations which bind state action, the parallel of the constructivist position that norms appropriate for an actor's identity help to constitute that actor's interests. Thomas Franck (1990) argues that international law gains legitimacy and so the power to obligate states to comply with it through four mechanisms: (1) determinacy – a clearly understood rule aids transparency in judging what obligations are and when they have been met; (2) symbolic validation by states reinforces their acceptance of a legal standard and the values it codifies; (3) coherence – a rule which is applied consistently in accordance with the principles motivating it both reflects existing legitimacy of the rule among states and reinforces it; and (4) adherence – the extent to which law is both supported by secondary rules that explain how to apply it and embedded within a larger structure of law to which it adheres. Franck does not argue that the compliance pull of international law is absolute, only that it is exists and strengthens with the legitimacy of that law as measured by his four mechanisms. States comply both because they believe the norms encased in legitimate law are proper and because they wish to affirm their identity as a lawful state with the privileges and obligations that come with that status.

The intersubjective nature of identities and the norms they entail is essential for them to operate as social structure. Actors cannot choose their identity freely for a given situation because if they could, identities and norms would not shape their choices. I have a large collection of baseball caps from the days when I attended games in many different cities, where the caps allowed me to assume the identity of a fan of the home team regardless of my true loyalties. If identities were like baseball caps, identities would not constrain actors because actors could change their identity freely, much in the way that I – simply by wearing a cap of the home team – can avoid any unpleasant consequences that might follow from being a fan of the visiting team in the midst of hometown fans who have been drinking.[6] Because identities are social phenomena (other actors recognize an actor's identity for a given situation and expect that actor to live up to the obligations of that role), an actor is not free to choose whatever identity suits its purposes of the moment. This is not to say that identities do not change; indeed, the central thrust of constructivism explores how identities and the norms associated with them are socially constructed over time. Instead, the intersubjective nature of identities and norms

---

[6] Having attended Dodger-Giant games in Candlestick Park in the past, I have seen the threat of violence present in the fans of the bucolic sport of baseball.

does not allow an actor to change them freely, and so they shape and limit what it can do. Furthermore, understanding identities and norms becomes critical for understanding how international politics works because these institutions shape everything about it.

## The Game-Theoretic Critique of Realism and Constructivism

If institutions create both institutional equilibrium (that is, behavior given the institution) and equilibrium institutions (the existing institutions are not changed because no set of actors both wants to change them and can do so), then political institutions depend on the two elements of equilibrium in game theory. First, the behavior under the institution forms a collection of mutual best replies, calculations of self-interest in which no actor wishes to change his or her strategy given the strategies of the other players. Second, the players share a common conjecture that they are playing that equilibrium of the game. The common conjecture is critical when a game has multiple equilibria because the players' best replies – the moves that are best for him or her – depend on which equilibrium the players understand that they are playing. The shared understanding of the common conjecture allows all players to understand which actions are in their interest. Institutions marry self-interest and a shared understanding in which both are essential and neither piece provides a complete picture on its own.

Both realism and constructivism are incomplete; each presents one side of the coin of political institutions. Realists correctly point to the importance of calculations of self-interest, whereas constructivists give pride of place to shared understandings. But neither of these essential factors of political institutions can operate without the other. They are fused together in the logic of political institutions. The game-theoretic understanding of political institutions allows us to understand how ideas and self-interest together motivate state action and the range of possible orders they can create, a marriage that neither realism nor constructivism can do alone.

The game-theoretic critique of realism concerns the range of possible worlds under anarchy. The realists' claim that shared understandings as institutions cannot lead actors to overcome the problems of anarchy can be interpreted as a claim that all equilibria of any game that satisfies their assumptions must be "competitive" in nature; equilibria with cooperative behavior cannot exist. This is a strong claim. It requires showing not that the worlds that have occurred have been competitive but that no game consistent with their assumptions has equilibria that vary in their level of competition or cooperation. Otherwise, how states act – whether they could cooperate for mutual gain – would depend on which equilibrium the players were actually playing. States could mitigate the effects of anarchy by playing an equilibrium in which competition was limited. Games with multiple equilibria mean the actors have different ways to compete or cooperate and their common conjecture about which equilibrium they are playing is essential to determining how they act, even though all continue to pursue their self-interest as they understand it within that equilibrium.

The game-theoretic critique of constructivism concerns the range of behavior that norms and identities can induce. Can norms and identities induce any pattern of behavior, or put another way, if you socially construct it, will they come? Constructivists do not address this point directly, although the precedence they give to norms and identities over interests suggests that any pattern of behavior could be supported by the proper set of norms and identities. A game-theoretic view of norms and identities limits the set of behaviors that could occur; even if a game has multiple equilibria, most combinations of strategies are not equilibria of that game (except for highly unusual games). Self-interest limits the possibilities of what norms and identities can induce actors to do. States may be able to play out the consequences of anarchy in different ways with important consequences for international politics, but they cannot make whatever they wish out of it.

A game-theoretic approach may also help us deal with two issues in determining how norms operate. Demonstrating that norms change behavior faces two related problems of empirical judgment. *Circularity* arises when norms and identities are inferred from observed behavior and then used to explain that behavior. Because norms and identities cannot be observed directly, we do not have evidence of them beyond how actors behave, including their public justifications as actions. Constructivists rely on justifications of actions to reveal identity, norms, and when actors consider them legitimate (cf. Kratochwil 1989). I do not deny that justifications can be useful, but they must be considered as strategic acts to be interpreted properly. Game theory can help us think through the complexities of how principles of proper behavior could be used by actors in their public justifications and so reveal how such acts reflect whether such principles are held.

Circularity would be less of an issue if actors always complied with the norms for the relevant identity. *Inappropriate behavior* poses the problem of judging whether norms influence behavior. Realists commonly critique constructivist arguments by pointing out cases in which the actors do not follow the prescripts of the putative norms (cf. Krasner's [1999] critique of sovereignty). Exceptions exist to sovereignty now and throughout the history of the sovereign state system. As constructivists point out, the existence of some violations of norms does not mean that norms have no effect. However, disentangling the puzzle posed by inappropriate behavior forces us to spell out when actors will see such violations as being in their interest. Constructivism does not provide a way to determine when actors will violate norms or what degree and level of violations renders norms and identities impotent. A central goal of this book is to explain when the laws of war have been violated and when they have been observed. That explanation requires both the shared understanding of the norms of such conduct and the calculations of state interest in the light of those norms.

Game theory does not solve either problem; it gives us a tool to model norms and identities formally and then derive how actors should behave if they held them. The precision of the analytic tools of game theory can help us cut through these problems to arrive at clear tests of when actors should observe norms and when they should not. These tools also allow us to ask what would happen under alternate sets of norms by examining the full set of equilibria of the game in question. In the words of Robert Powell, "formal models provide a kind of accounting mechanism that enables us to think through some issues more carefully than ordinary-language models can" (1999, 29). By thinking about norms and identities as being reflected in the common conjecture of the game in question, we have a way to model how actors would act if they held a particular set of norms and identities, addressing the circularity problem, and then derive how they should act, addressing when inappropriate behavior occurs.

The game-theoretic approach also undercuts the distinctive character of international politics as anarchic. Neorealists and constructivists agree that international politics is anarchic and that domestic politics has a legitimate central authority, even though they disagree about the consequences of anarchy. Contrary to received wisdom, the game-theoretic view sees no difference in fundamental character between domestic and international institutions; domestic politics is also anarchy.[7] Legitimate domestic authority exists in domestic politics only to the extent that the actors accept and enforce domestic institutions on one another; they cannot appeal to some outside power to enforce defections from the accepted order. All political institutions are tenuous, and their permanence is always something that must be explained. If institutions persist and succeed in enforcing their principles and rules, it is because the actors can enforce them on one another. The depth, breadth, and acceptance of domestic institutions is greater than international institutions, but this is a difference in degree not character. International relations theory can learn much about international institutions from the study of domestic institutions.

Furthermore, multiple institutional arrangements are always possible. The questions that drive men and women to form political order do not have unique solutions. The games that underlie these problems have multiple equilibria. Alternative political institutions are always possible, and such changes make some actors better off and others worse off. Additionally, the exact consequences of new institutional arrangements are unclear. Perhaps change is for the better, perhaps it is not.

This final point is the necessary consequence of multiple equilibria in games. Multiple institutions are possible in most social settings, with resulting different

---

[7] Goldsmith and Levinson (2010) make the parallel between international law and constitutional law that matches my point here that international and domestic institutions face the same problems. Also see Milner (1991) and Powell (1994) for similar critiques of the concept of anarchy in international relations.

behaviors. This point should be obvious if we think of domestic institutions. There are many different forms of government. Some work better than others, and some people are better off in one than another. This point is more difficult to see in international institutions because they do not vary cross-sectionally as governments do. But they do vary over time, demonstrating that a variety of international institutions is possible.

REALISM, IDEALISM, AND INTERNATIONAL LAW

The opposition between the realist focus on power and interest and the idealist focus on ideas extends to whether and how international law shapes what states do. From Louis Henkin's famous declaration that "almost all nations observe almost all principles of international law and almost all of their obligations almost all of the time" (Henkin 1979, 47), some believe that international law suffuses and structures international politics to the point where compliance verges on automatic. The managerial school (cf. Chayes and Chayes 1993) argues that when states fail to comply with their obligations in international law, they do not do so out of calculations of immediate self-interest. Instead, there are three causes of noncompliance. First, the language of the agreement might be imprecise, leading a party to commit acts that other parties see as a violation even though the first party had no intent to breach the agreement. Second, a party might lack the capability to carry out its obligations and so finds itself in violation even though it cannot follow through on those obligations. Third, conditions may change, leading a party that fully intended to comply to wish to end the agreement or at least hold it in abeyance until conditions change once more. These three causes of noncompliance suggest that absolute standards should not be applied when judging whether states live up to their legal agreements; instead, there are acceptable levels of noncompliance for each agreement. The agreement is breached only when violations exceed this level, with violations below it ignored. With the qualification for acceptable noncompliance, states in this view do live up to their legal obligations.

Others (e.g., Downs, Rocke, and Barsoom 1996) see the same pattern of widespread compliance with law and draw the opposite conclusion; law does not shape what states do because they choose to enter into legal obligations only when they see complying with those obligations as unproblematic. Cooperation through law is shallow; it does not address difficult issues in which there is a common benefit to be realized but a substantial risk of failure through noncompliance. There is widespread compliance with international legal obligations because states legalize only the issues for which compliance is easy. At the extreme, international law and, more generally, international institutions are epiphenomenal; they are a shadow, following the consequences of power and interests, instead of the form moving international politics (Mearsheimer 1995a, 1995b).

As is the case with realism and idealism generally, both of these views hold an incomplete portion of the truth. States have created international law to help them realize benefits from cooperation, but law helps to address some of the issues that make that cooperation difficult. Cooperative agreements face a host of problems, including but not limited to opportunistic defection, any one of which could cause an agreement to fail. Legal agreements are designed to help the actors create social mechanisms to address those problems. Without those agreements and mechanisms, cooperation is likely to founder. The realists correctly see that states select into legal agreements because they believe they will benefit from then, but fail to see that the resulting cooperation may require the mechanisms induced by those agreements. The idealists see that legal agreements structure international relations, but they fail to see the myriad problems that can impede cooperation, particularly when the mechanisms induced by legal agreements defuse those problems.

Limiting violence through the laws of war faces a number of these problems. States disagree about the appropriate standards of behavior during war. Some believe they gain from restraint, others from unrestrained combat. Even those who agree on the former may disagree about the exact nature of restraint. Those opposed to restraint may wish to portray themselves as favoring it and conceal their true views until wartime. How can those who prefer restraint identify one another, so they can anticipate when both will observe restraint and when they must protect themselves against an opponent who denies restraint? Even when both sides would prefer restraints on conduct during war, do they agree on what the limits are, what acts are allowable, and which fall outside the bounds of restraint? A vague agreement to cooperate on restraint might founder if one side took actions that it thought were acceptable but the other did not; the latter might retaliate out of a fear that the first was seeking to exploit its restraint. A preference for restraint, even one shared openly by both sides, may not be sufficient for them to realize those shared preferences.

Law can aid states in creating a restrained battlefield by clarifying what restraint means, who wishes to live within those limits, and how to respond to those who do not. Universal treaties define what proper conduct is, thereby reducing disagreement about the limits. Treaty ratification of that public standard screens out states that do not want restraint. By opting out, those states indicate that they will not live within the bounds of restraint. Others are then forewarned of the intention of a state to violate the standard, and so can prepare themselves for that, including possible responses in kind. This may lead to the unrestrained battlefield that is sought by the state that does not accept the standard. When both sides ratify a universal treaty, they create shared expectations that both sides will comply with that treaty standard to the best of their ability. If one party violates that standard, it should expect its opponent to respond in kind. This threat of retaliation could enforce their agreement to live up to the treaty standard that both accepted before the war. Treaty law could help the parties realize their shared preference for restraint in the face of the problem created by differences in the willingness of the parties to be restrained.

This example is only one facet of how international law might help states at war cooperate on restraint. This restraint is neither epiphenomenal as the realists declaim nor automatic as the idealists believe. It results from the design of the institutions of international law, principles which shape how states at war will act toward one another. Furthermore, compliance with the laws of war is problematic, with many warring parties violating those laws, including those who have accepted them. The problematic record of compliance contradicts both the realist and idealist views; cooperation on this issue is difficult to accomplish, yet states have created these laws and taken on the burden of complying with them, even given those difficulties. Law aids cooperation by creating shared understanding of proper conduct married to incentives created during war to follow that law when possible.

## LAW AS AN INSTITUTIONAL EQUILIBRIUM

This book examines the laws of war as an example of an international institution in light of the general argument about political institutions just presented. International law fosters the strategic expectations of the common conjecture underlying the equilibrium that international actors are playing. It shapes the actors' expectations of how they will play the game and allows them to anticipate one another's actions and reactions. Law goes beyond norms of conduct by adding precision to the terms, a sense of legal obligation to the provisions, and the possibility of enforcement through domestic legal and political processes. The treaties that embody the laws of war strengthen and refine the norms of proper conduct during wartime. These treaties have been negotiated and then ratified by states that wish to make that law binding onto themselves. Finally, such treaties resist change and thereby operate as equilibrium institutions; common conjectures of which equilibrium will be played also resist change because no actor can change them acting alone.

Law adds precision to norms as the common conjecture requires precision about behavior in all possible cases. An equilibrium specifies what each actor will do in all possible situations, including those that should not occur under that equilibrium. The common conjecture requires that the players share that understanding of how they will act even when some actor does not follow the prescribed behavior.[8] General normative principles, such as the protection of soldiers who have surrendered, lacks the precision of the Geneva Conventions concerning exactly how prisoners of war must be treated. Law in general moves beyond norms by adding precision; the law on homicide moves beyond the general norm of "[t]hou shall not kill" to explain the set of crimes which

---

[8] In the interest of a clean presentation, I do not discuss varieties of equilibria in which the players can hold discordant beliefs about what would happen off the equilibrium path.

homicides may fall into, how to judge which of those crimes a particular kill-ing is, including the possibility of justifiable homicide, and how those crimes should be punished.

Law also creates obligation even when the parties do not fulfill their obliga-tions. In international law, such obligations are formally binding when states ratify the relevant treaties. Common conjectures shape how an actor acts even if it does not agree with it. Because others will act in accordance with the common conjecture, an actor is not free to disregard the consequences of its behavior which are spelled out in the common conjecture. In this sense, com-mon conjectures create obligations for players even though they, like people under a system of law, are free to violate those obligations subject to the conse-quences that follow from such violations. Many students of international law argue that customary international law binds states even when they have not formally ratified it or even when it has not been negotiated into the form of a treaty. Customary international law captures the expectations created by stable patterns of behavior by states over time in absence of a formal treaty. Again, such law would have binding power on international actors to the extent that the system of behavior identified with that custom forms an equilibrium.

I focus, however, on formal treaties over customary law in this project. The dual process of formal negotiation followed by ratification means that the standards of the treaty and its acceptance by states are clearer than those in customary international law. The single public treaty produced through negoti-ation means that all states know what the standard is even if they do not accept it; ratification is public evidence that the ratifying state has accepted that stan-dard. Formal treaties help to address the problem of circularity facing explana-tions based on norms. We have a text that explains the standard independent of the acts of the states in question, and we have a clear public signal of which states have accepted the obligations of that standard through ratification. I can then match behavior against the standards of a treaty to determine when states have followed their standards in the laws of war.

Of course, behavior may differ from the standard because the parties do not wish to comply on their own and that standard does not produce sufficient incentives for the parties to comply. The formal model of the laws of war that I present in Chapter 3 provides a logical structure for thinking about incentives to comply. I use the ideas in that model to discuss the practical issues in com-pliance, leading to testable hypotheses about when states should comply and how bad their behavior is when they do not comply.

The formal model of the laws of war links three games representing the var-ious problems facing restraints on violence during wartime. States at war have to decide whether they can gain an advantage if their soldiers commit viola-tions. On the battlefield, soldiers of both sides have to worry about whether their enemies will commit violations against them and whether they should in turn protect themselves by violating the law. Within each state, the central political and military authorities can use military training and discipline to control violations by their own soldiers. How states and soldiers act in any one of these games depends on the other two. On the battlefield, there are multiple equilibria, so that strategic expectations determine the level of violations. Expectations of an unrestrained battlefield lead to further violations for self-protection, whereas expectations of restraint by the other side can lead to restraint. A state that sees restraint as advancing its chances of winning will discipline its soldiers to limit their violations, whereas one that seeks an unrestrained battlefield will not. The latter may refuse to ratify a treaty to induce expectations of a lack of restraint should war come, expectations that can be a self-fulfilling prophecy. Treaty ratification then screens out some states that do not intend to comply with that treaty during wartime. The characteristics of these three problems vary across the issues addressed by the laws of war, leading to predictions about which issues should pose greater challenges to compliance. The successes of the laws of war depend on the strategic incentives warring parties have to honor them during wartime, including their expectations for how the other side will act. The full range of incentives both to honor and violate these laws is wide, and simple generalizations do not follow about compliance, violations, and atrocities.

Law is more than just a collection of normative rules; it embodies a strategic logic of action. All law creates incentives for actors, which shape their actions. Successful law, particularly at the international level, requires a marriage of moral principles with strategic logic if actors are to follow those principles. An example from domestic law may help clarify this point. The legal systems of the United States and Great Britain draw on a shared common-law tradition, but differences in their specific laws produce different behavior both in the legal system and within its shadow. For example, it is more difficult to prove libel in the United States than Britain, as British defendants need to prove that they had good reason to believe their statements were true, whereas U.S. defendants need merely prove that they did not know their statements were false. This difference changes not only which libel cases are pursued through the courts; it also changes how news organizations collect, document, and justify their stories as they are prime targets for libel suits.

Law induces strategic dynamics of its own. Actors pursue their self-interest as they understand it in the shadow of the law, and the law shapes what they perceive as their self-interest and how they act. Self-interest and shared understandings of appropriate actions are not separable in such a system, because they are necessarily knitted together.

This view of law also explains why different areas of international law differ from one another. Different issues pose different collections of strategic problems that law can address and aid the parties in overcoming. These differences explain why international law varies across issues. Human rights law aspires to create ultimate and universal standards and is unilaterally binding; trade law seeks to create a uniform multilateral free trade zone that is enforced through bilateral sanctions. Human rights strike at the fundamental relationship between the state and citizen, and compliance cannot be enforced by international retaliation. All states commit some human rights abuses, in part because they cannot control their agents, such as the police. The standard is aspirational – a goal to work toward – rather than absolute. Trade advances the ideal of free trade; an ideal that seeks to remove barriers to the movement of thousands of goods and services that trade across borders. Bilateral enforcement puts the detection and response to violations on the parties who are harmed by a barrier to trade. Because the strategic problems posed by different issues vary, so does law across these issues. Yet they share the common logic of creating common knowledge about what the law is, even though the content and procedures of it vary from issue to issue. When both bodies of law succeed, they do so by fostering expectations that states and their agents will follow the law or have it enforced on them.

## THE ESSENTIAL SOCIAL NATURE OF GAME THEORY

This argument relies on a view of game theory different from that commonly held and taught. Game theorists have focused on the calculation of mutual best replies and the identification of equilibria because we have mathematical tools for these tasks. The logic of the enterprise is straightforward; think of a game that one believes represents the social situation of interest, find at least one equilibrium of that game, and then interpret the behavior in that equilibrium to explain behavior in the situation under examination. If there is a fit between the equilibrium and observed behavior, we then implicitly assume that the actors hold the common conjecture underlying that equilibrium. Although we sometimes look for multiple equilibria, only rarely are multiple equilibria treated empirically either by looking for regularities in behavior that hold across all equilibria or considering conditional hypotheses of multiple patterns in the data. The latter would occur when the players play different equilibria across the cases and we cannot distinguish when the different equilibria are being played except by observing what the actors did in a given case. In all of these analyses, calculation of mutual best replies takes precedence over determining the common conjecture. This approach to analysis has led many constructivists to assert that game theory is incapable of dealing with norms and identities because – they believe – games must assume identities and interests as given.[9]

Thomas Schelling first proposed an alternate view of game theory's ability to explain social issues that gives precedence to common conjectures over mutual best replies (Schelling 1960, chapter 6), although he did not use those words. Schelling addressed bargaining, arguing that simple bargaining games had a continuum of equilibrium; therefore, knowing which equilibrium was

---

[9] An example of such arguments can be found in Jepperson et al. (1996, 41, 43, 59), although they do qualify their criticism in important ways.

being played was far more important than understanding the logic of mutual best replies within that equilibrium. He argued that cultural features that made a particular equilibrium stand out from the others in the minds of the players would prove to be the real keys to predicting how players would play a game. Schelling's argument, like mine, gives pride of place to the common conjecture; it also, unlike my argument, makes the common conjecture more important than the strategic dynamics of mutual best replies. Schelling chose situations (such as bargaining or simple coordination) in which the strategic dynamics were trivial and gave rise to an infinite number of equilibria. Once we turn to a situation (such as the restraint of violence during wartime) for which where the strategic dynamics are more complicated, those strategic dynamics restrict the set of equilibria and therefore the common conjectures which could act as institutions.

Like Schelling, I give common conjectures a central place in game theory. In this sense then, many have failed to grasp the social nature of game theory. It is truly a theory of interdependent decisions; what the actors think one another will do is as central to their own calculations as their preferences over outcomes. Equilibrium in game theory is a social theory constructed around individual actors. Action by individuals isolated from the context of their interaction with the other players only makes sense in trivial games or those in which the player has a dominant strategy.[10] Equilibrium concerns stable shared expectations based in calculations of self-interest. The shared expectations then shape how the players understand their interests and how they can advance those interests. In that way, shared understandings can operate as institutions. At the same time, the expectations created by that shared understanding must respect the interests of the players and what they will do to advance them. The burden of this book is to demonstrate that this argument can be used profitably to understand an important, real phenomena – the laws of war.

THE PLAN OF THE BOOK

Several years ago, a satire on the field of international relations entitled "A Medieval Sociology of International Relations" circulated widely through email.[11] The elite scholars at the Ivy League universities were the nobles whose only skill was the ability to engage one another in paradigmatic combat; the mass of scholars doing quantitative work were the peasants working hard to assemble their data and publish their results in the slight hope that they might survive the rigors and whims of academia; the formal theorists were the clergy with their arcane language and impenetrable theories. Although I am one of

---

[10] A player has a dominant strategy if its payoff is always higher than that produced by its other strategies against all strategy combinations of the other players.

[11] It can be found at http://www.gotterdammerung.org/humor/medieval-ir.html, accessed July 12, 2011. I thank Randy Siverson for directing me to this site.

the high officials of the church of formal theory in international relations, I hope this book talks to all three classes in the medieval world of the study of international relations. For the nobles, I offer sweeping arguments about the role of norms and law in the international system that might end their eternal paradigmatic wars. For the peasants, I too have toiled in the fields of data collection as I tested the conclusions of my arguments against a dataset of compliance with the laws of war during the twentieth century. For the clergy, I hope to offer enough formal theory that they will not declare me a heretic for my deviations from the Holy Theory.

This introductory chapter lays out the broad argument. Chapter 2 discusses common conjectures in game theory and how they can be used to represent norms and identities as those concepts are understood in international relations. I discuss the theory behind common conjectures in the abstract, but the chapter concentrates on a variety of different equilibria of iterated Prisoners' Dilemma to show what the common conjecture does in each of those equilibria and how the shared understanding in that common conjecture works like norms and identities. Iterated Prisoners' Dilemma is particularly useful for this discussion because it has wide ranges of types of equilibria with very different behavior. The common conjecture induces strategic expectations of reciprocity – what the players have agreed to, what acts trigger a response, and the exact nature of any retaliatory response– that are necessary for the players to realize the benefits of reciprocal enforcement.

Chapter 3 offers a model of the laws of war that link three games on the three strategic problems faced by restraints on violence during war: between warring states, on the battlefield between soldiers, and within militaries when states seek to control their soldiers. I discuss the laws of war generally, the challenges that compliance with it face, and the three strategic problems captured in the model. I pull together the discussion of the laws of war both in the abstract and in practice to arrive at a set of hypotheses about how and when they are violated. Chapter 3 appears in dual form; the first Chapter 3 presents the argument in words with little mathematics to spare those readers who do not wish to delve into the technical detail, whereas Chapter 3' immediately afterward provides the formal details of the model for those who do.

Chapter 4 tests these hypotheses against a dataset of compliance with the laws of war during the twentieth century. I examine the effects of legal obligation through ratification of the relevant treaties, the political system of the country in question, and the relative power of the warring sides among the variables tested. The results support reciprocity generally and specifically the key role of variations in noise across issues in determining compliance. Legal obligations have little effect on their own; instead, law creates shared expectations of restraint that induce the sides' acts to move together; compliance matches compliance, violations are met with violations. Law also clarifies what acts are violations and which parties accept the obligations of treaty law. I also examine the questions of the timing of first violations during a war and whether obligation and compliance are separated across issues within a war. As with Chapter 3, Chapter 4 appears in dual form, the first presenting the results of the statistical analyses in graphical form to make them accessible to all readers, the second presenting the details of the analyses for specialists in quantitative international relations.

Chapter 5 tests the hypotheses about compliance by examining in detail the issue of prisoners of war. During the World Wars, there was substantial variation in how states treated prisoners. Strategic expectation for the treatment of those trying to surrender is critical for creating humane treatment of captured soldiers; legal commitment helps to create those expectations between states and on the battlefield. Compliance faces challenges in that some states seek an unrestrained battlefield in which it is difficult to surrender, whereas the realities of combat can corrode a commitment to take prisoners and treat them humanely. Ratification of the relevant treaties operates as a screen for intent during wartime, particularly in the face of differing views on how prisoners should be treated. I also consider cultural explanations for treatment of prisoners of war and explain why I reject them in favor of strategic expectations. The case material in this chapter complements and deepens the statistical tests in Chapter 4.

Chapter 6 briefly discusses four issues in the laws of war that have received more attention in the international relations literature: aerial bombing, chemical weapons, conduct on the high seas, and treatment of civilians. I do not analyze these issues in as great detail as I do prisoners of war, mainly seeking case support for the results of the statistical analysis and countering explanations for compliance that others have proposed.

These chapters explain how the laws of war work once in place; they seek to explain how they operate and how we can know that such norms have actual effects of behavior. Chapter 7 turns to the question of how norms change over time, again using the laws of war as the subject. I draw on theories of the sources of common conjectures to analyze how norms and identities change. I use results from evolutionary game theory to outline a theory of the rational evolution of institutions, applying that theory to the development of law concerning prisoners of war.

Chapter 8 concludes the book by examining some current issues in the laws of war. I discuss whether the results of the historical cases apply to recent wars. Terrorism poses particular problems for the dual legal systems of the laws of war and criminal law, suggesting that the evolution toward a third body of law on violence is appropriate. The push to universalism – the idea that all states must ratify the laws of war – poses dangers as well as the promise of the acceptance of humanitarianism as a central value in world politics. Finally, the book ends with some broad conclusions about normative standards shape world politics – that is, how and when ideals bring order to anarchy.

# 2

## Common Conjectures, Norms, and Identities

Constructivism focuses on how shared understandings shape social life, giving predictability to it. Stable social orders require shared understandings when multiple stable configurations of behavior exist. In the language of game theory, the existence of multiple equilibria in a game representing a social setting means that many sets of strategies could be stable. Which equilibrium the actors play depends on the common conjecture they share. This chapter examines the concept of common conjecture to show how such shared understandings capture social norms and identities.

A common conjecture is how the actors understand and anticipate one another's strategy and so know that their own strategy is what they should do. The common conjecture is specific to the equilibrium being played and coincides with the strategies the actors use in that equilibrium. Understanding the role of the common conjecture requires looking across multiple equilibria of a game to compare the shared understandings that the actors could hold in a stable social system. Because the common conjecture explains why the actors are playing one of a number of possible equilibria, its role can only be grasped by examining the content of different common conjectures of a single game. This variation in the actors' strategic expectations can change the actions that they believe to be in their own best interest.

The core of this chapter examines multiple equilibria of the well-known iterated Prisoner's Dilemma, in both its simple form and more complicated versions, to illustrate how common conjectures operate like norms and identities. Iterated Prisoner's Dilemma has many equilibria, indeed infinite ranges of equilibria in some versions. The equilibrium played depends on the specific common conjecture in force, and so behavior can vary greatly with the common conjecture. By comparing across the range of equilibria, we see how behavior can change even when the preferences of the actors are fixed. We see how anticipations of behavior and understanding of how that behavior should be interpreted can change an actor's view of which actions are in its interest. By examining the common conjecture of an equilibrium we can determine the principles and identities underlying a pattern of behavior.

Common conjectures set standards of acceptable behavior, prescribe appropriate and inappropriate responses, create anticipations about the behavior of others, allow the actors to comprehend each other's actions, and can differentiate the social roles of the actors even when they have no differences in their capabilities. This range of possible effect covers much of the role of norms and identities in international politics.

This chapter begins with a discussion of strategic expectations and the challenges actors face in forming them. The common conjecture solves this issue. I next describe the concepts of norms and identities in constructivism. The game of iterated Prisoners' Dilemma and its infinite number of equilibria are used to show how the common conjecture underlying different equilibria parallels norms and explains the logic of reciprocity. I turn to how identity as social roles can be captured in a common conjecture. Common conjectures also make communication possible by ensuring that actors share an understanding about what signals mean and what responses they should trigger; this parallels how norms enable justifications and support shared ideas of legitimacy. I end by drawing contrasts between law and common conjectures to clarify how law helps actors form strategic expectations, much as a common conjecture does.

This chapter and the next use formal models to analyze norms and identities in general here and specifically in the laws of war in Chapter 3. Formal models seek to clarify our understanding of a causal process by boiling down the complexities of reality into their simplest, most elemental form, allowing us to extract an exact and deep understanding of the logic of that process (cf. Powell 1999, chapter 1). Because models greatly simplify reality and focus on a single process at the expense of others, models present a thin version of reality, one that may seem a mere shadow of reality. This thinness is a strength because it makes it possible to understand exactly why things happen in the world of the model; this thinness is a weakness because it complicates the translation from the model to the real world. Chapters 4 through 6 seek to deal with the difficulties of translating the models back to understanding how the laws of war have worked in practice. For now, the reader is warned that the models of norms and identities presented in this chapter will seem like thin, watery gruel compared to the richness of the norms and identities that structure world politics. But the move to present these ideas in their purest form allows us to see clearly how and when shared understandings shape world politics.

Those readers whose interest is solely with the laws of war may wish to skip ahead to Chapter 3 to avoid this detour through the combination of game theory and international relations theory.

Player 2

Cooperate     Defect

|  | Cooperate | Defect |
|---|---|---|
| **Cooperate** | (1,1) | $(-\beta,\alpha)$ |
| **Defect** | $(\alpha,-\beta)$ | (0,0) |

Player 1

$\alpha > 1$ and $\beta > 0$

FIGURE 2.1 Strategic form of prisoners' dilemma.

## STRATEGIC EXPECTATIONS AND COMMON CONJECTURES

Game theory is a useful tool for understanding strategic interaction, situations where all the actors can affect the outcome and so each must consider what the others might do. These strategic expectations are central to deciding what each should do in the situation. Political institutions generally, and international law specifically, help actors form their strategic expectations and so bring predictability to politics, including the brutal politics of the battlefield in the case of the law of war.

Forming strategic expectations is not a straightforward matter of applying deductive rules to the incentives of others. This section considers the demands of strategic expectations in the series of games. Beginning with a simple example, the sequence of games explored here shows the difficulties of forming strategic expectations in social settings. All of them focus on equilibrium – a set of strategies for the players where no player wishes to change its strategy given the other players' strategies and the players' strategic expectations follow from the other players' strategies. Equilibrium describes a stable pattern of behavior in the game, one where every player is doing as well as they can and no one is systematically fooled about what others will do. It is an institutionalized pattern of mutually supporting behavior and belief.

It is not always the case that what players should do depends on their beliefs. Figure 2.1 gives the Prisoners' Dilemma. Both players choose Cooperate or Defect simultaneously, with Player 1 receiving the first payoff and Player 2 the second. Both players prefer to play Defect no matter what the other does because $\alpha > 1$ and $0 > -\beta$. In the terms of game theory, both players have a *dominant* strategy, and Prisoners' Dilemma is *dominance solvable*. The players' choices do not depend on what they expect the other will do in a single play of Prisoners' Dilemma; this will change when we consider repeated play of Prisoners' Dilemma later in this chapter.

Games that are dominance solvable are unusual, however. In most games, what strategy is best for a player depends on what the other does. Figure 2.2 gives a pure coordination game; if both players choose the same strategy, they receive one; if they do not, both get zero. Now what each does depends

Player 2

|   |   | A | B |
|---|---|---|---|
| Player 1 | A | (1,1) | (0,0) |
|   | B | (0,0) | (1,1) |

FIGURE 2.2 Strategic form of pure coordination game.

critically on what the other will do. If you will play A, I want to play A; if I will play B, you want to do the same. Strategic expectations – what each thinks the other will do – are critical in this game.

The idea that strategic expectations can coordinate self-enforcing behavior is widely understood and appreciated (Schelling 1960; Stein 1990; Ferejohn 1993). The choice of which side of the road we agree to drive on is the common example. If everyone agrees to drive on the right side of the road, it is in my interest to do so even if I have a right-hand-drive car.[1] To do otherwise risks a head-on collision. This example suggests that a coordination problem can be solved with a simple shared understanding that can be easily achieved. But this suggestion depends on several features of this pure coordination game, which are not general to all strategic situations.

First, both players make a move in all plays of the game and only hold expectations over moves that the other will make. Their expectations of how the other will act can be tested against the play that results, allowing the players to adjust their expectations over time to how the other is playing. In the language of game theory, all of the moves of the game are *on the equilibrium path*. For many games, the players need expectations about how the other will play for moves that should not happen if each plays according to the equilibrium, that is, those that are *off the equilibrium path*. Figure 2.3 gives the extensive from of the Chain Store Paradox, perhaps the simplest game where a player's strategy depends on moves off the equilibrium. This game has two equilibria, (Enter, Accept) and (Stay Out, Fight). In the first, Player 1 expects that Player 2 will accept its entry into the market, and so enters the market, leading Player 2 to accept that entry and confirm Player 1's expectation. In the second equilibrium, Player 1 expects that Player 2 will fight entry and so stays out, meaning that Player 1's expectation is never tested against what Player 2 would do in the event of entry. It is purely a hypothesis in Player 1's mind.

As readers familiar with game theory will know, the expectation in the second equilibrium seems incredible; Player 1 expects that Player 2 will act contrary to her interest if she found herself forced to choose between Accept and Fight (I adopt the convention of referring to Player 1 as "he" and Player 2 as "she"). In the terms of game theory, this is *subgame perfection*, which seeks to limit the

---

[1] But it still looks odd, as anyone who has seen a British car while on vacation in the French countryside will attest.

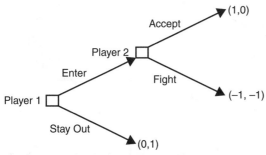

FIGURE 2.3 Extensive form of the chain store paradox.

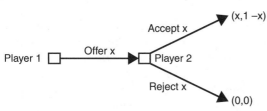

FIGURE 2.4 Extensive form of take-it-or-leave-it bargaining.

set of expectations that players can hold off the equilibrium path. For the Chain Store Paradox, this limit seems reasonable given that Player 1 knows Player 2's payoffs; he can judge that she will act in her own interest if forced to move. Consider the take-it-or-leave-it bargaining game in Figure 2.4. Player 1 makes an offer to divide a unit between the two, which Player 2 can accept or reject. What offer Player 1 makes depends on how he expects Player 2 will respond as he would like to make the offer that she will accept that gives him the most. Now Player 1 needs expectations across all possible offers, a continuum. The only expectation that is tested against Player 2's belief is the offer he makes.

Again, we can use subgame perfection to rule out expectations where Player 2 acts against her interests in this game. The game in Figure 2.5 adds uncertainty for Player 1 about Player 2's value for no deal; $t$ gives her value for rejecting his offer where $t$ is between zero and one with all values equally likely. Now Player 1 needs expectations about how every type of Player 2 will respond to all possible offers, this is a continuum of continua.[2] Subgame perfection can also be used here to rule out expectations where Player 1 thinks Player 2 will act against her interest, but the point is Player 1's expectations must address an immense set of contingencies and that experience playing can touch only on particular values.

Players could hold divergent expectations about a third player if there are more than two players in the game. Fudenberg and Levine (1998) present a game in which Players 1 and 2 can hold divergent expectations of what Player

___

[2] The set $[0,1] \times [0,1]$, to be precise.

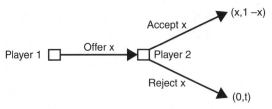

FIGURE 2.5 Extensive form of take-it-or-leave-it bargaining game with types.

3 will do, which prove self-confirming when they act according to those expectations, because Player 3 does not have to make a move when they do. As is generally the case in game theory, three is not just two plus one; it is fundamentally more complex.

The earlier examples are simple games with few moves and clear incentives that allow the players to form expectations about one another using subgame perfection. Social settings in practice are less clear, clouding the ability of actors to form clear expectations for one another. The range of moves off the equilibrium path, the things that are not supposed to happen but might, can be vast and unanticipated. Those unanticipated events may happen rarely, if at all, with no grounds for forming expectations. Everyone may interact with many other actors of unknown type, where their behavior varies greatly with those types. Often people violate subgame perfection in experiments (cf. Camerer 1997 for a review), and the models that attempt to account for these variations do so by including some uncertainty about the motivations of others (cf. Kreps et al. 1982 and Milgrom and Roberts 1982 for early examples). Attempts to produce a general theory that specifies a unique rational way to form strategic expectations have foundered (Kreps 1990, 95–128; Fudenberg and Levine 1998; Heath 2001, 130–135).

The assumption of a common conjecture resolves these dilemmas. Players should play a *best reply* – a strategy that gives the player as great a payoff as any other strategy does against the strategies of the other players. A *Nash equilibrium* is a set of strategies where each player's strategy is a best reply against the other players' strategy. An equilibrium is stable; no player wishes to change its strategy, and each correctly anticipates the other's strategy.

The concept of Nash equilibrium assumes that players correctly anticipate each other's strategy – that is, they hold a *common conjecture* about how the game will be played. That common conjecture must be at least mutual knowledge if there are two players (Brandenburger 1992; Aumann and Brandenburger 1995).[3] If there are more than two players, the common conjecture must be

---

[3] Something is *mutual knowledge* if all actors know it. Mutual knowledge is a weaker standard of shared knowledge than common knowledge is. Mutual knowledge does not require all actors to know that all other actors know the information being described, or any higher depth of shared understanding.

common knowledge. All actors hold the same conjecture about the play of the game, so their expectations of one another's behavior arise from the others' equilibrium strategies. Common conjectures cut the Gordian knot of how actors form expectations.

A common conjecture could arise for any number of reasons. The players could have prior experience playing with one another, they may share a common culture that distinguishes certain strategies, or they might have negotiated these strategies prior to playing the game (Kreps 1990, 140–145). For now, I will not consider the question of how common conjectures arise. I return to it in Chapter 7 when I discuss change in institutions.

The demands of a common conjecture can be extensive. As in the earlier examples, the players may need conjectures about a continuum of types making a continuum of moves where very few of those moves happen in equilibrium and those conjectures need to be common knowledge. Political institutions can help create common knowledge about how actors will act, allowing all to form accurate expectations about how others will act. These expectations assure each actor that it is acting in its own interest given what others will do. In this way institutions, including international law, bring predictability and stability to political life.

Equilibrium marries calculated self-interest in the form of mutual best replies and a shared understanding of mutual behavior that undergirds those calculations in the common conjecture. Institutions integrate self-interest with a shared understanding. By itself, neither is sufficient to understand a political institution. Self-interest is necessary to give the actors reason to act as the shared understanding prescribes and so to give the institution durability and persistence. The shared understanding allows the actors to anticipate one another's actions correctly and to judge their own self-interest correctly in response. Enduring and efficacious institutions require both an interest in living within the institution and its rules as well as a common understanding of those rules.

## SOCIAL FACTS: NORMS, IDENTITIES, AND JUSTIFICATIONS

Before turning to how common conjectures represent social facts, we need a closer understanding of norms, identities, and justifications as social facts. This section emphasizes the intersubjective nature of social facts, namely that they are common knowledge among the actors. I do so to make the correspondence between these social facts and the common conjectures of games clearer. This is not to claim that norms, identities, and justifications are always common knowledge in a society; they are not, which poses a tough challenge for studying them. At the end of the chapter I address the question of how knowledge of the law and the norms embodied in that law could differ from the common-knowledge status of common conjectures and the implications of those differences. For now, I put aside those important questions to allow a closer comparison between norms, identities, and justification on one hand and common conjectures on the other.

Norms are shared understandings about appropriate conduct and proper responses to inappropriate conduct.[4] They are shared across a wide range of actors, which makes them social facts rather than just personal normative beliefs and values. Their shared nature allows others to condition how they act based on whether an actor follows or breaches norms. The values encapsulated in norms may be moral imperatives, "Thou shalt not kill," or merely ideas about how one should conduct oneself, such as shaking hands as opposed to bowing when meeting someone. Humanitarianism – the protection of noncombatants and property – is a central norm in the laws of war.

Constructivists distinguish constitutive norms – those that define actions and provide them with common meaning – from regulative norms, which seek to regulate conduct among actors (Ruggie 1998, 862–874; Wendt 1999, 165–178). The rules of chess are often-cited example of constitutive norms; you are not playing chess if you do not follow the rules. Those rules constitute the game itself and allow players to know that they are playing chess as opposed to checkers or football. Sovereignty norms, the rules that both empower and limit state action as well as defining states, are often cited as the fundamental constitutive norms of international politics. In the laws of war, the definition of when a state of war exists would be a constitutive norm because an armed conflict must exist for the laws to apply; they do not apply to other forms of political violence.

Norms could shape action by changing the considerations in decisions or through the internalization of their prescriptions for behavior.[5] Those who wish to violate a norm could be dissuaded by the prospect of responses of others to compliance with or violations of that norm (Axelrod 1986). These others could be fellow members of society who engage only with those who they believe to follow the norms of their society or formal third-party enforcement, such as the police. Norms become internalized when actors incorporate them to the extent that breaking those norms is unthinkable. As one of my friends in graduate school put it, do you stop at a stop sign at two in the morning? Organizations internalize some norms through their internal rules and procedures. Both mechanisms may be necessary for many norms; while most of us do not contemplate killing another person, enforcement of the laws on homicide deter some who harbor such dark thoughts.

---

[4] For definitions of norms by constructivists, see Kratochwil (1989, 59), Finnemore (1996, 22), Jepperson et al. (1996, 54), Finnemore and Sikkink (1998, 891–893), and Tannenwald (1999, 436). Crawford (2002, 40–41) distinguishes between norms–dominant patterns of behavior–and normative beliefs–the beliefs that justify those acts are appropriate.

[5] Pouliot (2008) is an extreme example of the internalization of norms where actors follow norms entirely out of unconscious habit.

Identity is a supple concept that covers a wide range of concerns.[6] Here I focus on identity as social role.[7] Social roles define the expectations that people have for how one another should act in particular situations. These roles can be differentiated, such as the classical master-slave example. Both of those social roles require the other and entail expectations for how each acts within that relationship. Norms attach to social roles and create the expectations that actors have of one another. Furthermore, an actor can have multiple social roles, with different norms attached to those different roles. What others expect of an actor changes with the social role that they believe the actor fills in that setting. National identity, the idea that all the members of a given nation share membership in that nation and the values advanced as central to that identity, is a primary type of identity in international politics. National identity in the United States focuses on the acceptance of the political ideals of the nation, whereas Islam plays a central role in the Saudi national identity. These shared understandings of the purpose of the nation influence what their leaders can do by shaping how their citizens will view the policies those leaders pursue. Social roles can also be defined between countries as a whole, such as the shared acceptance of common interests between the United States and Saudi Arabia in spite of the conflicts in interests the two countries have faced over time. In the laws of war, combatant is a social role attached to protections from the law, limits on what a soldier can do under the laws, and what acts he is empowered to do, most notably to kill on the battlefield. Identity as social role has three key implications: (1) norms are attached to identities; (2) an actor cannot change its active identity easily because its role is a shared understanding; and (3) multiple identities create the possibility of changing expectations if all can be convinced that a different role is appropriate.

Because norms embody shared understandings of appropriate conduct, they provide a way for actors to justify their actions to one another. Norms provide general ideas of proper conduct rather than spelling out exactly which acts violate those standards. Furthermore, specific cases can fall into the "grey areas" where behavior might or might not be consistent with a norm. This uncertainty about how to judge a specific act allows the actor in question to justify what it has done to others. As shared standards of appropriate conduct, norms allow

---

[6] For constructivist discussions of the concept of identity, see Jepperson et al. (1996, 59–61), Reus-Smit (1999, 29–30), and Wendt (1999, 224–231).

[7] Wendt (1999) distinguishes four types of identities: personal or corporate, type, role, and collective. In my view, all four reduce to the concept of social role. A personal identity – the things that make an individual distinct – matters only when others accept that individual as an actor. Corporate identities require all those within the corporate body to accept them, their roles within it, and the ability of their collective to act as one. Types matter only when others attach expectations to those who exhibit a particular type. Collective identities create common social roles of shared membership in that collective, such as national identity. I also focus on identities as social roles because it is easier to show how the common conjecture can represent differentiated social roles.

for justifications. In international politics, those justifications could be made by one government to another or to its own citizens. The shared understanding in those norms allows others to judge whether they believe the acts in question can be justified under those norms. In the laws of war, for example, many inside and outside the United States rejected the justifications advanced by the George W. Bush Administration for its treatment of those it detained under the War on Terror.

Justifications rely on shared understandings of meaning. Otherwise, arguments advanced by an actor may not be understood by those to whom it directs its justification. Norms then also embody shared meaning and the ability to communicate created by that shared meaning, both the ability of the listener to understand what is being said and the ability of those talking to know how their message will be understood. They create a lifeworld (taken from Habermas) of shared meaning that allows individuals to understand one another and what they are doing. Norms tied to justification enable corporate actors to coordinate actions of their members to their common purpose as well as engage others (Crawford 2002, 68–71).

Justifications also allow norms to convey legitimacy on actions. Legitimacy – the belief that a norm ought to be obeyed (Hurd 2007, 30) – can be either specific to an actor or shared across actors. I focus on the latter, because if legitimacy solely resides within an individual, we would not be able to observe it; if legitimacy is a shared idea of the obligation to obey a norm, we could observe whether the actors appeal to that norm in their justifications of actions to others, as well as whether they follow it (Kratochwil 1989, 97). When others reject a justification, they see the action in question as a violation of a norm, and thus illegitimate. Legitimacy rests on shared understandings of what conduct is acceptable in concert with conduct that lives up to those norms. The laws of war allow actors to show that their use of force is restrained in compliance with the norms embodied in those laws and so meet a test of legitimacy in how they are using force, if not why.

Reality complicates this nice picture of norms, identity, justification, and legitimacy. First, compliance with norms is not universal. My friend in graduate school posed his question precisely because he never stopped at stop signs at two in the morning. Even constitutive norms are broken; there have always been exceptions to sovereignty for some polities (Krasner 1999), such as the current status of the non-states of Taiwan and Palestine. Noncompliance raises issues for the study of norms. How do we know that the norm influences behavior when some follow it and others do not? When do actors allow exceptions to norms that turn an apparent breach into compliance? How much compliance is enough?

Second, norms rarely spell out precise lines between appropriate and inappropriate conduct. This lack of clarity is part of the reason why actors justify their actions and why others may not accept the resulting justifications. Actors may well agree on a general norm, such as limiting the destruction of war, and still disagree on what specific acts are unacceptable. Normative agreement may break down because of these disagreements; both sides interpret the other as breaking the norms in question while following it themselves. Perceived violations may be evidence of lack of agreement on the precise boundaries of behavior rather than willful efforts to breach norms.

Third, there are often multiple norms relevant to the issue at hand, and those norms may conflict over what acts are appropriate. The laws of war incorporate norms against perfidy – using the protections of the laws to gain an unfair advantage on the battlefield – in addition to humanitarian norms. How should one respond when the other side uses an ambulance as an ammunition carrier? Actors may well disagree about which norm has priority. Similarly, conflict over the correct social roles in a setting can lead to conflict over which norms apply.

Fourth, some may not accept norms and so see no need to observe their boundaries. Norms are shared understandings, but are they shared universally? Some reject norms publicly whereas others register their objections only through their actions. Even when a state publicly accepts a norm, its agents may not and so act contrary to that norm. Conflict over which norms should hold has been one of the central issues in world politics; the norms underlying human rights are often claimed to be universal, even though a number of governments explicitly reject their general applicability. Some may reject the social role that others believe they must fill.

These four complications do not render norms empty and powerless, but they do make the study of how norms shape what actors do more demanding than simply specifying the norm and noting that many seem to comply. Joseph Heath summarizes the problem succinctly:

> The problem with the classical sociological theory of action is that its proponents have never been able to specify with any precision how values and norms interact with other intentional states – primarily beliefs and desires – in order to produce observed interaction patterns. When compared with, for example, contemporary rational choice theory, sociological models of action are woefully imprecise (Heath 2001, 17–18).[8]

Tracing the effects of norms requires careful study to determine which acts constitute compliance and the full range of behavior under their influence and how actors deal with the gray areas of conduct within them, the conflict among competing norms, and lack of universal acceptance of them. Formal models are one way to untangle this gnarl, which is why I turn to discuss common conjectures as a way to model norms and identities.

---

[8] Heath's (2001) primary focus is criticism of the rational choice program.

## COMMON CONJECTURES IN ITERATED PRISONERS' DILEMMA

I have argued that a shared understanding – the common conjecture – is essential to explanations of social regularities using game theory. I also claim that common conjectures capture norms and identities as understood by constructivists, and so game-theoretic models can usefully represent constructivist arguments. The claim requires us to examine the role of the common conjecture in different equilibria of the same game. Each of these different equilibria are possible patterns of stable behavior given the underlying interests in the payoffs. The variation in common conjecture – how the players expect that one another will behave – explains the variation in behavior. By comparing the content and consequences of the common conjectures of different equilibria of the same game, we can understand the role a common conjecture plays in determining behavior. The game I examine, iterated Prisoners' Dilemma, has many classes of equilibria, allowing me to illustrate the elements that a shared understanding must include to support reciprocal enforcement.

Figure 2.1 gives the strategic form of Prisoners' Dilemma in normalized form.[9] The players choose one of their moves, labeled C and D for Cooperate and Defect. If they both play Cooperate, they benefit from their cooperation, and the payoff for this outcome is normalized to one. If they both play Defect, each receives a payoff of zero. If one plays Defect while the other plays Cooperate, the former exploits the latter, providing a payoff of $\alpha$, with $\alpha > 1$ for the former. The player being exploited receives a payoff of $-\beta$, with $\beta > 0$.[10]

Prisoners' Dilemma has a single equilibrium; both players play Defect. Furthermore, Defect is each player's *minmax strategy* – the strategy that limits the other player to its smallest possible payoff given that the other player plays its best reply in response to that strategy. Minmax strategies are important because they are the severest punishment that one player can impose on the other in the game.

Prisoners' Dilemma has been extensively studied and applied to many different social problems.[11] It captures a problem of enforcing an agreement in the face of opportunism; both players are better off if they honor an agreement to play Cooperate than if they both play Defect. Each, however, has an incentive to cheat on the agreement by playing Defect. Such action not only allows a player to exploit the other if she plays Cooperate, it also protects the player against exploitation by the other.

---

[9] I present the normalized form rather than the better-known letter payoffs (*P* for Punishment, *R* for Reward, *S* for Sucker, and *T* for Temptation, with $T > R > P > S$) because the calculations are easier in this form.

[10] It is often assumed that $\alpha - \beta < 2$, so that both players are better off in the long run when they both play Cooperate every round instead of exploiting one another (one plays Cooperate while the other plays Defect) alternately.

[11] This literature is so large that I will not even bother to give representative citations.

Although we commonly think of the players as trying to enforce an explicit agreement, the dilemma merely requires that they share an understanding that both would like to play something other than both Defect in every round. The distinction between an explicit agreement and a shared understanding becomes more important in the cases that favor one player over the other. To reinforce the idea that the equilibrium requires only a shared understanding rather than an explicitly negotiated agreement, I refer to their arrangement about how they will play the game rather than their agreement on how to play it.

In iterated Prisoners' Dilemma, the players play the game repeatedly, with each play called a "round." Payoffs from future rounds are discounted by a common discount factor $\delta < 1$ and summed to give a player's payoff across this and all future rounds. Because the game is repeated, each player can condition his or her choice of move on the earlier plays of the game. Specifically, the players can impose reciprocal punishments to enforce an arrangement to play Cooperate. If both players begin playing Cooperate and respond to a play of Defect by both playing Defect in the next round, then both will honor their arrangement by playing Cooperate in all rounds if the following condition is true[12]:

$$1 + \delta(1) > \alpha + \delta(0)$$
$$\delta > \alpha - 1$$

Because I present many equilibria of iterated Prisoners' Dilemma in this chapter, I state each equilibrium in full to aid in comparing the common conjecture underlying each. Reciprocal strategies can be described by the actions to be taken in a punishment state and a normal state. The normal state occurs when their arrangement is in force, and the punishment state occurs when one of the players violates the arrangement. The strategies specify what each player should do in a round depending on the current state and rules for when the players shift between the states as a consequence of their actions. The first equilibrium is the subgame perfect version of the well-known strategy of Tit-for-Tat:

Tit-for-Tat: Normal State: Both players play Cooperate. If either player plays Defect in a round, switch to Punishment State. Otherwise, remain in Normal State.

Punishment State: Both players play Defect. Switch to Normal State no matter what the players play.

What does the common conjecture do in this equilibrium? First, it tells the players that they expect to cooperate with one another. Second, it specifies the consequences of breaking the arrangement: a punishment period of one

---

[12] Carrying out the punishment is self-enforcing because (Defect; Defect) is an equilibrium of the stage game.

round. Third, and most importantly, it allows the players to distinguish when a play of Defect is a violation of the arrangement and when it is acceptable, indeed even mandated, punishment of a violation; the former when they are in the Normal State and the latter in the Punishment State. Only the history of the game as understood through the common conjecture of this equilibrium allows the players to determine when a play of Defect is acceptable. This parallels the use of tariffs in the bilateral enforcement of arrangements to lower barriers to international trade under World Trade Organization (WTO) law. The same action, placing a tariff on goods imported from another country, can be an illegal violation in one case and acceptable retaliation in another. The shared understanding of when such retaliation is allowed allows governments to understand how tariffs will be perceived by other states and what the likely response to their use will be.

Furthermore, the common conjecture guarantees that both players understand how one another should perceive and react to a play of Defect by either of them. Neither player can credibly claim that a play of Defect in the Normal State was allowable retaliation, and they should therefore not be punished in the next round. The moves in the game are clear enough that the proper response to a play of Defect, including none, becomes common knowledge through the common conjecture and the public nature of events. Obviously, the real world is not so clear, and the creation of a common interpretation of what actions constitute violations of an arrangement is central to any system that uses punishment to enforce an arrangement, whether through reciprocity or a judicial system that uses third parties to carry out punishments.

The first variation on the Tit-for-Tat equilibrium increases the length of the punishment phase. There is a class of equilibria for longer but finite punishments:

> N-round Punishments: Normal State: Both players play Cooperate. If either player plays Defect in a round, switch to Punishment State. Otherwise, remain in Normal State.
>
> Punishment State: Both players play Defect. Switch to Normal State after $n$ rounds in a row in this state.[13]

This class contains an infinite number of equilibria; the only difference across their common conjectures is how long punishments last. Clearly, the precise

---

[13] To be careful, I should have *n+1* states, one Normal, and *n* Punishment states, labeled Punishment-1, Punishment-2, and so on up to Punishment-n. A play of Defect in the Normal state shifts to Punishment-1. Punishment-i shifts to Punishment-(i+1) at the end of a round, with Punishment-n shifting to Normal. This way the Punishment states count the rounds of punishment that have passed. This distinction becomes important if the players punished one another with minmax strategies that are not Nash. Then the player carrying out the punishment needs an incentive to carry through with the punishment.

For those interested, the condition that $\delta$ must satisfy for an n-round Punishment strategies to form an equilibrium is $\delta^{n+1} > \alpha(1 - \delta)$ .

nature of the common conjecture matters. The players need to know more than just that they will employ reciprocity to enforce their arrangement. If $n$ rounds of punishment are insufficient to deter breaking the arrangement, but $n+1$ are sufficient, the length of the punishments must be common knowledge for the arrangement to be enforceable.[14]

The common conjecture also needs to specify how the players will cooperate. Commonly, it is assumed that both players will play Cooperate on every round. There are, however, other ways to cooperate in iterated Prisoners' Dilemma. The players could agree to exploit one another on alternate rounds, that is, play (Cooperate; Defect) one round and (Defect; Cooperate) the next. This possibility is generally eliminated from consideration by assuming that both players do better if they both play Cooperate every round instead of alternating exploiting one another. Furthermore, arrangements that treat the players differently can also be supported in equilibrium, such as an arrangement that allows one of the players to Defect without retaliation every other round. The following equilibrium details this possibility:

> Player 1 Exploits Player 2: Odd-Round Normal State: Both players play Cooperate. If Player 1 plays Defect in a round, switch to Punish-1 State. If Player 2 plays Defect in a round, switch to Punish-2 State. Otherwise, shift to Even-Round Normal State.
>
> Even-Round Normal State: Player 1 plays Defect, Player 2 plays Cooperate. If Player 2 plays Defect in this round, switch to Punish-2 State. Otherwise, shift to Odd-Round Normal State.
>
> Punish-1 State: Both players play Defect. Switch back to Odd-Round Normal State no matter what the players play.
>
> Punish-2 State: Player 1 plays Defect, Player 2 plays Cooperate. If Player 2 defects, stay in this state; otherwise, switch back to Even-Round Normal State.

The arrangement in which Player 1 exploits Player 2 every other round can be enforced with this punishment scheme if both parties will play Cooperate on even-numbered rounds and Player 2 is willing to allow Player 1 to exploit her on the odd-numbered rounds rather than suffer punishment. The following three inequalities, the first two for Player 2 and the third for Player 1, are necessary:

$$\frac{\delta^2 (1 + \beta)}{1 + \delta} > \alpha - 1$$

---

[14] To be careful again, only common knowledge that punishments will last at least $n+1$ rounds is needed here. Because that length of punishment is sufficient to lead both parties to honor their arrangement, we never observe a play of Defect or a punishment in equilibrium. Common knowledge of the length of punishments becomes an important issue once we elaborate the model so that the arrangement is broken some times in equilibrium. Consider the problem of what happens if I think punishments last ten rounds while you think they last eleven.

$$\frac{\delta^2(1+\beta)}{1+\delta} > \beta$$

$$\delta > \frac{\alpha - 1}{\alpha}$$

Even if alternate exploitation cannot be enforced, less frequent exploitation can be enforced if an arrangement to play Cooperate on every round can be enforced. As with longer punishment periods, there are an infinite number of such equilibria in which one party exploits the other in some but not all rounds. If an arrangement by which Player 1 exploits Player 2 once every million rounds can be enforced, then so can an arrangement where he exploits her every million-and-one rounds, another where he exploits her every million-and-two rounds, and so on.

These asymmetric arrangements are in both players' interest in two senses. First, both receive a higher average payoff than if they both play Defect every round. Second, an asymmetric arrangement may be enforceable when a symmetric one is not. If one player does not value the future enough that the punishment deters him from playing Defect (i.e., $\delta_i < \alpha - 1$), increasing his average benefit by allowing him to exploit the other player occasionally might make the arrangement enforceable. Such situations can happen once the game is no longer symmetric in payoffs or discount factors.

A numerical example may help clarify asymmetric arrangements. Figure 2.6 gives a normalized Prisoners' Dilemma that is not symmetric in the payoffs or discount factors. The symmetric arrangement to play Cooperate in every round cannot be enforced with one-round punishments because Player 1 will want to play Defect (numerically, $\delta_1 = .85 < .9 = \alpha_{1-1}$). However, the asymmetric arrangement in which Player 1 exploits Player 2 every other round can be enforced. Substituting the relevant numbers into the three inequalities detailed earlier, Player 2 will play Cooperate in the rounds when both play Cooperate because

$$\frac{\delta_2^2(1+\beta_2)}{1+\delta_2} = \frac{(.8)^2(1+.5)}{1+.8} = .53 > .4 = \alpha_2 - 1$$

Player 2 will play Cooperate in the rounds when Player 1 exploits her because

$$\frac{\delta_2^2(1+\beta_2)}{1+\delta_2} = \frac{(.8)^2(1+.5)}{1+.8} = .53 > .5 = \beta_2$$

Player 1 will play Cooperate in rounds when both play Cooperate because

$$\delta_1 = .85 > .47 = \frac{\alpha_1 - 1}{\alpha_1}$$

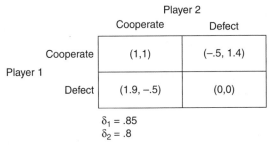

FIGURE 2.6 An asymmetric prisoners' dilemma that requires an asymmetric equilibrium.

In this example, the players will not live up to a shared understanding to play Cooperate every round in this game, but the asymmetric arrangement in which Player 1 gets to exploit Player 2 every other round can be sustained. I am not making any claims about how such an understanding arose; I am merely observing which shared understandings induce stable behavior in this situation.

Asymmetric arrangements can be sustained provided that both players receive average benefits beyond what they receive when both played Defect. Those benefits must be sufficient to deter defection from the arrangement accounting for the discounting of punishments in the future. There is a complete range of divisions of the gains of cooperation that can be split between the players and enforced given the appropriate cooperative arrangement. This result is the well-known Folk Theorem for repeated games (Fudenberg and Maskin 1986; see Morrow [1994a, chapter 9] for a non-technical discussion); any individually rational, feasible division of the payoffs can be enforced in a repeated game given a sufficiently high discount factor. The converse of this conveys my point; if any cooperative arrangement is enforceable for a given stage game and discount factors of the players, then an infinite number of such arrangements may generally be enforced.[15] Each equilibrium in this infinite set has a different common conjecture, therefore the specific common conjecture is essential to understanding what the players will do.

The common conjecture must specify how the players will cooperate and what behavior is acceptable and unacceptable under the arrangement. Occasional defection by a player is acceptable in an asymmetric equilibrium but not in the symmetric equilibrium. The degree and frequency of exploitation also must be specified. Both of these elements of the common conjecture look like a normative agreement between the players about appropriate behavior. It also helps them understand and interpret one another's behavior correctly.

---

[15] The exceptions occur when strict equality holds in the enforcement conditions or when there are no divisions when both players receive more than in the punishment strategy employed, whether it is a Nash equilibrium or a minmax strategy.

These asymmetric equilibria may be common in the real world; they represent situations in which one of the parties compensates the other to obtain its cooperation. In the model, occasional exploitation is the only way for the parties to redistribute the gains from their cooperative arrangement. Because Prisoners' Dilemma is typically presented as a symmetric game, attention is naturally focused on the symmetric cooperative arrangement. Situations that produce asymmetric gains for the parties from an arrangement may lead to efforts to redistribute those gains. Once in place, an asymmetric arrangement could be quite stable; it is Pareto optimal within the set of such equilibria.[16] Player 1 prefers an asymmetric equilibrium in which he gets to exploit Player 2 some of the time to the symmetric equilibrium where both players play Cooperate every round.

In its simplest form, iterated Prisoners' Dilemma has multiple classes of equilibria in which each class has an infinite number of possible equilibria. The common conjecture plays a critical role here because of this multiplicity of equilibria. The players cannot cooperate without a shared understanding of *how* they will cooperate, when a play of Defect is a violation of their arrangement, and what the consequences of such violations are. Among the asymmetric equilibria, there is great variation in behavior from rare acts of exploitation to frequent exploitation. The common conjecture, not the payoff structure of the game, drives this variation. Like a norm, it defines what behavior is appropriate and how to respond to inappropriate behavior, and allows actors to anticipate how one another will act.

## Elaborations of Iterated Prisoners' Dilemma

In the world of the model, the symmetric equilibria produce the same behavior – both players play Cooperate every round – when the punishment is sufficient to deter defection regardless of how long the punishments would last if they occurred. In the real world, we observe actions perceived to be violations of arrangements and punishments in response. We need to elaborate the model for these to occur in equilibrium.

The stage game of iterated Prisoners' Dilemma is simple; the common conjecture increases in complexity if we add additional complications to the stage game. These complications lead to behavior in equilibrium, such as defections and punishments, which the simple model does not produce. They add new features, such as larger strategy sets (more moves), limited information about moves and outcomes, and more than two players, while retaining the structure of the payoffs. They also lead to common conjectures that reflect norms more clearly.

The players know exactly what one another has done in iterated Prisoners' Dilemma. This certainty has three important effects on their ability to enforce

---

[16] *Pareto optimality* means that any change that makes one player better off makes the other worse off, so there are no changes that both would agree to.

an arrangement. First, certainty allows them to determine both when a violation has occurred and, therefore, when punishment is in order. Second, certainty allows them to know who has violated the arrangement, so that any retaliation can be directed at the violator if that is possible within the game. The difference between these first two may seem trivial in a two-player game, but it becomes important when there are more than two players. Third, certainty creates common knowledge of the status of a violation and any retaliation for that violation. The violator cannot attempt to claim that his actions were different from this shared history of the game.

These three effects become issues when the players are not perfectly informed of one another's actions. If the players are not fully aware of one another's actions, one could interpret the consequences of the other actions as violations when the other had no intention of violating the arrangement. This problem is commonly referred to as *noise* in a parallel to information theory, where noise – as in a radio signal – makes it difficult for the receiver to understand the information in a message. Imagine the players play iterated Prisoners' Dilemma with the added feature that there is a small chance that each move is switched, Cooperate to Defect and Defect to Cooperate, after the player makes it but before the outcome is realized. You are aware of the consequences of my move through your payoff, but you do not know if a move of Defect on my part was a deliberate violation or just a switch of my move outside my control. If we could know that perfectly and commonly, then we would shift to a punishment round only when my move was publicly known to be an intentional violation. Instead, you shift to the punishment phase any time my realized move is Defect because you cannot distinguish the deliberate defections from the unintended ones. We may still be able to enforce an arrangement to play Cooperate in every round by suspending the arrangement for a round if the chance of mistaken moves is not too large. The equilibrium is the same as Tit-for-Tat with the possibility that we move to the punishment stage because of a random switch of move:

> Tit-for-Tat with Errors in Moves: Normal State: Both players play Cooperate. If either player's effective move is Defect in a round, switch to Punishment State. Otherwise, remain in Normal State.
>
> Punishment State: Both players play Defect. Switch to Normal State no matter what the players play.

Notice that both players attempt to comply fully with their arrangement; punishment is always a mistake in equilibrium because neither player ever chooses to play Defect. The players carry out these unjustified punishments because if they did not punish all reported moves of Defect, even the unintended one, they could not deter deliberate plays of Defect.

Because the precise condition for both players playing Cooperate in every round is complicated, I do not present it here. As the chance of incorrect moves increases (chance of move changed close to one-half), the direct Tit-for-Tat strategy cannot deter violations of the arrangement; good intentions will often result in bad outcomes and resultant punishments, and bad intentions will not draw punishment sufficiently often. The connection between intentions and outcomes becomes difficult to perceive when there is a lot of noise in the decisional environment. Under these circumstances, the players wait and accumulate a pattern of possible violations before punishing. Consequently, punishments become irregular in that not every possible violation triggers an immediate response. To compensate for the irregularity of punishment, they increase the length of punishment periods. Both players, however, still continue to play Cooperate in every period; each player is deterred from playing Defect, and thus raising the chance that it exploits the other in that period, because that play increases the likelihood that it will accumulate enough plays of Defect over time – even if the rest of them are unintentional – to trigger punishment.

Lack of certainty about whether a violation has occurred need not prevent effective reciprocal enforcement, provided that the players have some idea when violations happen. They shift into a punishment period when sufficient public evidence of a violation exists. The risk of punishment must be high enough to deter intentional violations, and so sufficient evidence of a defection is defined by how often punishment must occur for successful deterrence. In the Tit-for-Tat with Errors in Moves equilibrium, for example, the players enter into punishment every time a play of Defect is observed outside a punishment round. No tolerance of defection is allowed.

This equilibrium, however, is not efficient because punishments will occur. Every round of punishment reduces the value the players could have received and divided through some complicated arrangement over time. Efficiency requires that the players be able to target perceived violators with specific punishments, rather than imposing costs on both players. In our example of iterated Prisoners' Dilemma with noise, both players play Defect when one or the other must be punished. This is inefficient because both players lose value during a punishment. The players can distinguish which player is more likely to have played Defect when an outcome in which one plays Cooperate and the other plays Defect occurs. Rather than shift to both playing Defect after such an occurrence, the players could instead allow the player whose realized move was Cooperate to exploit the other during the next round; the former plays Defect while the other plays Cooperate, raising the chance that exploitation of the latter by the former is the result. This punishment is efficient in the sense that the result is Pareto optimal. In essence, these punishments adjust the distribution of the value that the players generate through their arrangement, compensating the damaged party for its short-term loss. The logic of why the players are willing to allow themselves to be exploited matches the logic of the asymmetric equilibria earlier; violating the arrangement leads to a worse outcome for that player. Of course, all of these considerations are probabilistic. The players do not know that either has intentionally violated the arrangement. Instead, they, make judgments about when they should adjust the arrangement to favor an exploited party based on a pattern of such exploitation, whether intentional or not.

This punishment strategy of compensating the damaged party at the expense of the possible violator forms the base for a Folk Theorem for games in which moves are not directly observable but can be inferred from public actions (Fudenberg, Levine, and Maskin 1994). In general, the players can get as close as they want to any feasible, individually rational distribution of the payoffs through some equilibrium, even though the players cannot directly observe one another's moves, provided that the discount factor is high enough. This result requires that the players can discern which player is more likely to have caused each outcome that violates the terms of their arrangement, so that the distribution of payoffs can be adjusted to reduce that player's share in favor of the other players, if sufficient evidence of violations by that player accumulates.

This result also requires that the players be able to target those who have been judged to be violators through the accumulation of sufficient evidence. This is the second effect of noise on reciprocal enforcement. If the players cannot discern which player is responsible for violations or cannot target that player individually, reciprocal punishments must be inefficient. A simple public goods game is an example of these problems. Imagine that 100 of us play a game in which each round we either contribute or not to the public good. The amount of the public good purchased depends on the number of contributions. Each player's marginal benefit from his or her contribution is less than his or her personal cost of that contribution. Each player's payoff is, say, *(# of total contributions) − 2(if he or she has contributed)*. The well-known logic here matches the Prisoners' Dilemma; not contributing dominates contributing. The players may be to able enforce an arrangement by which all contribute by using a reciprocal strategy where they respond to a failure of any player to contribute by all refusing to contribute in the next round. This reciprocal enforcement is inefficient because everyone loses during a punishment round.

This inefficiency can be eliminated if the players can discern which player is likely to have caused any particular violation of the agreement and if they are able to punish that player selectively. Typically, we expect that neither is the case in public goods problems; our contributions are anonymous, and we cannot withhold the benefits of the goods from anyone. However, the absence of either of these conditions is sufficient to make reciprocity inefficient. Being able to target punishments does not help if we cannot come to a common understanding of who has violated our arrangement, and knowing who has done what does not help if we cannot target the party responsible for a violation.

The common conclusion of Folk Theorems is that any feasible, individually rational set of payoffs can be achieved through some equilibrium of the repeated game *provided* that the discount factor is high enough. Concern for future payoffs, as reflected in the discount factor, is central to any scheme of reciprocity. Because actors care about their future payoffs, threats to lower their payoffs in the future can deter intentional violations. Even if the benefits of exploiting the other player are great in the short run, long run reductions in payoffs can take away all of those benefits *provided* the discount factor is high enough. If it is difficult to tell who has done what because of noise, players are willing to wait for enough information to collect before punishing *provided* that the discount factor is high enough that the eventual punishment will remove the benefits of any exploitation. Actors can use reciprocity to enforce just about any division of the payoffs *provided* that the discount factor is high enough.

Unfortunately, actors cannot choose their own discount factors. In practice then, actors will not be able to produce efficient distributions of payoffs. Noise introduces inefficiency through unnecessary sanctions. In the limit, unnecessary sanctions can be controlled by collecting information over a longer period of time to determine significant violations of the arrangement (Abreu, Pearce, and Stacchetti 1990). Additionally, compensation can be fine-tuned across longer periods of time to allow any feasible distribution of the payoffs. Fixed discount factors reduce the efficacy of each of these measures by placing a limit on how long the actors can collect information before punishing and limiting their ability to use any feasible redistribution as a sanction.

I now return to the question of the role of the common conjecture in these systems of reciprocity under noise. Earlier, the common conjecture specified how the players would cooperate, when sanctions were triggered, and what those sanctions were. It does the same thing in these equilibria but in much greater detail. The common conjecture of an equilibrium of one of these repeated games with noise details not only what the players' arrangement is but also how it adjusts over time in response to perceived violations of the arrangement. It must also describe what evidence is considered sufficient to judge that a violation of the agreement has occurred. It acts like a norm that prescribes how the actors are supposed to conduct themselves. If such common conjectures do not derive from an explicit agreement of the players but are instead a feature of the existing strategic situation, the distinctions among acceptable and unacceptable behavior may seem as arbitrary as constructivists describe some norms.

The third element of iterated Prisoners' Dilemma that noise could undermine is the common knowledge of when punishments should occur. The results about noise that I have discussed so far assume that the players still share a public signal about what has happened. The players use this signal to make their own personal judgments about what has happened and to ensure that those judgments are common knowledge. For instance, the outcome of each round of iterated Prisoners' Dilemma with noise was made public. The players may not have known exactly what the other had done, but they both knew what the result of those moves and the noise combined was. They could then respond to any observed move of Defect with a punishment round, knowing that one another would correctly anticipate that punishment round.

Reciprocal enforcement generally becomes more difficult without such public signals of what has happened in the game.[17] Unfortunately, the actors in many situations do not have such public signals. For example, consider two countries trying to enforce a trade agreement to limit non-tariff barriers. Each country knows whether it has adopted such barriers, and each receives reports about whether the other has barriers in place. How should one respond to a claim by the other that it has sufficient evidence of the first one's barriers that it will raise its own barriers in response? Regardless of the actual policies, the second side does not know if the first has sufficient intelligence to conclude that it has adopted policies that violate their agreement. Perhaps the first side does not have that evidence and is using its claim to justify raising its own barriers. It seems likely that both will enter into a period of rising barriers, but who is the target of this punishment and how will they know when to end it? Furthermore, it will be difficult to use a scheme of compensation to enforce an arrangement because both sides may not agree on who should compensate whom. The essence of the problem is that private signals and messages based on those signals do not necessarily build a common understanding of the state of the game, specifically whether or not they are in a punishment phase. A public signal avoids this problem because both sides can refer to the public signal in light of their shared understanding. Even if the public signal is inaccurate in some cases, at least the current state of the game is common knowledge between the two parties. The dispute resolution procedure of the WTO produces a public signal of which side of a dispute is correct. That signal eliminates ambiguity about which party is in the wrong and can prescribe compensation through tariffs, which are then not violations.

An additional problem complicates the interpretation of private signals. Because each player's signal is coordinated with the other player's action, the first player's interpretation of that signal depends on his or her equilibrium anticipations of how the other player should play the game. Imagine that two players are playing iterated Prisoners' Dilemma, and both understand that they will play Cooperate on every round and enforce it with a reciprocal threat. What should one conclude if it receives a signal that the other has played Defect in a round? It could be that the latter has broken their understanding by playing Defect or that the signal is in error. Given that the first believes that the second is playing Cooperate, it should place great weight on the signal being in error, and consequently, it should not punish the second in the next round by playing Defect. But if the second player knows that the first will not punish it after one signal that it played Defect, the first cannot deter it from playing Defect once, and the arrangement to play Cooperate unravels.

This discussion should not be taken to suggest that the absence of public signals makes reciprocal enforcement impossible. Instead, a private signal with

---

[17] Kandori (2003) provides a good discussion of the literature and issues therein.

noise is a more difficult problem than a public signal with noise, and the former is not understood as well as the latter.

### Reciprocity, Common Conjectures, and Norms

Two main ideas need to be drawn from this discussion of iterated Prisoners' Dilemma and its variations. The first concerns the nature of reciprocity; the second concerns the role of the common conjecture in systems of reciprocity. The simple strategy of Tit-for-Tat in iterated Prisoners' Dilemma gives rise to what Robert Keohane has called specific reciprocity – "situations where specified partners exchange items of equivalent value in a strictly delimited sequence" (1986, 4). It is direct reciprocity; punishment is immediate and proportionate to a violation. The discussion in the prior section leads to what Keohane calls diffuse reciprocity – "the definition of equivalence is less precise, one's partners may be viewed as a group rather than as particular actors, and the sequence of events is less narrowly bounded" (Keohane 1986, 4). The reciprocity in the full range of models in the prior section is diffuse. The response to a perceived violation may come much later, only after sufficient evidence has accumulated. That response may take the form of compensation to the damaged party instead of punishment of the violator. These relations are regulated by complex shared understandings of acceptable behavior and responses to unacceptable behavior.

All of these issues have to be addressed in the common conjecture, which must be established before play begins. For a common conjecture to support effective reciprocal punishments, it must satisfy two conditions. First, *it must specify how the players will cooperate*. That specification determines what behavior is acceptable and what behavior is unacceptable. The latter are violations of the agreement and are subject to retaliation or compensation. It may be that a pattern of violations must accumulate before a response is warranted. Second, *it must specify how violations will be addressed*. Reciprocity is the central idea here; what unacceptable behaviors are states allowed to employ in response to a violation of the agreement? It could be that the existing pattern of acceptable behavior is altered to compensate a damaged party. The first condition delineates the agreement, and the second defines how the agreement will be enforced.

Because a wide range of possible arrangements are enforceable through some equilibrium of the repeated game, the common conjecture plays a large role in determining behavior. The standards of behavior incorporated in the common conjecture are as important as the underlying interests captured in the payoffs.

The common conjecture must also be common knowledge (only mutual knowledge is required if there are two players), that is, all must hold the same anticipation about one another's behavior and have all degrees of knowledge that they hold that anticipation. Simple declarations of intent are not sufficient to create common knowledge. For example, a state could declare that it will refrain from using a particular weapon during wartime. Such statements could be signals of its privately known information, thereby conveying information about its future actions. Of course, such signals face the question of credibility; will the other actors believe the message in the signal? Even if that declaration is completely credible, it does not create a common conjecture because it does not specify the behavior of other states. The creation of mutual knowledge typically requires more than simple declarations of future intent (Chwe 2001).

## IDENTITIES AND COMMON CONJECTURES

In Dr. Seuss' classic children's story "The Sneeches," there are two kinds of Sneeches, those with stars on their bellies and those "with none upon thars" (Seuss 1961). The Star-Belly Sneeches exclude those without stars from their parties and flaunt that they "are the best kind of Sneeches on the beaches." This system of discrimination is an example of identity as social role; the Star-Bellied Sneeches treat the Plain-Bellies differently, and their identification of the Plain-Bellies as inferior and unworthy of consorting with is understood by all in both groups (not that the Plain-Bellies like the distinction). Can such distinctions in social roles be captured in the common conjecture of an equilibrium?

To show that it can, consider iterated Prisoners' Dilemma with social matching. These models have a large number of players who are matched in pairs every round to play Prisoners' Dilemma. The matching can be done randomly (where the chance of meeting a particular player again depends on the number of players), or in turnpike fashion (where the players form two infinite lines that march past one another, guaranteeing that no pair will ever meet again in the future).

Whether the players meet again or not, some knowledge of prior plays is essential for reciprocal enforcement, although very little knowledge of prior plays may be necessary for effective enforcement (Ellison 1993). If every player's complete history of play is public knowledge, defectors can be punished by the players they meet in the future. On the other hand, if all histories of play are private and players never meet again, enforcement requires a complicated pattern of play to make it possible.[18] Without such a pattern, the players need

---

[18] Ellison (1993) describes such an equilibrium, proves it always exists for Prisoners' Dilemma, and shows that it is robust to noise. Every player shifts to playing Defect after experiencing a play of Defect either by herself or the other player in any round. One play of Defect then propagates across the players over time, creating an indirect punishment for the player who first played Defect. This descent into defection is not permanent, however. There is a public signal at the start of each round, and all players return to playing Cooperate when it has particular values. These values effectively cap the expected duration of the spread of defection and are calculated to give penalty that is large enough to deter an initial play of Defect and small enough that players are willing to participate in the descent into defection.

I find it hard to see how such a common conjecture would arise in practice. The real question is whether this sort of arrangement or one that relies on a formal institution, such as the Law Merchant (Milgrom et al. 1990), is more likely to arise over time.

some way to credibly communicate their prior plays to inform others when to punish the player they face in a round. Institutions could aid in the collection and dissemination of information as in the example of a model of the medieval Law Merchant (Milgrom, North, and Weingast 1990). The Law Merchant registers a record of play, specifically a list of all players who have played Defect when they were supposed to play Cooperate. Players can pay the Law Merchant to check the record of the player they will play in the current round. Should the report indicate that the other player has played Defect in the past, the player knows to play Defect against that player. In essence, the merchants no longer trade with any merchant who has a record of cheating another.

I will assume for now, however, that all players know the complete history of all opponents in their social matching game. My interest is not in the interesting informational problems posed in a social matching game but on the existence of equilibria in which the players have different social roles. If all moves are public knowledge, each player knows what moves her current partner has made in every round to date. Players can separate all other players into two groups; Normal players who have honored the arrangement in the previous round, and Shunned players who have not. As a group, all of them can then use simple reciprocal strategies to enforce an arrangement to play Cooperate:

> Social Matching Tit-for-Tat: If neither player is currently Shunned (both players are Normal): Both players play Cooperate. Any player who plays Defect in a round becomes Shunned. Otherwise, remain as a Normal.
>
> If either player is currently Shunned: Both players play Defect. Switch both players to Normal no matter what the players play.

The conditions for this equilibrium are the same as Tit-for-Tat with two players. With the knowledge of who has cheated, the players can enforce an arrangement to play Cooperate even if no two players ever meet again. The punishments are decentralized to whoever plays a defector in the next round.

Asymmetric equilibria of a social matching game have a similar logic to the asymmetric equilibria of the two-player game in which one player had the right to exploit the other under conditions that both understood. The following equilibrium has two different groups of players, Star-Bellies and Plain-Bellies, and the Star-Bellies exploit the Plain-Bellies:

> The Sneeches Equilibrium: Normal round: Both play Cooperate if both players are from the same group. If not, the Star-Belly plays Defect and the Plain-Belly Cooperate. Any player who deviates from these moves becomes Shunned.
>
> Round Facing a Shunned Player: Both play Defect. The Shunned player returns to the group it came from afterward.

The Shunned category is necessary for punishing those who do not follow the arrangement. A straightforward calculation for the Plain-Bellies gives the following conditions on the discount factor where $p$ is the fraction of Star-Bellies in the population:

$$\delta > \frac{\beta}{1-p(1+\beta)} \quad and \quad \delta > \frac{\alpha-1}{1-p(1+\beta)}$$

Because the discount factor has to be less than one, we have the following conditions on the maximum proportion of Star-Bellies in the population:

$$p < \frac{1-\beta}{1+\beta} \quad and \quad p < \frac{1-(\alpha-1)}{1+\beta}$$

Under these conditions, the Plain-Bellies will accept exploitation when they meet a Star-Belly out of fear of being Shunned and missing the value of interacting with the other Plain-Bellies. In essence, the Plain-Bellies are enforcing the system that oppresses them. We typically think that the superior group enforces an oppressive order; here the inferior group has to enforce it because the superior group does not have a punishment worse than exploitation.[19]

The common conjecture of the Sneeches Equilibrium requires that the players be able to distinguish the members of each group on contact. The central characteristic of a Sneech is the visible star or absence thereof on their belly. The presence or absence of a star allows both members of each pair to know on inspection the group of each new partner, and therefore, how to act with that partner. It defines the social role of each individual immediately on inspection. In "The Sneeches," the discriminatory system breaks down once Sylvester McMonkey McBean arrives with his Star-On and Star-Off machines. The Plain-Belly Sneeches are willing to pay to make themselves indistinguishable from the Star-Bellies, who pay even more to try and reestablish the visible distinction that the system requires. Sylvester McMonkey McBean uses their desires to extract all their money, leaving the Sneeches in the position that the presence or absence of a star has no connection with their original group membership, and the system ends by common agreement (Seuss 1961).

I hope the point of this story is obvious to the reader. The only difference between the system of equals in the Social Matching Tit-for-Tat equilibrium and the system with sharply differentiated social roles in the Sneeches Equilibrium is the common conjecture. There is no difference in the game being played; the identities of the players are endogenous to the equilibrium being played. I am not asking how such a system arose, merely that once in place, the common conjecture explains the difference in identity across the two equilibria.

---

[19] One could create an equilibrium in which the Star-Bellies enforce the system by punishing deviant Plain-Bellies themselves if the Star-Bellies did not exploit every Plain-Belly they meet. Then the Plain-Bellies might allow themselves to be exploited so as to not lose the benefits of the times that a Star-Belly will not exploit them. Dr. Seuss' story implies that interaction with a Star-Belly is better than with a Plain-Belly, but he does not explain the off-the-equilibrium-path strategy that enforces the system of discrimination.

The idea of reflecting differences in social roles in the common conjectures of different equilibria has been used to explain social phenomena. Barry O'Neill (1999) creates equilibria with differences in players to represent systems of honor, where the players behave against their short-term interest to protect their long-term interest in defending their social position. He lays out an equilibrium with a hierarchy of six roles. My own model of coordination in the face of distributional and informational issues (Morrow 1994b) has four classes of equilibria, three in which the players hold identical roles and a fourth in which their roles are differentiated into a leader and follower. Milgrom et al. (1990) use the creation of the novel social role of the Law Merchant to explain the shift that provides the information on prior play necessary for reciprocal enforcement of long-distance trade. Institutionalization can create novel social roles that shape and support different social orders, and these changes can be thought of as shifts in the common conjecture that lead to the players adopt new social roles without changing their incentives or available actions.

## COMMUNICATION AND COMMON CONJECTURES

Constructivists believe that norms play a large role in shaping communication (cf. Risse 2000; Crawford 2002). Much communication is symbolic rather than verbal, and the lexicon of available symbolic acts may constrain and shape what we can communicate with one another. The structure of the language we use may also constrain and shape what we communicate and how we do it. Can the common conjecture of an equilibrium capture these ideas?

Communication in games concerns future moves. In signaling games, one player (called the "sender") attempts to convey something about the game to another player (called the "receiver"). In more general games with communication, all players will be both senders and receivers at some time during the game. In some cases, the sender tries to inform the receiver what moves she will make in response to possible moves he may make. In other cases, the sender may know something about the consequences of moves available to the receiver that could alter his choice if he knew the information. Two things are true in all cases of communication; there are multiple possibilities known to both the sender and the receiver, and the receiver does not know which possibility is true or will happen. The interests of the sender and receiver may be identical as in games of pure coordination, but they typically have a conflict of interest at some level. Differences in interests allow us to explore strategic information transmission, where the sender may attempt to bluff or dissemble to advance her interests at the expense of the receiver. Knowing this, the receiver may be inclined to discredit the signals of the sender.

Two types of communication are commonly considered in game theoretic models. Costly signals are actions that convey meaning because the sender must pay some cost to perform the act. Only a sender with this particular information would be willing to pay the cost to send the message, and so sending

|            |   | Player 2 A | Player 2 B |
|------------|---|------------|------------|
| Player 1   | A | (2,1)      | (0,0)      |
|            | B | (0,0)      | (1,2)      |

FIGURE 2.7 Strategic form of battle of the sexes.

that signal convinces the receiver of the sender's information. Some gifts and favors operate as costly signals in ordinary life. In Chinese cuisine, for example, there are many rare and expensive dishes that are used as signals of the high esteem the host has for the guest. I attended a conference in Taiwan at which we were served sea cucumber at every dinner. Although the preparations were excellent in every case, I attach little value to eating sea cucumber even when it is well-prepared. However, sea cucumber is rare and expensive, so the host serves it to send the message "See how important you are to me? I even bought sea cucumber for you!"[20] In the extreme, one can think of costly signals as "burning money," destroying value simply to send a message.

Cheap talk involves actions that impose no cost whatsoever to send the signal. Much verbal communication is thought of as cheap talk. Costly signals transmit information because both parties know of the cost of sending the message. Cheap talk transmits information because it has effects on the moves the players make later in the game; it generates costs within the game itself even if sending the message is free. The original example of cheap talk (Farrell 1987) addressed coordination of moves in the game known as Battle of the Sexes depicted in Figure 2.7. Both players would like to make the same move, A or B, but Player 1 prefers they coordinate on A, Player 2 on B. If Player 1 tells Player 2 that he will play B in the game, this cheap talk signal can lead both players to play B by producing a shared expectation that they will play that combination of moves. Because that combination of moves is a Nash equilibrium of the game, both players' strategies after the signals are received are best replies.

Cheap talk is meaningless if the players deliberately ignore it. If both know that Player 1's announcement has no correlation with his move, then it should have no effect on Player 2's move because it does not change her expectation about what move Player 1 will make. Games with cheap talk always have multiple equilibria because there is always a "babbling equilibrium," where the players ignore the messages. In this sense, cheap talk models show that communication requires both a common language and a shared understanding to use it.

---

[20] My cynical, Western tastes make me wonder, "Have they never heard of French wine?" One can spend vast amounts of money on French wine, and I actually enjoy consuming it, unlike sea cucumber.

Additionally, models with cheap talk always have equilibria in which the understanding of the message is reversed. Because a cheap talk message is free, its content can be changed as long as the common conjecture that allows the players to interpret those messages changes with it. In everyday life, turn signals are an excellent example of cheap talk. On the freeway, signaling the intent to change lanes can help avoid collisions. In the United States, one turns on the turn signal on the side of lane that the driver intends to change into. Other cars can anticipate the lane change and avoid a collision. Activating the turn signal does not lock me into turning, making it cheap talk. Nor is it necessary to signal to change lanes; indeed, many drivers never signal their intent. Still, accurate use of turn signals can be in all drivers' interests.[21] Furthermore, there are multiple ways to signal changes of lane. In the United States, one puts on the signal before moving and turns it off after the change is complete. In France, where drivers are supposed to stay in the right lane and only use the left lane to pass slower cars, one turns on the left signal before entering the left lane, leaves the signal on while in the left lane, and only turns it off when the car is back in the right lane after the pass is complete. Either system of signals works provided that *everyone understands the system*.

Cheap talk models can also have a variety of systems with completely different interpretations of the messages. James Morrow (1994b) presents a model of coordination in the face of distributional and informational problems based on the Battle of the Sexes game. The players are uncertain about the exact nature of the game they are playing, and each has some information about it. No matter what game they are playing, both would like to play the same move as in the Battle of the Sexes. The model has at least four classes of equilibria, one of which is the babbling equilibrium. Two classes of equilibria use cheap talk signals to the players' mutual benefit. In one of those systems, the signals are used only to coordinate the players on one of the two available moves; in the other, the signals attempt to communicate each player's private information about the exact game they are playing to the other. If successful, both may benefit by coordinating on the superior pair of moves. The common conjecture determines which system of communication they are using, along with the signals they send and the moves they make. Additionally, the specific system they use limits what types of messages can be sent. If the players are playing the equilibrium in which the signals merely coordinate their moves, then they cannot use those signals to communicate their private information. The shared understanding of the system of signals limits their actions.

---

[21] The added value of turn signals depends on how other drivers react to a car signaling a turn. Some drivers respond to a signal of a lane change on the freeway by a car ahead of them by speeding up into the empty space, cutting off the car trying to change lanes. Understandably, drivers become reluctant to signal lane changes after experiencing this reaction a few times. Meaningful signals depend on the sender also gaining some benefit from its signal.

The common conjecture of a cheap talk equilibrium captures the shared understanding of the available messages and how they should be interpreted. That common knowledge is necessary; without it, the sender does not know which message to send, and the receiver does not know how to interpret the sender's message. Cheap talk messages are an extremely sparse language, but effective systems of cheap talk exhibit the principle of how shared understandings about how information is conveyed are essential to communication.

## IDENTITIES AND INTERESTS VERSUS PREFERENCES

Constructivists claim that rational choice models, including game theory, are unable to capture the source of interests through change in identity because such models require assumptions about actors' preferences; they believe that they can endogenize interests (Jepperson et al. 1996, 54–65; Wendt 1999, 231–233). What is the relationship between interests as understood by constructivists and preferences in rational choice theory? Is the latter silent concerning the former?

Rational choice theory assumes that an actor holds preferences over outcomes, a set of actions that it can choose (also called choices, strategies, or policies), and beliefs that relate the actions to the outcomes. An actor chooses the action it believes provides it with the most attractive option to achieve its preferred outcomes given the risk inherent in its choices. (I will not go into the details of expected utility theory or alternative ways of assessing what choice is "best" as those details are unnecessary for this discussion.) We derive an actor's preferences over strategies from its preferences over outcomes and how it believes those strategies are linked to the outcomes.

Constructivists tie interests to identities; the identity of an actor in a social setting determines its preferences. Wendt's example of pairs of states as enemies, rivals, or friends reflects this notion (Wendt 1999, 246–312). Enemies have no interest in any form of cooperation because they view one another as implacably hostile. Rivals may be able to cooperate on small issues to defuse and control their relations, but they still consider their interests to be opposed fundamentally. Friends cooperate extensively and deeply because they see their interests as shared and mutual. A variety of mechanisms – socialization, selection, imitation, and learning – could explain why and how state relations become locked into one of the identities (Wendt 1999, 318–336).

"Interests" as a concept are rarely defined, whereas preferences are clearly defined as a complete ordering over all outcomes. Interests as defined in the three categories discussed earlier allow for substantial variation in preferences. Preferences require a more detailed ordering over outcomes than just a simple belief that the other state is a rival; for instance, a choice whether to use force requires a comparison of the outcomes of winning, losing, and a peaceful, moderate settlement. Even if all agree on the order of those three outcomes, whether they agree that force should be used or not depends on how they judge the acceptability of different risks, which are part of preferences. Interests are broader than preferences because many preference orders are consistent with those interests, and interests alone are insufficient to understand choices.

Because people in the same country can hold different preferences while sharing the same ideas of national interest, divergence of preferences across actors and the resulting uncertainty that others must hold about how they will act are key in world politics. Even if U.S. policymakers all agreed that the Soviet Union was their rival during the Cold War, they had to judge the balance between hawks and doves in the Soviet leadership when judging how they thought the Soviet Union might respond. That is, Soviet leaders held different preferences even if they all agree that the United States was their rival, and U.S. leaders were uncertain about how the Soviet Union would act. Judging uncertainties about others' preferences is a central problem in world politics. So is the communication of one's own preferences to persuade others to act as one wishes.

The diversity of preferences within a country concerning exactly how shared national interests should be pursued leads to another way that ideas shape interests. They provide a shared basis for the evaluation of policies to achieve national interests. States are corporate actors, and those who compose the state and act in its interest need to justify the interests they pursue and the policies they adopt. Ideas allow them to coordinate on policies to fit specific situations and justify those policies to the politically relevant audience. Containment of communism played such a role in the United States during the Cold War. It provided both a direction to international policy and a means to explain that policy to the electorate to secure its support.[22]

Finally, the concept of preferences is more flexible than commonly realized. Nothing in division of decisions into outcomes, strategies, and beliefs specifies what those outcomes are. As analysts, we are free to choose them as we wish. Preferences that appear to be fixed can be endogenized by changing the outcomes; preferences over fixed outcomes of war and peace could instead be thought of as postwar consequences of each, where the actor in question could change its evaluation of each if it changes what consequences it believes follows from each course of action. Andrew Kydd uses a series of models to show how two states can develop a rivalry through escalation or defuse one through reassurance, thereby endogenizing their shared understanding of their relationship (Kydd 1997, 2000a, 2000b). The actors learn about one another's intentions through their actions and so revise how they are willing to act toward one another. The rivalry that is often assumed in the preferences of models of international conflict arises from the choices of the actors.

---

[22] Bukovansky (1997) has a constructivist argument for how the concept of neutrality shaped U.S. interests and policy in the early Republic.

## COMMON CONJECTURES AND LAW

Norms and common conjectures aid actors in forming strategic expectations. But the demands of a common conjecture are strong; the players must know what strategies all other players will play in all situations, and it all must be common knowledge. Law helps to establish this common knowledge by codifying norms. Writing down these understandings of proper conduct allows the actors to have a clearer idea of what those standards of conduct are, what acts breach them, and how others might respond. The ratification of treaties gives a public signal of the acceptance of that explicit standard in the treaty language. Law strengthens norms through specificity and public commitment. These two features – specificity and public commitment – make the operation of international law in practice easier to study than that of international norms. The substance of this book focuses on law for this reason.

Law, however, is not exactly a common conjecture of a game. It is an "incomplete contract" in three ways (cf. Williamson [1985] and Hart and Moore [1988] on incomplete contracts). To remind the reader, a common conjecture specifies what should happen at each move, including those off the equilibrium path, and those expectations are common knowledge.[23] It would be a complete contract among the players because they know what to do in all possible circumstances and can anticipate what others will do in those circumstances. Law, in contrast, does not detail contingencies for all possible occurrences, does not ensure that players hold the same beliefs about what should happen in unanticipated situations, nor does it ensure that all accept the law or share a common interpretation of it.

Games pose simplified structures of interrelated but limited choices. The players can only do what the game allows them to do. Actors in the real world can innovate in unanticipated ways; events never anticipated and outside their control also occur. Because no one can anticipate all possibilities in life, law cannot specify what the actors should do in all situations that might arise. Law in some cases provides specific contingent understandings about how some, well-known, and anticipated situations should be handled. The 1949 Geneva Convention on the treatment of prisoners of war (Roberts and Guelff 2000, 299–369) provides specific rules for what effects and articles can and cannot be taken from prisoners (Article 18), that prisoners cannot be denied the use of tobacco (Article 26), and the exact amounts in Swiss francs that each prisoner by rank will be paid by the detaining power (Article 60). In other cases, law instead seeks to create principles that the actors can use to judge how these situations should be handled. The 1949 Geneva Convention says only that food for prisoners must be "sufficient in quantity, quality and variety to keep prisoners of war in good health and to prevent loss of weight or the development

---

[23] Moves *off the equilibrium path* are decision nodes that are not reached when all players play their equilibrium strategies.

of nutritional deficiencies" (Article 26). Faced with an actual situation, the warring parties and any neutral monitor might be able to agree on whether the diet provided by a captor nation is sufficient from this principle. Because not all conditions can be foreseen, law offers principles for judging novel cases in the place of the complete statement of what should be done in all contingencies in a common conjecture.

Legal principles, however, do not ensure that the parties will share expectations of how novel cases should be handled. They may disagree about how to apply it to a specific situation, which principle applies when multiple principles might, and even on the general interpretation of a principle. The result is that actors disagree about what should be done and whether the rules have been broken. Even if the parties have a history of living up to the principles in a legal standard in common, anticipated cases, they might disagree when they face a novel situation. Both the Hague and Geneva conventions provide for the classic four conditions that soldiers and irregulars must meet to qualify as prisoners of war: be commanded by a responsible officer, carry a distinctive sign or emblem recognizable at a distance, carry their arms openly, and conduct themselves within the customs and laws of war. In the aftermath of the 9/11 attacks, the Bush Administration claimed that Al Qaeda operatives were "unlawful combatants" who should not receive the protections and rights of the Geneva Convention because they violated one or more of these conditions at the time of their capture. Others, including many international lawyers, disagreed, arguing that detainees either had to be tried under criminal law, be handled as prisoners of war, or be released. Without going into the lengthy evolution of the handling of detainees over two administrations, the discrepant beliefs about how this novel situation should be handled illustrate the difficulties of the application and interpretation of legal principles in specific novel cases.

Actors could further disagree about the interpretation of legal principles in general. Reprisals, violations in response to violations of the other side, were long considered an acceptable form of enforcement of conventions limiting war. The understanding of law of war has turned against reprisals, now seeing them as illegal violations rather than tolerable retaliatory enforcement. Even before reprisals became seen as illegal, states disagreed about when they could be applied. The German army during World War I saw reprisals as a necessary tool to control irregular violence in occupied areas; the Western Allies did not. Britain and France viewed the executions of Belgian and French civilians as atrocities even though the Germans justified them as reprisals.[24]

Even if the interpretation is common, the parties may not know that others have accepted them. States choose to take on legal obligations through

---

[24] As we will see in Chapter 6, most of these executions occurred even though no real attack had taken place on German soldiers. In that sense, these executions were not reprisals, even though the Germans justified them as such.

ratification, and not all have accepted all treaties. Even if ratification signals acceptance of a treaty standard, states can and have ignored those commitments during wartime. Unlike a common conjecture, the status of law, its interpretation, and its application cannot be taken for granted as common knowledge. Treaty negotiation and ratification are tools to help create common knowledge of a standard and its acceptance, but they do not create the certainty of common knowledge inherent in a common conjecture.

## Appendix

This appendix contains the more complicated calculations for the results in this chapter.

Limits for Player 1 Exploits Player 2: First calculate the continuation value to Player 2 in equilibrium as it differs from odd to even rounds:

$$V_2\left(odd\right) = 1 + \delta V_2\left(even\right) \quad and \quad V_2\left(even\right) = -\beta + \delta V_2\left(odd\right)$$

Solving these two equations simultaneously, we get

$$V_2\left(odd\right) = \frac{1-\delta\beta}{1-\delta^2} \quad and \quad V_2\left(even\right) = \frac{\delta-\beta}{1-\delta^2}$$

Player 2 will play Cooperate in an odd round if

$$V_2\left(odd\right) > \alpha - \delta\beta + \delta^2 V_2\left(even\right)$$

$$\frac{\delta^2\left(1-\beta\right)}{1-\delta} > \alpha - 1$$

Player 2 will play Cooperate in a Punish-2 state if

$$-\beta + \delta V_2\left(even\right) > 0 - \delta\beta + \delta^2 V_2\left(even\right)$$

$$\frac{\delta^2\left(1+\beta\right)}{1+\delta} > \beta$$

Note that if this is true, Player 2 will then play Cooperate in an even round as well. Player 1 will play Cooperate in an odd round if

$$1 + \delta\alpha > \alpha + 0\delta$$

$$\delta > \frac{\alpha-1}{\alpha}$$

# 3

# The Laws of War in Their Strategic Context

The laws of war are effective to the extent that they change how states and their soldiers fight. How the law plays out in practice – that is, how warring parties and their soldiers observe or violate the abstract principles in combat – hinge on the marriage of the abstract principles of the law to the practical situations faced on the battlefield. The practical implications of the abstract principles of that law aid the formation of expectations of conduct on the battlefield. These strategic expectations of how the other side will act shape calculations to observe or violate the law. These shared expectations can create either a battlefield limited by the restrictions of the law or one governed solely by the logic of kill-or-be-killed. Public acceptance of treaties by both sides creates expectations that the limits of the law will be observed by both sides to the best of their abilities. Such expectations may not be realized in practice because of the difficulties of limiting violence during war.

This chapter presents the general norms of the law of war and the strategic problems that make their implementation problematic. These problems occur between states at war and between their soldiers on the battlefield. Even if both warring states desire a limited battlefield, realizing one requires controlling their soldiers so they limit violence. Limiting violence during war at the state level faces the possibility of deliberate violations, opportunistic violations for short-term military advantage, and self-interested interpretations of the law. Soldiers on the battlefield may commit violations on their own initiative against state policy; they may commit inadvertent violations or use perfidy to gain an unfair advantage in combat. Any of these problems can cause the limits of the laws of war to be broken and even to fail completely if the other side retaliates in kind.

The arguments of this chapter are based on a model of the laws of war with multiple equilibria presented in the companion chapter that follows. I have separated the technical discussion of the model to spare those readers who do not wish to read the mathematical details of the formal model. This model has three separate games within it: (1) between warring states, (2) between soldiers of the two sides on the battlefield, and (3) concerning the discipline of violations within each country's military. Each individual model has its own strategic dynamics, which are described in this chapter. Multiple equilibria on the battlefield create the need for the two sides to understand which equilibrium they will play. The exact dynamics depend on what happens in the other two games. State authorities can limit violations by their own soldiers, pushing both sides toward lower levels of violations on the battlefield. At the same time, one side may believe that it will benefit during the war from violations by its own troops and so not seek to control them. Although each side knows whether or not it views limiting violations as being in its own interest, its opponent will not. There are two reasons for the sides to seek to create an agreement on conduct before war breaks out. First, both sides need to share an understanding of what will be tolerated on the battlefield. Second, each side would like to have a better idea of how the other will act so as to anticipate what will happen and how they should respond.

In this sense, the laws of war help states and their soldiers form strategic expectations of conduct during war. They establish which acts are violations, those acts that are acceptable, and what level of violations is allowable without rupturing the standard. These norms shape how states fight wars not by compelling states to follow their dictates but by shaping the strategic incentives they have during wartime. Treaty ratification of a common standard clarifies what behavior is allowable and which parties intend to adhere to that standard, subject to the limits of monitoring and enforcement. A side that believes it gains militarily from violations would like to signal that intent to ensure that both sides commit high levels of violations on the battlefield. Ratification of a fixed standard operates as a screen that separates those states willing to observe that standard from those who are not.

Testing this model requires examining the treaties that address conduct on particular issues in the laws of war to determine the standard in them. The treaty explains where the line is drawn between acceptable and unacceptable conduct. Ratification of the relevant treaty standard is a public signal by a state that it plans to honor that standard during wartime. Chapters 4 through 6 present tests of whether treaty standards and ratification explain compliance with the law. The compliance of warring parties should move together; violations by one beget violations by the other. This correlation in compliance should be stronger when both sides have ratified the relevant treaty for a given issue. Because the issues vary in their characteristics in the model (such as strategic gain from violations for a state, the vulnerability of soldiers to violations by the other side, and the ease of monitoring violations by one's own soldiers), there are systematic differences in compliance across issues. States that believe they can gain from violations should commit violations early in the fighting, and those who suffer from such violations should respond quickly, if they do so at all. Chapter 4 reports the results of large-n statistical analysis of the patterns of compliance including tests of timing of first violations. Chapter 5 compliments the statistical analysis with a close analysis of the treatment of prisoners of war (POWs) during the World Wars. POWs are a particularly useful issue to study because there is wide variation in conduct toward enemy soldiers taken prisoner even by the same state in some wars. This issue demonstrates the range of strategic responses during wartime and how law can shape those responses or fail on the individual level as well as the state level. Chapter 6 presents brief analyses of four other issues in the laws of war – chemical weapons, submarine warfare, aerial bombardment, and the treatment of civilians – that have received more recent attention in the literature. I include these issues to demonstrate the differences between my explanation and those in the literature and demonstrate why my explanation better accounts for the record. This discussion also completes the picture of how the laws of war work in practice across a number of issues.

This chapter explains the laws of war as the codification of their norms, which shape conduct on the battlefield. I begin by discussing briefly the laws of war and their central concepts. I review the reasons why states might violate those laws and the practical difficulties of implementing them when a state wishes to comply with them. Deliberate state violations and individual violations against state policy are both key issues here. I distill three strategic problems – on the battlefield, between states at war, and within each side's military – that are the basis of the three games in the model. I present the formal model of the laws of war through an informal description of it and the character of its equilibria. I lay out the logic of each of the three games separately and show how they change when the three games are combined into one model. I summarize how issues in laws of war differ on the parameters of the model and the consequences of those differences for compliance. I examine when states should be willing to make such agreements about appropriate conduct in advance of war. States are not willing to signal their intentions when entering war; instead, ratification of treaties screens out those who do not intend to comply from those who do. Finally, I argue that states have created separate treaties to act as "firewalls" to prevent the breakdown of a treaty standard on one issue from causing a breakdown on other issues. I end the chapter summarizing the implications of the model that I test in the following chapters.

THE LAWS OF WAR

The laws of war, or more properly international humanitarian law, are the body of treaty law that seeks to regulate conduct during wartime. It is traditionally separated into two parts: *jus ad bellum*, when it is lawful to use force and begin the state of war; and *jus ad bello*, lawful use of force during wartime. My interest is in the latter because I wish to focus on when states can enforce such agreements on one another. Additionally, law during wartime is applied more often and is accepted more widely than law regulating when war can occur. The Hague and the Geneva Conventions are the main sources of this law of war, although I also examine how other related treaties have worked during wartime. Levie (1986) and Detter Delupis (2000) provide good discussions of this law within their analysis of the complete range of law of war. Best (1980) gives an excellent discussion of the issues raised by the restriction of violence during wartime. Roberts and Guelff (2000) is a source for the key portions of the treaties in this area, with the Web site of the International Committee of the Red Cross (ICRC) providing the full texts.

Modern law of war traces its roots back to the middle of the nineteenth century. Henry Dunant founded the Red Cross because of his horror at the suffering of the wounded and dying at the Battle of Solferino in 1859. President Lincoln asked Francis Lieber, a law professor at Columbia University, to draw up the Lieber Code to regulate how the government treated Confederate soldiers held as prisoners during the Civil War. These early developments led to various parties drafting conventions to regulate conduct during wartime. The two Hague Conventions of 1899 and 1907 form the initial core of the modern laws of war. They cover a wide range of issues, including limitations on "the launching of projectiles and explosives from balloons" in the 1899 Convention for the following five years. The interwar period saw efforts to revise this body of law through the negotiation of new treaties, most notably the 1925 Geneva Protocol for the Prohibition of the Use of Asphyxiating, Poisonous or Other Gases, and of Bacteriological Methods of Warfare (henceforth 1925 Geneva Protocol on CBW) which outlawed first use of chemical and biological weapons and the 1929 Geneva Convention relative to the treatment of Prisoners of War (henceforth 1929 Geneva Convention). Other draft treaties, such as those addressing submarine warfare and aerial bombardment, failed to gain acceptance through ratification. The horrors of World War II led to a substantial increase in the laws of war, primarily through the 1949 Geneva Conventions, which address conduct on the high seas (II) and treatment of civilians (IV), POWs (III), and enemy wounded (I). The 1949 Geneva Conventions added detail on how exactly governments at war were supposed to handle prisoners in their control and civilians in areas under military occupation. The body of treaty law continued to develop in the following decades.

The laws of war seek to restrict the violence of war in two ways. First, they create classes of protected people and sites, including civilians, POWs, hospitals, and cultural property. Second, they limit what weapons and methods can be used in combat. Chemical weapons are an example of a limited weapon; unrestricted submarine warfare is a method of war that violates the laws of war. The laws of war seek to create a battlefield in which military personnel face off in their deadly contest. Protected people and sites cannot always be removed from the modern battlefield, so they receive legal protection. Methods of war are limited both to shield protected groups and to prevent the use of objectionable weapons. Unrestricted submarine warfare increases the risk that sailors on torpedoed ships will drown as submarines attack without warning and rarely pick up crew members of their prey from the water.

Maintaining these restrictions during wartime requires the ability to distinguish those who receive protection from combatants and military targets. Combatants are supposed to meet four tests: answer to a commanding officer, wear a distinctive and visible uniform or emblem, carry their arms openly, and follow the laws of war. The Red Cross emblem was created so that protected medical personnel and sites, including hospital ships, could be easily identified at a distance. Soldiers need to be able to distinguish protected people and sites in a combat zone if they are to avoid attacking them.

Even with these efforts to make those protected easy to identify, the application of the laws of war recognizes that not all efforts to protect them will succeed. There is collateral damage as a consequence of combat. Battles are often fought where people live, and those who live in active areas of combat cannot always get away. Honest mistakes of targeting may take place. Sometimes, defeating the enemy entails damage to protected people and sites. Whether a specific attack which damages those protected violates the law depends on two tests. First, was the attack militarily necessary? Was there another way to accomplish the mission without the damage to those protected? Although military necessity is often seen as an excuse for negligence, the original use of the concept in the early development of the law of war restricted military action from wanton destruction (Carnahan 1998). Second, was the military objective proportionate to the damage done? Destroying a city block to get one sniper is hardly proportionate. The law of war does not mean that any violence against a protected person or site is a war crime; it depends on the specific details of the action in question. The protection of the laws of war is not absolute.

The creation of protected status for some people and places also faces the problem of perfidy; those who seek to use protected status to gain an unfair advantage on the battlefield. I discuss some examples of perfidy in combat in the following sections. The laws of war also seek to prevent perfidy to prevent the breakdown of protected status. Protection of noncombatants and the prevention of perfidy are two competing and conflicting norms at the heart of the laws of war. Absolute protections could encourage perfidy, while allowing soldiers to ignore clear indications of those who are to be protected undermines their protection from combat. Strengthening one weakens the other.

Reciprocity is an unstated but necessary norm underlying the laws of war. Reprisals – violations committed in direct response to violations of the other side – played an important role historically in the enforcement of conventions to limit violence during war. The need for reprisals was recognized in the early development of the law, but later development has sought to eliminate them as a tool of enforcement. Nevertheless, retaliation for violations still occurs on the battlefield. Anticipations of retaliation shape how states and soldiers fight on the battlefield and when they commit violations. These anticipations can push in both directions, toward greater or lesser control of violations. Soldiers may control themselves out of the fear of retaliation or they may seek to act before they become victims themselves.

Reciprocity implies that the actors see one another as equal. Superiors do not have reciprocal relations with their inferiors; they command them. The laws of war rest on the assumption that states and soldiers from the warring sides see one another as equals. For states, legal equality is a central tenet of sovereignty. Compliance with the laws of war in civil conflicts poses a greater problem than in interstate wars in part because governments rarely view rebels as having the same legitimacy as the state. On the battlefield, soldiers recognize their enemies as those who they fight as combatants rather than noncombatants. One reason why soldiers follow the laws of war is to receive their protection from the enemy. That reciprocity requires a common recognition of one another as legal combatants. When the soldiers of one side view those of the other as beneath contempt, they have no reasons to honor any protection for them.

The laws of war create rights and obligations for states and individuals. States can wage war regardless of their justification. The laws only limit how states and their soldiers fight. Individual soldiers are obligated to follow the laws; they, for example, are supposed to take enemy soldiers prisoner if the latter make a recognized signal of surrender. They do not always do so in practice, however. Soldiers also gain rights, such as that to refuse to answer questions beyond identifying themselves to their captors. Soldiers gain the unstated but important right to use deadly force on the battlefield. They can kill the enemy when possible, acts that are crimes in everyday life. They do not need to give the enemy any warning or an opportunity to surrender before killing them, even if they are obligated to take prisoner those who signal their desire to surrender. The soldier then has a distinctive social role tied to permissions and obligations that define that role. Of course, soldiers often violate their obligations and take liberties with their permission to use deadly force. What are the practical problems facing the implementation of the laws of war under the conditions of combat?

## PROBLEMS FACING THE LAWS OF WAR AT THE STATE LEVEL

Effective limits on violence during wartime face a variety of problems of implementation. States and their agents may break the rules for a wide range of motivations, from seeking an advantage on the battlefield to a lack of control over subordinates. This section lays out the range of such motivations and provides examples of each from history.

### Deliberation Violation as State Policy

On September 22, 1980, the armed forces of Iraq attacked Iran after a period of prolonged tension across their common border. Iraqi forces occupied border regions including the city of Khorramshahr and laid siege to Abadan. Iran, however, fought back and began to mobilize its larger population into its army. The Iranians often used primitive tactics, relying on the fervor of their volunteer Basij militia. Their numbers turned the tide, pushed Iraq's army back across the border, and carried the war into Iraq despite heavy casualties. Iraq began to use chemical weapons, primarily mustard gas delivered by aerial bombing and artillery, to halt the Iranians. Iran had charged that Iraq used chemical weapons within the first two months of the war, but the first cases of use documented by outside experts came on March 13, 1984. Iraq sought to compensate for its weakening position on the battlefield, although it denied using chemical weapons publicly. One Iraqi general put the matter succinctly: "We have not used chemical weapons so far and I swear by God's Word I have not seen any such weapons. But if I had to finish off the enemy, and if I am allowed to use them, I will not hesitate to do so" (Robinson and Goldblat 1984). Iran retaliated with its own use of chemical weapons later in the war, although Iraq's use of these weapons was much more extensive. Both countries were party of the 1925 Geneva Protocol banning the use of chemical weapons.

Deliberate state violations pose the most direct challenge to the laws of war. A government which deliberately and systematically violates its legal obligations flouts the shared commitment to limit violence of those laws. Furthermore, its open action demonstrates that any retaliatory response is insufficient to deter that action. In some cases, such as Iraq's use of chemical weapons, the violations reflect a strategic calculation of military advantage. In other cases, these violations reflect a rejection of the norms and principles underlying the law. Japan did not ratify the 1929 Geneva Convention, a rejection that presaged its mistreatment of POWs during World War II. Deliberate state violations also include the worst and most extensive violations of the laws of war. Although they are the type of violation that come to mind easily, other types of violations also pose challenges for the limitation of violence through international law.

## Opportunistic Defection

On April 7, 1982, Great Britain declared a maritime exclusion zone (MEZ) of 200 miles around the Falkland Islands in response to the Argentine invasion of those islands on April 2 of that year. Argentine warships and naval auxiliaries within that zone were liable to attack from British forces beginning April 12. After the range of ships liable to attack in this zone was extended by the end of that month, Britain had effectively declared a blockade of the islands. Such blockades are regulated by the relevant treaties concerning conduct on the high seas.[1]

On May 1, the British submarine *HMS Conqueror*, under orders to intercept and sink the Argentine cruiser *General Belgrano* if it should enter the

---

[1] For details of the Maritime Exclusion Zone and the sinking of the *General Belgrano*, see Freedman and Gamba-Stonehouse (1990, 248–269).

MEZ, sighted its target and began to trail it. A debate now ensued among the British admirals in command of the task force off the Falklands. The *Belgrano* was Argentina's second most powerful warship, after the aircraft carrier *25 de Mayo*, and it posed a serious threat to the British task force off the islands. The British Government had already declared that the *25 de Mayo* was liable to attack even outside of the MEZ, given the threat it posed to British naval forces in the vicinity. Additionally, the Argentine Navy appeared to be maneuvering both these ships to converge on the British task force and attack in a pincers movement. But the *Belgrano* still lay outside the MEZ and might succeed in eluding the *Conqueror* before entering the MEZ. The decision to target the *Belgrano* outside the MEZ was taken to the Cabinet, and Prime Minister Margaret Thatcher approved of a change in the rules of engagement, making all Argentine ships liable to attack even outside the MEZ. Captain Wreford Brown of the *Conqueror* received the orders changing the rules of engagement at 1330 on May 2 and torpedoed the *Belgrano* around 1600. It sank within an hour with a loss of 321 Argentine sailors. Unknown to the British, Captain Lombardo of the *Belgrano* had orders to stay out of the MEZ.

Afterwards, many felt that the British had not exactly played fair; the *Belgrano* had been sunk when it had reason to believe it was safe from attack. But this attack does not appear to be a violation of Britain's treaty obligations because those treaties do not obligate member states to create zones in which enemy ships will be safe from attack. Given the threat posed by the *Belgrano* to the British task force, Howard Levie argues that the attack on it was not a violation of the laws of war (Coll and Arend 1985, 66).

This attack raises the question of states violating the laws of war to gain an advantage on the battlefield. Such opportunistic defections are one main threat to compliance with the laws of war. States may believe that they are better off not living up to their obligations because they are more likely to win the war by doing so. Opportunistic defection occurs when a state's forces violate the laws of war because the temporary advantage of doing so is great. Such violations are not part of a deliberate policy to breach the rules, but rather submission to the temptation to seize the immediate gain. Opportunistic defections threaten general compliance with the laws of war when the victim retaliates, particularly when it triggers a spiral of retaliation. They also undermine the confidence the opposing side has that the violator will honor its legal obligations as the fighting continues.

## Self-Interested Interpretation of the Rules

In 1602, the Duke of Savoy sent an army to conquer the Free City of Geneva. They attempted to scale the city walls and were repelled only through some legendary responses by alert Genevans, most notably Madame Cheynel who dumped her kettle full of vegetable soup on the heads of the Savoyards. An annual festival in Geneva remembers this event, which – I suspect – is popular with the Swiss because they figured out a way to make chocolate in the form of little chocolate soup pots filled with marzipan vegetables that the children smash before eating, a central part of the commemoration.[2] One element of the story that the Genevans do not deny but do not commemorate in their festival was the trial and execution in one day of thirteen Savoyards they took prisoner in the assault. There are pictures in the Museum of Art and History in Geneva depicting the hangings of the prisoners and the display of their severed heads on fence posts outside the city. To this day, the Genevans claim that those executed did not deserve prisoner of war status because the Duke of Savoy had not declared war on Geneva before the attack, and so the men they took prisoner were criminals and not entitled to prisoner of war status. These were unlawful combatants 400 years before the Bush Administration, if you will.

Effective rules require a shared understanding of how they apply to specific cases, both so that actors can take account of those rules and the consequences of breaking them and so that others know how to respond. More detailed and specific rules help to produce such a shared understanding by clarifying what the rules mean. Increasingly detailed treaties lay out proper conduct in many areas of the laws of war precisely to reduce the range of possible interpretations of what is appropriate conduct. No treaty and no law can anticipate all possible situations, however. In domestic law, the creation of a common interpretation of laws is one of the central roles of courts, in addition to reaching judgments. In international law, the practice of states and international law professionals plays some of the same role. Nevertheless, those interpretations never fully anticipate all possible cases and leave scope for interpretation by actors.

Self-interested interpretation of the law – the effort to justify acts in the gray areas of the law – pose two related problems for an effective system of law of war. The most famous example of a self-interested interpretation was the German claim that their first use of chemical weapons against the British and French armies at the Second Battle of Ypres in 1915 did not violate the 1899 Hague Convention. The gas was released from cylinders rather than projectiles (which were explicitly banned), leading to the claim that they had not violated the treaty. First, self-interested interpretations provide an opportunity for actors to push the boundaries of acceptable conduct, as the Germans did with poison gas. When such actions trigger a response in kind or worse, both sides may find themselves in a downward spiral.[3] Second, self-interested interpretations induce skepticism in the other side, straining the commitment of both sides to the agreed standard. Both the British and French began using chemical weapons once they had developed the capability to do so, at first using

---

[2] In case you did not guess, my children loved this aspect of the Escalade celebration, making us buy multiple chocolate pots.

[3] I note in passing that the Genevans did not have to worry about the Savoyards retaliating against them for their execution of their prisoners.

cylinders as the Germans had. The explicit prohibition on gas shells was first breached by France in February 1916.

## PROBLEMS FACING THE LAWS OF WAR AT THE INDIVIDUAL LEVEL: AGENCY AND NOISE

The laws of war create obligations and rights for individuals as well as states. The classic case of "Name, Rank, and Serial Number" – the only three pieces of information that a soldier taken prisoner is obligated to provide to his captors – exemplifies the individual soldier's rights and responsibilities. This dual nature of obligations under the laws of war produces two related strategic problems. Agency is the first. How does the state control its agents – soldiers – to do as it wishes? As shown in Chapter 5, state policy to observe the Geneva conventions for prisoners of war means little if the men at the front generally kill enemy soldiers when they attempt to surrender. Noise, the second problem, arises because states must judge the intent of the opponent from what they do. When pressed by the United States and its allies early in 1942, Japan stated publicly that it would comply with the 1929 Geneva Convention *mutatis mutandis* even though it had neither signed nor ratified the treaty. In practice, they did not even come close to complying with that treaty. Because POW camps are behind enemy lines and the willingness to take prisoners can only be judged from what happens on the battlefield, the United States and its allies could not verify the Japanese statement directly. They had to judge Japanese intent to comply from what they could see. As described in Chapter 2, reciprocal strategies of enforcement rely on the ability of the parties to judge when one another has violated their agreement. Noise – the difficulty of judging what the other side is exactly doing – complicates reciprocal enforcement by muddying the lines when an actor should retaliate to enforce an agreement.

The problem of agency compounds the problem of noise. When soldiers commit violations on the battlefield, the other side must judge whether such violations are deliberate policy or the result of individuals acting against the policy of their government. If individual violations are widespread, it may be impossible to distinguish these two possibilities. That distinction matters because the two outcomes require different responses. Violations as a matter of state policy call for a response in policy, even if such is unlikely to induce compliance from the violating government. Individual violations call for efforts to convince the other side to get its soldiers to live up to their legal obligations and commitments through training and discipline.

Noise complicates reciprocal enforcement. How should a state respond to a pattern of violations by the other side? There is a tradeoff between two risks. The first is the risk of overreaction. Large responses in kind may be misinterpreted as unjustified violations on their own requiring a response. Additional reciprocal reactions could create a spiral of retaliation which neither side wants or seeks. The second risk is a failure of deterrence through the lack of a response. A warring party that received no response when its soldiers commit violations might make no effort to control their future bad behavior. This is not to say that reciprocal enforcement can never work under noise, only that its use cannot be fully effective. In some cases, the dynamics of the battlefield will lead to a collapse of a legal standard in action.

## Violations by Individuals

After his first experience in combat in the Philippines, General George C. Marshall remarked:

> Once an army is involved in war, there is a beast in every fighting man which begins tugging at its chains. And a good officer must learn early on how to keep the beast under control, both in his men and himself.[4]

Historically, war has been an opportunity for the armed man to use armaments to take what he would like. Loot, rape, and murder have been the prerogatives of the soldier through most of history. It is only recently that this has changed in principle. It has not, however, completely changed in practice. To the extent that the armed man is restrained and responsible for his actions, military discipline and training are key.[5] Even the best disciplined armies today commit some violations of the laws of war, violations considered to be crimes. Armies use systems of military justice – courts-martial – to try and convict those soldiers whose transgressions go beyond the limits of acceptable military conduct. Even so, the ability of armies to control their own soldiers is limited. They depend on reports from other soldiers, who are often reluctant to report the misconduct of their comrades in arms. Those in charge may prefer to look the other way when those under their charge take liberties with the armed power granted to them. The question is when such violations by individual soldiers rise to the level where the system fails to restrain them.

## Inadvertent Violations

> Each commander must weigh, on the one hand, those necessities [of the military situation] and, on the other hand, the imperative demands of suffering humanity and so far as possible spare the places in which the wounded are gathered and the persons who are engaged in caring for them. Manifestly, it is not always possible during the course of an engagement to accord them the immunity which considerations of humanity dictate. Naturally, also, regrettable mistakes are inevitable, and hospitals are sometimes fired upon unintentionally. Their flags are not always

---

[4] Quoted in Luke Mogelson, "A Beast in the Heart," *The New York Times Magazine*, May 1, 2011, 40.

[5] Watson (2008, 56–61) provides an excellent discussion of the role of training and discipline in sustaining military organizations.

visible, and not infrequently they are located near the lines and within the range of necessary military action. Belligerents are also under a strong temptation to employ the insignia of the Geneva convention for purposes for which it was not intended, and it may be assumed that sometimes the places over which it was hoisted or the persons bearing it were fired upon in the sincere belief that it was being improperly used, when in reality it was not (Garner 1920, 1:504).

Accidents happen in wartime. Most weapons are not guided onto their targets, and they hit whatever they land on. Mistaken targets occur in the fog of war, meaning that even guided munitions hit things that should not be targeted. The combat environment is confused and confusing, and soldiers must often make split-second decisions with their lives on the line. Even when there is time to contemplate what should be targeted, the uncertainty of identification and the inaccuracy of weapons mean that protected sites and people will be hit. These inadvertent violations, these mistakes of targeting and delivery of munitions, rarely appear to be accidental to those on the receiving end. Even in the broader picture, at higher levels, mistakes happen. During the 1991 Gulf War, the U.S. Air Force targeted the Ameriyaa bomb shelter in Baghdad, which it believed sheltered officials of the Iraqi regime and military. Almost 300 Iraqi civilians died when the shelter was bombed. Mistaken attacks can take many forms during wartime. Japan used merchant vessels to transport U.S. and Commonwealth soldiers they had taken prisoner from camps in the Philippines and what is now Indonesia to camps in Japan and Manchuria, packing men into the holds under inhuman conditions. The United States conducted unrestricted submarine warfare against Japanese merchant shipping during the war. At least five ships carrying prisoners were torpedoed and sunk by U.S. submarines. Not knowing the cargo, the submarine captains thought they were carrying out their mission (Vance 2000, 294–295).

## Perfidy

The television show "Saturday Night Live" once ran a satire of World War II documentaries on "The Walker Brigade," complete with an over-the-top imitation by Bill Murray of Sir Richard Burton as narrator.[6] "The Walker Brigade" was supposed to be a collection of wounded and crippled soldiers so named because many of them required the aid of walkers. They would attack the Germans counting on the protections under the Hague Conventions to prevent the Germans from firing on them in battle. As one might imagine, the Germans in the sketch did not respect their protected status, and "The Walker Brigade" slipped into the mythical pages of history.

Perfidy – the use of the protections of the laws of war to gain an unfair advantage on the battlefield – strikes at the principle of discrimination between

[6] It was on episode 125, originally aired on February 10, 1979; http://www.nbc.com/saturday-night-live/recaps/#cat=4&mea=125&ima=89940, accessed on May 28, 2013.

protected sites and people and legitimate military targets. The laws of war recognize the use of camouflage, ruses, and ambush as legal forms of deception during wartime. However, the use of protected status – such as the Red Cross symbol for medical sites, vehicles, and personnel – to cover military activities is forbidden as an unfair deception of the enemy. Nevertheless, perfidy occurs in most wars in some form. Cultural sites are used to shelter military assets from attack, like the archeological sites that Iraq parked jet airplanes next to during the Gulf War in 1991 in the hope that Coalition forces would not bomb them. Uniforms of the enemy disguise surreptitious acts, such as German infiltrators who sought to misdirect U.S. troops during the Battle of the Bulge. Japanese soldiers during World War II would sometimes pretend to signal an intent to surrender (such as waving a white flag) to lure U.S. soldiers into the open where they could be killed (Linderman 1997, 152). Perfidy abuses the rules to protect military targets from enemy attack and to secure an advantageous position from which to attack the enemy.

Acts of perfidy corrode the willingness of the other side to respect the lines of discrimination between military targets on the one hand and protected people and sites on the other. They often trigger responses by the other side that violate the principles of discrimination as well. Perfidy by one side puts soldiers of the other at risk, leading the latter to violate the laws of war to protect themselves. U.S. soldiers and marines ignored white flags and stopped taking Japanese prisoners in response to Japanese perfidy. In extreme cases, these responses and the acts that trigger them cause the complete breakdown of discrimination between military targets and protected people and sites, making the latter effectively the former.

Perfidy also operates like noise by making it difficult to tell whether or not the other side is observing the rules. Tales of perfidy spread rapidly, leading to snap judgments that the other side is widely engaging in perfidy. When a medical team comes under fire, is the attack deliberate or a result of the confusion of the battlefield? The former is easier to believe when you think the enemy has engaged in perfidy before. Suspicions of perfidy corrode standards on the battlefield.

## THREE STRATEGIC PROBLEMS FACING AN EFFECTIVE SYSTEM OF LAW OF WAR

There are three interrelated strategic problems facing the enforcement of the laws of war in practice. First, there is a question of compliance at the level of state-to-state policy. One or both sides may believe they can gain an advantage through violations. These violations could produce a military advantage on the battlefield or raise the costs of fighting to the other side in the hope of convincing it to surrender sooner. Second, there is the question of compliance on the battlefield between the soldiers of the warring parties. Agreement by states to follow the rules means little if soldiers do not abide by that agreement. The cruel logic of battlefield – kill or be killed – produces an incentive for soldiers to break the rules for their own protection. Third, there is the question of enforcement and discipline within each army. If the leadership wishes to follow the rules, they need a system to train their soldiers in the rules and proper conduct on the battlefield, to monitor violations by them, and discipline at least some who break the rules.

The solutions to these three problems are interrelated. State commitment to abide by international humanitarian law means little when the logic of the battlefield breaks down cycles of violations between the soldiers of the two sides. Implementation of the laws of war requires training of soldiers and a system of military justice. Strategic expectations of how the other side will act influence whether soldiers and their leaders will follow treaty standards. Public commitment to treaties can screen out those states with little or no intention to follow the standards embodied in those treaties. Screening of states that will not comply is useful because states differ in whether they perceive an advantage in following a standard and what they believe that standard should be. They also provide common sets of standards that can help remedy self-interested interpretation through greater legal clarity and allow for precise training on the rights and responsibilities of soldiers.

Different issues in the laws of war pose different challenges to compliance. The parameters of the model, factors that vary from issue to issue, reflect these different challenges. Limiting the use of chemical weapons poses different issues than the protection of civilians. These different characteristics explain in part why compliance varies across these issues. Additionally, the precise characteristics of compliance with an issue vary with the warring parties because some see an advantage in violations or do not create effective systems of military discipline. These differences across actors explain why a system of universal treaty standards makes sense. Such a system uses public acceptance of a standard through ratification to screen out those who will not comply.

I now turn to an informal description of each of the separate models with an emphasis on explaining how each represents the problems of compliance with the laws of war, the range of behavior by the actors in each, and why they do what they do. The following companion chapter provides full details of each model and their combination. Each state is composed of a government or central military authority that makes the state-level decisions and a large number of soldiers that compose its army.[7] The combatants of each side are the agents capable of committing violations on their own discretion. For some issues, they will be individual soldiers; for others, they will be officers in

---

[7] Assuming the number of soldiers is large also allows me to avoid the question of the elimination of soldiers from either military. Obviously, some soldiers die, are incapacitated, jailed for misbehavior, or captured in the course of fighting. But if they are replaced by others with the same distribution of types, their elimination from the game makes no difference to the strategic logic of matching. It could make a difference if there was systematic selection, such as the elimination of types likely to commit violations because of temptation.

a position to order violations. Ship captains in naval warfare are an example of the latter as they, instead of individual sailors, make the decisions whether to rescue enemy sailors from a sunk ship and whether to respect the rules for sinking unarmed merchant ships, two of the prime obligations of the laws of naval warfare. The three separate models address the three strategic problems previously described. I discuss their combination and how the three problems are solved together, giving rise to various possibilities. I characterize the parameters for different issues in the laws of war to allow me to make predictions about the patterns of compliance for each issue. I also point out the testable implications of the models.

As with all formal models, this effort seeks to distill the essence of the strategic interactions in making the laws of war work during wartime.[8] The model is not a literal description of the complexities and difficulties of an effective system of law of war. Instead, it reduces these complexities to a simple form that allows us to analyze why states and soldiers comply or violate within that simple form. If successful, the model allows us to examine the strategic logic of the situation so we can understand it more fully.

## On the Battlefield

The laws of war mean little if soldiers do not carry out their responsibilities and respect the rights of enemy soldiers and noncombatants. I model the battlefield as repeated encounters by soldiers of the two sides represented in the matrix game in Figure 3.1. Each army has a large and equal number of soldiers who are paired up randomly in each round of the model. As the number of soldiers is large, none of them expects to encounter their opponent from the current round in a future round (more accurately, the chance any two combatants meet again is insignificantly small). Each soldier has an encounter with a soldier from the other side in each round of the game. In an encounter, each soldier simultaneously decides whether or not to commit a violation. The consequences of a pair of combatants' choices depend on what both do. Violations by both are worse for both than neither committing a violation (the payoff to non-violations is set to $0$ and for joint violations to $-1$ for convenience). If one combatant commits a violation while the other does not, the first may benefit while the second suffers. The *temptation (T)* to violate is the possible benefit; *vulnerability (V)* is cost of suffering a violation without a response in kind. Not all combatants will act on the temptation to violate. There is a range of types of combatants for both sides, where each combatant's type reflects his personal inclination to act on the temptation to violate. The larger $T$ is for an issue, the greater the number of combatants who are willing to commit unilateral violations. Even with temptation, some soldiers will not violate even if

---

[8] See chapter 1 of Powell (1999) for a defense of the role of formal models in international relations.

| | Honor | $b_j$ Violate |
|---|---|---|
| Honor | (0,0) | $(-V, T-t_j)$ |
| Violate | $(T-t_i, -V)$ | $(-1, -1)$ |

$a_i$

FIGURE 3.1 Battlefield violation game.

they anticipate no reaction from the other side; that is, there are combatants who will comply on their own. Issues in which the temptation to violate is larger would include treatment of civilians where individual soldiers benefit from looting and other crimes against civilians. This temptation would also cover the lack of care and discrimination in targeting that lead to collateral damage to civilian targets. It also covers unilateral violations by individuals such as the killing of soldiers attempting to surrender not provoked by a fear of perfidy. Vulnerability reflects soldiers' exposure to violations by the other side. When $-V$ is worse than the consequence of mutual violations $(-1)$, soldiers have an incentive to violate for self-protection if they believe their opponent in this round will violate. Vulnerability is greater for issues like prisoners of war where soldiers themselves are at risk than for issues such as protection of civilians where they are not. Temptation and vulnerability reflect the personal consequences to soldiers on the battlefield, not the larger strategic effect of these violations on the course of the war.

How combatants act depend on their vulnerability, the temptation to commit violations, and their anticipations of how combatants from the other side will act. When the other side is unlikely to violate, temptation determines what a combatant will do. Some types will commit violations, others will not, with the number of violations growing with temptation. When the other side is likely to commit violations, vulnerability drives the response to those violations. If vulnerability is low, soldiers of the other side may simply ignore the violations and not respond. More common, though, vulnerability leads to anticipatory violation in kind. These violations are not reciprocal punishments in the sense that they seek to respond to violations in previous rounds. They are violations that seek to limit damage to the individual soldier given the anticipation of violations from the other side. Strategic expectations of violations drive further violations when vulnerability is large enough.

Equilibrium requires that these strategic expectations and behavior match one another. Although individual soldiers may be fooled some of the time, they will learn how the enemy acts and what they must do in turn. The most-common case has high vulnerability $(V > 1)$ and some but not overwhelming temptation (the exact condition is in the companion chapter). In this case, expectations of violations can be high, medium, or low. Low expectations can be sustained if only those tempted to violate on their own break the rules. High expectations of violations lead combatants to commit violations to protect themselves, which create the expectations needed to justify violations to limit damage to one's self. Medium expectations lead some but not all to violate, falling in between the other two. Expectations of how the other side will act determine what unfolds on the battlefield, giving both sides an incentive to clarify those expectations before combat.

The other cases occur when the parameters differ from this most-common case of high vulnerability and some temptation. If vulnerability is very large with sufficient temptation, expectations and behavior converge on all violating. The consequences of not protecting one's self are too large to honor the limits. When vulnerability is lower than the cost of mutual violations ($V < 1$), violations either occur at low levels or there can be asymmetric situations in which the soldiers of one side all comply while the other side commits a low level of violations. In this situation, soldiers prefer not responding to violations by the other side, with only those most susceptible to temptation committing violations. Again, the multiple equilibria in the case of low vulnerability provide a reason to clarify those expectations before war.

## Military Discipline

States can attempt to limit the violations of their soldiers through military justice. Military discipline is a classic example of a principal-agent problem in which the principal attempts to induce the agent to act on its behalf as it desires. Soldiers are the agents of each state with the central military and political authorities of the state their principal. Soldiers as agents have interests of their own that may lead them to act against the interest of the principal. Here the state would like to prevent violations in the face of the temptation for individual soldiers to commit them. The process takes place within the military of each warring party. Military authorities have access to both suspects and the likely witnesses if they choose to punish soldiers who commit violations. Detection of violations on the battlefield is a serious impediment to such enforcement. Military authorities set a level of costly monitoring, followed by decisions by the combatants whether or not to violate. Temptation again is soldiers' incentive to commit violations with soldiers' varying in the willingness to commit violations by type as in the battlefield model. Afterward, the state detects some of the violations based on their monitoring, which is not perfect. The state punishes the violators it detects among its soldiers. The combatants have incentives to violate from temptation and their type, with some types unwilling to commit violations under any circumstances. Monitoring and enforcement for the state is costly to create and carry out. The state would like to minimize the number of violators in its army but also pays a cost to establish a system of monitoring and discipline, a cost that increases more rapidly with the degree of monitoring. The cost of monitoring and the temptation to commit violations are the two parameters of this model. The cost of monitoring increases as the scope for violations by individual soldiers grows. Issues in which the control of violations is easily limited to high-level officers (such as the use of chemical weapons) are easier to monitor and enforce than those in which every soldier has the ability to commit violations (such as protection of civilians).

Whether the state enforces the rules depends on the cost of monitoring. When the cost is low, the state raises the risk of detection and punishment high enough to deter all violations. When the cost of detection is higher, the state engages in some monitoring but not enough to deter all violations. The benefit of stopping all violations is not enough to justify the cost. Combatants follow the incentives set by the system of monitoring. When it is lax, it fails to deter violations. Otherwise, the risk of being caught is high enough to deter all violations.

This model does not examine whether states can use discipline to induce soldiers to commit violations. In the battlefield model, this is an issue only when vulnerability is low. When vulnerability is high, combatants are willing to commit violations if they believe the other side will as well. A state that wants its soldiers to commit violations seeks to create expectations that violations would be committed in any war. Such a state might very well take public actions, such as failing to ratify the relevant treaty, to establish those expectations before war broke out. It might also conduct military training to encourage violations in the hope of shaping the expectations of further violations in combat. This logic of creating the anticipation of violations could explain why those states that plan to commit violations do not ratify treaties. Ratification could create an anticipation that the standards will be followed, an expectation that such a country does not want to produce.

### State-to-State Compliance

The laws of war can also affect the course of fighting in a war. A war can be modeled as a series of battles (Smith 1998a; Wagner 2000), leading to the total conquest of one side if it loses enough battles. These battles are not predictable, giving both sides some reason to continue fighting in the hope that it will win enough battles to win the war. These battles are costly to both sides, a cost that provides an incentive to end the war by surrendering the stakes to the other side. The two sides fight a series of battles until one side quits or wins by eliminating the other. Each battle moves the state of the war one notch toward the winner and away from the loser. In equilibrium, sides do not generally fight to the death. Instead, each has a break point at which it quits once the tide of battle turns far enough against it. Each side's break point depends on the costs of fighting, its chance of winning each battle, and the other side's break point.

Broadly speaking, the acts that violate the laws of war have three consequences for the conduct of a war. Violations could increase a side's chance in winning a battle. Violations by the other side would reduce its chance of winning a battle.

Violations also raise the costs of battles, both for the side suffering them and the side carrying them out. Raising the other side's costs of fighting might induce it to drop out of the war earlier than it would in the absence of those added costs. These three effects of violations – the greater chance of winning a battle, the higher costs the other side suffers, and the higher costs a side's violations impose on itself – are parameters of this model. Some issues have little effect on which side wins battles or little effect on the violator's costs of war. Others raise the costs of fighting substantially, such as aerial bombing did during World War II, particularly when the other side retaliates in kind. Some issues in particular wars, such as submarine warfare during the World Wars, have asymmetric effects, helping one side win battles while providing little advantage on the battlefield to the other. Each side chooses how many of its soldiers will commit violations during the current battle, with its chance of winning rising with the number of violations along with the costs of both sides.

When will states choose to violate in an effort to gain an advantage at war? A straightforward comparison determines this choice. A state compares the added costs it will suffer from its acts to the added chance of its winning a battle. If this ratio exceeds the consequences of winning this battle to losing it, the cost will be too high for the benefit, and it will not commit violations. If the ratio is less than the difference between winning and losing today's battle, it will order all its soldiers to commit violations. The implications of this result are straightforward. States at war are most likely to commit violations when those violations improve their chances of winning battles and do not create substantial costs on their own.

This simple and straightforward logic has an important implication for when states break the rules for the first time in a war. If this condition holds for a state, it should commit violations from the first day of fighting. To wait costs the advantage gained from violating the rules from the first day. If neither side benefits from violations at the beginning of the war, both sides' incentive to break the rules increases the closer they come to victory. The difference between winning and losing today's battle influences the choice to violate because it is the gain from raising the chance of winning today's battle. This difference increases the closer a side comes to winning the war. The biggest difference comes when the other side is on the verge of quitting; it will surrender after one more loss. When a side must win many more battles to win the war, the difference in value between winning and losing this battle is small. If you win, you still have to win many more battles to prevail. The chance of doing so before the other side wins enough battles to force you to quit is not great, whether or not you win this battle. Pulling these points together, warring parties should commit violations from the beginning of a war. If they honor such limits early in the war, the side close to winning is more likely to commit a first violation than the side losing.

This logic examines just the incentives of each party acting on its own in the absence of a prewar agreement not to violate. Whether a party gains from its own violations is independent of the other side's violations. Violations by one side, however, increase the costs to the other. Because the strategic logic of violations leads both sides either to not commit any violations or to go to the furthest extent possible, their simultaneous decisions whether to violate in a given battle have the form of a two-by-two game. There are three variations on this game. It could be the case that both players prefer not to commit violations; the costs of such violations exceed their gain no matter what the opponent does. These situations do not require a deal for compliance. The second situation is asymmetric – one side prefers restraint while the other does not. The latter is unlikely to abide by any prewar agreement because it gains from its violations and the other side is unwilling to retaliate in kind. The third case – both sides prefer to commit violations – can pose the familiar strategic logic of Prisoners' Dilemma. Both sides gain from their own violations but lose more from the violations of its opponent. Both could gain from a deal not to commit violations which is enforced by an agreement to respond in kind in the next round to such violations. But this third case does not necessarily have this dynamic of the Prisoners' Dilemma. It can be the case that one side prefers committing violations even if the other side will respond in kind. A reciprocal response will not deter such a side from committing violations. It cannot be the case, however, that both sides prefer committing violations no matter how the other side responds. At least one of the sides in this third case must prefer joint restraint to joint violations.

### Fusing the Models into One

Each of the three models described are part of the complete model. There are four sets of actors, the political/military leadership of the two sides and the soldiers of each. The leaders set the level of monitoring of violations of their own soldiers in order to influence the level of violations committed by their soldiers. The soldiers of the two sides meet in combat as in the earlier battlefield model with the addition of the monitoring and discipline imposed by their own leaders. The leaders can no longer directly set the level of violations of their soldiers. They can reduce violations by increasing monitoring. If they believe they would benefit from violations by their own soldiers, they can seek to encourage play of one of the equilibria of the battlefield game with higher levels of violations.

The willingness of national leaders to control violations is the key to the model. When the leaders of a side wish to control violations, they invest in monitoring and discipline needed to limit the violations of their own soldiers. The level of monitoring depends on its cost, with more provided for issues in which it is easier to monitor and discipline soldiers. If the cost is low enough, the leadership may raise monitoring to a level to deter all violations, even by the type most willing to commit violations. Full compliance is possible when the leadership wants to limit violations and monitoring is relatively cheap.

Furthermore, when at least one side wants to control its soldiers through monitoring, it can raise the monitoring to the level at which high levels of violations on the battlefield are no longer an equilibrium. Its own soldiers no longer prefer to respond in kind to violations by the other side's soldiers. This change stops the self-preservation dynamic of the battlefield equilibria with high levels of violations.

As in the model of state-to-state compliance, there are three combinations of the willingness of the two sides' leadership to limit violations. When both sides wish to limit violations, both monitor and discipline their soldiers, and the result is a battlefield with low levels of violations. When one side wishes to limit its violations but the other does not, the former monitors and disciplines its soldiers while the other does not. The result differs but still has low levels of violations. The control of the soldiers of the first side reduces the need for the soldiers of the latter to commit violations for self-defense. When neither side wishes to control the violations of its own soldiers, there can still be restraint on the battlefield. If both sides have Prisoners' Dilemma preferences in which they prefer mutual restraint to mutual violations, they can gain by coordinating on the battlefield equilibrium with low levels of violations. Neither will seek to control its own soldiers, so altering soldiers' expectations of what to expect on the battlefield is the only way to control violations. When one side prefers to commit violations even if the other side responds in kind, then the two sides can differ on what equilibrium of the battlefield game they play. The side that prefers to violate no matter how the other side responds prefers an equilibrium with a high level of violations; the other will have Prisoners' Dilemma preferences and prefer an equilibrium with a low level of violations. It cannot be the case that both sides prefer high levels of violations. If both sides commit violations, the net effect on the chance of winning the next battle increases for one and decreases for the other. The side whose chance of winning goes down would then have Prisoners' Dilemma preferences and prefer mutual restraint.

## Screening through Ratification

These differences in the willingness to control violations and their consequences for what happens on the battlefield create a need for states to indicate their interest in restraint prior to war. The previous argument assumed that state leaders knew how one another views the benefits and costs of violations, and so could tell whether prospective opponents would fight with restraint. It is unlikely, however, that national leaders know exactly whether one another will follow conventions of restraint during war. The precise advantage the leaders of one state see in violations is known only to them. Leaders of other states have some ideas about their views, but those judgments are based on general beliefs about their intent. Asymmetric effects of violations on the chances of winning battles can be anticipated, but not fully. Britain, for example, sought to restrict submarine warfare during the interwar period, but Germany and France resisted these efforts because they believed those rules would only benefit Britain. The exact consequences on the battlefield and costs of violations are private information to the leaders of each state. Because many states could benefit from restraint while others do not, all could benefit if they could communicate that interest in advance of war.

If the leaders of each state know the added chance of winning a battle and the costs they suffer from their own violations, they know whether they gain from their own violations and whether they are willing to control their own soldiers. Those that know they lose from the violations of their own soldiers will control their own soldiers and would prefer any opponent to do so as well. Those that know they can gain from the violations of their own soldiers do not know whether or not they prefer mutual restraint because they do not know how much the other side gains from its violations. Both sides might prefer mutual restraint and not know that. Communication of their interest in restraint might persuade one side that restraint was definitely not in its interest.

There are different ways for states to communicate their interest in restraint. They could signal, that is, announce their costs and benefits from their own violations at the outbreak of war. Honest announcements of interest in restraint, however, cannot be sustained. Types that lose from their own violations are willing to reveal their intent, as do types that believe they will gain from their own violations even if the other side responds in kind. The types that know they will benefit from their own violations but lose more from the violations of the other side will not reveal that honestly. They are better off pretending to be a type that will discipline its own soldiers as that signal leads to restraint on the battlefield even if the other player gains from violations.

The incentives that undermine honest signals suggest that screening in advance of the outbreak of war could communicate sufficient information to allow the players to coordinate on restraint that benefits both. In signaling, the informed parties indicate their types through their actions; in screening, uniformed parties create a screen with the informed parties opting in or out. A fixed treaty standard that states accept through ratification acts as a screen on their preference for restraint during wartime. The logic that undermines signaling leads to separation in screening as states separate themselves into either types that prefer restraint or those that do not. The status of both sides' ratification indicates what should happen on the battlefield. When one side will discipline its own soldiers, it will ratify and monitor its soldiers conduct, and the level of violations should be low. If neither side is willing to discipline its soldiers, joint ratification leads to play of the battlefield equilibrium with low levels of violations. Their shared desire to limit violations leads to shared expectations of restraint, even though neither side punishes violations by its own soldiers. If one side believes it will benefit from its own violations in any case, a failure to ratify indicates that the equilibrium with a high level of violations will be played during war.

The model of screening through ratification answers a key puzzle in treaty law; it provides a positive reason why some states would not ratify a treaty. A state that has no intention of following a treaty might gain by deceiving possible opponents by ratifying that treaty. After all, there is no external agency to enforce the obligation it undertakes through ratification. It might gain some advantage through the surprise of first violation. In the model, however, ratification creates expectations in the state's military forces in addition to other states. A state that intends to violate a treaty standard wants to create the expectation of violations on the battlefield among its own troops. Ratifying a treaty sends them the wrong message. Failure to ratify signifies the intent to violate, an intent that a state's leader wishes to send. Those state leaders want and need to opt out of the treaty standard.

## Firewalls

Separate treaties codify the laws of war. Although the Hague Conventions covered the range of issues in the laws of war, developments after World War I separated the issues into different treaties: the 1925 Geneva Protocol on CBW, the 1929 Geneva Convention, and so on. The 1949 Geneva Conventions addressed treatment of civilians, prisoners of war, enemies wounded on land, and enemies shipwrecked and wounded sailors in separate conventions, although almost all member states ratified them as a set (Roberts and Guelff 2000, 355–361).[9] Other issues, such as the protection of cultural property, have their own conventions.

The separation of issues poses a puzzle in explaining the institutional design of the laws of war. This separation focuses responses to violations within each issue rather than across issues. Cross-issue responses might deter some violations when responses in kind are insufficient (McGinnis 1986). One example was the vague threat made by U. S. Secretary of State James Baker to Tariq Aziz, the Foreign Minister of Iraq during their meeting in Geneva before the war:

> The United States will not tolerate the use of chemical or biological weapons, support for any kind of terrorist actions, or the destruction of Kuwait's oil fields and installations. Further, you will be held directly responsible for terrorist actions against any member of the coalition. The American people would demand the strongest possible response. You and your country will pay a terrible price if you order unconscionable acts of this sort (quoted in Roberts [1994, 149–150]).

This statement leaves open the response of the United States, from retaliation in kind, use of nuclear weapons, or simply just a commitment to overthrow and punish the regime. Although Iraq lit many oil wells in Kuwait on fire, the United States did not respond in any of these ways.

---

[9]  The only exceptions are Sri Lanka, Djibouti, Trinidad and Tobago, and the Philippines.

Separating issues and denying cross-issue responses prevents the outbreak of violations on one issue from spreading to others. This separation acts as a firewall that prevents the spread of violations, preserving restraint on one issue even when it fails on another. Cross-issue retaliation would break down agreed and mutually beneficial restraint. Noise makes the problem of the spread of violations from one issue to another worse. If violations occur outside the control of state authorities, cross-issue responses could lead to a total breakdown that no one sought.

### Elements of the Laws of War Not in the Model: Drawing "Bright Lines"

The model focuses our attention on the interplay of the decisions of state leaders and what happens on the battlefield. State decisions influence the restraint of soldiers in combat, but the dynamics of the battlefield limit what can be accomplished even when both sides prefer restraint. The laws of war aid restraint by allowing states to reveal their desire to limit violence on the battlefield through treaty ratification. Public acceptance of a treaty standard creates shared expectations and understandings of what will happen on the battlefield.

The laws of war also clarify what acts constitute violations and what is allowable. In the model, the definition of violations is given and known to all parties. In practice, the definition of violations is a critical role of the treaties. Bright lines have to be negotiated; they are not self-evident to all. Thomas Schelling stated the idea that some bright lines are natural focal points even when many limits might be acceptable to both sides in a war:

> It is interesting to speculate on whether any alternative agreement concerning poison gas could have been arrived at without formal communication (or even, for that matter, with communication). "Some gas" raises the complicated questions of how much, where, under what circumstances; "no gas" is simple and unambiguous. Gas only on military personnel; gas used only be defending forces; gas only when carried by projectile; no gas without warning – a variety of limits is conceivable. Some might have made sense, and many might have been more impartial to the outcome of the war. But there is a simplicity to "no gas" that makes it almost uniquely a focus for agreement when each side can only conjecture at what alternative rules the other side would propose and when failure of coordination on the first try may spoil the chances for acquiescence in any limits at all (Schelling 1966, 131).

The "no gas" rule, however, leaves a critical question unanswered.[10] What chemicals constitute "gas"? The United States did not ratify the 1925 Geneva Protocol, which bans the use of chemical and biological weapons, until 1975 because it argued that the use of riot control agents, commonly known as "tear

---

[10] To be fair to Schelling, his concern was primarily with the use of nuclear weapons, for which the chances of a treaty outlawing their use seemed remote, leaving tacit agreements as the only option.

gas," should be allowed during war just as they were used by governments within their own countries. Other ratifying states, particularly Britain and France, disagreed, contending that riot control agents violated the Protocol. The United States used both riot control agents and defoliants during the Vietnam War (Harris and Paxman 2002, 193–198).

Norms for restraint in war rarely spell out exactly which acts violate those norms. Law expressed in treaties seeks to do so, drawing "bright lines" for ratifying states. Although the model does not capture this key feature of the laws of war, bright lines are relevant to its concern with noise. Lack of clarity about where the lines of conduct are exacerbates noise. One side could believe it is following the rules while the other side views those acts as unacceptable. Cycles of retaliation could result, an escalation in violations that neither side sought nor wanted. Such spirals of retaliation are more likely on the issues where noise is greatest because individual soldiers possess the ability to violate on their own.

## ISSUES IN THE LAWS OF WAR FROM THE PERSPECTIVE OF THE MODEL

The eight issues for which attempts have been made to negotiate treaties to produce the laws of war – aerial bombing, armistices and cease fires, chemical and biological weapons, treatment of civilians, protection of cultural property, conduct on the high seas, prisoners of war, and treatment of enemy wounded – differ in the characteristics reflected in the parameters of the model. This section discusses the parameters for each issue, using the model to predict patterns of compliance with the laws of war for that issue. To reiterate for the reader's benefit, *temptation* reflects how often soldiers will commit violations when the other side does not. *Vulnerability* is the loss soldiers feel when they do not respond in kind to violations of the other side. *Military advantage* reflects the increase in the chance of winning the next battle from committing violations. Table 3.1 shows both the typical value of military advantage and whether it is asymmetric in some cases. When one side believes it gains greatly from violations while the other side does not, the former has a strong incentive to encourage violations as a matter of state policy. State leaders also see *costs* from the violations of their own soldiers as well as those of the enemy. *Ease of monitoring* captures the scope for individual violations and the ease of monitoring and controlling those violations. Table 3.1 gives the expected levels of violations for that issue and whether the variation across cases is high.

Aerial Bombing: Temptation and vulnerability are low in aerial bombing. Aircrew have little incentive to bomb inaccurately unless antiaircraft fire is strong, and violations by the other side do not change their personal incentives for bombing inaccurately. The inaccuracy of aerial bombing for most of the twentieth century is a larger source of violations by aircrew against state policy, albeit inadvertent violations. Precision-guided munitions only entered into

TABLE 3.1. *Parameters and predictions for issues in the laws of war*

| Issue | Temptation | Vulnerability | Military advantage from violations | | Cost of one's own violations | Cost of other side's violations | Ease of monitoring | Expected levels of violations | Consistency of violations across wars |
|---|---|---|---|---|---|---|---|---|---|
| | | | Average | Asymmetry | | | | | |
| Aerial bombing | Low | Low | High | Low to high | Low | High | Medium | Medium | Low when asymmetric |
| Armistice/Cease-fire | Medium | Medium | Medium | Low | Low | Medium | Medium/low | Medium | High |
| CBW | Low | Medium | Medium | Low to high | Medium | High | High | Low | Low when asymmetric |
| Treatment of civilians | Very high | Low | Low | Low to high | Medium | High | Low | Very high | High |
| Protection of cultural property | Medium | Medium | Low | Low | Low | Medium | Medium | Medium | High |
| Conduct on the high seas | Medium | Medium | Medium | Low to high | Low | Medium | Medium | Medium | Low when asymmetric |
| Prisoners of war | High | High | High | Low to high | Medium | High | Low | High | Medium |
| Treatment of wounded | High | Medium | Low | Low | Low | High | Medium | Medium high | Medium |

service at the end of the Vietnam War. State leaders, however, have often seen substantial military advantage in strategic bombing, which proved to be indiscriminate in practice if not intent. Furthermore, there have often been large differences between warring parties in the advantage they can gain from strategic bombing. Aerial bombing imposes few costs on the side committing the violations but high costs on the side suffering the bombing. This combination suggests that states should generally have Prisoners' Dilemma preferences over aerial bombing with the costs suffering from the enemy's bombing outweighing the benefits of one's own. Agreements to limit aerial bombing, however, suffer from the inaccuracy of most bombing, large asymmetries when one side is invulnerable to it, and the absence of any international convention in force on the issue, as is shown in Chapter 6.

Armistice/Cease-Fire: Temptation and vulnerability are medium on whether warring parties respect armistice agreements and short-term cease-fires on the battlefield. Individual shooting incidents are common during cease-fires, but they rarely become widespread unless one side chooses to make them so. Some strategic advantage can be gained by violating a cease-fire, but there is little difference in the advantage that either side can gain. Perfidy during a cease-fire is a common concern. The cost to the violating side is low, but the cost from being the target of violations is higher. As cease-fires on the battlefield are negotiated to allow the removal of wounded and dead from the battlefield, the side fired on is often in a vulnerable position. Armies have some ability to monitor whether their own soldiers follow a cease-fire agreement, with violations by officers ordering their troops to break a cease-fire more important than individual incidents of shooting under the white flag. Expected compliance is medium on average because of violations by individuals and lower-level officers.

Chemical and Biological Weapons (CBW): These weapons are controlled centrally, so regular soldiers lack the ability to violate on their own. Temptation is low. Vulnerability is medium because officers want to respond in kind if they have been authorized to use chemical weapons. There are military advantages to using chemical weapons, as demonstrated in Chapter 6. These advantages are largest when one side has a chemical weapons capability and the other does not. Chemical weapons impose some costs on those who use them, from the difficulty of handling the agents to the possibility of accidental exposure. Their use imposes high costs on those who suffer from chemical attacks. In addition to the gruesome nature of exposure to chemical weapons, they also produce substantial incapacitated casualties. Central control and authorization of the use of chemical weapons means that the cost of monitoring is very low; soldiers cannot use weapons they do not have. In general, chemical weapons should have very low levels of use. Individual violations are not a problem, and their high costs create Prisoners' Dilemma incentives for both warring states. Provided that both sides understand that one another will not use chemical weapons, both should comply with that understanding. Biological weapons differ by imposing a high cost on those who use them out of the fear that the agents will spread to their own troops.

Treatment of Civilians: Soldiers commit just about every crime imaginable against civilians within combat zones. Temptation is higher for treatment of civilians than any other issue. Vulnerability is low compared to other issues because soldiers do not suffer from the violations of the other side against those same civilians. In some cases, there is a desire for revenge for earlier atrocities of the enemy once the battle moves into their territory. The military advantage on the battlefield from harming civilians is generally low, although there are notable cases where at least one side believed it could gain from targeting enemy civilians on the battlefield. Treatment of civilians concerns conduct on the battlefield, so this does not include civilians victimized by aerial bombing or blockade, only direct killing and other atrocities on the battlefield. It includes internment of enemy civilians during wartime. The cost of violations by one's own soldiers is the loss of discipline in the ranks. The cost of enemy violations is high. The cost of monitoring is high because fellow soldiers are often the only living witnesses of these atrocities. The combination of high temptation and high costs of monitoring make treatment of civilians the most problematic issue in the laws of war for compliance.

Protection of Cultural Property: Perfidy is the central concern in protecting cultural property. Individuals and small units may take shelter in such sites to avoid attack. Charges of such perfidy often occur. The temptation is moderate (as is vulnerability) to attack protected sites when they are used perfidiously. The military advantage of abusing the protection of cultural property is limited because such sites are relatively few in number. Only sides that are at a great military disadvantage systematically use protected sites for perfidious protection, such as Iraq did during the Gulf War in 1991. The cost of one's own violations is low, but the costs of enemy violations can be high. Compliance with the protection of cultural property falls in the middle of the issues. Concerns with perfidy, often imagined rather than real, reduce compliance.

Conduct on the High Seas: Violations on conduct on the high seas focus on attacks on merchant shipping without warning and failure to recover shipwrecked sailors. The temptation for ship captains, particularly submarine captains, to engage in both types of violations is high because the attacked ship may warn friendly warships in the vicinity and the attacker may lack time and space to take on the shipwrecked. Ship captains make these decisions on these individual violations, and so the scope for individual violations is less than if individual sailors could do so. Vulnerability is medium for reasons of self-defense and revenge. The strategic advantage on the battlefield from violations can be substantial, and it is often different across the sides as one may be more vulnerable than the other. The cost of one's own violations is low, but the cost of enemy violations rises above that level. Asymmetry of interest in restraint at the state level is the primary problem facing conduct on the high seas. Other violations, such as Q-ships and blockades, are also state-level decisions. State decisions to violate often have an element of retaliatory response to violations of the other side.

Prisoners of War: On the battlefield, the temptation to wreak havoc on enemy soldiers attempting to surrender is high. So is vulnerability, both from revenge for enemy atrocities and in protection against perfidy during surrender. Once behind the lines and in the collection point, the risk of individual violations from guards drops but does not disappear. States widely differ in whether they see an advantage in humane or inhumane treatment of enemy POWs. Some believe that taking prisoners and treating them well encourages enemy troops to surrender; others want to encourage their own soldiers to fight to the death and abuse POWs as a source of labor. The cost of one's own violations is the loss of military discipline, while the cost of enemy violations is paid in human lives. Because individual soldiers possess the ability to kill enemies trying to surrender or to abuse them afterwards, monitoring compliance and enforcing discipline on this issue is as difficult as it is with civilians. Compliance with POWs faces the twin difficulties of controlling behavior on the battlefield with states that see violations as being in their interest.

Treatment of Enemy Wounded: The obligation to treat enemy wounded is closely related to prisoners of war. Soldiers are rarely hospitable to those who have been trying to kill them moments before. The role of medical personnel and the incapacity of enemy wounded to fight back make control more likely on the battlefield. There is little gain from not taking care of enemy wounded, except in cases in which medical facilities are crowded with your own wounded. The cost of one's own violations is low, but the cost of enemy violations is high, particularly if the wounded are abused rather than neglected. Because medical personnel commonly handle enemy wounded soldiers, control within a military is easier on this issue than POWs. Treatment of enemy wounded poses more problems for compliance than most issues, except civilians and POWs.

The issues covered by the laws of war differ both in their characteristics and in their compliance. Violations arise both from soldiers on the battlefield and from national leaders seeking a military advantage. The ease of monitoring and disciplining soldiers is critical to limiting individual violations. If not, the battlefield can deteriorate into spirals of retaliation. Controlling violations as state policy depends on clear public commitments to limit violence and the will to carry out those commitments.

## SUMMARY OF TESTABLE HYPOTHESES FROM THE MODEL

How would we know that the model matches reality? We compare the implications of the model that we can compare to the patterns and details of compliance. These tests are the object of the next three chapters. To set the stage, I review the testable hypotheses and why they should hold.

1. Compliance by parties at war are correlated.

The violations of the two sides in the model move together because of reciprocity and strategic expectations. On the battlefield, fear of enemy violations drives some individual violations. At the national level, anticipations of whether the enemy will be restrained affect each side's own efforts at restraint. The level of compliance of warring parties should be similar. I will call this *reciprocity* even if it does not require reciprocal responses to violations. Strategic expectations of violations trigger violations in anticipation.

2. Joint ratification of the relevant treaty strengthens the correlation of compliance and overall compliance by both sides.

Restraint requires a shared understanding between states and the soldiers at war. Treaty ratification indicates that the ratifying state accepts the treaty standard. When both sides ratify the relevant treaty, they create the shared expectation that one another will comply up to the limits of their control. Violations are likely to be met with violations. Across cases, compliance under joint ratification should be higher than when one or both do not accept the standard through ratification.

3. When one side ratifies the relevant treaty but the other does not produces the lowest correlation of compliance and the lowest level of compliance.

Those states that do not ratify the relevant treaty standard indicate that they do not intend to follow that standard. They believe they benefit from violations, even when they are reciprocated. When their opponent has ratified, it may control its own violations despite those of the other side. The compliance of the two sides then should be lower than other cases. Further, the violations of the non-ratifying side provoke some response on the battlefield from the soldiers of the ratifying country.

4. Average compliance varies across issues, with those issues where there is greater scope for individual violations and higher monitoring costs having lower average compliance than other issues.

The issues of the laws of war vary greatly in their characteristics, as the previous section argued. Individual violations pose an important problem for control. The cost of monitoring influences how much states will invest in controlling their soldiers. Temptation and vulnerability also influence the level of violations on the battlefield. Those issues for which centralized control is easiest should have the best record of average compliance.

5. Control of individual violations is critical to control of violations on the battlefield.

For the issues for which individual violations pose an important problem, the creation of systems of monitoring and discipline are necessary to limit individual violations. Not all state authorities will create such systems, either because of their cost or because they believe they gain from the violations of their own soldiers. Those states that create systems of monitoring and discipline should have better records of compliance.

6. First violations occur early in wars.

States violate the laws of war as a matter of policy because they believe they will gain from those violations. If that is the case, they should commit those violations as soon as the fighting begins to gain as large an advantage as possible. If individuals acting against state policy are the primary source of violations, they should commit violations from the outbreak of fighting.

7. When first violations come late in a war, the side winning the war at that time is more likely to commit that first violation than the side that is losing.

Each side's calculation of whether it gains by following the laws of war depend in part on the value of winning the next battle. The larger this is, the greater the gain from the violation. The value for winning the next battle increases the closer a side gets to winning. Sides closer to winning can gain more from a first violation of an agreement that has held up to that point in the war.

Chapters 4, 5, and 6 assess these testable hypotheses against the historical record of compliance with the laws of war in interstate wars during the twentieth century. Chapter 4 examines the statistical patterns of compliance across all wars. Chapter 5 delves into the specifics of prisoners of war during the World Wars, both on the battlefield and once prisoners move into state custody. Chapter 6 briefly analyzes four other issues in the laws of war – aerial bombing, chemical weapons, conduct on the high seas, and treatment of civilians.

# 3'

# Modeling Minutia

This chapter presents the formal details of the mathematical model of the laws of war discussed in Chapter 3. It is intended for those interested in those details. Other readers may wish to skip ahead to Chapter 4, which presents the patterns of compliance with the laws of war. I present each of the three models separately and examine their equilibria. The first focuses on soldier-to-soldier interaction on the battlefield as a matching model between the two infinite sets of soldiers. The second models military discipline within a state's military as a principal-agent model. The third model builds on Smith's (1998a) model of war as a gambler's ruin problem where the parties can influence their chance of winning by having their soldiers commit violations. The sides' interests in limiting violence divide into three cases: (1) neither side wishes to commit violations, (2) both sides would like to commit violations on their own, and (3) one side would like to commit violations and the other does not. An agreement to limit violence is self-enforcing in the first case, and reciprocity could be used to enforce such an agreement in the other two cases.

After presenting the three models separately, I examine their interaction. The battlefield model has multiple equilibria with some having higher levels of violence than others. Additionally, states that wish to control the violations of their own soldiers can use military discipline to do so. Because the battlefield model has multiple equilibria with different levels of violations, states may wish to signal their preference for a restrained or an unrestrained battlefield. They lack the incentive to reveal this information on their own, but public acceptance of a treaty standard through ratification can screen out the parties that want an unrestrained battlefield. Those parties reject the treaty standard to induce the unrestrained battlefield equilibrium.

THE THREE MODELS

There are four actors, or set of actors, in the three models. I refer to the two countries with the colorful names of **A** and **B**. Each country has a government, labeled $A$ or $B$, and an army which is a very large set of individuals, $\{a_i\}$ or $\{b_j\}$, respectively, with equal numbers of soldiers in each army. Individual soldiers have type $t_i$ drawn from a uniform distribution on $[0,1]$. The number of soldiers in each army is assumed to be very large so that any soldier can be treated as a draw from this distribution without worrying about whether certain types are removed from the distribution over several rounds of the games. All three models are kept simple to emphasize the interaction of their equilibria. For each model, I describe the game and then present the equilibria of the game in isolation.

## On the Battlefield

The soldiers of the two armies meet on the battlefield. The combat environment is represented by randomly matched soldiers into pairs with one soldier from each side. They then play the simultaneous game as in Figure 3.1. Each soldier chooses between $H$ (honoring the existing treaty standard) and $V$ (violating that standard by committing an atrocity). The game has two parameters, $T$ with $0 < T < 1$ for the temptation to commit violations and $V > 0$ for the vulnerability to violations (the payoff is $-V$, demonstrating that suffering unreciprocated violations is a loss). These parameters vary with the issue-area covered by the game. $T$ would be higher for issues in which an individual soldier could benefit from a violation, such as looting, on the issue of treatment of civilians. I restrict $T$ to be less than $1$ so that some $a_i, b_j$ prefer not committing violations. $V$ would be greater in magnitude for issues in which the soldier suffers greater consequences as a victim of a violation, such as on treatment of prisoners of war or enemy wounded. Each soldier's type $t_i$ gives his "personal cost" for committing opportunistic violations, with higher values denoting less willingness to violate.

This game has multiple equilibria, with the character of the equilibria depending on whether $V < 1$ and $(T-V)^2 + 4 - 4V > 0$. In each symmetric case, because $b_j$ plays the same strategy based on its type that $a_i$ does, I omit the strategy of $b_j$ to save duplication. For the asymmetric equilibrium, I list only one of each pair; the other can be found by reversing $a_i$ and $b_j$.

$\underline{\text{Equilibria:}}$   Let   $t_{crit}^{-} = 1 + \dfrac{1}{2}(T-V) - \dfrac{1}{2}\left((T-V)^2 + 4 - 4V\right)^{\frac{1}{2}}$   and

$$t_{crit}^{+} = 1 + \frac{1}{2}(T-V) + \frac{1}{2}\left((T-V)^2 + 4 - 4V\right)^{\frac{1}{2}}$$

Case 1: If $V < 1$, then:

(a) There is a symmetric equilibrium: $a_i$ plays Honor when $t > t_{crit}^-$, Violate otherwise.

(b) If $V \leq T$, there are two asymmetric equilibria: $a_i$ plays Honor when $t_i > T$, Violate otherwise; $b_j$ plays Honor for all types and a second reversing $a$ and $b$.

Case 2: If $V \geq 1$ and $(T - V)^2 + 4 - 4V > 0$, then there are three symmetric equilibria (ranked from the lowest frequency of violations to the highest):

(a) $a_i$ plays Honor when $t > t_{crit}^-$, Violate otherwise;

(b) $a_i$ plays Honor when $t > t_{crit}^+$, Violate otherwise; and

(c) all $a_l$ play Violate.

Case 3: If $(T - V)^2 + 4 - 4V < 0$ (this implies $V \geq 1$), then all $a_i, b_j$ play Violate.

Proof: When $V \geq 1$ (Cases 2 and 3), Violate is a best reply to itself for all types. Honor is not a best reply to itself for types $t < T$. To find mixed strategies across types, let $a,b$ be the cut point of types for each side respectively playing Honor for $t > a$ and Violate otherwise. Setting expected utility of both strategies equal to find the cut points, we have the following pair of equations:

$$a(1-b) = T - b(T - V + 1)$$
$$b(1-a) = T - a(T - V + 1)$$

Symmetric equilibria are found by setting $a = b$ and solving the resulting quadratic equation to get $t_{crit}^-$ and $t_{crit}^+$. Because $(T - V)^2 + 4 - 4V$ is the discriminant of this quadratic equation, it has real roots when the discriminant is positive in Cases 1 and 2. Subtracting the second equation from the first leads to

$$(a - b)(T - V) = 0,$$

which implies that asymmetric equilibria where $a \neq b$ are not possible except when $T = V$ (which I do not consider here).

When $V < 1$ (Case 1), Violate is no longer a best reply to itself. Honor dominates Violate for all $a_i, b_j > T$. This leads to the symmetric equilibrium for $t_{crit}^-$; $t_{crit}^+ > 1$. The asymmetric equilibrium arises when type $t = 0$ of one player prefers Honor to Violate given that types of the other player with $t < T$ will Violate. The condition of the asymmetric equilibrium matches the indifference condition between Honor and Violate for $t = 0$.

The strategic logic of the cases is simple. The first case has dynamics similar to the two-by-two game of Chicken in the sense that being a victim is preferable to both playing Violate. The symmetric equilibrium has low levels of violations, although violations by those with low costs for committing violations (low types) cannot be deterred. The asymmetric equilibrium comes from the Chicken dynamics. When one side will always play Honor, low types of the other side will commit violations. These violations are common enough to deter even the lowest type of the first side from committing violations. The use

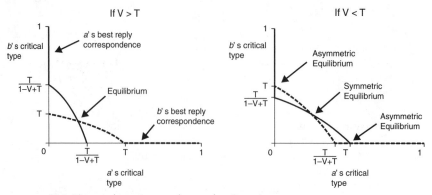

FIGURE 3'.1 Best reply correspondences for Case 1.

of chemical weapons could be such a case where from the individual soldiers' view, it is preferable to run a small risk of suffering a chemical attack to the certainty of a battlefield in which both sides use chemical weapons regularly. The second and third cases have Prisoners' Dilemma payoffs for low types ($t < T$), those who are willing to commit violations. They always prefer Violate. The risk of facing such a type leads some types to play Violate to avoid the worse payoff of being a victim (you play Honor, opponent plays Violate, payoff $T$) even though they prefer the outcome in which both play Honor (payoff 0) to their own unilateral violation (payoff $T - t_i < 0$). Case 3 is the extreme case for which the risk that the other side will violate is so high that all types play Violate to protect themselves; $V$ is noticeably greater than 1 for the condition of this case to hold. The consequences of being a victim are large enough that everyone commits violations to protect themselves from being a victim.

The strategic logic of the cases can be understood by examining the best reply correspondences of the players in the different cases. Figure 3'.1 shows the best reply correspondences for Case 1 in which vulnerability is low enough that soldiers prefer to Honor even when the soldiers of the other side will Violate. The two equations in the previous proof lead to the best reply correspondences (because they are symmetric, I show the equation only for the soldiers of $A$):

$$a = \frac{T}{1-b} - \left(\frac{b}{1-b}\right)(1 - V + T) = T - \left(\frac{b}{1-b}\right)(1 - V)$$

Differentiating the best reply correspondence, we derive how the cut point that defines the strategy of the $a$'s varies with the cut point of the $b$'s.

$$\frac{da}{db} = \frac{V-1}{(1-b)^2}$$

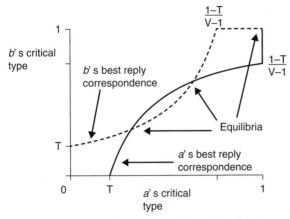

FIGURE 3′.2  Best reply correspondences for Case 2.

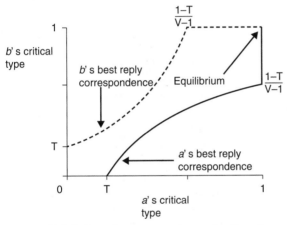

FIGURE 3′.3  Best reply correspondences for Case 3.

When $V < 1$, as in Case 1, this derivative is negative, and $a$'s best reply declines as $b$'s increases. When $b \geq \dfrac{T}{1-V+T}$, $a = 0$ is a best reply, and when $b = 0$, $a = T$ is a best reply. When $T \geq V$, this cut point is less than $T$, which creates the asymmetric equilibria, which are depicted on the right side of Figure 3′.1. The best reply for the $a$'s is given by the solid curve in Figure 3′.1, while that of the $b$'s is given by the dashed line and curve. The single, symmetric equilibrium is circled where the best reply correspondences cross in both sides of Figure 3′.1.

Figures 3′.2 and 3′.3 show the best reply correspondences for Cases 2 and 3. In these cases, the derivative of the best reply correspondences is positive because $V > 1$, leading to their upward slope. In Case 2, the best reply correspondences cross twice and meet at $a = b = 1$, meaning all types of both sides play Violate. In Case 3, the best reply correspondences do not cross, so the only equilibrium is at $a = b = 1$.

Strategic expectations, not reciprocity, drive the behavior in this game. The multiple equilibria in Case 2 have different strategic expectations from the common conjectures underlying them. In the first subcase, violations are rare, leading to restraint by those who do not want to commit violations. In the second subcase, the expectations of violations from the other side are higher, leading to violations for protection from being a victim. The third subcase is the complete breakdown with anticipations that violations will always be committed. Similarly, the common conjecture drives whether the symmetric or asymmetric equilibrium is played under Case 1, along with which side will not commit violations under the asymmetric equilibrium. Although the game is considered to be repeated, only the anticipation of what the other side will do in this round affects the players' choices. No one ever suffers retaliation in a future round for violations in this round.

## Military Discipline

Each government and its soldiers have a principal-agent relationship in which soldiers are agents of the state. For ease, we will assume the state is **A**. The government $A$ would like its soldiers $\{a_i\}$ to comply by playing Honor rather than Violate. Many but not all $a_i$ would play Honor left to their own devices; they have the same payoff structure as in the battlefield game if the opponent plays Honor. $A$ can monitor the soldiers, choosing a probability of detection of those who Violate, denoted by $p$ with $0 \leq p \leq 1$. Monitoring is costly for $A$; creating the capability for monitoring costs the probability of successful detection, $p^2 D$, where $D$ represents the cost of detecting violations on that given issue. This cost increases in the level of monitoring to represent the difficulty of monitoring all violations. For convenience, I assume the punishment of any soldier $a_i$ detected committing violations is $-1$.

The time line of the monitoring and discipline game is as follows:

1. $A$ chooses $p$ and announces it publicly.
2. All $\{a_i\}$ choose Honor or Violate.
3. Nature determines whether each $a_i$ who played Violate is detected with probability $p$ of detection. Payoffs are received as follows:

   $a_i$ played Honor: $0$
   $a_i$ played Violate and not detected: $T - t_i$
   $a_i$ played Violate and detected: $T - t_i - 1$

   $A$: $\dfrac{\#(a_i\ played\ Honor)}{\#(a_i)} - p^2 D$.

   The equilibrium of the monitoring game is straightforward. It depends on the cost of monitoring as follows:

   <u>Equilibrium:</u> $A$: Choose $p = min\left(T, \dfrac{1}{2D}\right)$ $a_i$: Violate if $t_i < T - p$.

<u>Proof</u>: Proceed by backward induction. $a_i$ plays Violate if $T - t_i - p(1) > 0$. Given $a_i$'s best reply correspondence, A's expected utility for setting detection at $p$ is as follows:

$$(1 - T + p) - p^2D \quad \text{if } p \leq T, \quad \text{and} \quad 1 - p^2D \quad \text{if } p > T$$

The first order condition is as follows:

$$0 = 1 - 2pD,$$

leading to $p_{opt} = \dfrac{1}{2D}$. If $p_{opt} > T$, $p = T$ also produces full compliance at lower cost.

The level of monitoring rises as the cost of monitoring decreases. If the cost of monitoring is low enough, A raises it high enough to deter all violations.

## State-to-State Deterrence

The war between A and B is represented by a model in the spirit of Smith (1998a). I present the full model in a series of steps, beginning with the basic model of war, adding decisions to commit atrocities in the effort to prevail, and end by examining prewar agreements to limit such violations. The sides fight a series of battles over an ordered set of fixed points in discrete time. The endpoints of the set represent total victory for one side or the other. The initial state of the war is one of these points. Each battle moves the state one position closer to the victory outcome for the winning side. The winner of each battle is determined by a given and known probability $q$ with $\frac{1}{2} \leq q < 1$ (I assume that A is stronger than B and so more likely to win any individual battle for convenience). There are then $N+1$ states to the game, the set $\{0,1,\ldots,N\}$, where state $N$ represents complete victory for A and $0$ complete victory for B and initial state $k$. Refer to any state as $S_i$. In each round, both players choose simultaneously whether to continue fighting or quit. Quitting gives the entire stakes to the other side, which both sides value as $1$. Each side pays costs of $c_A, c_B > 0$ for each round. If side $i$ quits in round $N+1$, its payoff is $-Nc_i$ and the other side's payoff is $1 - Nc_j$. The costs per round are assumed to be small enough that both sides are willing to continue to fight if they could win in the next round; $c_A < q$ and $c_B < 1 - q$.

I focus on the monotone equilibria of the game (Smith 1998a). The players have cut point strategies in these equilibria in which they play Continue for all states on one side of the cutpoint and Quit for those on the other.

Equilibrium: Let

$$F_A(k) = \left( k + \sum_{j=1}^{k} \sum_{i=1}^{j} (2k - (2i-1)) \alpha^i \right) c_A \text{ and}$$

$$F_B(k) = \left( k + \sum_{j=1}^{k} \sum_{i=1}^{j} (2k - (2i-1)) \alpha^i \right) c_B$$

for non-negative integer $k$ and $\alpha = \dfrac{1-q}{q}$. Define $K_A$ as smallest $k$ such that $F_A(k) \geq 1$ and $K_B$ parallel for $F_B$. The following are monotone equilibria of the game:

Case 1:  $K_A > K_B$. A plays Continue for all $k > 0$. B plays Continue for $k < K_B$, Quit otherwise.

Case 2:  $K_A < K_B$. A plays Continue for all $k > N - K_A$, Quit otherwise. B plays Continue for all $k < N$.

Case 3:  $K_A = K_B$. For $M$ such that $K_A \leq M \leq N$, A plays Continue for all $k > M - K_A$, Quit otherwise. B plays Continue for $k < M$, Quit otherwise.

Case 3a:  If $K_A \geq N$ and $K_B \geq N$, A plays Continue for all $k > 0$, B plays Continue for all $k < N$.

Proof: First, show that both players play monotone cut point strategies defined by a state in which the player plays Continue if the state is higher (for A, lesser for B) than that and Quit otherwise. Let $V_A(k)$ be A's continuation value for playing the game from state $k$ and $V_A(\sigma,k)$ be A's continuation value for playing $\sigma$ from state $k$ (parallel notation will be used for B). Let $k$ be the lowest state in which B always quits or N if no such state exists. $V_A(k) = 1$ by definition. $V_A(Continue, k-1) \geq q - c_A > 0$, so A must play Continue in equilibrium in state $k-1$. There is then a range of states $\{l,l+1,...N\}$ for which A plays Continue, $V_A(l) > 0$, and $l \leq k-1$. Because B plays Continue with positive probability at $k-1$, $V_B(k-1) \geq 0$.

Note that if a player plays Quit at two states, $l$ and $m$, and the other player never plays Quit for any state $l \leq k \leq m$, $V(k) = 0$ and the first player must play Quit for all such $k$. From any such state $k$, all histories of play lead to the first player quitting before the other, because either $l$ or $m$ are reached before any state in which the other player plays Quit. The value and optimal play of Quit at all these states immediately follows.

Furthermore, there cannot be ranges of states for which both players mix between Continue and Quit. If there were, then $V_A(s) = 0 = V_B(s)$ for all such states $s$. Let $k$ be the least such state for which B plays a mixed strategy. At least one player plays Continue with probability 1 in state $k-1$ because both playing Quit is not a mutual best reply. If only one player plays Continue at $k-1$ (say B for convenience), then $V_A(k-1) = 0$. But then $V_A(k,Continue) = (1-q)V_A(k-1) + qV_A(k+1) - c_A = (1-q)*0 + q*0 -c_A < 0$, and Continue is not a best reply for A at state $k$. This contradicts that A plays a mixed strategy at $k$. If both players play Continue at $k-1$, then both players play Quit with positive probability for some state less than $k-1$. Otherwise, $V(k-1,Continue) < 0$. The states lower than $k-1$ in which each player quits cannot be the same because Quit is not a best reply to itself nor may they be mixed for both because $k$ is the lowest state in which both players mix. For the player who quits at the higher state of these two, $V(i) = 0$ for all states between $k$ and this Quit state, implying that $V(i,Continue) < 0$ for these states and Quit is best reply. This contradicts this player playing Continue with positive probability at $k-1$.

In a monotonic equilibrium, each player's value increases or decreases across the set of states with $V(s) = 0$ for any state in which the player quits and $V(s) = 1$ for any state where the other player quits. Because $V_A(N) = 1$, $V_A(0) = 0$, $V_B(0) = 1$, and $V_B(N) = 0$, $V_A$ is increasing and $V_B$ decreasing. Each player's value function satisfies the following nonhomogeneous difference equation (I drop the subscript denoting $A$ or $B$ because the equation holds for both):

$$V(s+1) - V(s) = \alpha\big(V(s) - V(s-1)\big) + (1+\alpha)c$$

The solution to the nonhomogeneous equation is

$$V(k) = C\left(k + \sum_{j=1}^{k}\sum_{i=1}^{j}\big(2k - (2i-1)\big)\alpha^i\right)c +$$

$$(1-C)\left(n - k + \sum_{j=1}^{n-k}\sum_{i=1}^{j}\big(2(n-k) - (2i-1)\big)\alpha^{-i}\right)c$$

The corresponding homogenous difference equation is

$$V(s+1) - V(s) = \alpha\big(V(s) - V(s-1)\big)$$

with a family of solutions: $A + B\alpha^k$. Any sum of these two solutions for values of $A,B,C$ are solutions of the nonhomogeneous difference equation (Elaydi 2005, Theorem 2.30, 84). The first part of $V(k)$ is increasing in $k$, while the second part is decreasing. Calculations show that the first part of $V(k) = F_A(k)$ gives $A$'s value for state $m+k$ when $A$ quits at state $m$; the second part then gives $B$'s value for state $k$ if $B$ quits at state $n$ and equals $F_B(k)$. (These functions can be found by solving the nonhomogeneous difference equation recursively from $F_A(0) = 0$). $K_A, K_B$ give the states in which each player's value for playing Continue exceeds 1, and so specifies the number of states that each player has positive value for playing Continue from the state in which the other player Quits. For instance, if $A$ Quits at state $k$, $B$'s best reply plays Quit for state $k + K_B$ and Continue for all states less than $k + K_B$. When $K_A = K_B$, any pair of states $k, l$ form an equilibrium of Quit points when $|k - l| = K_A$. When $K_A > K_B$, the only mutual best replies are $A$ quitting at $0$ and $B$ quitting at $K_B$. When $K_A < K_B$, the only mutual best replies are $A$ quitting at $N - K_A$ and $B$ quitting at $N$.

Note: When $K_A = K_B = K$ and $N \geq 3K$, there are equilibria in which $A$ and $B$ alternate ranges of states where they Quit. For example, $A$ plays Continue for states *(1,2K–1)* and *(2K+1,N)*, Quit for *2K*, and $B$ plays Continue for *(0,K–1)* and *(K+1,N-1)* and Quit for *K* can form an equilibrium. I do not consider equilibria like this because they are equivalent on the equilibrium path to an equilibrium given in the proposition depending on the initial state of the game or produce counterintuitive behavior. An example of the latter occurs in the range of *(K,2K)* in the previous equilibrium in which both players gain by losing battles rather than winning them.

Note: The value functions for both players in an equilibrium in which $A$ Quits for $s \leq m$ and $B$ Quits for $s \geq m + K$ can be found from the full set of solutions of the nonhomogeneous difference equation by setting *C = 1* for $A$ and *C = 0* for

*B* and then solving for *A,B* given the boundary conditions that $V_A(m) = 0$ and $V_A(m + K) = 1$ or $V_B(m) = 1$ and $V_B(m + K) = 0$. Solving, we have the following value function for $V_A$ (using definition of $F_A$ in statement of equilibrium):

$$V_A(k) = \begin{cases} 0 & \text{if } k \leq m \\ F_A(k-m) + \left(\dfrac{1-F_A(K)}{1+\alpha^k}\right)\left(1+\alpha^{k-m}\right) & \text{if } m < k < m+K \\ 1 & \text{if } k \geq m+K \end{cases}$$

I add the choice of committing violations to each round of this game. In addition to the choice whether to Continue or Quit, both players decide what proportion of their soldiers they wish to commit violations. These violations affect both the probability of winning the current battle and the costs of fighting for both sides. The transition probability from state to state depends on how many of the country's soldiers Violate rather than Honor the treaty standard: $p(S_{i+1}) = q + r\left(\dfrac{\#\,a_i\,violate}{\#\,a_i}\right) - s\left(\dfrac{\#\,b_j\,violate}{\#\,b_j}\right)$

with $p(S_{i\text{-}1}) = 1 - p(S_{i+1})$ and $r,s > 0$. Both players' costs of war are increased by the number of soldiers who commit violations on both sides; specifically, *A*'s costs equal $c_A + d_A\left(\dfrac{\#\,a_i\,violate}{\#\,a_i}\right) + w_A\left(\dfrac{\#\,b_j\,violate}{\#\,b_j}\right)$; *B*'s costs are

$c_B + d_B\left(\dfrac{\#\,b_j\,violate}{\#\,b_j}\right) + w_B\left(\dfrac{\#\,a_i\,violate}{\#\,a_i}\right)$ with $d_A, d_B, w_A, w_B > 0$. Each player's

strategy maps the state into how many soldiers it will order to Violate in the current round and whether the player Quits or Continues. Refer to the fraction of soldiers that *A* orders to violate to be *x*, with *y* being the same fraction for *B*.

Lemma: In equilibrium, *A* plays $x = \{0,1\}$ and has a state $L_A$ such that *A* plays $x = 0$ for all states $k < L_A$ and $x = 1$ for all $k \geq L_A$. (The parallel result holds for *B*.)

Proof: *A*'s value from state *k* is

$$V_A(k) = (q + rx - sy)V_A(k+1) + (1-q-rx+sy)V_A(k-1) - c_A - d_A x - w_A y.$$

The first order condition for maximizing this value with respect to *x* is positive if

$$V_A(k+1) - V_A(k-1) > \frac{d_A}{r}$$

and negative if the inequality is reversed. Optimal levels of *x* are then the extreme values of the range, *0,1*, depending on the direction of this inequality, with $x = 1$ if the first order condition is positive and $x = 0$ otherwise.

$$V_A\left(k+1\right)-V_A\left(k-1\right)=\left(2+\alpha^{k+1}+4\alpha^k+4\sum_{i-1}^{k-1}\left(k+2-i\right)\alpha^i\right)c_A$$
$$+\left(\frac{1-F_A\left(K\right)}{1+\alpha^k}\right)\left(\alpha^{k+1}-\alpha^k\right),$$

which is increasing in $k$. This implies that if $x = 1$ is optimal for some state $k$, it is optimal for all states greater than $k$.

This first order condition leads directly to comparative statics for the states in which a side will commit violations. As in the previous lemma, the closer a side is to winning, the more likely the inequality will be satisfied. This is because the differences in the value function increase as a side gets closer to victory. Second, violations become more attractive the larger the battlefield advantage produced by them ($r$). Third, the lower the cost a side suffers for committing violations, the more attractive it is to do so.

The state-to-state game of compliance reduces to a two-by-two game because each player plays $0$ or $1$ in each round. For convenience, I call these moves *Not Violate (NV)* or *Violate (V)*. Refer to each player's value for each of the four outcomes as $V_A(s_A,s_B,k)$ or $V_B(s_A,s_B,k)$, where $s_A,s_B$ are the strategies and $k$ is the current state. Both players prefer outcomes in which the other does not violate, $V_A(s_A,NV,k) > V_A(s_A,V,k)$ for $A$ for instance, because their costs are higher and probability of winning each battle lowers when the other violates. The other comparisons of outcomes depend on the exact values of the parameters. $V_B(s_A,s_B,k)$ is increasing in the probability $A$ wins the next battle, $q + rx - sy$, and decreasing in $A$'s costs, $c_A$, directly from the generating equation of $V_A$.

Each player's decision whether or not to violate does not depend on the other player from the earlier lemma. There are then three possible cases in the two-by-two game:

1. Both players prefer to play Not Violate.
2. One player prefers to play Violate while the other prefers to play Not Violate.
3. Both players prefer to play Violate.

The first case covers issues in which neither player would commit violations on their own. The second case is asymmetric when one can benefit from violations while the other does not. The third case covers those issues in which both players can benefit from violations. This case has the familiar Prisoners' Dilemma dynamics when $V(NV,NV,k) > V(V,V,k)$. It need not have such dynamics when this inequality is reversed for one of the players. It cannot be the case that both players have $V(NV,NV,k) < V(V,V,k)$. This preference is possible only when a player's probability of winning is higher when they both play Violate than when they both play Not Violate because costs increase. If one player's probability of winning a battle increases, the other's must decrease and then the latter cannot prefer $V(V,V,k)$ to $V(NV,NV,k)$. Finally, each of these two-by-two games is defined for each state $k$ where both players play Continue. It need not be the case that the same preference order, and hence the same game, holds for all such states. The previous lemma shows that a player's preference between Not Violate and Violate can change as it approaches victory (as the current state approaches the state in which the other player will Quit).

When can prewar agreements to play Not Violate be enforced through reciprocity? The first case requires no such agreement; both players comply out of their own interests. The asymmetric cases of the third type cannot be enforced through reciprocity. The player that prefers $V(NV,NV,k)$ to $V(V,V,k)$ lacks a reciprocal threat to play in the face of defection from $V(NV,NV,k)$. Retaliating makes the other player better off because it prefers $V(V,V,k)$ to $V(NV,NV,k)$. In the second case, this player has the reciprocal threat to play Violate, and so might be able to use that threat to induce the other player to play Not Violate. This player, however, lacks the incentive to play Violate in the round following the other player playing Violate because it prefers Not Violate no matter what the other player does. The threat would not be carried out in equilibrium and so will not deter the play of Violate by the other. This leaves only the set of the third case in which the game is Prisoners' Dilemma. The hardest case for reciprocity occurs when a player is one state away from winning. Its benefit from violating is two-fold: it increases the chance of winning and so avoiding retaliation, and the difference between winning and losing the battle is larger than at any other point. Calculating the value for violating and not violating for $A$ at state $K-1$ (one winning battle away from winning the war) and reducing, we have the following condition for when $A$ will honor an agreement not to violate:

$$(1-q)\big[V_A(NV,NV,K-2)-V_A(V,V,K-2)\big] \geq r_A\big[1-V_A(V,V,K-2)\big]-d_A.$$

The right-hand side is positive because the first order condition for violating is satisfied. If this condition holds, the threat of a response in kind for one round is sufficient to deter $A$ from playing Violate from any state.

The comparative statics of this inequality follow from the first order condition. Higher costs for committing violations ($d$, remember that this is the cost the violating side pays for its own violations) and less strategic benefit ($r$, the increased chance of winning a battle from violations) make honoring the agreement more likely by reducing the right-hand side. The relative strength of the parties enters into the left-hand side in two ways. It changes the probability that the side in question will lose the current battle and so face the reciprocal sanction. This means that the condition is more likely to bind the weaker side than the stronger, and the effect increases with the underlying chance that the stronger side wins a battle (i.e., no violations by either side). The stronger side then is more likely to break such an agreement, all else equal.

These results rely solely on one-round reciprocal punishments for enforcement. Agreements for this form of enforcement could be ad hoc, through wartime negotiations. Because they hold only when both sides share an interest in limiting the costs of war, they are weaker than the treaties of international humanitarian law. Later, I discuss how universal treaties could be modeled as prewar agreements as a mechanism of screening out types that intend to commit violations. Before doing so, we consider combinations of the equilibria of the three games to show their interactions.

### VIOLATIONS AND COMPLIANCE ACROSS THE THREE MODELS

Each of the three models captures a different portion of the strategic problems posed by the limitation of violence during wartime. How do the equilibria of the separate models depend on one another when the three games are linked? Linking the games together changes the choices for states and the consequences for states and their soldiers. States can no longer choose the level of violations (i.e., fraction of soldiers who commit violations). Instead, they influence the level of violations through their probability of detecting violations. This probability of detection may deter some of their soldiers from committing violations, and so reduce the level of violations. The conditions on the battlefield and which equilibrium the soldiers believe they are playing also influence both how many soldiers commit violations and the strategic consequences on the battlefield.

Begin with the soldiers' decisions on the battlefield given level $p$ of monitoring. Soldiers only face punishment when they violate and are detected with probability $p$ set by their national leadership. Figure 3'.4 demonstrates the battlefield game including the risk of being caught and punished. Soldiers treat the risk of detection and punishment as given when they meet on the battlefield.

Let $a,b$ be the critical types that are indifferent between Honor and Violate with $p_A$, $p_B$ being the probability that a violation is detected. The indifference condition is as follows for side $A$ with a parallel calculation for side $B$:

$$(1-b)(0) + b(-V) = (1-b)(T - a - p_A) + b(-1 - p_A)$$

|  | $b_j$ | |
|---|---|---|
|  | Honor | Violate |
| Honor | $(0,0)$ | $(-V, T - t_j - p_B)$ |
| Violate | $(T - t_j - p_A, -V)$ | $(-1 - p_A, -1 - p_B)$ |

$0 < T < 1, V > 0, t \sim U[0,1]$

FIGURE 3'.4 The Battlefield game with monitoring.

This condition holds for both sides in equilibrium and this pair of equations simplifies to the following system of equations:

$$a(1-b) = T - p_A - b(1 + T - V)$$
$$b(1-a) = T - p_B - a(1 + T - V)$$

State leaders choose the level of detection of violations to reduce the number of their soldiers that commit violations, provided that they prefer to control violations. State $A$'s value in a given round is the following:

$$V_A(p,k) = (q + ra(p_A) - sb)V_A(k+1) + (1 - q - ra(p_A) + sb)V_A(k-1) - c_A$$
$$- d_A x - w_A y - D p_A^2,$$

where $x,y$ is the type for $a_i, b_j$ respectively that is indifferent between committing violations or not (there is, of course, a parallel calculation for state $B$).

Solving the first order condition for maximizing $V_A$ with respect to $p_A$ leads to the following:

$$p_A^* = \frac{1}{2D}\left(\frac{da}{dp_A}\left(r[V_A(k+1) - V_A(k-1)] - d\right)\right)$$

When $p_A^* \geq T - b(1 - V + T)$, all types of $a$ prefer Honor to Violate. This implies $A$ will set $p_A = min(p_A^*, T - b(1 - V + T))$. From implicit differentiation of the first equation in the previous system and the Envelope Theorem, we have

$$\frac{da}{dp_A} = \frac{-1}{1-b}$$

Because $D > 0$, this implies that $p_A{}^* > 0$ requires

$$r[V_A(k+1) - V_A(k-1)] - d < 0,$$

which is the same condition as $V_A(NV,s_B,k) > V_A(V,s_B,k)$. Let $\Phi_A(k) = -(r[V_A(k+1) - V_A(k-1)] - d)$ with a parallel definition of $\Phi_B(k)$, the value for not committing violations for $A$, and we get the following simplification:

$$p_A^* = \frac{1}{2D}\left(\frac{\Phi_A(k)}{1-b}\right)$$

With these expressions, we can find the best reply correspondences for $a$ and $p_A$ as functions of $b$. When $\Phi_A(k) < 0$, $p_A = 0$ because $A$ gains from more violations by its soldiers, and best reply correspondence for $a$ matches the

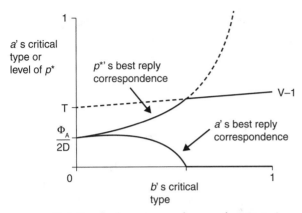

FIGURE 3′.5 Best reply correspondences when $\Phi_A > 0$.

conditions of the case of the battlefield model described earlier. When $\Phi_A(k) > 0$, $p_A > 0$ because $A$ wants to discourage violations by its soldiers. Figure 3′.5 shows the best reply correspondences for $p_A$ and $a$ as functions of $b$. The best reply correspondence for $p_A$ is the minimum of the line from $(0,T)$ to $(1,V-1)$, which gives the level of monitoring that deters all violations by soldiers of $A$, and the hyperbola for $p_A{}^*$ in the previous equation. Both are given as thin, dashed lines in the figure to show how the best reply correspondence arises from them. The intersection of the two is found by setting them equal and solving the resulting quadratic equation. This gives the following, with the positive root if $1-V+T < 0$ and the negative root if $1-V+T > 0$ ($b'$ is defined in a parallel fashion):

$$a' = \frac{1}{2} + \frac{T}{2(1-V+T)} \pm \frac{1}{2(1-V+T)}\left((1-V+T)\left(1-V+T+\frac{2\Phi_A}{D}\right)+T^2\right)^{\frac{1}{2}}.$$

The best reply correspondence for $a$ follows from the optimal level of $p_A$ and the first equation in the system that defines $a$ and $b$. In equilibrium, monitoring of one's own troops rises with the level of violations by the other side until monitoring rises to the level at which all violations are deterred.

There are some variations on Figure 3′.5 depending on the values of the parameters. If $\dfrac{\Phi_A}{2D} > T$, the hyperbola lies above the line that is then the best reply correspondence. If $T > V-1$, the line slopes downward rather than upward, but the best reply correspondence remains at the lower level of the line and the hyperbola.

The equilibria of the model can be drawn from these best reply correspondences. There are four cases based on the values of $\Phi_A(k)$ and $\Phi_B(k)$, where $k$ is the initial state of the model.

<u>Proposition</u>: The following strategies are equilibria of the complete game:

Case 1: $\Phi_A(k) > 0$ and $\Phi_B(k) > 0$ (both sides prefer their soldiers to honor the standard). Let $a^*, b^*$ solve the following system of equations:

$$a(1-b) = T - \frac{\Phi_A(k)}{2D(1-b)} - b(1+T-V)$$

$$b(1-a) = T - \frac{\Phi_B(k)}{2D(1-b)} - a(1+T-V)$$

(a) If $\dfrac{\Phi_A(k)}{2D} < T$ and $\dfrac{\Phi_B(k)}{2D} < T$, $A$ sets $p_A = \dfrac{\Phi_A(k)}{2D(1-b^*)}$ $B$ sets $p_B = \dfrac{\Phi_B(k)}{2D(1-a^*)}$ ;

$a_i$ plays Violate if $t_i < T - p_A$ ($= a^*$ in equilibrium), Honor otherwise; and $b_j$ plays Violate if $t_j < T - p_B$ ($= b^*$ in equilibrium), Honor otherwise.

(b) If $\dfrac{\Phi_A(k)}{2D} \geq T$ and $\dfrac{\Phi_B(k)}{2D} < T$, $A$ sets $p_A = T$; $B$ sets $p_B = \dfrac{\Phi_B(k)}{2D}$ ; $a_i$ plays Violate if $t_i < T - p_A$ ($= 0$ in equilibrium), Honor otherwise; and $b_j$ plays Violate if $t_j < T - p_B$ ($= b^*$ in equilibrium), Honor otherwise.

(c) If $\dfrac{\Phi_A(k)}{2D} < T$ and $\dfrac{\Phi_B(k)}{2D} \geq T$, $A$ sets $p_A = \dfrac{\Phi_A(k)}{2D}$ $B$ sets $p_B = T$; $a_i$ plays Violate if $t_i < T - p_A$ ($= a^*$ in equilibrium), Honor otherwise; and $b_j$ plays Violate if $t_j < T - p_B$ ($= 0$ in equilibrium), Honor otherwise.

(d) If $\dfrac{\Phi_A(k)}{2D} \geq T$ and $\dfrac{\Phi_B(k)}{2D} \geq T$, $A$ sets $p_A = T$; $B$ sets $p_B = T$; $a_i$ plays Violate if $t_i < T - p_A$ ($= 0$ in equilibrium), Honor otherwise; and $b_j$ plays Violate if $t_j < T - p_B$ ($= 0$ in equilibrium), Honor otherwise.

Case 2: $\Phi_i(k) > 0$ and $\Phi_j(k) < 0$ (one side prefers honoring the standard while the other prefers violating it). For convenience, assume $\Phi_A(k) > 0$ and $\Phi_B(k) < 0$, the opposite case parallels this. Let $a^*, b^*$ solve the following system of equations:

$$a(1-b) = T - \frac{\Phi_A(k)}{2D(1-b)} - b(1+T-V)$$

$$b(1-a) = T - a(1+T-V)$$

(a) If $b' < T$, $A$ sets $p_A = \dfrac{\Phi_A(k)}{2D(1-b^*)}$; $B$ sets $p_B = 0$; $a_i$ plays Violate if $t_i < T - p_A$ ($= a^*$ in equilibrium), Honor otherwise; and $b_j$ plays Violate if $t_j < b^*$, Honor otherwise.

(b) If $b' \geq T$, $A$ sets $p_A = T$; $B$ sets $p_B = 0$; $a_i$ plays Violate if $t_i < T - p_A$ ($= 0$ in equilibrium), Honor otherwise; and $b_j$ plays Violate if $t_j < T - p_B$ ($= T$ in equilibrium), Honor otherwise.

Case 3: $\Phi_i(k) < 0$ and $\Phi_j(k) < 0$ (both sides prefers violating the standard to honoring it).

(a) If $V \le 1$, then

    (1) $A$ sets $p_A = 0$; $B$ sets $p_B = 0$; $a_i$ plays Honor when $t_i > t_{crit}^-$, Violate otherwise.

    (2) If $V \ge -T$, there are two asymmetric equilibria: $A$ sets $p_A = 0$; $B$ sets $p_B = 0$; $a_i$ plays Honor when $t_i > T$, Violate otherwise; $b_j$ plays Honor for all types and reversing $a$ and $b$.

(b) If $V > 1$ and $(T - V)^2 + 4 - 4V > 0$ then there are three symmetric equilibria:

    (1) $A$ sets $p_A = 0$; $B$ sets $p_B = 0$; $a_i$ plays Honor when $t_i > t_{crit}^-$, Violate otherwise;

    (2) $A$ sets $p_A = 0$; $B$ sets $p_B = 0$; $a_i$ plays Honor when $t_i > t_{crit}^+$, Violate otherwise; and

    (3) $A$ sets $p_A = 0$; $B$ sets $p_B = 0$; all $a_l$ play Violate.

(c) If $(T - V)^2 + 4 - 4V < 0$ (this implies $V > 1$), then $A$ sets $p_A = 0$; $B$ sets $p_B = 0$; all $a_i, b_j$ play Violate.

Proof: Follows straightforwardly from best reply correspondence described previously.

The willingness of both sides to limit violations determines the level of violations through the monitoring and discipline of soldiers who violate. The costs of monitoring limit the ability of a side to deter violations by its soldiers. For issues with low costs of monitoring relative to the gains from preventing violations, the leadership can raise monitoring enough to deter all violations and ensure full compliance. When the costs of monitoring are higher, the leadership will accept a low level of violations rather than raise monitoring high enough to deter all violations. These motivations hold even when the other side makes no effort to police its own soldiers.

When a side believes it will gain from violations, it puts no effort in monitoring what its soldiers do. Whether its soldiers commit many or few violations depends on what the other side's soldiers do. When the other side tries to control its soldiers, they will commit few violations. The lack of violations by the other side reduces the incentive the first side's soldiers have to commit violations to protect themselves against anticipated violations by the other side's soldiers. This dynamic results in a low level of violations because of the restraint of the other side, although the violations by the first side are higher than if it sought to enforce the standard on its own troops. The side that wants to violate the standard gains from the restraint of the other side as all sides prefer their opponents to commit fewer violations. It is unable, however, to take full strategic advantage of its breach of the standard because it cannot induce more of its soldiers to commit violations.

When both sides ignore the standard and seek to violate it, multiple equilibria on the battlefield can aid or frustrate their attempts to gain an advantage through violations. When vulnerability is low ($V < 1$), all of the equilibria have low levels of violations. When vulnerability is high ($V > 1$), the second case has three equilibria with low, medium, and high levels of violations. When both sides have Prisoners' Dilemma preferences over violations (both prefer committing more violations but prefer that neither violate over both doing so), they are better off coordinating on the equilibrium with a low level of violations. But if one prefers high levels of violations even if the other responds in kind, they may disagree about which equilibrium to play. Let $P_A(k) = (r - s)[V_A(k+1) - V_A(k-1)] - d - w_A$ with a parallel definition for $P_B(k)$. $A$ has Prisoners' Dilemma preferences when $\Phi_A(k) < 0$ and $P_A(k) < 0$.

### Screening through Ratification

A possible disagreement about which equilibrium the players wish to play provides them with a reason to communicate their intentions before war breaks out. The value that each side places on violations or restraint depends on the parameters of the model, some of which are common knowledge whereas others are private information. The issue determines cost of monitoring, $D$, meaning it is the same across actors and is therefore commonly known. Those issues for which individual soldiers possess the ability to violate on their own are more difficult and costly to monitor than those for which military and political authorities have the ability to control whether to violate directly. The strategic cost or benefit from violations depends on whether they contribute to winning battles ($r$ or $s$ for $A$ and $B$, respectively) and the costs a side suffers from its own violations ($d_A$ or $d_B$). The consequences of the other side's violations are irrelevant because each side would like to see the other side reduce its violations. Both of these parameters contain some private information. States vary in whether they see violations as advancing their chances in battle or whether they believe they gain from compliance. In some cases, the military advantage of violations may be clear to all, such as Britain's vulnerability to submarine warfare. In others, the military advantage a side perceives from violations may not be seen by others in advance. The costs of committing violations, in contrast, are likely to be private information, with the balance between any perceived strategic benefit and those costs known with certainty only to the government in question. Furthermore, this calculation is specific to the particular opponent; the same government may wish to be restrained against one and not against another.

The critical elements in a side's decision whether it gains from its own violations – $r$ and $d_A$ for $A$, for example – are known to it but not others. At the same time, one side does not know the type of its prospective opponent because the key parameters, $s$ and $d_B$ for $B$, in the other side's decision are its private information. Additionally, the first side, $A$ in this example, does not know whether the violations of the other side will lead it to prefer restraint by both to violations by both. That is, it cannot know whether it has Prisoners'

Dilemma payoffs $(P_A(k) < 0)$ or prefers to commit violations regardless of what the other side does $(P_A(k) > 0)$.

This private information about whether a side intends to comply with a standard creates a need to communicate it in advance of war. Additionally, prewar communication could allow the players to coordinate on which equilibrium they will play during a war, presumably one that both prefer to the other possibilities. First, we consider whether the parties would signal their private information at the outbreak of a war; that is, just announce their values accurately and fully. If both players knew all values, the mapping between their values and equilibria is straightforward:

Cases 1 and 2: Unique equilibrium given in prior proposition

Case 3, subcase a: Play symmetric equilibrium

Case 3, subcase b: Play equilibrium 1 (low violations) if $P_A(k) < 0$ and $P_B(k) < 0$; play equilibrium 3 (high violations) if one player has $P_i(k) > 0$

Case 3, subcase c: Unique equilibrium

In a separating equilibrium, both players would fully reveal their type. Unfortunately, a separating equilibrium does not exist if there is a need to signal types; that is, there are types that wish to limit their violations $(\Phi_A(k) > 0)$ and other types that do not $(\Phi_A(k) < 0)$; and some of the latter types do not have Prisoners' Dilemma preferences for some types versus some types of the other side which do not want to limit their violations $(P_A(k) > 0)$. Let $\Phi_A(t_A,k) = \Phi_{At}(k)$ when $t_A$ is $A$'s type, which gives $A$'s value for its own violations with a parallel definition for $\Phi_{Bt}(k)$. Let $P_A(t_A,t_B,k) = P_A(k)$ when the players' types are $t_A$ and $t_B$ with $P_B(t_A,t_B,k)$ for $B$.

Proposition: A separating equilibrium does not exist if there exists positive probability of types of both players with $\Phi_{it}(k) < 0$ and $\Phi_{it}(k) > 0$ and $P_A(t_A(max), t_B,k) > 0$ for some $t_B$ with $\Phi_B(t_B,k) < 0$.

Proof: Any type with $\Phi_{At}(k) > 0$ will reveal its type because the resulting equilibrium has low levels of violations (Cases 1 and 2). Consider type $t_B$ with $\Phi_B(t_B,k) < 0$ and $P_A(t_A(max), t_B,k) > 0$. This type prefers signaling that it is a type with $\Phi_B(t_B,k) > 0$. If it signals its true type, there is a positive probability that will be as in Case 3. If it signals falsely, it will fall in Case 2 instead of Case 3 with this positive probability. For the complementary probability, the inaccurate signal will not change equilibrium behavior after the signals as $A$ will set $p_A = 0$ no matter what the signals are. $A$ also prefers Case 2 in all three subcases of Case 3. For Case 3a, $t_{crit}^- < T$, so signaling incorrectly leads to higher violations by $A$ and lower violations by $B$, both of which benefit $A$. In Cases 3b and 3c, the signal to play Case 2 instead lowers both sides' violations compared to accurate signaling, which benefits $A$ because $P_A(k) < 0$.

Honest and complete revelation of type is not possible because types with Prisoners' Dilemma preferences prefer to signal that they will control their violations. Such a false signal creates expectations that it will control its own violations. This expectation induces a lower level of violations from the other side. The side making the false signal then completes the deception by not monitoring and disciplining its own soldiers. This deception requires some chance that the other side prefers to commit more violations, even when the first side responds in kind.

This strategic logic of deception suggests that weaker forms of communications could be supported in equilibrium. Specifically, a screening equilibrium, similar to ratification of a treaty standard, could hold where parties either opt in or out. Opting in implies that they prefer low levels of violations and will control the violations of their own soldiers during wartime. Opting out indicates that the party does not intend to observe the standard should war break out.

Proposition: There exist two screening equilibria by which each player either opts in or out. If both ratify, they play in accord with Cases 1, 2, 3a-1, 3b-1, or 3c based on the values of $\Phi_A(k)$, $\Phi_B(k)$, $T$, and $V$ as follows:

$\Phi_A(k) > 0$ and $\Phi_B(k) > 0$, Case 1
$\Phi_i(k) > 0$ and $\Phi_j(k) < 0$, Case 2
$\Phi_A(k) < 0$ and $\Phi_B(k) < 0$, Case 3a-1, 3b-1, or 3c based on the values of $T$ and $V$.

If one or both do not ratify, they play in accord with Cases 1, 2, 3a-1, 3b-3, or 3c based on the values of $\Phi_i(k)$, $\Phi_j(k)$, $T$, and $V$ as follows:

$\Phi_A(k) > 0$ and $\Phi_B(k) > 0$, Case 1
$\Phi_i(k) > 0$ and $\Phi_j(k) < 0$, Case 2
$\Phi_A(k) < 0$ and $\Phi_B(k) < 0$, Case 3a-1, 3b-3, or 3c based on the values of $T$ and $V$. If side $i$ ratifies and side $j$ does not and the conditions for Case 3a hold, play asymmetric equilibrium with $t_i = 0$ and $t_j = T$.

In one screening equilibria, all types with $\Phi_i(k,t_j) > 0$ ratify and those with $\Phi_i(k,t_j) < 0$ do not for both players. In the other, there are critical types of each player $t^*_A, t^*_B$ with $\Phi_i(k,t^*_j) < 0$ for both such that all types $t_i$ with $\Phi_i(k,t_j) > \Phi_i(k,t^*_j)$ ratify and those types $t_i$ with $\Phi_i(k,t_j) < \Phi_i(k,t^*_j)$ do not.

Proof: Denote ratification by $\rho_A$, with $\rho_A = 1$ meaning ratification and $\rho_A = 0$ non-ratification. The following integral gives the expected value for ratifying under the described strategies (written for $A$, parallel holds for $B$):

$$U_A(\rho_A = 1) = \int_{\rho_B=1} \left(ra_1 - sb_1(s)\right)\left(V_A(k+1) - V_A(k-1)\right) - da_1 - w_A b_1(s)\, dP(s)$$

$$+ \int_{\rho_B=0} \left(ra_2 - sb_2(s)\right)\left(V_A(k+1) - V_A(k-1)\right) - da_2 - w_A b_2(s)\, dP(s)$$

where $a_i$, $b_i$ give the level of violations in the relevant case and $dP(s)$ gives the density function of $A$'s beliefs over $B$'s type, $s$. Note that the level of the other side's violations depends on its type. The following gives the expected value for not ratifying:

$$U_A(\rho_A = 0) = \int_{\rho_B=1} (ra_2 - sb_2(s))(V_A(k+1) - V_A(k-1)) - da_1 - w_A b_1(s) dP(s)$$

$$+ \int_{\rho_B=0} (ra_2 - sb_2(s))(V_A(k+1) - V_A(k-1)) - da_2 - w_A b_2(s) dP(s)$$

The difference for not ratifying over ratifying is

$$\Delta U_A = \int_{\rho_B=1} (r(a_2 - a_1) - s(b_2 - b_1))(V_A(k+1) - V_A(k-1)) - d(a_2 - a_1)$$

$$- w_A(b_2 - b_1) dP(s) + \int_{\rho_B=0} (r(a_3 - a_2) - s(b_3 - b_2))(V_A(k+1) - V_A(k-1))$$

$$- d(a_3 - a_2) - w_A(b_3 - b_2) dP(s)$$

Each of the differences $(a_2 - a_1, a_3 - a_2, b_2 - b_1, b_3 - b_2)$ are non-negative. Because $\Delta U_A \leq 0$ for any type with $\Phi_A(k) > 0$, we assume all such types prefer to ratify. $\Delta U_A$ increases as $r$ increases and $d$ decreases. For types with $\Phi_A(k) < 0$, this difference reduces to

$$\Delta U_A = \int_{\rho_B=1} -\Phi_A(k)(a_2 - a_1) - (s(V_A(k+1) - V_A(k-1)) - w_A)(b_2 - b_1) dP(s)$$

$$+ \int_{\rho_B=0} -\Phi_A(k)(a_3 - a_2) - (s(V_A(k+1) - V_A(k-1)) - w_A)(b_3 - b_2) dP(s)$$

The type with maximum $\Delta U_A$ prefers not ratifying if the probability that it faces a type $t_B$ with $\Phi_B(k) < 0$ and $P_A(t_A, t_B) > 0$ is sufficiently large. There is then a type of A with $\Phi_A(k) < 0$ that is indifferent between ratifying and not. This critical type depends on the parallel critical type of B which ratifies in the screening equilibrium. If this type is that with $\Phi_B(k) = 0$, so that no types with $\Phi_B(k) < 0$ ratify, then the critical type of A is $\Phi_A(k) = 0$ as ratification has no effect on play when $\Phi_B(k) > 0$ and only hurts types of A with $\Phi_A(k) < 0$ when $\Phi_B(k) < 0$ and B does not ratify. If all types of B ratify, then maximal types of A may benefit from not ratifying. Because the same logic holds for the critical type of B, there are two screening equilibria: one in which no types with $\Phi_{i,j}(k) < 0$ ratify and another in which some types of both players with $\Phi_{i,j}(k) < 0$ ratify. The latter Pareto dominates the former for these types.

The two screening equilibria explain why states can benefit from a fixed, common standard embodied in a universal treaty which states opt into or out of through ratification. One equilibrium uses ratification to separate those states which intend to control their soldiers from those that will not. This standard is strict, but some types of states that could benefit from communicating their type in advance cannot do so. Those types which benefit from their own soldiers' violations but only slightly ($t_i$ with $\Phi_i(k, t_i) < 0$ but only slightly smaller than 0) are likely to have Prisoners' Dilemma preferences against types of the other player with $\Phi_j(k,t_j) < 0$. Both these types of players prefer a lower standard that they will join because it allows them to coordinate on the battlefield equilibrium with lower levels of violations. The second screening equilibrium does this. The break point between ratifying and not ratifying depends on how likely it is that each player holds Prisoners' Dilemma preferences. If this is high enough, there can be universal ratification, which will not eliminate violations but will reduce them greatly.

Ratification has no effect when at least one side wants to control its own violations ($\Phi_i(k,t_i) > 0$). Regardless of what the other side does, it will monitor its soldiers and discipline at least some violators. This reduces the incentive for the soldiers of the other side to commit violations to protect themselves, and produces higher levels of compliance on the battlefield by both sides. Discipline of soldiers, not ratification, is key here. Ratification is just a way to signal their intent. Such signaling could be useful when the sides can only infer whether the other side is controlling its soldiers from what happens on the battlefield, but the model does not address this problem of inference. If most of the types of both players will control their troops, ratification effectively becomes unilaterally binding. Under these conditions, states could adopt treaties that are unilaterally binding.

# 4

# Patterns of Compliance with the Laws of War during the Twentieth Century

This chapter begins the task of evaluating the evidence on how the laws of war work in practice by testing the hypotheses at the end of Chapter 3. The ratification of these treaties creates a common conjecture that both sides will follow them if war should break out. The threat of reciprocity enforces this shared expectation of restraint when self-control fails. The possibility of strategic advantage gained from breaking these rules along with noise produced by individual violations mean that these commitments will be broken by some parties in some wars. In response, the other side should respond in kind to these violations.

The key questions addressed in this chapter are:

1. Does the compliance of the warring parties move together?
2. How does joint ratification of treaties, which produces a common conjecture that the treaty rules will be followed, affect compliance and the correlation of the warring parties' compliance?
3. Does unilateral ratification of a treaty standard change the pattern from joint ratification?
4. Does greater scope for individual violations across issues lead to less compliance?
5. Do warring parties respond more strongly to clear legal violations as opposed to violations whose legal status is open to question?
6. Are there firewalls between the different issue areas, so that violations by one side on one issue are not correlated with violations by the other side on different issues?
7. Do defections from treaty standards come early or late in wars?

This chapter presents statistical results that seek to answer these questions from a dataset of compliance with the laws of war during the interstate wars of the twentieth century. Because of the large number of cases covered (all interstate wars according to the Correlates of War project from the Boxer Rebellion in 1990 to the Gulf War in 1991), compliance is assessed in general terms across the entire war as opposed to listing specific atrocities. Chapter 5 examines in detail the issue of prisoners of war during the World Wars; as such, it complements the results of this chapter. Chapter 6 presents shorter case studies of four other issues in the laws of war during the World Wars to show variation across issues in detail. This chapter provides a broad analysis of the patterns of compliance; the next two chapters discuss the details of particular cases. The combination of these chapters gives us confidence that the results have both external validity (that is, we can be confident that the argument will hold for cases beyond those examined) and internal validity (we can be confident that the results do reflect what happened in those cases).

I have divided this chapter, like the previous one, into two parts; one written for a general audience and another aimed at the academic political science audience. This chapter presents the central results of the statistical analysis using graphics to show the estimated effects and tables to show patterns in the data. It covers the main results of the statistical analysis presented in detail its companion, Chapter 4', which provides a complete description of the statistical estimations and tests of the theory. This chapter allows those readers who do not wish to review the full statistical analysis to understand the patterns uncovered by those techniques and their importance. I have striven to use graphics that should make those effects and the conclusions that follow from them clear even to the reader lacking in technical training. This chapter also provides the central discussion of the significance of these results and their implications for the theory presented in the preceding chapters.

I begin by discussing the factors that could influence compliance and reciprocity. This discussion expands on the hypotheses deduced from the model in the previous chapter to consider elements that lie outside the model, followed by a brief description of the data. The graphical presentation of the key results on compliance and how it varies come next. I examine discordant and outlying cases to see whether they are consistent with the expectations of the model. The lack of evidence of systematic retaliation across issues is evidence of "firewalls" between those issues. I then turn to presenting the results of when first violations occur and the timing of responses to those first violations. I conclude this chapter by summarizing the results.

## FACTORS THAT MIGHT AFFECT COMPLIANCE AND RECIPROCITY

States live up to their legal obligations during wartime when they believe a restrained battlefield is in their interest, either because their leaders see restraint as always in their interest or they fear a response in kind by the other side. But states see those advantages in different ways. The effect of most of the state-level variables in a statistical analysis is difficult to predict; there are often arguments that point in opposite directions. This section lays out the arguments for the different effects that the candidate explanatory variables could have on compliance and its correlation across warring parties. The precise measures used for these concepts are presented in the companion chapter.

## Legal Obligation

The central puzzle of this book is whether international law shapes state behavior, and if so, when and how. If law matters, a state's conduct during wartime should depend on its obligations. There are two different views of international law as legal obligation. One view assumes that legal obligations matter only when states agree to be bound by the standards in a treaty. This view puts the acts of treaty ratification as a signal that a state accepts the legal standards of the treaty. The second view asserts that legal obligations affect states as norms that shape their behavior even when states have not publicly accepted those standards.

The mechanisms of legal obligation or constraint through shared norms are audience costs and internalization of standards. Both views see both mechanisms as working and effective in shaping state behavior, although they disagree about how each operates. As such, the evidence presented in this chapter cannot separate the details of these mechanisms. The analysis can allow us to see if acceptance of legal obligations is necessary to limit state behavior by including cases in which states have not accepted the current treaty in an issue. The analysis also includes an issue – aerial bombing – for which no formal treaty has ever entered into force and so no legal obligations exist, even if norms against the indiscriminate bombing of civilians exist.

The status of legal obligation can be specific to a state or dyadic if a state is committed to observe a treaty obligation only when the other side has also ratified the treaty in question. In the analysis, I test for both unilateral ratification and joint ratification of the relevant treaty.

Legal obligations could also depend on the political system of a state as described earlier; democracies could care about and honor their legal obligations while autocracies do not (Hathaway 2002, 2005).

## Regime Type

International relations scholars conventionally distinguish between democracies and autocracies, with the well-known democratic peace – the observation that democracies are much less likely to fight one another even though they fight roughly as often as nondemocracies – being the focal result from that distinction. Why the democratic peace occurs has been a central issue of debate in the literature for more than two decades. Some believe that democracies are better at generating audience costs and so can signal their resolve more clearly (Fearon 1994; Schultz 2001), whereas others think the pattern is a spurious result of common interests among democracies during the Cold War (Farber and Gowa 1995), and many more such arguments have been advanced to account for the pattern described earlier. These arguments matter for my questions because the various arguments imply different patterns among regime types. The model of the laws of war is agnostic about these arguments, and so am I in this section.[1]

First, democracies may be more likely to comply with their legal obligations. If democracies externalize their domestic norms of limited competition, they would be more willing to limit how their military forces conduct combat (Maoz and Russett 1993). If democracies are law-bound states (those that respect international law and commitments because they are governments in which law presides over men), they would be more likely to comply with international humanitarian law during wartime (Slaughter 1995; Hathaway 2002, 2005; Simmons 2002). The former argument implies that democracies would be willing to comply with international humanitarian norms even if they had not ratified the current treaties, and acceptance of law through ratification would be critical for a law-bound state.

Second, autocracies may be less likely to comply because they hold human life in lower regard. This is the reverse of the normative argument of constrained competition in democracies. Autocracies are more likely to engage in mass killings of their own civilians (Harff 2003). Furthermore, because autocracies see law as a tool the leader uses to retain his hold on power, and not as a system of principles that limit the leader's power, autocracies will not take their international legal commitments seriously. They will feel free to ignore those obligations as suits their purposes of the moment.

Third, audience cost arguments suggest that democracies are more likely to live up to legal obligations that they have accepted before the war began. It is commonly argued that democratic leaders face greater audience costs for escalating a crisis and then backing down (Fearon 1994; Schultz 2001) because the domestic audiences can remove them from office more easily than those audiences in other systems (B. Bueno de Mesquita et al. 2003). Similarly, others argue that democracies are more likely to honor their alliance commitments to defend their allies because of such costs (Leeds 2003). In both cases, the clear public act of accepting the obligation combined with the public act of subsequently failing to live up to it signal to the domestic audience that the leader should be removed.[2]

All three of these arguments suggest that democracies are more likely to honor the laws of war than autocracies are, although each casts a different light as to why. Whether democracies retaliate when they suffer violations against

---

[1] As readers may know, I have strong views about why the democratic peace occurs (B. Bueno de Mesquita et al. 1999; Morrow 2002). For now, I am putting aside my own view about how democratic politics affects foreign policy.

[2] For a possible explanation why domestic audiences might remove leaders who break public commitments, see Smith (1998b).

their troops does not follow as clearly from these arguments. If democracies are unwilling to engage in unlawful acts, they may not respond to atrocity in kind. Of course, they could find other forms of response besides retaliation; recently, war crimes trials after the war have been threatened to deter autocratic leaders from committing atrocities. The current analysis is incapable of judging whether such threats deter violations because threats of postwar trials are a recent phenomenon. Law-bound states might be quite willing and capable of responding to violations in kind, particularly when the treaty in question provides for reprisals in the original meaning of the term – a violation that retaliates against other violations so as to induce future compliance. In some areas of the law of war, such reciprocal responses lift the protections of the law when the other side abuses that protection for a military advantage. Whether democracies are able to carry out reciprocal responses to violations is not obvious as different arguments point in different directions.

Finally, I turn to another way to think about how domestic regimes might influence a state's willingness to comply with the laws of war. All political leaders answer to a set of supporters – that is, their support coalition. To stay in power, a leader must keep his or her supporters from defecting to a challenger. Leaders can use public policy to reward their supporters with combinations of public goods – policies that benefit all in society – or private benefits – policies that directly or indirectly reward specific individuals. A central insight into politics is that public policy shifts away from the provision of private benefits and toward the provision of public goods as the size of the support coalition that the leader requires to hold power increases (B. Bueno de Mesquita et al. 2003). Leaders of modern mass democracies require a large support coalition, roughly half of the electorate of their states. Autocratic leaders, on the other hand, rely on a much smaller set of supporters to retain power, and so are less likely to provide public goods to all in society. In this view, democracies are law-bound states because the rule of law is a public good, and leaders of democracies have created institutions to enforce law to provide that public good.

This view of domestic politics has similar implications for compliance with the laws of war as more general views of democracies versus autocracies. First, no leader in any system draws support from enemy soldiers or civilians; their willingness to limit violence against the enemy arises from the benefits such limits produce for their own supporters in terms of shortening the war or reducing the costs of fighting. Democratic leaders may care more about both sides complying than autocratic leaders because it is more likely that their own people who suffer from violations will be supporters of the current leader. Because the supporters of the leader are more likely to suffer the consequences of atrocity when the winning coalition is large, leaders who answer to a large winning coalition should be more likely to comply but also more likely to retaliate. It may also be the case that leaders who answer to a large winning coalition are less likely to commit the first violation of an agreement during war, as they would like to uphold those standards, but are more likely to retaliate against a violation. Put another way, autocrats are less predictable than democratic leaders; they have more latitude to do as they wish because they answer to fewer supporters.

### Different Issues

State compliance with the laws of war should vary with the issue. In Chapter 3, I argued that violations by individuals produce noise, making reciprocal enforcement more difficult. Because various issues provide varying levels of opportunities for individuals to commit violations, overall levels of compliance should vary across issues. Some issues, like prisoners of war and treatment of civilians, provide individual soldiers with frequent opportunities to commit violations on their own initiative. Other areas, such as chemical and biological warfare, have little scope for such individual violations because soldiers can only commit violations if the command authority gives them the means to do so. Other areas, such as conduct on the high seas, are less prone to violations by individuals because the ability to commit individual violations lies in the hands of officers higher up the chain of command than the common soldier. The magnitude of these problems depends also on whether the states in question adopt military training and discipline that can reduce violations by individuals. I do not have direct measures of those instruments of control, so I cannot test for their ability to limit violations and prevent spirals of escalation on the battlefield. I expect to find substantial differences in compliance across issues independent of the legal status of those areas, and I expect that average compliance should decline as the role of noise from individual violations rises by issue.

### Relative Power

The relative power between the warring parties could also affect their willingness to comply. Here the arguments point in both directions. If the sides are roughly equal, then both possess the ability to retaliate in some form, enhancing reciprocal deterrence of violations. In contrast, the consequences of any military advantage gained from breaking a convention for which side wins the war might be more significant when the sides are equal. When one side is much stronger than the other, it might be restrained because it knows it is likely to win without violating any conventions. In contrast, a much stronger side might violate conventions to raise the cost of fighting, and so shock the weaker side into conceding quickly. As with democracy, I am agnostic on which of these effects dominates. It could be that although each of these arguments appears to hold in some cases, in general, they cancel one another out and there is no systematic pattern.

There is one exception to my agnosticism here because the model does have a clear prediction concerning which side is responsible when the first violation comes late in the war. A side close to victory can benefit from raising the costs of war by breaking a convention. Because this observation opposes the common wisdom that losing states break conventions in an attempt to stave off defeat, I test it separately.

## A BRIEF DESCRIPTION OF THE DATA

The data assesses compliance with the laws of war during the interstate wars of the twentieth century. The companion chapter (Chapter 4') gives full details on this collection. From the interstate war data of the Correlates of War project (henceforth COW), each war is broken down into warring dyads, accumulating states that fight under unified command into one side. The observation is the directed warring dyad for a given issue, so how France treated German prisoners during World War I is one observation.

Eight issues – aerial bombardment, armistice/ceasefire, chemical and biological weapons (CBW), treatment of civilians, protection of cultural property, conduct on the high seas, prisoners of war (POWs), and treatment of wounded – cover the range of issues examined here. The companion chapter also analyzes compliance with declaration of war; I exclude it from the analysis because the strategic dynamics of that issue differ from the others.

Coding rules of violations were developed from the treaties that address each issue, including draft treaties that never entered into force. Evidence on violations was collected from historical sources using the coding rules to identify major and minor violations of the treaty standards. Four dimensions of compliance – magnitude, frequency, centralization of violations, and legal clarity of violations – were coded from the collected evidence. The quality of the information used in the coding was also assessed, ranging from sketchy information to excellent documentation. Even with these efforts, a substantial amount of the observations are missing data; for some issues, standardized coding was used to complete both sides of a dyad for which there was information on the compliance of the other. The robustness of the results with respect to the quality of the data was extensively tested, and they do not vary substantially based on how the quality of the data is treated. When possible, dates of first violations were also collected to assess whether violations come early or late in a war.

A four-point scale of compliance – full compliance, high compliance, low compliance, noncompliance – was created from the data by combining the magnitude and frequency scores. These four levels of compliance are clearly distinguished from one another, although the differences across categories may not be the same. Of the 947 cases with coding based on evidence (not standardized coding except for CBW), 41 percent (385 cases) have full compliance, 32 percent (306) high compliance, 21 percent (195) low compliance, and 6 percent (61) noncompliance. As noted at the beginning of the book, the record of compliance with the laws of war is mixed. Whereas full compliance is common, low or noncompliance is not rare.

The analyses focus on whether the compliance of one side on a given issue moves with the compliance of the other because that pattern is a primary prediction of the model in Chapter 3. The correlation of compliance is assessed both between directed dyads (where the compliance of the other side is a predictor of that side's compliance) and by creating dyadic scores of total compliance across the sides and reciprocity measured by the difference in their compliance.

There are three threats to the validity of the statistical analyses reported here. The four-level scale of compliance and the estimation of reciprocity pose two different threats to inference. The scale of compliance is ordinal; the categories are ranked from highest to lowest compliance, but there is no guarantee that the separation of the categories is equal. The second threat is simultaneity bias, because the victim's compliance and the violator's compliance should cause one another. The third issue is the quality of the data, which I check by running each analysis three ways. *The results I present in the following graphics are robust in the face of all of these issues.* Although the specific coefficients vary from analysis to analysis, the patterns and estimated effects are similar across all of them. Consequently, the results reported are not the result of the ordinal nature of the compliance scale, simultaneity bias, or the erratic quality of the data. The companion chapter presents the full results of these analyses and a lengthier discussion of these methodological issues.

Finally, I would like to make clear what the dataset is not. As mentioned previously, it is not a comprehensive listing of all violations for a given warring directed dyad-issue. Such a comprehensive listing would be wonderful for testing the dynamics of reciprocity, but it is impossible to collect for even a small set of the cases. Second, the data is not based on a precise legal analysis of whether particular acts constitute violations of the treaty in question. The legal statuses of some acts are contested, particularly when questions of military necessity and proportionality arise. Instead, the coding captures whether the broad pattern of acts by a warring party are consistent with the standards of the relevant treaty. When such acts are not agreed to be clear legal violations, the score for the legal clarity of the violations reflects that uncertainty. At the level of aggregation of the data, precise legal analysis of all acts is not necessary to make broad distinctions between behavior that is compliant and that which is not. These limitations are important to remind us what we can learn from this data and what we cannot. The data can help us see broad patterns in how the laws of war have worked during wartime. Because they cannot show the full dynamics of those laws in practice, I complement this chapter with the two following chapters of case studies.

## THE CORRELATION OF COMPLIANCE

Table 4.1 matches the compliance of both sides of each warring dyad, excluding cases for which we have only standardized coding for both sides and declaration of war. If both sides of a warring dyad have a standardized coding, those

TABLE 4.1 *Cross-tabulation of the compliance of both warring parties in a directed dyad*

| | | Compliance of victim | | | |
|---|---|---|---|---|---|
| | | Full compliance | High compliance | Low compliance | Non compliance |
| Compliance of violator | Full compliance | 270 | 105 | 14 | 2 |
| | High compliance | 105 | 218 | 76 | 22 |
| | Low compliance | 14 | 76 | 80 | 24 |
| | Noncompliance | 2 | 22 | 24 | 12 |

*Notes*: $\Pi^2$ = 397.8 w/9 d.f.s Significance probability < 0.0001.
tau-b = 0.517 Significance probability = 0.020.

scores are equal by definition. Including them in the analysis would inflate the effect of reciprocity in the table. I refer to the side in an observation as the violator and the other side as the victim. Table 4.1 includes each dyad for which we have data twice, once for each direction of the dyad. Hence the table is symmetric about the main diagonal by construction. I have shaded the cells in the main diagonal in Table 4.1 to aid the reader.

The pattern in Table 4.1 shows that the compliance of the two sides is correlated in the data. The $\chi^2$ test shows that the compliance of the two sides is not independent of one another, and the tau-b statistic shows the positive relationship in the table. Of the 1,066 cases in Table 4.1, more than one-half (580) fall on the main diagonal of the table. Only seventy-six of the cases fall further than one cell off the diagonal. In more than 90 percent of the cases then, the compliance of the warring sides does not differ by more than one level. What factors influence this pattern?

### Ratification Status and Regime Type

Ratification status and regime type interact in important ways. Figure 4.1 shows the interactive effects of regime type and legal obligation through joint ratification in the directed-dyad analysis. The rows in the array of six separate diagrams show whether or not the state in question is a democracy, and the columns specify which parties (neither, just the violator, or both) had ratified the most recent treaty on the issue in question. Each individual diagram shows how the violator's compliance varies with the victim's compliance by showing the estimated probability of each level given the victim's level of compliance. The darker shaded regions indicate higher levels of violations. The amount of shading denotes the severity of the acts of the violator, with more of the darker shading indicating less compliance. The probabilities of each level of compliance are connected to show reciprocity, with steeper lines between the shared regions indicating a closer correspondence between the violator and victim's compliance.

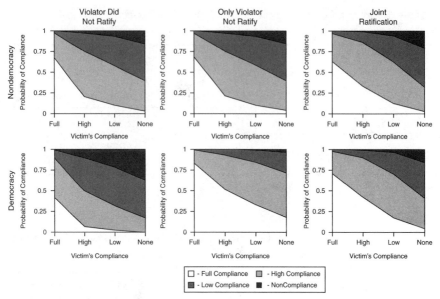

FIGURE 4.1 Estimated effects of democracy and ratification on compliance.

*Note*: Probabilities calculated from estimates of Table 4'.3 weighted for the quality of the data (the second column of that table). Probabilities assume clarity of victim's violations are definite legal violations (= 4), victim's violations were state policy (= 1), power ratio and battle deaths per 1,000 population set to their means (0.5 and 10.63, respectively), violator is not an initiator (= 0) nor a loser (= 0), and the issue is treatment of the wounded.

Legal obligation through ratification has two important effects. First, joint ratification strengthens reciprocity. The borders between the regions are steeper, particularly when the victim is less compliant, in the two pictures in the right column than in the other four. When both sides are obligated through joint ratification, both respond to substantial violations in kind. All the pictures have relatively steep drops when the victim's compliance moves from full to high compliance. Reciprocity matters more when the other side commits substantial violations. This stronger reciprocity under joint ratification does not depend on whether the violator is a democracy; the two pictures on the right reflect comparable strengths of reciprocity. Reciprocity still works to some extent, even when at least one side has not ratified the most recent treaty, but it is weaker in those cases. Reciprocal responses under joint ratification are 28 to 162 percent stronger than the other cases, with cases for which only the initiator has ratified have the weakest reciprocal responses.[3]

---

[3] The reciprocal responses are calculated as the difference in the average compliance when the victim has high compliance and noncompliance. The percentages compare the increases in these

The stronger reciprocal responses under joint ratification also produce more compliance through effective deterrence. The white areas in both of the pictures in the right column are larger than in the other four pictures, showing that full compliance is more likely. The deterrent effect of joint ratification is not strong as the differences in the white area are not large, but it is noticeable.

Second, ratification and restraint go together for democracies but not for other systems. Of the six pictures in Figure 4.1, a democracy which has not ratified the relevant treaty – the bottom picture in the left column – has the worst record of compliance, as can be seen from the small amount of white and large amount of black in that picture. In contrast, the other two pictures for when the violator is a democracy show more white and less black, and hence have better records of compliance. We do not see the same pattern looking across the top row corresponding to a nondemocracy. Ratification makes little difference on the behavior of a nondemocracy beyond added deterrence under joint ratification.

The tendency of democracies to comply less when they are not legally bound through ratification of the most recent treaty results partially from the issue of aerial bombing. The companion chapter reports results that exclude that issue, which reduces the increase in violations for democracies that have not ratified by about one-third. There has never been a formal treaty signed, much less ratified, to address aerial bombing. The major aerial bombing campaigns of the twentieth century were generally carried out by democracies; the United States has conducted extensive aerial bombing campaigns in every war it fought beginning with World War II. Chapter 6 discusses aerial bombing in detail.

The effect of reservations on compliance shows the logic of ratification as a signal of intent to comply with an agreement. Because the effects are small, I do not depict them in a figure or report their results in the tables of the companion chapter. Nondemocracies that have lodged a reservation to the most recent treaty commit more violations than those that have not, and – although it is not large – the effect is statistically significant. Reservations by democracies, however, do not lead to lower compliance. Reservations slightly improve compliance by democracies but the effect is not statistically significant. This pattern suggests that reservations are a signal by nondemocracies that they will not fully comply with the treaty. For democracies, on the other hand, reservations signal that they take the treaty seriously and lodge their reservation only to clarify the portions of the treaty with which they have a specific problem.

Does unilateral restraint by democracies lead to a more restrained battlefield? Figure 4.2 shows the effect of regime type on total compliance and

average compliance rates. Responses under joint ratification are stronger than if neither has ratified by 26 percent for a democracy and 43 percent stronger for an autocracy. The reciprocal response of a democracy is 162 percent stronger under joint ratification compared to the situation in which only it ratified; the reciprocal response of an autocracy is 117 percent stronger under joint ratification compared to the situation in which it has ratified but its opponent has not.

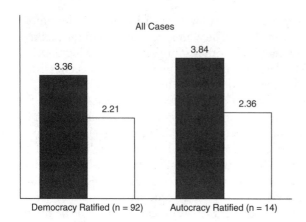

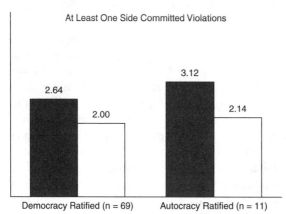

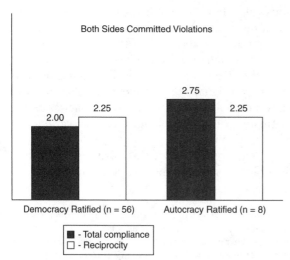

FIGURE  4.2 Reciprocity and total compliance for unilateral ratification by regime type.

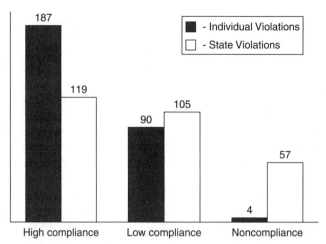

FIGURE 4.3 Compliance by centralization of violations.

*Note*: The height of the bars demonstrates the relative percentage of cases that fall into that level of compliance for each type of violation, and the numbers on the bars give the number of cases. The figure does not include cases with a standardized coding. Individual violations are scored as 2 (individual violations punished by state authorities) or 3 (individual violations against state policy but not punished by state authorities). State violations are scored 4 (probable state decision to violate) and 5 (state decision to violate with clear evidence of the decision). The difference in compliance between individual and state violations is statistically significant at the 0.0001 level ($\chi^2 = 62.3$ with 2 d.f.s).

reciprocity in the cases for which only one side has ratified the relevant treaty. Total compliance is eight minus the sum of the two sides' compliance scores, so that higher values indicate greater compliance; reciprocity is three minus the difference in the two sides' compliance scores, so that higher scores indicate a closer correspondence in the behavior of the two sides. There are three graphs for all cases: cases in which at least one side commits violations; cases in which both sides commit violations; total compliance is worse and reciprocity weaker when the democracy is the sole ratifying party. Because the number of cases is small, the only difference that is statistically significant is the difference in total compliance when both sides commit violations. Unilateral restraint by democracies produces a less restrained battlefield.

## State versus Individual Violations

Do states that ratify treaties control violations by their soldiers? Figure 4.3 compares the level of compliance based on whether the violations were committed by individual or as a matter of state policy. When the violations are committed by individuals, the state is still in high compliance approximately two-thirds of the time. When the violations are a result of state policy, those violations rise to the level of low or noncompliance nearly three-fifths of the time. Although reciprocal responses to individual violations may match those violations more closely, the worst violations are generally the result of state policy.

Figure 4.4 breaks down reciprocity and total compliance by whether the violations were committed by individuals or state policy and by ratification. Reciprocity is stronger and total compliance better when the violations are committed by individuals rather than state policy. When states deliberately violate treaty standards, they are not restrained by joint ratification, as can be seen in the graph to the right of the third figure. But deliberate state violations are less common under joint ratification (18 percent of cases, 24 out of 136) than when neither side has ratified the most recent treaty (25 percent of the cases, 19 out of 77). The prospect of retaliation may convince a government to institute disciplinary measures to stop violations committed by their soldiers in violation of state policy, whereas retaliation is insufficient to deter those governments that see an advantage in violating a treaty they have ratified.[4]

### Legal Clarity

Treaties add precision to norms of proper conduct. Does legal clarity reduce violations? Figure 4.5 examines the differences in reciprocity and total compliance between dyads in which neither side ratified and those in which both sides ratified, controlling for the greatest legal clarity of violations by either side. Controlling for legal clarity, reciprocity is stronger and total compliance better under joint ratification than when neither has ratified the relevant treaty in almost all situations.[5] Lower levels of legal clarity also have better records of compliance, largely because low levels of compliance are violations that are clear legal violations of existing standards. The cases in which the legal status of violations are in question are less likely to be major violations nor are they likely to be frequent, which means these cases show higher reciprocity and compliance. These cases predominantly occur when neither side has ratified the relevant treaty. If violations occur under joint ratification, they are clear legal violations in 84 percent (164 of 195) of the cases; when neither side has ratified the relevant treaty, less than 50 percent (60 of 121) of the cases of violations are clear legal violations. The better record of compliance under joint ratification is statistically significant at the 0.06 level for the second and third figures in Figure 4.5.

---

[4] I am indebted to Ryan Goodman of the NYU Law School for this argument.
[5] I omit the cases in which the greatest legal clarity of violations is none because neither side committed any violations in such cases, making both reciprocity and compliance perfect.

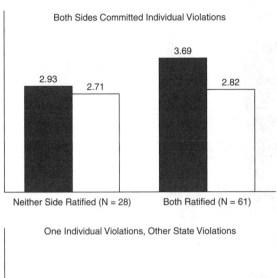

Both Sides Committed Individual Violations

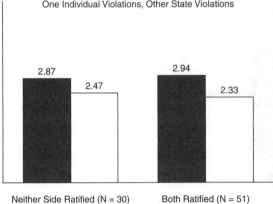

One Individual Violations, Other State Violations

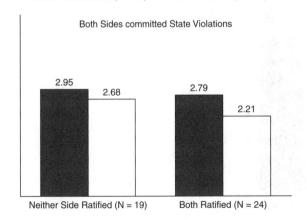

Both Sides committed State Violations

FIGURE 4.4 Reciprocity and compliance by ratification status and type of violation.

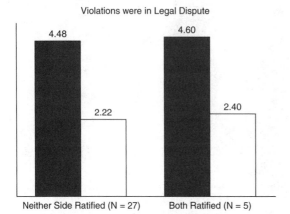

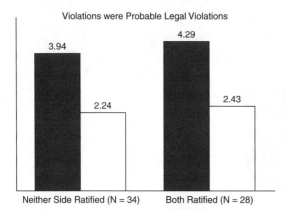

FIGURE 4.5 Reciprocity and compliance by ratification status controlling for greatest legal clarity of violations.

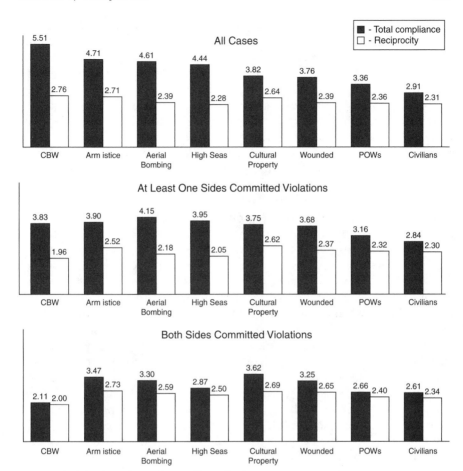

FIGURE 4.6  Reciprocity and compliance by issue.

### Differences across Issues

Figure 4.6 depicts average levels of total compliance and reciprocity across issues in the laws of war. I have placed the pictures of the issues in the order of the degree of compliance in the top graph which shows averages for all cases. Chemical and biological warfare (CBW) has the best record of compliance and is on the left of the figure. Average compliance declines moving right, with treatment of civilians having the worst record of compliance. The difference in average total compliance between CBW and treatment of civilians is large. Ranking all eight issues from the highest average compliance to the lowest, they are chemical and biological weapons, armistice/cease fire, aerial bombing, conduct on the high seas, protection of cultural property, treatment of the wounded, prisoners of war, and treatment of civilians.

This order corresponds to the scope for violations by individuals across issues. Individual soldiers cannot use chemical weapons unless their commanders give them the weapons to use, whereas every soldier on the battlefield has the ability to kill civilians and enemy soldiers attempting to surrender. The intermediate issues often provide opportunities for lower-level commanders to commit violations. Ship captains can violate the rules for conduct on the high seas by refusing to take on enemy sailors whose ships they have sunk. Individual violations make it difficult to tell whether the other side is trying to comply with an existing standard, which can lead to escalation in violations through tit-for-tat feuds on the battlefield. The pattern of compliance across issues suggests that such noise and the resultant difficulties it poses for reciprocal enforcement is key to how the laws of war can regulate combat.

If we break the issues into two groups based on average compliance that reflects the scope for individual violations, the issues with the least scope for individual violations (CBW, armistice/cease fire, aerial bombing, and conduct on the high seas) exhibit less reciprocity than those with a larger scope for individual violations (treatment of civilians, POWs, treatment of wounded, and protection of cultural property). The low-noise issues have average reciprocity of 2.58 when all cases are included, 2.16 when at least one side commits violations, and 2.52 when both sides commit violations; the parallel values for the high-noise issues are 2.63, 2.62, and 2.71, respectively. The last two differences are statistically significant at the .02 level, but the difference if all cases included is not. This pattern is consistent with the expectation in Table 3.1 that three of the low-noise issues – aerial bombing, CBW, and conduct on the high seas – have low consistency of violations in asymmetric situations. Total compliance is higher for the low-noise issues, except in the cases in which both sides commit violations. All three of these differences are statistically significant.

The effect of noise across issues also depends on ratification status and regime type. Figure 4.7 presents reciprocity and total compliance comparing high- and low-noise issues broken down for ratification status: neither or both ratified. Although joint ratification does not generally produce stronger reciprocity than neither ratifying, it does generally produce better total compliance. Four of the six differences in total compliance, comparing across ratification status, are statistically significant at the 0.02 level or higher. The two exceptions are on the low-noise issues in which violations occur (the left side of the second and third figures). Joint ratification has the greatest deterrent and restraining effect on the high-noise issues. On the low-noise issues, joint ratification leads to full compliance by both sides in 57 percent of the cases (59 out of 104), whereas only 37 percent (44 out of 119) of the low-noise cases whether neither side has ratified have full compliance by both sides. When violations occur on a low-noise issue, joint ratification does not strengthen reciprocity or improve compliance. Instead, it discourages any violations to begin with.

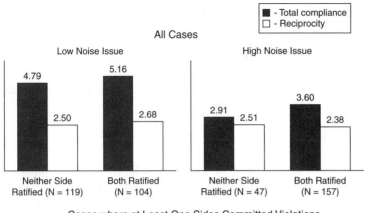

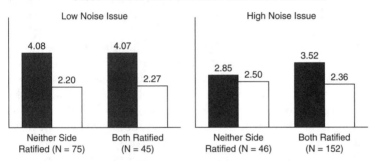

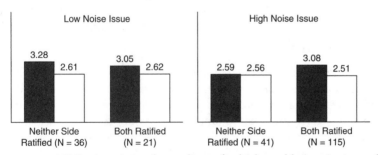

FIGURE 4.7 Reciprocity and compliance for high- and low-noise issues by ratification status.

## Other Variables

The effects of relative power on compliance are reduced by legal obligation through joint ratification. Legal obligation through joint ratification effectively eliminates the tendency of stronger states to commit more violations. When the violator loses the war, violations rise as the losing violator becomes weaker.

Compared to the other variables considered so far, relative power has no substantial effect on compliance. Intensity has a noticeable effect on compliance as more intense wars as measured by battle deaths per 1,000 prewar population have worse records of compliance. This effect is comparable to that of a democracy that has not ratified the relevant treaty. To avoid taxing the reader, I do not provide graphics showing these effects; those interested in these results should see the companion Chapter 4' for full details.

## Comparisons across Variables

How important are these different effects? What factors play the largest role in compliance? Such comparisons can be found from the estimated coefficients in Table 4'.3. The issue has the largest impact; the difference in average compliance between CBW and treatment of civilians is larger than any of the other differences considered here. Next and comparable in magnitude to the issue is reciprocity when both parties are legally obligated through joint ratification. The effects of the issue and reciprocity under joint ratification are roughly one level of compliance; changing the issue from chemical and biological warfare to treatment of civilians reduces compliance by one level, such as from high to low, and shifting the victim's compliance from full to none has about the same effect. After these two, the unilateral restraint of a democracy that has ratified the relevant treaty has the next biggest effect. Losing the war at hand and increasing the intensity of the war produce similar and lesser reductions in compliance. The strength of reciprocal responses does not vary appreciably with either legal clarity or whether the violations are state policy or the result of individual acts, nor does relative power have much effect on compliance.

### EXPLAINING THE PATTERNS

What do these results tell us about the hypotheses of the model from Chapter 3? First, compliance of the two sides is correlated. Violations are met with violations, providing one motivation to comply with existing treaties. Reciprocity, however, often fails, and both sides commit many major violations. We cannot tell from the data how often reciprocity succeeds in enforcing a standard because such cases are those in which both sides comply, which could also be the result of mutual self-restraint. Total compliance of the two sides is higher when their levels of compliance are closer, what I have called reciprocity.

The presence of noise introduced by violations by individuals shapes how reciprocity works in practice to produce compliance. *The degree of compliance across issues matches the scope for individual violations in those issues.* The issue with the most compliance – chemical and biological weapons – is the issue for which individual soldiers have the least ability to commit violations by acting on their own. They can only use such weapons if the command structure distributes them. At the other end of the spectrum of compliance is treatment of civilians, an issue in which every armed soldier has the ability and opportunity to kill and plunder civilians. Furthermore, civilians, unlike enemy soldiers, often lack the ability to retaliate against those that commit violations against them, undermining any sense of immediate retaliation that might deter violations. Between these extremes, the issues which have higher levels of compliance – aerial bombing, armistice/cease fire, and conduct on the high seas – allow greater scope for individual violations than CBW but still place that opportunity at the level of officers – pilots, local commanders, and ship captains, respectively – than the other issues in which the individual soldier has the ability to commit violations (even in violation of their orders). These other issues – protection of cultural property, prisoners of war, and treatment of the wounded – often break down on the battlefield because of individual violations, as discussed in Chapter 5.

The pattern of evidence does not support the argument that states live up to their legal obligations out of a sense of moral restraint. Legal obligation through joint ratification has no effect on its own; it works by strengthening reciprocity. Democracies comply somewhat more when they are legally obligated to do so; however, they commit more violations when they are not. This pattern contradicts the argument that the norms of appropriate conduct are more important than their legal implementation. Aerial bombing accounts for much, but not all, of the pattern that democracies without a legal obligation are less likely to comply. Chapter 6 takes up the specifics of aerial bombing and how democracies have viewed it. For now, I point out that democracies should be more likely than other systems to follow general normative principles, yet the wartime behavior of democracies depends on their legal obligation. The pattern of evidence is consistent with both audience costs and the law-bound nature of democracies producing compliance. Both arguments predict that legal obligation is the trigger for compliance by democracies. Legal obligation signals democratic audiences about which commitments their leaders are supposed to follow; law-bound states will try to live up to their legal obligations. Both arguments require that violations by the other side free a democratic state from its legal obligation to account for the pattern of reciprocity found here.

The effects of power provide some support for an argument about moral restraint. More powerful states are more likely to commit violations; presumably, they have greater opportunity than their weaker opponents to commit violations. The laws of war often seek to protect vulnerable targets, both military and civilian. Stronger states are more likely to win on the battlefield, providing them with access to enemy targets while protecting their own. Legal obligation and winning on the battlefield reduce – but do not eliminate – the effect of greater power on violations. This combination suggests that moral restraint may play a role. Audience costs, however, could also explain the pattern as the leaders of winning states have to worry about the reaction of their domestic audiences to how they fight in a way that losing leaders do not. This evidence is insufficient to allow us to judge between these arguments.

## Analysis of Outlying and Discordant Cases

The outlying cases in which the statistical model does not fit well could be helpful in separating these arguments. I focus on dyads for which either the model does not explain either side's compliance well (the outlying cases) or those cases for which reciprocity is not present (the discordant cases). The logic of reciprocity could explain why these cases either do not fit the statistical model or account for why one side refuses to respond to extensive violations of the other side. I use the instrumental variable analysis using the interaction of clarity with the victim's compliance with weighted data (second cell in the middle column of Table 4'.4) to judge outlying cases.[6] I begin by looking for all the cases for which the residual from this model exceeds two standard deviations of all the residuals. Out of these fifty-one cases, I next look for pairs of these cases that represent the two sides of a dyad for a given issue. These pairs of cases are those dyads in which the compliance of both sides deviates substantially from the prediction of the model.

Four dyad-issues are identified by this procedure. The use of chemical weapons between Germany and Great Britain during World War I is a case in which the conduct of both sides was much worse than the model predicted.[7] This case is the greatest use of chemical weapons, when the use of such weapons became commonplace on the Western Front. Any use of chemical weapons is unusual, and such use tends to be one-sided (as demonstrated in Chapter 6). The other three cases occur when one side's conduct is much better than expected and the other's is much worse. These cases are the failure of the former side to make a reciprocal response to the atrocities of the latter. Listed in the order of the side with much better conduct followed by the side with much worse conduct, they are: treatment of civilians by Russia and Turkey during World War I, conduct on the high seas between Italy and the Western Allies during World War II, and aerial bombing between North Korea and the UN during the Korean War. The first case is the Turkish atrocities during World War I against Armenian civilians where Russia saw no interest in retaliating. The Russians sought to protect Armenians and recruited troops from them. In the second case, Italy was the victim of submarine attacks on its merchant shipping and had no real chance to retaliate.[8] North Korea in the third case lacked any real capability to retaliate for extensive aerial bombing of its cities. The paucity of these cases in which one side does not retaliate against atrocities of its opponent suggests that unilateral moral restraint occurs very rarely.

---

[6] I chose this instrumental variable analysis because it has the largest $R^2$.

[7] The France-Germany dyad for CBW during World War I almost makes this set as well, with the residual for Germany being slightly smaller than two standard deviations.

[8] The Western Allies – that is, Great Britain, the United States, and the members of the British Commonwealth – are coded as not complying with the standard of conduct on the high seas through their unrestricted submarine attacks in the Mediterranean and their use of Q-ships.

TABLE 4.2 *List of cases in which one side complies fully while the other is noncompliant or has low compliance*

| War | Issue | Compliant side | Noncompliant side |
|---|---|---|---|
| World War I | Chemical warfare | Belgium | Germany |
| World War I | Conduct on high seas | Italy | Germany |
| World War I | Conduct on high seas | Italy | Austria-Hungary |
| World War I | Conduct on high seas | Greece | Germany |
| World War I | Treatment of wounded | France | Germany |
| Italo-Ethiopian | Aerial bombing | Ethiopia | Italy |
| World War II | Aerial bombing | Italy | Western Allies |
| World War II | Conduct on high seas | Italy | Western Allies |
| Korean War | Aerial bombing | North Korea | United Nations |
| Korean War | Treatment of wounded | United Nations | North Korea |
| Korean War | Treatment of wounded | United Nations | China |
| Vietnam War | Aerial bombing | North Vietnam | United States and Allies |
| Vietnam War | Treatment of wounded | United States and Allies | North Vietnam |
| Yom Kippur | Treatment of wounded | Israel | Egypt and Allies |
| Israel-Syria (Lebanon 1982) | Aerial bombing | Syria | Israel |
| Israel-Syria (Lebanon 1982) | Treatment of civilians | Syria | Israel |

The discordant cases are defined using the ordinal measures of compliance. I look for cases in which one side fully complied with the standard or had high compliance while the other engaged in violations at the level of noncompliance. As a reminder to the reader, a side is coded as being noncompliant when it commits major violations frequently. These cases are listed in Table 4.2. The cases fall into two rough groups. First, there are cases in which the compliant side had little capability to retaliate. The aerial bombing cases in Table 4.2 are cases in which the compliant side did not use what little air capability it had to engage in aerial bombing outside of the battlefield.[9] The compliant side in the cases of conduct on the high seas did not deploy its naval forces where they could attack merchant shipping, greatly reducing the opportunity for violations. The second group concern treatment of the wounded in which the compliant side committed itself to humane treatment despite the violations of the other side. In the first group, the compliant side has little ability to respond; in the second group, it has made a conscious decision not to respond. Only seven

---

[9] A side that lacks any capability or the ability to produce any capability to commit violations is coded as missing for that issue. In all of these cases, the compliant side possessed some airplanes.

cases fall into this second group, again implying that unilateral restraint in the face of frequent major violations is rare.[10]

SEARCHING FOR FIREWALLS

In Chapter 3, I argued that the laws of war separate issues to channel when and how reciprocity occurs. Reciprocal responses occur on the issue in which the violation occurs. Actors, whether states or individual soldiers, do not retaliate to a violation by committing violations on a different issue. These firewalls between the issues prevent the spread of violations from one issue to another, so that some standards of conduct are still honored even if others are not.

I test this claim against the patterns of conduct captured in the data. If actors respond across issues, compliance on a given issue should be positively affected by compliance of the other side on other issues, above and beyond that predicted by the compliance of the other side on that issue. If firewalls exist between the issues, we should find that the compliance of the other side on other issues is not correlated with compliance on the given issue once we control for the other side's compliance on that issue. I look for cross-issue correlations in the residuals of the instrumental variable analysis in Chapter 4' – that is, the part of compliance that is not accounted for by the variables in the statistical analysis. If states often retaliate against violations by the other against their soldiers held prisoner by attacking the civilians of the latter, for instance, the residuals of compliance on prisoners of war should be positively correlated with those of compliance with treatment of civilians. When the compliance of one side on one issue is much higher or lower than expected from the model, then the compliance of the other side on the other issue should be also. This test is conservative in the sense that it would miss cross-issue retaliation if the variance from such is correlated with one of the exogenous variables in the instrumental variable analysis used to calculate the residuals. I am conservative in interpreting the correlations. Furthermore, a negative result means only that there is no evidence of cross-issue retaliation occurring regularly; a negative result would not exclude individual cases of cross-issue retaliation. Firewalls, if they exist, merely try to separate issues so that retaliation operates only within them and not across them.

The observation in this test is the directed warring dyad, not the warring directed dyad-issue.[11] I take the residuals of the best instrumental variable

[10] These cases in Table 4.3 are nonuse of CBW by Belgium against Germany in World War I, treatment of the wounded by France versus Germany in World War I, UN forces versus both North Korea and China in the Korean War, U.S.-led forces versus North Vietnam in the Vietnam War, Israel versus Egypt and allied forces in the Yom Kippur War. Treatment of civilians by Syria versus Israel during the 1982 Invasion of Lebanon may count, although fighting between Syrian and Israeli forces was limited geographically compared to combat by Israeli forces against Palestinian combatants.

[11] I exclude declaration of war from the analysis as I do in the analysis of compliance.

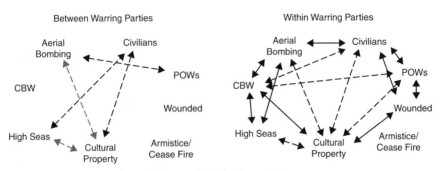

FIGURE 4.8 Pattern of correlations of residuals across issues.
*Note*: A black line indicates a positive correlation, a gray line a negative one. Solid lines indicate correlations significant at the 0.001 level or higher, and dashed lines correlations significant at the 0.1 level.

analysis and collapse the dataset so that I have the residuals on all issues for both sides for each directed dyad. The picture on the left of Figure 4.8 shows the pattern of correlations among the residuals of different issues between warring parties. I plot statistically significant correlations, using a dashed line to indicate statistical significance at the 0.1 level and a solid line for the 0.001 level. A black line indicates a positive correlation; a gray line indicates a negative correlation. Of the twenty-eight correlations across warring sides and issues, only five are statistically significant at the 0.1 level and only one at the 0.05 level.[12] The largest correlation, that of protection of cultural property and conduct on the high seas, is negative, contradicting cross-issue retaliation as an unusually high level of violations by one side on one issue is linked to the other side have an unusually low level of violations by the other. Two of the five statistically significant correlations are negative. There is no systematic grouping of issues and few of the correlations are significant at even the 0.1 level. There is little evidence consistent with cross-issue retaliation generally, and so we have some evidence, albeit weak, that firewalls exist between different issues in the laws of war.

To check that the lack of significant results here is not just a property of the randomness of residuals, I also calculate the cross-issue correlations for each warring side on its own. Do sides that tend to commit high levels of violations on a given issue consistently commit more violations on another? The picture on the right side of Figure 4.8 shows the patterns of correlations of residuals across issues for the same warring party. Here the evidence is much stronger that compliance by warring states is correlated across issues. Of the twenty-eight correlations, fifteen are positive and statistically significant at the 0.1 level, and nine of those are statistically significant at the 0.001 level. There are no statistically

---

[12] If the residuals were simply random numbers, we would expect about three of the twenty-eight correlations to be statistically significant at the 0.1 level and one of those at the 0.05 level.

significant negative correlations. In general, those states that comply at a higher level than they should on one issue tend to do so for more issues. Furthermore, the issues fall into two groups which state compliance is highly intercorrelated among all the issues. The first set – aerial bombing, chemical and biological weapons, and conduct on the high seas – are all issues with low levels of noise. The second set – treatment of civilians, prisoners of war, and treatment of the wounded – are all high-noise issues. Noise could explain this grouping of issues. Once a side decides it is going to violate on the low-noise issues, its violations are clearly the act of the central government, and so it might as well violate on the other low-noise issues as well. The correlation on the high-noise issues would be the result of a collapse of these standards generally, whether a deliberate act of policy or inadvertent escalation induced by noise on the battlefield. Another possible explanation lies in the willingness of states to impose discipline on their own soldiers. Large scale violations on the second set of issues – civilians, POWs, and enemy wounded – often result from a breakdown of discipline in an army or the lack of any discipline to begin with. The first set of issues would be the result of a government simply ignoring the standards generally.

We have some evidence that firewalls exist in the laws of war. States exhibit patterns in their own compliance or the lack of it across issues, but there is little evidence that such patterns exists across issues between states. Again, this test looks for systematic patterns of cross-issue retaliation but does not find any. It could still be the case that warring parties retaliate in particular cases across issues, but there is no evidence that such retaliation occurs regularly. The laws of war in practice have been upheld on some issues, even while they were failing on others.

## TIMING OF FIRST VIOLATIONS

The model in Chapter 3 predicted that if a state violates a treaty standard, it would do so early in wars so as to gain the strategic advantage of that violation as soon as possible. When violations come late in a war, the side winning on the battlefield, not the loser, should be more likely to break the standard. The winning side could use such violations to raise the cost of continuing the war to its opponent, pushing the latter to agree to terms to end the war. These hypotheses contradict the view that the first violations come from states desperate to stave off defeat. This section presents the results of a survival analysis on dates of first violations to test these hypotheses.

I collected dates of first violations where possible. Survival analysis estimates the hazard rate – the chance that a country will commit its first violation on a given day – and how it changes over time and with the conditions of the war. The model predicts that first violations should come early in the war – that is, that the hazard rate is falling as the war lengthens. The companion chapter (Chapter 4') provides full details of the analysis used to calculate the graphics of the hazard rate shown in this section.

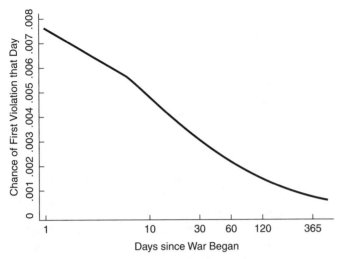

FIGURE 4.9 Estimated hazard rate for first violations.

*Note*: This figure is calculated from the Lognormal Model with correction for non-proportional hazards in Table 4'.10. All independent variables are set to their mean values.

Figure 4.9 depicts the estimated hazard rate for first violations by length of the war in days. The quick drop in the hazard rate can be easily seen in the graph of the estimated hazard rate. I have plotted the passage of time on a logarithmic scale to spread out the quick decrease in the hazard rate in the first days of the war to make the magnitude of the change easier to see if far less dramatic graphically.[13] The hazard rate drops quickly from its original high on the first day of the war. It drops by more than one-third in the first ten days of the war and is less than one-half of its initial value within one month of fighting (the tick at thirty days in Figure 4.9). Within two months, the hazard rate has almost dropped to one-quarter of its initial level, and within a year, it has dropped to one-eighth of its initial high value.

The hazard rate is the daily risk of a first violation, and although it is highest early in the war, there is still a significant chance of first violations later in the war. Figure 4.10 gives the chance that a side will not have committed any violations as a function of time passed during the war. The scale of the time axis is linear rather than the logarithmic scale used in Figure 4.9. There is about a 15 percent chance of violation within the first month of the war; the risk of a violation rises to more than 30 percent within the first six months of the war. After a year, the risk of the standard being violated is more than

---

[13] The nonlinearity of the log-normal distribution shows up in the first day of the war as the hazard rate rises from the first to the second day of the war. A violation on the first day of the war occurs at time zero in the model.

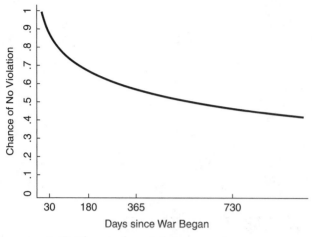

FIGURE 4.10 Chance of no violation over time.

*Note*: This figure is calculated from the Lognormal Model with correction for non-proportional hazards in Table 4'.10. All independent variables are set to their mean values.

40 percent, which rises higher than 50 percent after two years. (These points in time correspond to the vertical ticks in Figure 4.10.) Figure 4.10 overstates the chance that violations will occur at some time during a war because it does not account for the fact that most wars are shorter than the period of time depicted in the figure. The median duration of a war in the dataset is 237 days. About 45 percent of the wars last one year, and less than one-third last two years or longer (32.9 percent to be exact). The picture remains the same; warring parties are much more likely to violate the laws of war early rather than late in the course of their war.

I can also test for reciprocal responses using survival analysis. I separate first violations into whether they were the initial violation in the warring dyad or a response to an initial violation by the other side. Cases in which both sides committed first violations on the same day were not considered as reciprocal responses to one another. Including a variable for whether the other side has already committed a first violation allows me to see how quickly states respond to first violations by the other side. The more quickly the response comes, the more immediate the reciprocity.

Reciprocal responses are swift. Figure 4.11 shows the estimated hazard rates for first violations and reciprocal responses after a first violation by the other side. The estimated chance of responding to a first violation during the day immediately after is *more than 40 percent*. The chance of a reciprocal response falls off very quickly so that two months after the initial violation, it is not greatly higher than the chance of a first violation. Figure 4.12 shows the chance that a side will not have committed a violation as a function of time because

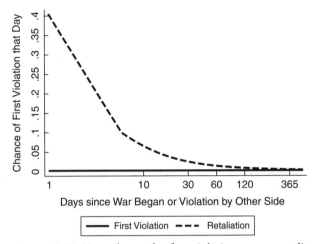

FIGURE 4.11 Hazard rates for first violations versus retaliatory responses.
*Note*: This figure is calculated from Table 4'.11. All independent variables are set to their mean values.

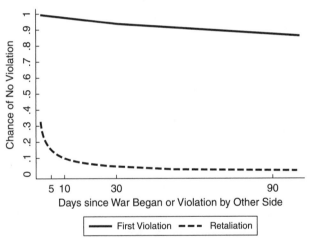

FIGURE 4.12 Probability of no violation over time for first violations versus retaliations.
This figure is calculated from Table 4'.11. All independent variables are set to their mean values.

either the war began or the other side has committed its first violation. I have shortened the time period shown in Figure 4.12 compared to Figure 4.10 to show how rapid reciprocal responses are. There is almost five-sixths chance that a side will respond to a first violation within *five* days. There is a 95 percent chance of a response violation within one month of the initial first violation.

TABLE 4.3 *Cases of late first use classified by status of fighting at the time of the first violation*

| War | Side committing first violation | Other side | Issue | Date of first violation |
|---|---|---|---|---|
| Violator favored | | | | |
| World War I | Turkey | United Kingdom | POWs | November 10, 1915 |
| World War I | Germany | Italy | POWs | October 24, 1917 |
| Violator unfavored | | | | |
| Iraq-Iran | Iraq | Iran | CBW | October 21, 1983 |
| Violator clearly losing | | | | |
| World War I | Serbia | Austria-Hungary | POWs | November 18, 1915 |
| Violator neither losing nor winning | | | | |
| World War I | Italy | Austria-Hungary | POWs | June 29, 1916 |
| World War I | France | Turkey | POWs | September 1, 1916 |
| Vietnam | North Vietnamese | United States, South Vietnam, and Allies | Civilians | December 5, 1967 |
| Vietnamese-Cambodian | Cambodia | Vietnam | Civilians | April 30, 1977 |
| Iraq-Iran | Iran | Iraq | POWs | March 15, 1983 |

This analysis does not tell us about the size of the reciprocal response nor does it demonstrate that the responses were adopted as retaliatory responses. But it does show that first violations are often met quickly by violations.

## Cases of First Use Late in a War

As the survival analysis shows, first violations tend to come early, not late, in wars, as the model in Chapter 3 predicted. A side might choose to violate an agreement that had held throughout the war in a last effort to affect the outcome of war that was almost decided. Although some argue that losers in such situations should be those who break a standard in order to stave off defeat, in the model, victors might do so to force their opponent to surrender and end the war. To test these two possibilities, Table 4.3 lists all the cases in which both the first violation by either side on the given issue occurred at least one year into the war and that side's compliance was low at best.[14] I exclude cases for which the violator committed only isolated violations

[14] In the dataset, the first violation by North Vietnam against civilians in South Vietnam produces two cases, one against the United States and its allies and one against South Vietnam because the South Vietnamese did not fight under U.S. command. I have grouped these two cases as one because they are coded off the same incident.

because such violations could not be part of a campaign to influence the outcome of the war. This measure excludes cases of accidental sinking of hospital ships for instance. I have classified these cases of late first use based on the military position of the violator in the war at the time of the first violation; were they clearly winning or losing or were the two sides relatively even in the results of battle? Table 4.3 uses five levels to describe the military situation at the time of the first violation: the violator was clearly winning, the violator was favored on the battlefield, the violator was neither winning nor losing, the violator was unfavored, or the violator was clearly losing. There are no cases of the first violator clearly winning, and five of the nine cases are even on the battlefield.

Of these nine cases, only one in which a clear decision reached on the battlefield before the first violation was Serbia's violations against Austro-Hungarian prisoners. Serbia was overrun quickly by after Bulgaria joined the Central Powers by a combination of German, Austrian, and Bulgarian troops. The violations in this case occurred when the Serbians forced around 40,000 Austrian POWs to march with their retreating forces across the mountains into Albania (Fryer 1997). Given the difficult conditions of a forced march across the Albanian mountains as winter approached, many of both sides died. The two cases in which the violator was favored – Turkish treatment of British POWs after the surrender of Kut in Iraq, and German treatment of Italian POWs after the Battle of Caporetto – are also the first occasions when these violators took large numbers of prisoners from the forces of the victim. The case that most closely fits the picture of a losing side violating a standard to prevent defeat is Iraq's use of chemical weapons against Iran. Although the Iranians were gaining ground when Iraq used mustard gas in 1984, the fighting was still along their border, meaning that Iraq was not close to defeat. Most of the cases occur in situations in which the battle results do not clearly favor either side. The conservative coding used for dates of first violation also mean that some of these cases may have had earlier violations for which I was unable to pin down an explicit date. I would be surprised, for example, if the first atrocity by North Vietnamese forces against civilians during the Vietnam War happened in 1967; however, that is the date of the first atrocity that I could verifiably document. The cases of late first use do not help us judge the conclusion of the model that late violations are committed by those winning the war, nor its alternative that the losers break the rules to stave off defeat. First violations come early, not late in war.

## Cases of Early First Use

The model in Chapter 3 argued that a side would be willing to violate a standard if it saw a clear strategic advantage in doing so. One way to test this conclusion is to examine the cases in which a side committed a first violation when the survival analysis predicted it should not. To find these cases, I examine the

TABLE 4.4 *List of outlying cases of first violations*

| War | Side committing first violation | Other side | Issue | Date of first violation | Violator favored even if victim retaliates |
|---|---|---|---|---|---|
| Second Balkan | Bulgaria | Serbia | POWs | June 30, 1913 | No |
| Second Balkan | Bulgaria | Serbia | Wounded | June 30, 1913 | No |
| World War I | France | Germany | Civilians | August 3, 1914 | Yes |
| World War I | France | Austria-Hungary | Civilians | August 3, 1914 | Yes |
| World War I | France | Germany | High Seas | August 15, 1914 | Yes |
| Italo-Ethiopian | Italy | Ethiopia | Aerial Bombing | October 3, 1935 | Yes |
| Sino-Japanese | Japan | China | CBW | July 18, 1937 | Yes |
| Changkufeng | Japan | Soviet Union | POWs | July 29, 1938 | No |
| World War II | Germany | Western Allies | High Seas | September 3, 1939 | Yes |
| World War II | Western Allies | Italy | High Seas | June 10, 1940 | No |
| World War II | Germany | Soviet Union | POWs | June 22, 1941 | No |
| World War II | Germany | Soviet Union | Aerial Bombing | June 24, 1941 | Yes |
| World War II | United States | Japan | High Seas | December 10, 1941 | No |
| Six Day | Israel | Jordan | Armistice | June 7, 1967 | Yes |
| Six Day | Israel | Syria | Armistice | June 9, 1967 | Yes |
| Turco-Cypriot | Turkey | Cyprus | Armistice | July 21, 1974 | Yes |
| Israel-Syria (Lebanon 1982) | Israel | Syria | Aerial Bombing | June 4, 1982 | Yes |

deviance residuals of the survival analysis including reciprocity. Table 4.4 lists the cases for which the deviance residual exceeded two, the side in question committed the first violation, and its violations rose to the level of low compliance or noncompliance (magnitude and frequency greater than or equal to 3). These are the cases in which a side was the first to commit frequent major violations early in a war when the survival analysis predicts that they were unlikely to commit violations at all. The model suggests that there should be many cases in which the strategic effect of breaking the standard was asymmetric and favored this side.

Of the seventeen cases in Table 4.4, I judge that at least eleven were cases in which the effect of breaking the standard favored the violator over the victim even if the victim retaliated. France placed strong restrictions on German and Austrian civilians at the outbreak of World War I out of fear of espionage and sabotage, interning 45,000 enemy aliens in concentration camps. The number of French citizens in Germany and Austro-Hungary at the outbreak of war was much smaller, and Germany did not intern French citizens in camps until after the German public became aware of France's policy of internment of German citizens (Garner 1920, 1:74–80). Although France gave German merchant ships a grace period of seven days before they were subject to seizure in French ports and by French warships on the high seas, the seizure of merchant shipping violated the 1907 Hague Convention (VI) relative to the Legal Position of Enemy Merchant Ships at the Start of Hostilities and greatly favored France over Germany because the German fleet was contained in harbor by the British while the French fleet had free access to the high seas (Garner 1920, 1:149–156). Germany lost almost two-thirds of its merchant shipping to seizures and internment in neutral ports within one month of the outbreak of war (Herwig 1996, 288). Ethiopia lacked sufficient airplanes to retaliate against Italian bombing of civilians (Sbacchi 1997, 71), and China lacked chemical weapons to match Japan's extensive use of poison gas against them beginning in 1937 (Harris and Paxman 2002, 50–51). The adoption of unrestricted submarine warfare favored Germany over Britain in World War II. The destruction of much of the Soviet Air Force on the first days of Operation Barbarossa met that the Soviets lacked the capability to retaliate against German air attacks on their cities in the first years of the war known to the Soviets as the Great Patriotic War. The three cases of armistice violations in Table 4.4 are cases in which the violator used a local superiority to gain territory by breaking or refusing to enforce a cease-fire (Oren 2002, 244, 291–292 for the Six Day War; Polyviou 1980, 157–159 for the Turco-Cypriot War). Israel shot down twenty-nine Syrian aircraft with no losses early in their 1982 war in Lebanon; after that, the Syrian air force ceased operations in Lebanese air space, giving Israel freedom to conduct aerial attacks without fear of retribution in kind. Of the other six cases, the two POWs cases involving Japan and Germany have violators who clearly decided that humane treatment of POWs was not in their interest, as shown in Chapter 5. Perhaps the most interesting case here is the adoption of unrestricted submarine warfare by the United States against Japan shortly after Pearl Harbor. The United States was quite vulnerable to retaliation in kind against its own merchant shipping needed to transport troops and supplies in the Pacific, but the Japanese did not use their submarines to attack Allied shipping, providing the U.S. with a huge strategic advantage from its own submarine war against Japanese shipping, as shown in Chapter 6. Similarly, Great Britain and its allies gained a small strategic advantage from adopting unrestricted submarine warfare against Italy because Italy did not commit its submarine fleet to the Battle of the Atlantic in response. At least eleven, and perhaps as many as fifteen, of the nineteen cases in Table 4.4 have asymmetric strategic effects, supporting the argument of the model from Chapter 3.

CONCLUSION

This chapter has been awash in the results of statistical results, and I realize I have tested the patience of the reader with them. What is the big picture of these results?

First, there is clear evidence of reciprocity in the laws of war. Warring parties respond to violations on an issue with violations of their own, and they respond to first violations very quickly. Reciprocity produces better compliance.

Second, joint ratification strengthens reciprocity and produces higher levels of compliance. Ratification is a signal that a state will comply with the treaty standard if the other side will as well. Joint ratification creates the expectation of reciprocal enforcement and hence better compliance.

Third, noise introduced by violation by individuals is essential to the dynamics of reciprocity. The issues with the greatest scope for individual violations have lower levels of reciprocity and the worst record of compliance.

Fourth, treaty law matters indirectly by clarifying what acts are violations and by inducing restraint in actors that would otherwise violate. Legal clarity helps the sides understand when they need to respond to the acts of the other side. They respond more strongly to violations by individuals than those of state policy.

Fifth, unilateral legal obligation does matter for democracies, but democracies do not feel a moral obligation to follow general norms of conduct in the absence of legal obligation. Legal obligations also restrain the tendency of the powerful to use their power to coerce their weaker opponents through atrocities. Situations in which only one side has ratified the relevant treaty have the worst records of reciprocity and compliance, implying that unilateral restraint is not a good thing.

Sixth, there is no evidence that sides systematically retaliate across issues. Firewalls exist between different issues in the laws of war.

Seventh, first violations come early in wars if they happen at all. If a side sees an advantage in violating a treaty standard, it grabs that advantage quickly.

Eighth, first violations trigger responses by the other side quickly. Vengeance is swift in the laws of war.

These results are consistent with the view of the laws of war as formalized conventions of allowable conduct during wartime. Actors, whether states or soldiers, comply with such standards when doing so is in their interest, considering the consequences of any response from the enemy. The laws of war, and international law more generally, rely on both shared understandings of right and wrong and self-interest, a marriage between power and principle.

These results broadly support the view of reciprocity under noise in Chapter 2 and the model of the laws of war in Chapter 3. Having shown that the broad pattern of wartime acts fits these views, I now turn to a detailed examination of some cases of a few issues to show how well the details of these cases fit these views. Chapter 5 addresses treatment of prisoners of war, and Chapter 6 briefly discusses chemical weapons, conduct on the high seas, aerial bombing, and treatment of civilians. Both chapters focus on the World Wars because there is plenty of evidence for a detailed analysis of these issues for those wars.

I end this chapter by reminding the reader of some brief qualifications on the data analysis. The data covers a period of history and therefore describes how states and their militaries operated in this period. In the concluding chapter, I discuss current issues in the laws of war in which I consider how these current issues differ from those during the period of time covered by the data. Simple-minded extrapolation does not account for how current situations differ from those covered by the data. Second, the data aggregates many events both within each war and across many wars to look for the general patterns reported in this chapter. The data used here was difficult to collect and required compromises on what one would like to be able to collect to fully test the theories presented so far. In most cases, the compliance scores are aggregates of many actions, and the dates of first violations are just that. Ideally, one would like detailed time series of all violations to test reciprocity. That cannot be collected from the historical record, and so the data and its analysis is a compromise between what one would like to be able to do and what one can do. I have strived to be careful about the strength of conclusions I have drawn from this data and remind the reader of the limits of this data analysis. Now I turn to some case material to complement and buttress the arguments I have made here, to reveal the strategic dynamics of how law shapes whether and how states and their soldiers limit their use of violence during war.

# 4'

## Statistical Gore

Chapter 4 presented the patterns of compliance graphically and in simple tables. This companion chapter provides the details of the statistical analysis for readers interested in seeing "what is going on underneath the hood" of these results. I discuss issues of research design and the coding rules for the data, and present the tables of the estimated coefficients and additional tests of the results reported in the prior companion chapter. I understand that some readers will not be interested in the material presented here and so may wish to skip ahead to Chapter 5 on the detailed analysis of prisoners of war.

I have broken this chapter into sections to allow the reader to move directly to particular topics of interest. The order of the section generally matches the order of Chapter 4, although this chapter also includes analyses, such as that of declarations of war, that were not discussed in the companion chapter. The presentation here follows the standards of statistically oriented political science, as it is written for that audience.

This chapter presents the central statistical results from the dataset, those underlying the graphics of the previous companion chapter and demonstrating that they are robust. In doing that work, I explored many other possible specifications of the statistical models. Space, and the interest of most readers, precludes me from presenting all these combinations in these pages. Dina Zinnes once said that she figured that for every regression published in an article, ninety-nine others went into the trash can. I do not think my ratio of specifications tried and discarded to those reported is quite that high, but my statistical trash can is hardly empty. In the spirit of allowing the interested reader to rummage through my statistical trash can, I have created a Web site (http://sitemaker.umich.edu/jdmorrow/lawsofwar) that contains a wide range of supplementary analyses to those reported here. I refer to some of these estimations in the text and footnotes. This Web site also contains the original dataset as a spreadsheet, the dataset including all the variables used here, and documentation of both to enable those who would like to conduct their own analyses with this data. John Ferejohn once remarked that "every scientist knows that the thing that keeps you honest is that there is a graduate student out there with your name on it." These materials are now available for all, named and unnamed, even tenured professors, who might wish to labor in the muddy fields of data analysis.

## THE DATA COLLECTION

These analyses use data I collected on compliance with the laws of war. The time period covered is the twentieth century because the formal body of international law of war begins with the Hague Convention of 1899 and grows with the Geneva Conventions and other treaties regulating conduct between warring parties. The basic unit is the directed warring dyad-issue area; that is, what did each warring party do to each of its enemies on each particular issue in the laws of war. The question is what leads to compliance. A fuller discussion of the coding can be found in Morrow and Jo (2006).

This coding effort relied on many research assistants, whom I acknowledge in the preface. My primary assistant in this effort, Hyeran Jo, worked closely with me during the coding of the cases to ensure consistency to the point of being an equal participant in the process. In recognition of her work on the data collection, I discuss our procedures using "we" rather than "I" in this section.

First, we consider all COW interstate wars from the Boxer Rebellion to the Gulf War in 1991. Each multilateral war is broken into all warring dyads by pairing off each member of each side with every member of the other side. Additional research determined whether military action occurred between the members of each of the possible warring dyads. When neither state in the dyad engaged in military action against the other, the dyad is dropped. For example, World War I expands to a full set of forty-four dyads matching each of the eleven states that were members of the Allies with the four states of the Central Powers. From this set, dyads (such as United States-Bulgaria) are dropped if they did not actually fight one another.

The set of dyads is reduced further by consolidating states that fought under unified command into one actor. States that fight under united command have a single leader or leadership group that has the power to order subordinate units to comply and therefore do not have separate policies. This process reduces over-counting of observations that are not independent of one another. Additional research determined when such unified command existed. For example, all dyads in World War I between Portugal and the various Central Powers are absorbed into the corresponding dyads with Great Britain because Portuguese forces fought under British command.[1] This consolidation also eliminates some cases for which it may be difficult to determine if the two

---

[1] Although, it might be more accurate to say the Portuguese ran under British command.

states in question actually fought, such as United States-Hungary during World War II, as Hungary – in this example – fought under the command of Germany, which clearly fought the other member of the directed dyad.

The period of fighting for a particular warring dyad may differ from the general dates of the war; each is dated from the beginning of military action until fighting ends by agreement.[2] For example, the Netherlands and Germany fought one another from May 10, 1940 to May 14, 1940 in World War II. States that reentered World War II are dropped (e.g., Vichy France in 1940 and the Free French in 1942); consolidation under unified command leads to the acts of these forces being included in the command under which they served. Each warring dyad produces two directed dyads. For instance, Germany and France fought against one another in World War I, giving rise to the directed dyads of Germany → France and France → Germany.

For each warring directed dyad, we code behavior of the first member toward the second member on nine different issue areas in the law of war:

1. Aerial bombardment
2. Armistice/Ceasefire
3. Chemical and biological weapons (CBW)
4. Treatment of civilians
5. Protection of cultural property
6. Conduct on the high seas
7. Prisoners of war (POWs)
8. Declaration of war
9. Treatment of wounded

Each of these issues is defined by the set of treaties, including draft treaties, in the issue. We used the text of treaties found at the Web site of the International Committee of the Red Cross, grouped into these nine issues.[3] Issues such as neutrality law were dropped because they do not address the conduct of one warring party toward another. Genocide was also dropped as acts that could be considered genocide on the battlefield were subsumed under the treatment of civilians. These issues encompass those with well-developed treaty law and some issues that lack any formal treaty law, notably aerial bombardment. This design allows a test of whether the existence of a formal treaty aids compliance with the norms of proper conduct in an issue.

The relevant treaties in each issue were read to identify major and minor violations. Table 4′.1 gives examples of major and minor violations for each issue and the corresponding treaty that is the source for that violation. These coding rules structured the collection of information on violations and compliance for each directed warring dyad. Historical works and contemporary

---

[2] This is typically the surrender of one party to the other, but we also end fighting when one side is no longer capable of resisting the other even if there is no formal surrender document.

[3] http://www.icrc.org/ihl.nsf/WebFULL?OpenView.

TABLE 4'.1 *Examples of major and minor violations in each of the issue areas*

| Issue area | Example of violations | Treaty referenced |
|---|---|---|
| Aerial bombardment | Major: Bombing civilians, civilian installations | Amsterdam Draft Convention for the Protection of Civilian Populations Against New Engines of War, 1938 (never signed) |
| | Minor: Deceptive or improper use of safety zones | Amsterdam Draft Convention for the Protection of Civilian Populations Against New Engines of War, 1938 (never signed) |
| Armistice/flag of truce | Major: Attacks on individuals under a flag of truce | Hague Convention (II) with Respect to the Laws and Customs of War on Land and its annex: Regulations concerning the Laws and Customs of War on Land, 1899 |
| | Minor: Use of flag of truce as ruse | Hague Convention (II) with Respect to the Laws and Customs of War on Land and its annex: Regulations concerning the Laws and Customs of War on Land, 1899 |
| Chemical and biological weapons | Major: Use of projectiles, the sole object of which is the diffusion of asphyxiating or deleterious gases | Hague Declaration (IV,2) concerning Asphyxiating Gases, 1899 |
| Treatment of civilians | Major: Torture or inhumane treatment of civilians | Geneva Convention (IV) relative to the Protection of Civilian Persons in Time of War, 1949 |
| | Minor: Detention of enemy civilians at the outbreak of war, except for military personnel and security risks | Tokyo 1934 Draft International Convention on the Condition and Protection of Civilians of enemy nationality who are on territory belonging to or occupied by a belligerent, 1934 (never entered into force) |
| Cultural property | Major: Failure to take care to avoid destruction of cultural property | Hague Convention (II) with Respect to the Laws and Customs of War on Land and its annex: Regulations concerning the Laws and Customs of War on Land, 1899 |
| | Minor: Use of cultural property for military purposes when so marked | Hague Convention (II) with Respect to the Laws and Customs of War on Land and its annex: Regulations concerning the Laws and Customs of War on Land, 1899 |

*(continued)*

TABLE 4'.1 *(cont.)*

| Issue area | Example of violations | Treaty referenced |
|---|---|---|
| Conduct on the high seas | Major: Detention of enemy merchant ships at the outbreak of war | Hague Convention (VI) relating to the Status of Enemy Merchant Ships at the Outbreak of Hostilities, 1907 |
| | Minor: Destruction of any submarine cable | Oxford Manual of the Laws of Naval War, 1913 (not a treaty, does reflect treaty interpretation) |
| Prisoners of war | Major: Summary execution on the battlefield, no quarter | Hague Convention (II) with Respect to the Laws and Customs of War on Land and its annex: Regulations concerning the Laws and Customs of War on Land, 1899 |
| | Minor: Failure to separate races or nationalities | Geneva Convention relative to the Treatment of Prisoners of War, 1929 |
| Declaration of war | Major: Sneak attack without declaration of war | Hague Convention (III) relative to the Opening of Hostilities, 1907 |
| Treatment of wounded | Major: Reprisals against the wounded | Geneva Convention (I) for the Amelioration of the Condition of the Wounded and Sick in Armed Forces in the Field, 1949 |
| | Minor: Use of medical signs as military ruse | Geneva Convention for the Amelioration of the Condition of the Wounded and Sick in Armies in the Field, 1906 |

journalistic sources were searched for examples of violations and general judgments on degree of compliance by each warring party toward the other member of a directed dyad. We coded the following dimensions of compliance:

- Magnitude: How bad were the violations?
  A four-point scale from none to many major violations such that compliance does not matter.
- Frequency: How frequent were violations?
  A four-point scale from none to massive violations to the point where the standard is ignored.
- Centralization: What was the role of central military and political authorities concerning violations?
  A five-point scale from no violations to central authorities punishing individual violators to positive identification of state intent to violate.
- Clarity: Did the actions clearly violate the treaties?
  A four-point scale from no violations to definite legal violation.

When a state commits violations, we also attempt to determine the date of first violation. This breakdown of compliance into four dimensions is designed to make the coding more reliable than a single scale of compliance. Each dimension can generally be coded when we have available evidence on the acts.

This design does not allow me to test direct reciprocity because the coding includes judgments about compliance across the entire period of fighting. Ideally, one would like to have a complete list of all instances of violations for which one could directly trace the patterns of reciprocal responses. Although such sequences can be found in some cases, it is impossible to find them for even a notable set of cases. Understandably, those who commit atrocities often attempt to conceal their participation in them – that is, many violations are not recorded. Charges that the other side has committed atrocities are also common; sorting out what actually happened can be difficult. We prefer secondary historical sources, particularly academic works written decades after events, because the authors of such sources have often done the difficult work of separating truth from unfounded accusation. They also often make judgments about the nature and extent of violations from an examination of many incidents.

Only violations that occurred *during* the conflict period were coded. Because we are strictly interested in compliance with *jus in bello*, events before and after the war are eliminated.[4] For this reason, we do not consider POW repatriation or postwar civilian treatment of occupiers, even though both are important issues for the laws of war.

We benchmark the most recent treaties in coding violations. We do not follow the principle of intertemporal law,[5] but ask how warring parties in the twentieth-century wars fought by the contemporary standard of the laws of war. In practice, this decision does not have a great impact on what acts constitute violations. The general principles underlying the laws of war have been largely consistent throughout the twentieth century. We use the principle of intertemporal law in judging legal clarity. The law of war has developed over time to clarify acts as violations that have been found to be ambiguous, meaning their legal clarity was in doubt at the time of the violation.

We sort out violations of different magnitude and frequency by the following priorities: (1) most prevalent, (2) highest magnitude, and (3) highest quality of evidence. These priorities were used when a warring party committed many minor violations and a few major violations. One example is how French policy in the use of chemical weapons evolved during World War I. The use of CBW by the French was decentralized with a few minor violations at first,

---

[4] The only exception to this rule is "declaration of war" for which skirmishes prior to the starting date help to determine the magnitude and frequency of violations at the start date of the war.

[5] Intertemporal law is the legal rule that the validity of a state's action is determined by the accepted rule of international law at the time the action was taken and not by a rule of law adopted later.

but became centralized with more intense and clearly illegal use of chemical weapons beginning with the Battle of Verdun in 1916. Our coding is based on French conduct after Verdun under these priorities.

Coding decisions were based only on available information in the sources we collected. The notes section of the dataset explains when our coding is based on an inference from the information in the sources.

Quality and coverage of the data are key questions facing any analysis on this topic for two reasons. Violations are not possible for some issues in some wars. Missing data is an immense problem for any comprehensive study of compliance with the laws of war. Atrocities are often not reported. Some of these wars are obscure – that is, little or no information is available. Because the amount of information available to use in coding varies greatly from observation to observation, each directed-dyad-issue area is also coded by the quality of the data used in the coding, resulting in a fifth variable:

• Quality of the data: Do we have confidence in the coding because it is based on substantial and reliable information?
  A four-point scale from sketchy evidence to excellent documentation providing strong confidence in coding.

The quality scores reflect our preference for secondary historical sources over primary and journalistic sources. If multiple sources substantiate each other with concrete evidence, the case received the highest score of 4 for quality of information. Journalistic sources with unsupported allegations or sketchy evidence receive quality score of 1. In extreme cases, some coding is based on a single sentence in a source or a judgment from a simple statistic. For instance, a report that a very small number of prisoners were exchanged at the end of a war with significant fighting suggests that the side that took the prisoners did not comply with the 1929 or the 1949 Geneva Conventions on POWs because they would otherwise have taken more prisoners and those prisoners would have survived the war. We use the score for the quality of the data in some analyses to place greater weight on the cases for which we have confidence in the coding.

Given the amount of directed-dyad issues where we had no evidence on which to base a judgment, we employed standardized coding for the following issues: treatment of civilians, cultural protection, conduct on the high seas, prisoners of war, and treatment of the wounded. This standardized coding reflects the view that even the best disciplined armies commit some violations. The codes suggest that civilians, soldiers surrendering, and wounded enemies are killed during combat, and that such acts are against state policy and may be punished. The coding for the conduct on the high seas assumes that naval forces conduct themselves properly when naval combat occurred during the war. The standard coding for cultural property protection assumes that a few protected sites come under fire during combat. These standardized coding are superseded if any information is available. In the analyses, we drop a warring-

TABLE 4'.2 *Standardized coding used for cases lacking evidence*

| Issue area | Frequency | Magnitude | Centralization | Clarity | Data quality |
|---|---|---|---|---|---|
| Civilians | 2 | 3 | 2 | 4 | 0 |
| POWs | 2 | 3 | 2 | 4 | 0 |
| Wounded | 2 | 3 | 2 | 4 | 0 |
| High seas | 1 | 1 | 1 | 1 | 0 |
| CBW | 1 | 1 | 1 | 1 | 2 |
| Cultural | 2 | 2 | 2 | 3 | 0 |

dyad-issue if both sides have a standardized coding on that issue. These standardized coding allows us to use warring dyads where we have information only about what one member of the dyad did. The standardized coding is given data quality 0, which matters when analyses are weighted by the quality of the data. Table 4'.2 summarizes the standardized coding.

A standardized coding is also used for the issue of chemical and biological weapons when we had no reports of use by a side. Accusations of the use of such weapons have been extensively investigated by others (e.g., SIPRI 1971; Harris and Paxman 2002), allowing us to conclude that a side did not use such weapons if the sources that focus on chemical and biological warfare do not mention that it used such weapons in that war. For the issue of chemical and biological warfare, a warring party is coded as having no violations if there are no reports in these sources. Data quality is rated as a 2 for such cases.

Violations are not possible for some issues in some cases because the sides either lacked the capability to carry out such violations or no fighting of the type in question occurred during the war. All the fighting in the Hungarian-Allies War of 1919 was on land, making violations of conduct on the high seas impossible.[6] Similarly, sides that had no air force, like the Chinese during the Boxer Rebellion, could not commit violations of aerial bombing. Cases in which parties did not have capabilities are coded as missing data (–9) for all five measures of compliance; the absence of violations when the parties had capabilities or the ability to create them is compliance, not missing data. For the issue of CBW, we assumed that parties could create such capabilities even if they did not possess them.

We collected the first date of violation by a warring party on a given issue whenever possible to test hypotheses about timing of first violations. When a side commits both major and minor violations, the date for the first major violation is coded. When the date of first violation is unclear in the sources, we used the closest date of the associated battle or event. In the Second Balkan War of 1913, for example, the date of the first Turkish violation against Bulgarian

[6] Out of 222 cases of high seas cases, 80 cases do not involve any naval engagement and thus are not applicable.

POWs was determined by the date of Turkish occupation of Adrianople because that was the first documented time when the Turks took Bulgarian soldiers prisoner. Dates were coded conservatively in the cases for which a precise date could not found. When we could narrow a violation down to a month but not a date, we used the last day in the month. In some cases, the first date is set at the last date of war because the date of event could not be established (e.g., violations against Chinese wounded by the Relief Expedition forces during the Boxer Rebellion).

### Clarifications of What Acts Are Violations

When the higher military and civilian authority of a warring party adopts a policy to not violate an aspect of the laws of war, that case is judged to have no violations unless historical sources report violations by individual combatants. Examples include Austria-Hungary explicitly refusing to attack hospital ships in the World War I (Halpern 1987, 319–320), and Saudis not using the few planes they had in Saudi-Yemeni war of 1934 (Kostiner 1993, 170). A contrary case is the destruction of Iraqi infrastructure by the United States during the Gulf War, even though the United States adopted the Joint No-Fire Target List (Lewis 2003, 487).

Inadvertent violations are recorded as violations. For example, we code the destruction of the National Museum in Budapest by the Soviet military during the Russo-Hungarian War of 1956, even though the Soviets did not intend to destroy it (Mikes 1957). We do so because the laws of war create obligations for individual soldiers against committing violations and for states to take steps to reduce inadvertent violations by their military forces.

Some violations could be classified in more than one issue area, raising the possibility of double coding. We explain what these incidents are and how we handled them in the following section on specific issues in the coding.

### Coding Decisions for Specific Issue Areas

We report coding rules and judgments specific to a particular issue area and address special and difficult coding issues and cases. We also present some interesting cases to illustrate coding decisions.

#### *Aerial Bombardment*

The coding rules for aerial bombardment are based on draft treaties that sought to address the bombing of nonmilitary or civilian areas. Legal clarity of violation is 3 by default, because of the lack of any ratified treaty on aerial bombing. When it is unclear whether the town was defended at the time of violation or when the civilian casualties are not specifically reported with the bombing of civilian areas, clarity is rated as 2. When the air force of a belligerent is destroyed in the initial phase of war, no violation is recorded unless some bombing cases are reported. If a warring party has no or nominal air force, not applicable/available codes (-9) are assigned.

Aerial bombing of civilian areas are prohibited under treaties pursuant to aerial bombardment as well as those that address treatment of civilians. We code the aerial bombing of civilian areas under aerial bombardment because (1) the primary purpose of the draft treaties addressing aerial bombardment is to distinguish civilian areas from military installations, and (2) there are many violations against civilians other than aerial bombardment. Methods of warfare distinguish the violation in the area of aerial bombardment from that of civilian treatment. Aerial bombardment includes missiles and rockets if fired from a great distance so that they act like bombers rather than artillery. Artillery attacks are coded under the treatment of civilians. Syria's conduct during the Six Day War illustrates this. Syria bombed Israeli civilians from the air on the first day; from the second day on, Syrian artillery barraged them (Barker 1980), which is coded under treatment of civilians.

## Armistice/Ceasefire

Armistice violations are of two types: (1) violation of official ceasefire before the agreed denouncement, and (2) failure to respect white flags by individuals. We focus on the first and code the second only when sources report individual violations. Only armistice/ceasefire agreements *during* war are coded, following the general principle to code violations during war. Violations of preexisting armistice lines are not coded; for example, the Israeli violation of 1947 armistice line in Sinai War of 1956 is not coded. These events at the origin of the war are addressed in the area of war declaration.

## Chemical and Biological Weapons

The laws of war specify what is allowed and what is not as a method of war. For the practical matters with respect to CBW, it is less clear which items are prohibited because the list is not exhaustive. Two such weapons whose use is often alleged are dumdum bullets and tear gas. The use of dumdum bullets is a violation (e.g., Ethiopian use during the Italo-Ethiopian war of 1935–1936), but many reports of dumdum bullet use are unsupported allegations, which are dismissed if not supported by concrete evidence of use. Use of tear gases is a minor violation with dispute over its legal status to reflect disagreement about whether such chemicals violate the relevant treaties.

## Treatment of Civilians

Civilians suffer in almost every war. Civilians include all the protected persons of nonmilitary personnel in war zones; local residents, foreign nationals, diplomatic persons, religious missionaries, and international aid workers. We therefore consider civilians in combat zones who are not the nationals of the warring parties. For instance, Italy and Turkey fought the Italo-Turkish War of 1911–1912 in the Turkish Provinces in North Africa (modern Libya), and we code how Italy treated local Libyans as well as the Turks. How warring parties treat enemy civilians also matters. Although World War II was not fought on the U.S. soil, treatment of enemy civilians resident in the U.S. by the government of the U.S. counts as a violation. The internment of Japanese was therefore coded as a major violation.[7]

## Protection of Cultural Property

We pay special attention to two aspects of the violation of cultural properties. First, we check whether the destroyed property fits the definition of "cultural property" as defined in the 1954 Hague Convention for the Protection of Cultural Property in the Event of Armed Conflict. Second, we separate out looting of cultural property – such as art – that took place during wartime from those acts during postwar occupation. Similar to treatment of civilians, we code the destruction of cultural property in war zones in which both warring parties fought, even if the property was that of a third-party state in which the sides were fighting. The destruction of the Abbey at Monte Cassino in 1944 is coded as a violation by the Western Allies against Germany even though the cultural property was Italian because the Allies were fighting the Germans when they bombed the Abbey to rubble.

## High Seas

The majority of violations of conducts on the high seas concerned illegal naval mining, naval bombardment of civilian areas, and attacks on merchant or hospital ships. We identify violations on international waters; we do not consider any engagement that occurred on rivers. As a consequence, many incidents occurred on Yangtze River (Hsèu and Wen 1972) in the Sino-Japanese war of 1937–1945 are excluded. For naval blockades, sources rarely provide sufficient evidence about the effectiveness of blockades for us to judge whether the blockade is effective, and hence legal or not.[8] We reflect this uncertainty in our codes for legal clarity of these cases.

## Prisoners of War

Commonly reported violations of POWs are maltreatment or summary executions. We make some inferences in the absence of detailed information on treatment of POWs. The death rate of POWs while held often provides a general view of their treatment (Morrow 2001). We lack detailed accounts of Serbian treatment of Austria-Hungary POWs in the World War I but base our coding on the death rate of more than two-thirds (Fryer 1997; Vance 2000). We

---

[7] Internment of civilians is classified as a major violation except when it is absolutely necessary. Detention of enemy civilians at the outbreak of war, except for military personnel or security risks is a minor violation.

[8] To be lawful, a naval blockade has to be formally declared and effective; that is, it has to be properly enforced by warships of the blockading state.

distinguish treatment of nationals, because the treatment of nationals differs even when held in the same camps.

The first dates for POW treatment are often difficult to track down. If the exact date of maltreatment is not available, we trace the date to the most relevant incident, often the date of the first major battle. The first German violation of Italian POWs in World War I is dated to the Battle of Caporetto (October 24, 1917) at which a large number of Italian soldiers were taken prisoner by German forces.

As noted before, POW repatriation is not an issue in the dataset because it is an incident after the war is over. The Soviet Union did not return Japanese POWs until 1956 after the Soviet Invasion of Manchuria in August 1945 (Tucker 2004, 307), but these reports of bad treatment of Japanese POWs and delayed repatriation by Russia after World War II were not coded.

### Declaration of War

The laws of war do not provide clear guidance on practical problems that arise with respect to the declaration of war, so we had to render judgments in assigning codes. The foremost criterion concerns whether a state formally declares war before hostility in compliance with the 1907 Hague Convention (III) relative to the Opening of Hostilities. Violations of this convention involve judgments about the incidents that led to the first hostile military action: from ultimatum or diplomatic warning, expiration of ultimatum at the proposed deadline, and formal declaration of war prior to full scale war.

Taking the chain of events in mind, we classified major and minor violations in the act of declaring war and determined the magnitude of violation, including its legality. Frequency gives size/number of attacks launched at the start of hostilities. Attack without any warning is magnitude 4 and clarity 4. An attack launched after ultimatum but much earlier than deadline is magnitude 3 and clarity 3. Failure to communicate an ultimatum in a timely fashion to the other belligerent falls into this category. The allied ultimatum that led to the interstate war portion of the Boxer Rebellion was delivered so late that the local Chinese forces could not consult central authorities before the deadline. The Relief Expedition is then responsible for the breakout of hostilities without adequate prior warning. Attack in response to an ultimatum by the other side is magnitude 2 and clarity 2, as are attacks after the issuance of an ultimatum but before its expiry or formal declaration of war. An example of this last case was Germany's cross-border attacks into France before its declaration of war on August 3, 1914 but after the ultimatum to France to declare its intentions (Gray and Argyle 1990, 1:14, 16; "France Orders Mobilization after Germany Asks Her Intentions," *New York Times*, August 2, 1914). Sides that declare war before taking military action have committed no violation, as are the targets when war is initiated entirely by the other party.

War often develops from initial skirmishes in which identification of the initiator is difficult and both sides make allegations of aggression by the other.

Slow escalation of fighting from border struggles without a clear attack is magnitude 3 and clarity 3; an example is the Chaco War of 1931–1933. Border clashes often involve decisions of local commanders rather than higher authority and are coded centralization 3. Frequency of violations is 2 or 3, depending on the size of initial attack that marks the beginning of the war. In the Assam War of 1962, China's initial attack covered several areas, whereas the Indian attack was restricted (Eekelen 1964, 94), and – therefore – the frequency of China's violation is coded 3 and the India's 2. Declaration of war is the only issue for which the coding rules require that magnitude and clarity have the same values; they vary on the other eight issues.

### Treatment of Wounded

Violations in the treatment of the wounded include general maltreatment by individual enemy soldiers and the destruction of hospitals or hospital ships, including Red Cross hospitals or personnel. Destruction of hospitals potentially falls under three issue areas: treatment of civilians, prisoners of war, or treatment of wounded. Because the treaties related to wounded and sick cover both combatants and noncombatants, we decided to code the hospital bombing under the treatment of wounded. Destruction of hospital ships are double coded under the treatment of wounded as well as the high seas, because the treatment of hospital ships is a specific action on the high seas. We coded wounded POW cases under both the treatment of wounded and POWs. Some cases lack information on how the wounded and sick were treated. The treatment of wounded POWs thus provides an indicator about how the wounded were generally treated.

Finally, I would like to make clear what the dataset is not. As mentioned earlier, it is not a comprehensive listing of all violations for a given warring directed dyad-issue. Such a comprehensive listing would be wonderful for testing the dynamics of reciprocity, but it is impossible to collect for even a small set of the cases. Second, the data is not based on a precise legal analysis of whether particular acts constitute violations of the treaty in question. The legal status of some acts are contested, particularly when questions of military necessity and proportionality arise. Instead, the coding captures whether the broad pattern of acts by a warring party are consistent with the standards of the relevant treaty. When such acts are not agreed to be clear legal violations, the score for the legal clarity of the violations reflects that uncertainty. At the level of aggregation of the data, precise legal analysis of all acts is not necessary to make broad distinctions between behavior that is compliant and that which is not. These limitations are important to remind us what we can learn from this data and what we cannot. The data can help us see broad patterns in how the laws of war have worked during wartime. Because they cannot show the full dynamics of those laws in practice, I complement this chapter with the following two chapters of case studies.

MEASURING COMPLIANCE

The variables in the dataset are defined for the ease and clarity of collection and coding from the historical sources used. Compliance with the laws of war is the central variable of the analysis. A compliance score needs to combine the scores for magnitude and frequency of violations into one. Ideally, the categories of compliance should have large differences across levels compared to the variance in compliance within levels. Table 4'.3 presents the cross-tabulations of magnitude and frequency of violations in the dataset, the first with the standardized coding included and the second excluding them. These tables are helpful in grouping the scores into distinct levels. A score of 1 for either frequency or magnitude means the other must also score 1 as both reflect no violations by the state in question on that issue. By construction of the measure, the top row and leftmost column of these tables have 0 for every cell, except the top leftmost cell. Looking across the rows, minor violations are almost always infrequent (216 of 221 if standardized coding is included, 35 of 40 if not) and even major violations are likely to be infrequent from the third row of the table (534 of 688 including standardized coding, or 240 of 394 cases when excluding them). This pattern suggests that frequent major violations differ from these less frequent and severe violations. Similarly, massive major violations constitute almost one-half of the cases with many major violations across the fourth row (61 of 128 cases in both tables). These patterns suggest the following ordinal scale of compliance with four levels given by different shadings in Table 4'.3:

1. Full compliance, where no violations are reported,
2. High compliance, where only minor violations are reported or infrequent major violations,
3. Low compliance, where major violations occur frequently but the standard is not ignored,
4. Noncompliance, where violations are both major and frequent.

This ordinal scale of compliance is robust in its separation and order of categories even if we cannot say that the differences in compliance between the levels are comparable.[9]

I exclude declaration of war from the analysis of compliance because it is only judged at the outbreak of war and reciprocity is not possible. That issue is included only in the summary statistics reported in this chapter. I analyze violations of declaration of war separately later in this chapter.

---

[9] I have also run the analyses using scales with three levels (combining low compliance and noncompliance into one level) and five levels (dividing high compliance into a level with only minor violations and another with only infrequent major violations). The results of such analyses are generally similar to those I report and can be found at the Web site with the data and replication information.

TABLE 4′.3  *Cross-tabulations of magnitude and frequency of violations*

All observations including standardized coding

| | | Frequency | | | |
|---|---|---|---|---|---|
| | | 1: None | 2: Infrequent | 3: Common | 4: Massive |
| Magnitude | 1: None | 438 | 0 | 0 | 0 |
| | 2: Minor violations | 0 | 216 | 4 | 1 |
| | 3: Some major violations | 0 | 534 | 145 | 9 |
| | 4: Many major violations | 0 | 26 | 41 | 61 |

All observations excluding standardized coding

| | | Frequency | | | |
|---|---|---|---|---|---|
| | | 1: None | 2: Infrequent | 3: Common | 4: Massive |
| Magnitude | 1: None | 385 | 0 | 0 | 0 |
| | 2: Minor violations | 0 | 35 | 4 | 1 |
| | 3: Some major violations | 0 | 240 | 145 | 9 |
| | 4: Many major violations | 0 | 26 | 41 | 61 |

Declaration of war is excluded from the tables.

Legend:

Full compliance
High compliance
Low compliance
Noncompliance

## MEASURES OF INDEPENDENT VARIABLES

The analysis seeks to determine when states comply with the laws of war. Reciprocity complicates the analysis because noncompliance could result either from a unilateral desire to violate these norms and legal obligations or from retaliation against the violations of the other side. The essence of the analysis is to separate which conditions lead to violations regardless of the other side's acts from those that trigger reciprocal responses. The basic model of compliance has two parts, one concerning unilateral incentives to comply or violate, and a second that responds to the opponent's acts:

$$Comply_{i \to j} = \beta_{unilateral} X_{i,j} + \beta_{reciprocal} \left( X_{i,j}^{'} \right) \left( Comply_{j \to i} \right) + \varepsilon_{i \to j}$$

where the $\beta$'s and $X$'s are vectors of coefficients and independent variables. The $X_{i,j}$ are those variables that lead to compliance or violations unilaterally, and the $X'_{i,j}$ are those that effect whether $i$ responds to $j$'s violations. Later I discuss the issues involved in estimating such a model; for now, I want to discuss the various explanatory variables examined in the analysis.

### Treaty Status of Both States in Question

I have argued that international law can create a shared understanding of which acts are acceptable and which are unacceptable during war. Treaty ratification is central to the creation of such a shared understanding because the act of rat- ification signals that the state in question accepts its legal obligation to live up to the standards set out in the treaty in question. The first set of explanatory variables addresses the legal acceptance by the state of the most recent treaty in that issue area in question.

For each warring state, I code whether each warring party has accepted existing law in each issue area through ratification. This variable is coded as 1 if the state has ratified the most recent treaty which has entered into force on the date when the war begins, and 0 otherwise. I also collected information on whether warring parties had signed the treaty and whether they lodged reservations to it when they ratified it. Under these coding rules, a state that has accepted an earlier standard but does not accept the most recent treaty is coded as not having signed or ratified the standard. Japan, for example, ratified the 1907 Hague Convention (IV) respecting the Laws and Customs of War on Land that covered prisoners of war with a reservation but only signed the 1929 Geneva Convention on POWs. For World War I, Japan is coded with SIGN, RATIFY, and RESERV all equal one, whereas for World War II, the codes for Japan are SIGN equals 1, while RATIFY and RESERV are coded 0.

For some issue areas at some times, there are multiple treaties that all entered into force at the same time. A state must sign or ratify all treaties to qualify as having signed or ratified the current standard in that issue area. It is coded as having a reservation if it registers a reservation to any of the treaties in ques- tion. This issue primarily arises with conduct on the high seas under the 1907 Hague Conventions, where the obligations were broken into different agree- ments. A number of states, including notably the United States, signed and rat- ified only some of these obligations, leading to this situation.

As described earlier, states that fight under joint military command are treated as a single actor in the collection of the compliance data. For cases in which some states under the joint command ratified the relevant treaties as others did not, I average the ratification, signing, and reservation scores for all members of the joint command by the relative military capabilities that they contributed in the war. The strongest states in the joint command are consid- ered to set the tone for the allied forces in this method. The resulting scores fall between 0 and 1 if the members of the joint command do not all have the same treaty status.

The analyses reported here focus on ratification by the violator and by both sides as measures of legal acceptance and legal obligation, respectively.

Ratification is the public act that the state in question accepts the most recent legal standard. I report analyses using signings and reservations among the additional analyses that can be found at my Web site.

## Power Relationship

The balance of forces between the two sides, and hence their chance of winning the war, could affect the willingness of both sides to comply with the laws of war. To measure the rough power relationship of the warring sides, I use the Composite Capabilities indicators developed by the COW project (Singer, Bremer, and Stuckey 1972; Singer 1987). They collected annual data on six indicators of national capabilities (two demographic, two industrial, and two military):

Demographic: Total Population, Urban Population
Industrial: Iron/Steel Production, Energy Consumption
Military: Military Expenditures, Military Personnel

For a given state, each of these indicators is divided by the world total of that indicator to give the state's proportion of the world share of that indicator, and hence its capabilities on that dimension relative to other states. These six proportions are then averaged to give the state's composite capabilities, its share of the total capabilities in the system.[10]

Where the state fights also enters my measure because it is difficult for states to project their full capabilities at a great distance from their homeland. I use the loss-of-strength gradient first introduced by Bruce Bueno de Mesquita (1981) in *The War Trap*. First, the state in which the fighting generally took place is determined for each warring dyad. The distance from each state's capital to the location of the fighting is calculated. If a state is contiguous with the state in which fighting took place, the distance is considered to be 0. Each warring state's composite capabilities are then adjusted for how far the state was from the fighting:

$$Adjusted\,Capabilities_{i\,at\,j} = \left(Composite\,Capabilities_i\right)^{log_{10}\left(\frac{distance\,from\,i\,to\,j}{miles\,per\,day}+10-e\right)},$$

where miles per day is 250 before 1919, 350 from 1919 to 1945, and 500 thereafter. These adjusted capabilities give the effective power that the state in question can generate on the battlefield.

When several states fight under a unified command, I have treated them as one actor when collecting the compliance scores. To calculate the capabilities of a unified command, I added together the adjusted capabilities of all the member states of the command at the location of the fighting. I also used the adjusted capabilities as a measure of each state's contribution to the joint

[10] Capabilities and distance data were obtained from EUGene version 3.04 (Bennett and Stam 2000).

command when measuring the domestic system and status of legal obligations of that command.

To measure the power relationship between two warring sides, whether each is a state or a unified command, I calculated the ratio of each state's capabilities to the total of both sides. This value ranges between 0 and 1 and gives the proportion of the capabilities on the battlefield that each side possesses. This measure has been used as a measure of the probability that each side will win the war in other research (B. Bueno de Mesquita 1981). By construction, if $p\left(=\dfrac{AdjCapA}{AdjCapA + AdjCapB}\right)$ is this proportion or probability for one side of a warring dyad, then $1 - p$ is its value for the other side.

### Regime Type

I use the Polity data for measures of regime type (Marshall and Jaggers 2002), which has collected measures of competitiveness of executive recruitment (XRCOMP), openness of executive recruitment (XROPEN), constraints on the chief executive (XCONST), competitiveness of political participation (PARCOMP), and regulation of participation (PARREG) for all states from 1800 to 1999 (for Polity 4). Particular scores on the first four are combined into a measure of democracy that runs from a low of 0 to a high of 10, with higher scores indicating open and free political competition for election to a constrained chief executive. Particular scores of all five measures are combined to produce a measure of autocracy that also runs from a low of 0 to a high of 10 with higher scores indicating political systems in which the leader's power is unconstrained, and he or she is selected through a closed process in which few members of society participate. As these measures are well-known, I will not give the details of how each of the indicators is accumulated from these five measures (interested readers should see Marshall and Jaggers 2002). Following common practice, I judge a state to be a democracy if its democracy score minus its autocracy score is greater than or equal to 7. I also ran alternate analyses judging a state to be a democracy if the difference in its democracy and autocracy scores was 6 or greater, and other analyses entering the democracy and autocracy scores independently. Because these alternate analyses produced very similar results to those reported here, I only discuss them in footnotes when they differ. Interested readers can find the results of those analyses at the Web site with extensions and replication materials.

### Other Independent Variables

I also examined other independent variables drawn from the COW data that address the characteristics of the war itself (Small and Singer 1982). First, I examined which side initiated the war. In the COW coding, the initiator is the side that takes the first military action of the war, such as having their troops cross the border and attack. For the World Wars, COW only coded the states that began the fighting as the initiator, so Austria-Hungary is the initiator of World War I and Germany the initiator of World War II. As I am working with warring dyads, I have also coded as initiators any state that attacked a neutral or created a new front of the war through its intervention into the war. An example of the former is when Germany attacked the Netherlands in 1940, Germany initiated that dyadic war. An example of the latter occurs when Japan attacked the United States and the British Commonwealth in 1941, opening up new fronts in the Pacific and Southeast Asia. I do not code states that intervene in an ongoing war on existing fronts as initiators. For instance, China is not coded as an initiator when it intervenes in the Korean War. There are then dyadic wars in which neither side is the initiator. Full details of these decisions can be found at the Web site.

I also looked at the outcome of the war. COW codes each warring state in terms of the final outcome for its side of the war: victory, defeat, draw, or ongoing. However, these codes are based on the final result of the entire war and do not therefore reflect the dyadic wars I examined. Poland, for example, is coded by COW as a victor in World War II. I have coded the date of termination and outcome of each dyadic war based on the surrender of one side to the other or the end of effective combat if there is no formal surrender. This coding of the World Wars is based on the outcome when the losing side surrenders, even if its side won the war in the end. For instance, Germany and Austria-Hungary defeated Russia in World War I as a consequence of the Treaty of Brest-Litovsk. Again, documentation of these decisions can be found at my Web site.

Finally, I also added the battle deaths per 1,000 prewar population of each warring party as a measure of the intensity of the war. The battle death data and prewar population for each warring state comes from COW. Their measure of battle deaths does not try to collect civilian deaths as a consequence of the war, but in many cases, civilian deaths from bombings or counterinsurgency warfare are indistinguishable from battle deaths. Again, I aggregate these average deaths for unified commands, weighting by the capabilities that each member brings to the unified command.

## ESTIMATION ISSUES

The nature of the data on compliance and the presumption of reciprocity pose two issues for the statistical estimation of the relationships in the data. As described earlier, for the measure of compliance, I used is a four-point scale ranging from full compliance to noncompliance.[11] Because it is an ordinal

---

[11] It would be more accurate to describe the variable as "noncompliance" because higher values represent less compliance with existing treaties or norms. However, it is easier to say "compliance," and I will do so throughout this chapter. I will frequently remind the reader that higher values means worse violations and hence less compliance.

measure and cannot be treated as a ratio-level variable, techniques that assume a ratio-level variable – such as linear regression – are inappropriate. I analyzed compliance using ordered multichotomous probit, which assumes that the four categories result from an unobserved underlying variable modeled as a linear function of the independent variables with a normally distributed error term. In this case, we can think of the underlying variable as a full measure of compliance. We observe where a given case falls with respect to the four categories, based on where the underlying variable (including error term) falls with respect to three cutoff points. If it is lower than all three cutoff points, we observe full compliance; if it is between the first and the second, we observe high compliance; if it is between the second and the third, we observe low compliance; and above the third cutoff point, we observe noncompliance. I estimated the coefficients of the underlying function and the cutoff points. The use of ordered probit addresses the question of our confidence in the measure of compliance.[12]

Testing for reciprocity leads directly to the second issue, simultaneity bias. If reciprocity exists, then side $i$'s violations against side $j$ depend in part on side $j$'s violations against side $i$, and vice versa. The dependent variable, $Comply_{i \to j}$, appears on both sides of the equation as can be seen after we substitute for $Comply_{j \to i}$ into the previous equation:

$$Comply_{i \to j} = \beta_{uni} X_{i,j} + \beta_{recip}\left(X'_{i,j}\right)\left(Comply_{j \to i}\right) + \varepsilon_{i \to j} = \beta_{uni} X_{i,j}$$
$$+ \beta_{recip}(X'_{i,j})(\beta_{uni} X_{j,i} + \beta_{recip}(X'_{j,i})(Comply_{i \to j}) + \varepsilon_{j \to i}) + \varepsilon_{i \to j}$$

where $\beta_{uni}$ are the coefficients for the unilateral effects on compliance and $\beta_{recip}$ are the coefficients for the reciprocal effects. The consequence of running a model with the simultaneity bias is twofold. First, the estimated coefficients will be biased; that is, their expected values will differ from the true values. In this case, the bias will be upward because we anticipated positive effects from reciprocity ($\beta_{recip} > 0$). Second, the estimated standard errors of the coefficients will underestimate the true variability of the estimates. The combination of these two effects will be that we will reject the null hypothesis of no reciprocal effects too easily. In statistical terms, the chance of Type I error, believing our hypothesis to be supported by the evidence when it is not, is increased.

The standard response to simultaneity bias is to create instrumental variables for the included endogenous variables, here $Comply_{j \to i}$ in the equation predicting $Comply_{i \to j}$. Instruments are constructed by regressing the included endogenous variables on the included exogenous variables and several other variables not included in the regression and keeping the predicted values of that regression as the instrument for the included endogenous variable. By construction, the instrument is uncorrelated with the error terms, eliminating the

---

[12] I have also conducted analyses using three- and five-point scales of compliance. Those results can be found at the Web site.

bias introduced by the correlation of the included endogenous variable, here *Comply*$_{j \to i}$, with the error term of the equation, $\varepsilon_{i \to j}$. Instrumental variables add random variance to our estimation because the instruments cannot be as accurate as the true values of the included endogenous variables. This added variance increases the standard errors of our estimated coefficients. Using instrumental variables produces a tradeoff in terms of mean squared error; it eliminates bias in our estimates but increases variance.

I addressed these two issues of estimating reciprocal models on my compliance scores by performing two sets of analyses and seeing if the results are robust across them. I ran ordered probit including the endogenous variable of the other side's compliance in the estimated equation. The estimated coefficients from these runs should be biased upward, and their standard errors should be underestimated. I also ran two-stage least squares, which create instruments for the other side's compliance. These estimates will not be as precise as those produced by ordered probit, but they will be unbiased. Furthermore, the set of excluded variables that can be used to construct the instruments is limited because the analyses include a large number of exogenous variables. Consequently, I am only able to include one reciprocal term in each instrumental variable analysis. Two less than perfect estimation techniques will be better than one alone.

## WHEN DO STATES COMPLY?

I now turn to the analysis of when states have complied with the laws of war. This section presents the full analysis underlying the figures of the companion chapter, explaining how I arrived at those results. The key questions are:

1. Does the compliance of the warring parties move together?
2. How does joint ratification of treaties, which produces a common conjecture that the treaty rules will be followed, affect compliance and the correlation of the warring parties' compliance?
3. Does unilateral ratification of a treaty standard change the pattern from joint ratification?
4. Does greater scope for individual violations across issues lead to less compliance?
5. Do warring parties respond more strongly to clear legal violations as opposed to violations whose legal status is open to question?

The analyses of this section examine what factors influence the compliance of one side, which I refer to as the violator. To test for reciprocity, I also included the compliance of the other side, referred to as the victim. I also remind the reader that the compliance score might more accurately be called "lack of compliance" as the score increases with the severity and frequency of violations by the party in question. Sometimes I talk about the violations increasing under certain conditions; these comments should be understood as denoting lower levels of compliance. Again, positive coefficients in these analyses indicate that compliance decreases and violations increase; negative coefficients correspond to improvements in the compliance of the violator.

### Declaration of War

I began my analysis by separating out one issue-area – declaration of war – that needs to be studied separately from the others. Declaration of war is only an issue at the outbreak of war, and – as such – reciprocity is not an issue. Additionally, the coding of compliance with declaration of war force the scores of two sides to either move together or in opposite directions. The canonical case concerns whether the initiator declares war before it attacks. The target is coded as being fully compliant because it was attacked. If the initiator declared war before its attack, the scores of the two sides are the same. If not, magnitude is scored as a 4 and the frequency gives the scale of the initial attack, meaning that the initiator's score for noncompliance is high. But many cases do not look like the canonical case; they involve a slow buildup of fighting along a shared border. In these cases, it is often difficult to tell which side began the fighting or even when the war began. Both sides are coded with magnitude 3 in such cases, again with frequency giving the scale of this initial fighting.

I analyzed whether states declare war separately from the other issues in the laws of war. I tested to see if legal commitments, regime type, initiation, and the power relationship affect whether a state declares war. I expect that states will be more likely to declare war when they have ratified the 1907 Hague Convention (III) relevant to the Opening of Hostilities, the more democratic their system, and when they have not initiated the war. I also tested for the interaction of democracy and legal commitment to see if democracies are more likely to uphold their legal commitments. I have no clear expectations concerning the power relationship because there are two contrary arguments concerning power and declaring war. On one hand, it might be that stronger states are more willing to declare war because of they do not need the advantage of a surprise attack. On the other hand, stronger states are more likely to initiate and so more likely to launch undeclared wars.

Table 4′.4 presents the results of three ordered probit analyses of when states declare war. The dependent variable is the four categories of compliance described before, where full compliance is lowest, high compliance next, followed by low compliance, and noncompliance is the highest category. The coefficients predict the likelihood of not declaring war at its outset. I refer to the state in question as the violator and the other side as a victim, although both sides are in the analysis in different directed dyads, each as the violator in one and the victim in the other. Whether a state enters into war without a declaration is closely related to whether it initiates the war. States that do not initiate a war or new front to an existing war are likely to declare their entrance before beginning fighting. Whether or not the violator initiated the war swamps all the other variables, so

TABLE 4′.4 *Ordered probit analysis predicting failure to declare war*

| Variable | All cases | Just initiators | No initiators |
|---|---|---|---|
| Violator ratified treaty? | −.246, .190, n.s. | .261, .274, n.s. | −.748, .297, .016 |
| Violator democracy | −.070, .244, n.s. | .235, .357, n.s. | −.517, .372, n.s. |
| Violator democracy times ratification | −.824, .398, .039 | −1.343, .692, .052 | .295, .452, n.s. |
| Power ratio | .951, .300, .002 | .790, .479, .099 | .062, .452, n.s. |
| First cutpoint ($\mu_1$) | .368 | −.181 | .242 |
| Second cutpoint ($\mu_2$) | 1.324 | .959 | 1.505 |
| Third cutpoint ($\mu_3$) | 1.809 | 1.486 | none: only 3 levels |
| N | 222 | 86 | 136 |
| Log-likelihood | −232.1 | −109.7 | −88.88 |
| $\chi^2$ | 21.48 w/4 d.f. | 7.44 w/4 d.f. | 10.75 w/4 d.f. |
| Significance probability of model | .0003 | n.s. | .030 |
| Pseudo $R^2$ | .044 | .033 | .057 |

*Notes:* Each cell gives estimated coefficient, standard error, and significance for a two-tailed test that the coefficient is different from 0 if the statistical significance exceeds the 0.1 level.
Constant is set to 0 to identify cutpoint parameters.

I present three separate analyses: one of all cases that omits whether the violator initiated the war, and two other analyses that examine either just initiators or just states that did not initiate.[13] The pattern in Table 4′.4 is robust across the three analyses; the states most likely to comply and declare war are democracies that have ratified the relevant Hague Convention. For both the analyses of all cases and just initiators, only the interaction of democracy and ratification is statistically significant. For the analysis of non-initiators, ratification is the only statistically significant predictor of a declaration of war.

Because initiation is the strongest predictor of whether a state enters war without a declaration, Table 4′.5 presents an analysis of whether a state is an initiator in terms of the same variables in Table 4′.4. Power overwhelmingly determines initiation of war; the stronger a state is relative to its target, the more willing it is to initiate new hostilities. Again, democracies that have ratified the relevant Hague Convention are less likely to initiate war. The pattern across Table 4′.4 and 4′.5 is that the combination of democracy and treaty ratification does restrain surprise attacks.[14]

---

[13] There are dyadic wars when neither side is considered the initiator, such as dyadic wars that arise from the intervention of a state into an ongoing war. Hence, there are more cases in the analysis without initiators than the analysis of only initiators.

[14] That is, analyses that use joint ratification in place of whether the violator had ratified produce similar results. See the Web site for these.

TABLE 4'.5 *Probit analysis predicting war initiation*

| Variable | |
| --- | --- |
| Violator ratified treaty? | −.205, .214, n.s. |
| Violator democracy? | −.012, .282, n.s. |
| Violator democracy times ratification | −.748, .438, .088 |
| Power Ratio | 1.349, .340, >.001 |
| Cutpoint | .807 |
| N | 222 |
| Log-likelihood | −136.47 |
| $\chi^2$ | 23.47 w/4 d.f. |
| Significance probability of model | .0001 |
| Pseudo $R^2$ | .079 |

*Notes*: Each cell gives estimated coefficient, standard error, and significance for a two-tailed test that the coefficient is different from 0 if the statistical significance exceeds the 0.1 level.
Constant set to 0 to identify cutpoint parameter.

## The Main Analyses

The central arguments of Chapter 3 address how states and the soldiers will act during war and how the laws of war could help produce a restrained battlefield. States respect these prewar agreements to limit violence during war because they prefer to fight under the constraints than fight an unconstrained war. Reciprocity exists in that states tend to respond to their opponent's violations with violations of their own. The first question I address in this analysis is whether compliance met with compliance and violations with violations?

Law clarifies what acts are violations and what responses are appropriate to violations. Law can help warring parties form shared expectations about what the limits are and whether the other side intends to observe them, including imposing discipline on their own soldiers. Ratification of a treaty signals other states that the ratifying state intends to live up to its obligations under the treaty. Joint ratification of a public treaty creates a common conjecture that both sides will fight under the constraints of the treaty. If one side violates its commitment, the other should respond in kind. I tested these arguments by including whether the violator has ratified the most recent treaty on the issue and whether both sides have (that is, joint ratification). I also tested to see if legal commitments strengthen reciprocity by interacting these variables with the compliance of the victim. If reciprocity under joint ratification has a deterrent effect, joint ratification should correspond to higher levels of compliance on average.

Treaties could also strengthen reciprocity by creating bright lines of conduct that clarify when retaliation is called for. I tested for this possibility by interacting the legal clarity of the victim's violations with various reciprocal terms, the victim's compliance alone, with joint ratification and the victim's compliance, and with whether the violator has ratified the victim's compliance. This combination of interactive terms allowed me to test when legal clarity strengthens reciprocity.

Noise complicates the logic of reciprocity. When actors cannot be certain whether the violations they observe on the battlefield are the deliberate policies of the opposing state or simply individual enemy soldiers committing atrocities on their own, they cannot be certain whether they should respond on the battlefield. The logic could go either way. It could be that only deliberate state violations call for a reciprocal response, with retaliation against individual violations presenting the further problem of inadvertent escalation. The other possibility is that states may believe that there is no chance of deterring deliberate state violations, while retaliation against individual violations could convince the other side to police its own soldiers. I tested to see if reciprocal responses are stronger against individual or state violations by creating dummy variables for each type.[15]

Beyond the tests of reciprocity, which are interactions of the victim's compliance with other variables, I also tested for the separate effects of these variables on compliance. I included the ratification status of the violator alone, joint ratification, whether the violator is a democracy, and the interactions of democracy with the two types of ratification status. These interactions allowed me to see if democracies behave differently than other systems and if democracies take their legal obligations more seriously than other types of states.

I included seven dummy variables for issues to test for differences in average compliance across them. Because I analyzed declaration of war separately from the other issues, there are eight issues in the analysis. Dummy variables for the first seven issues give how they differ on average from the excluded issue, treatment of the wounded, with an assumed coefficient of 0. Negative coefficients denote issues with better records of average compliance than treatment of the wounded, positive coefficients denote worse records.

The power ratio measures the relative power of the sides. I included it to see if stronger sides commit more violations and interact it with joint ratification to see if legal restraint reduces any such tendency.

I also included other variables (mentioned earlier) that have a significant impact on compliance: battle deaths per 1,000 prewar population as a measure of the intensity of the war, whether the violator initiated the war, whether the violator lost the war, and the interaction of whether it lost with the power ratio.

As discussed earlier, the model of reciprocity is estimated in two different ways. The first estimation is an ordered probit on the four categories of compliance. Because this analysis includes the other side's level of compliance directly, it suffers from simultaneity bias. The second estimation tries to deal with this

---

[15] Individual level violations score 2 or 3 on the centralization variable, whereas state violations score 4 or 5.

bias by creating instruments for the other side's compliance and estimating a linear regression of the four-point scale of compliance. The instrumental variables analyses suffer from a lack of unincluded variables that could be used to construct instruments. These analyses assess reciprocity by only including one interaction of the victim's compliance with different combinations of legal clarity and joint ratification.

I conducted both sets of analyses in three ways to test for the robustness of the results against the quality of the data. The first two columns in Tables 4′.6 and 4′.7 report analyses with and without weights for the quality of the data from the data collection. The weighted analyses weight observations supported by more extensive historical documentation than those based on sparse documentation. These weights are equal to the sum of the quality of the data for both sides of the directed dyad and therefore range from 1 to 8. Observations in which both sides have only standardized coding for their compliance are dropped from all analyses. The third column of results in these tables reports results when all cases whether either the violator or the victim has a standardized coding are dropped from the analysis. These analyses are not weighted by the quality of the data remaining.

Table 4′.6 presents the results of the ordered probit estimations. The patterns are robust across all three variations of controls for the quality of the data. As I have discussed these patterns already in the preceding companion chapter, I do not repeat that discussion here. The full effect of reciprocity requires adding together all the relevant reciprocal terms, which are separated out at the top of Table 4′.6. The effects of ratification status, regime type, and relative power on overall compliance come next in the table. The dummy variables for the seven of the eight issues follow, with treatment of the wounded as the omitted base line category. The table ends with variables on the conditions of the war – initiation, intensity, and defeat, followed by the summary measures of each analysis.

The simultaneity bias present in the ordered probit models should inflate the estimated coefficients of the reciprocal terms and gives us some pause before we accept the results reported in Table 4′.6 as definitive evidence about compliance with the laws of war. Instrumental variable analysis creates instruments for the reciprocal variables to address the simultaneity bias. Table 4′.7 provides the estimated coefficients for the reciprocal terms in four instrumental variable analyses under each of the three treatments of the data quality issue, which means that twelve different analyses are reported in the table. I do not report the coefficients for the exogenous variables in these analyses. They are the same as in Table 4′.6, and those that are interested can find the full tables of results at my Web site. The excluded exogenous variables available for the construction of the instrumental variables limit the interactions of the reciprocal variables that we can include in any estimation.[16] The full set of exogenous

---

[16] These variables are the parallel of the included exogenous variables for the victim, such as its democracy score.

TABLE 4'.6 *Ordered probit analysis of noncompliance with the laws of war*

| Variable | Cases unweighted by data quality | Cases weighted by data quality | Only cases without standardized coding |
| --- | --- | --- | --- |
| Reciprocal variables | | | |
| Victim's noncompliance | –.288, .289, n.s. | –.516, .282, .067 | –.434, .349, n.s. |
| Clarity of victim's violations times victim's noncompliance | .173, .051, .001 | .181, .049, <.001 | .240, .058, <.001 |
| Joint ratification times victim's noncompliance | 1.153, .353, .001 | 1.415, .343, <.001 | 1.637, .435, <.001 |
| Clarity of victim's violations times joint ratification times victim's noncompliance | –.232, .069, .001 | –.280, .069, <.001 | –.339, .085, <.001 |
| Individual violations times victim's noncompliance | .164, .158, n.s. | .317, .154, .040 | .158, .181, n.s. |
| State violations times victim's noncompliance | .078, .168, n.s. | .261, .164, n.s. | .115, .191, n.s. |
| Non-reciprocal variables | | | |
| Joint ratification | –.396, .372, n.s. | -.737, .373, .048 | –.658, .461, n.s. |
| Violator ratified | –.006, .167, n.s. | –.011, .175, n.s. | –.211, .210, n.s. |
| Violator democracy | .608, .140, <.001 | .668, .135, <.001 | .632, .155, <.001 |
| Violator democracy times joint ratification | –.001, .298, n.s. | .273, .306, n.s. | .359, .404, n.s. |
| Violator democracy times violator ratified | –.814, .304, .007 | –1.153, .312, <.001 | –1.240, .407, .002 |
| Power ratio | .628, .234, .007 | .588, .235, .012 | .521, .273, .056 |
| Power ratio times joint ratification | –.670, .287, .019 | –.490, .293, .094 | –.387, .351, n.s. |
| Aerial bombing | –.192, .194, n.s. | –.155, .198, n.s. | –.207, .230, n.s. |
| Armistice | –.502, .185, .007 | –.440, .188, .019 | –.562 .213, .008 |
| Chemical and biological warfare | –1.138, .167, <.001 | –1.023, .169, <.001 | –1.101, .199, <.001 |
| Treatment of civilians | .440, .134, .001 | .483, .146, .001 | .359, .183, .049 |
| Protection of cultural property | –.005, .185, n.s. | –.013, .207, n.s. | –.025, .322, n.s. |
| Conduct on the high seas | –.341, .164, .038 | –.207, .169, n.s. | –.349, .204, .087 |

| Variable | Cases unweighted by data quality | Cases weighted by data quality | Only cases without standardized coding |
|---|---|---|---|
| Prisoners of war | .215, .135, n.s. | .297, .147, .043 | .179, .179, n.s. |
| Violator initiator | .319, .079, <.001 | .368, .078, <.001 | .514, .093, <.001 |
| Violator battle deaths per 1,000 population | .024, .0029, <.001 | .024, .0028, <.001 | .026, .0035, <.001 |
| Violator lost | .602, .158, <.001 | .524, .158, .001 | .488, .191, .011 |
| Violator lost times power ratio | −.772, .272, .005 | −.639, .277, .021 | −.594, .336, .077 |
| First cutpoint ($\mu_1$) | 0.81 | 0.70 | 0.93 |
| Second cutpoint ($\mu_2$) | 2.45 | 2.17 | 2.37 |
| Third cutpoint ($\mu_3$) | 3.65 | 3.44 | 3.81 |
| N | 1066 | 1066 | 798 |
| Log-likelihood | −935.44 | −955.33 | −645.93 |
| $\chi^2$ | 702.0 w/24 d.f. | 795.0 w/24 d.f. | 636.9 w/24 d.f. |
| Significance probability of model | <.0001 | <.0001 | <.0001 |
| Pseudo $R^2$ | .273 | .294 | .330 |

*Notes:* Each cell gives estimated coefficient, standard error, and significance for a two-tailed test that the coefficient is different from 0 if the statistical significance exceeds the 0.1 level. The omitted category for the dummy variables of the issue-areas is treatment of the wounded. Constant is set to 0 to identify cutoff parameters.

variable available for the construction of instruments lacks the variation to estimate more than one of the reciprocal variables effectively; a table of the statistical tests demonstrating this can be found at my Web site. Each analysis then includes only one term for reciprocity, which is interacted with joint ratification and clarity. All twelve terms are positive and statistically significant. The evidence of positive reciprocity in the ordinal probits is not the result of the upward bias induced by simultaneity. The common pattern across all these estimations is what we seek; I now turn to a technical discussion of the patterns I presented graphically in the companion chapter.

### Reciprocity
Tables 4′.6 and 4′.7 show reciprocity. Table 4′.8 sums the various reciprocal effects under different combinations of legal obligation and clarity and centralization of the other side's violations. The figures in the table give the slope of the increase in the latent variable in the ordinal probit for the compliance of the other side and the estimated standard error of each sum calculated from the variance-covariance matrix of the analysis. For instance, the latent variable

TABLE 4'.7 *Coefficients for reciprocal variables from instrumental variable analyses of noncompliance with the laws of war*

| Instrumented reciprocal variable | Cases unweighted by data quality | Cases weighted by data quality | Only cases without standardized coding |
|---|---|---|---|
| Victim's noncompliance | .203, .102, .046 | .330, .091, <.001 | .349, .107, .001 |
| Clarity of victim's violations times victim's noncompliance | .043, .021, .042 | .072, .020, <.001 | .077, .023, .001 |
| Joint ratification times victim's noncompliance | .368, .178, .039 | .650, .172, <.001 | .655, .199, .001 |
| Clarity of victim's violations times joint ratification times victim's noncompliance | .074, .036, .040 | .134, .036, <.001 | .134, .043, .002 |

*Notes*: Each line reports the estimated coefficients for an instrumental variable analysis where the listed variable is the endogenous variable. I have omitted the estimated coefficients for the exogenous variables that are the same as those included in the analyses reported in Table 4'.6; they and summary statistics can be found in Supplemental Tables 2 through 5. Supplemental Table 6 provides tests of the strength of the instruments. All supplemental tables can be found at sitemaker. umich.edu/lawsofwar.

Each cell gives estimated coefficient, standard error, and significance for a two-tailed test that the coefficient is different from 0 if the statistical significance exceeds the 0.1 level.

underlying the violator's compliance rises by 0.963 for each increase in the level of the victim's violations when both sides have ratified and the violator's violations are state policy but their legal status is in dispute (the upper right cell of Table 4'.8). They are calculated from the second column of Table 4'.6. These numbers cannot be interpreted directly as an increase in violations in response to those of the victim because they are probit coefficients. They do reflect how the compliance of two warring parties move together.

Legal obligation through joint ratification strengthens reciprocity, as can be seen by comparing across the columns of Table 4'.8. Although warring states do not match one another's compliance exactly, there is a strong tendency to meet violations with violations and compliance with compliance. These differences across the columns are statistically significant at the 0.004 level or higher, with the closest comparisons occurring when the victim's violations are definite legal violations. The added strength of reciprocity under joint ratification can be seen in Table 4'.7 by comparing the coefficients of the reciprocal effects in the bottom two rows (where the victim's compliance is interacted with joint ratification) and the top two rows (where it is not). These coefficients can be read directly as decreases in compliance because the analysis is a regression rather than a probit. Joint ratification roughly doubles reciprocal responses.

TABLE 4′.8 *Estimated reciprocal effects of ratification, legal clarity, and centralization*

| | Without joint ratification | Joint ratification |
|---|---|---|
| Legal clarity of victim's violations with state violations | | |
| Violations in legal dispute | .108, .136 | .963, .170 |
| Probable legal violations | .289, .102 | .865, .123 |
| Definite legal violations | .470, .084 | .766, .090 |
| Legal clarity of victim's violations with individual violations | | |
| Violations in legal dispute | .164, .149 | 1.019, .180 |
| Probable legal violations | .345, .117 | .921, .136 |
| Definite legal violations | .526, .100 | .822, .106 |

*Notes*: Each cell reports the estimated derivative of Violator's Compliance followed by its estimated standard error. These estimates are calculated from the estimates of Table 4′.6 weighted for the quality of the data (the second column of that table) and the estimated variance-covariance matrix of that analysis. These estimated derivatives are probit coefficients and so do not directly translate into changes in compliance. They do allow a comparison of relative magnitudes of reciprocal effects across these nine situations.

The evidence on whether legal clarity strengthens reciprocity is not so clear. In Table 4′.8, legal clarity strengthens responses only when the parties are not bound by joint ratification, and the differences across the levels of legal clarity are statistically significant at the 0.001 level. Increasing legal clarity of violations strengths reciprocal responses, as can be seen in the second and fourth rows (which interact legal clarity with the victim's compliance) and in the fourth row (joint ratification) of Table 4′.7. The resulting effect at the clearest level of violations, when clarity equals 4, is less, however, than the terms above them, where legal clarity is not interacted with the other side's behavior. This suggests that legal clarity does not have the expected effect of strengthening reciprocity, but this unexpected result may occur because of a lack of variation in the dataset. Under joint ratification, most violations are definite legal violations. There are only ten cases of violations in clear legal dispute under joint ratification, and both sides have high or full compliance in these cases. The reversed sign of legal clarity under joint ratification is based on only a few cases, and so we should place little weight on it.

The effects of the centralization of violations on reciprocity are negligible. The coefficients in Table 4′.6 for the interactions of the victim's compliance with individual violations is higher than that with state violations, although the difference is not statistically significant in any analysis.

### Democracy and Legal Obligation
Because the effects of ratification mediate the effects of regime type and relative power, I discuss these together. Table 4′.9 sums the baseline effect of the

TABLE 4'.9 *Estimated unilateral effects of ratification status and regime type*

|  | Violator did not ratify | Only violator ratified | Joint ratification |
|---|---|---|---|
| Democracy | .668, .135 | –.496, .268 | –1.205, .312 |
| Nondemocracy | 0 | –.011, .175 | –.993, .298 |

*Notes*: Each cell reports the estimated unilateral effect of ratification status for regime type followed by its estimated standard error. These estimates are calculated from the estimates of Table 4'.6 weighted for the quality of the data (the second column of that table) and the estimated variance-covariance matrix of that analysis. Power ratio is set to its mean of 0.5 for the third column. These estimated derivatives are probit coefficients and so do not directly translate into changes in compliance. They do allow a comparison of relative magnitudes of reciprocal effects across these six situations.

six combinations: two types of regimes – democracy and nondemocracy – matched with each of three types of legal status – violator did not ratify, only the violator ratified, and joint ratification. These effects do not include reciprocal effects that vary with joint ratification. Democracies are *more* likely to commit violations than nondemocracies when they have not ratified the most recent treaty on the issue at hand, but commit fewer violations when they have. The effect of ratification on the baseline behavior of a democracy (the difference between the left and middle cells in the top row of the table) is statistically significant at more than the 0.001 level. Ratification by itself has no real effect on the behavior of a nondemocracy. Joint ratification, and presumably the anticipation of reciprocity, is necessary to restrain a nondemocracy. The difference between joint ratification and when the violator alone has ratified for nondemocracies is statistically significant at the 0.002 level.[17] This difference is statistically significant for democracies at the .078 level.[18]

Aerial bombardment accounts for part of this pattern, but not all of it. No party in the dataset ever has a legal obligation on aerial bombardment because the draft treaties from the 1930s, 1956, and 1970 were never signed, much less ratified. Historically, democracies have conducted most of the large campaigns of aerial bombardment against civilians. To check this possibility, Table 4'.10 reports the results of replications of Table 4'.6 excluding all

[17] This test is whether the sum of the coefficient for joint ratification and power ratio times the interaction of power ratio and joint ratification is different from 0. I set power ratio to its mean of 0.5 for the test. The difference between the violator not ratifying and joint ratification, the sum of these two terms and violator ratified, is statistically significant at the 0.001 level.

[18] We should not read too much into the better baseline compliance under joint ratification. It is consistent with deterrence through reciprocity. The coefficients in Table 4'.9 do not include the effects of reciprocity which is part of the effect of joint ratification. Returning to Figure 4.1, there is little visible difference in compliance behavior between joint ratification and not when the victim fully complies. The visible trace of deterrence through reciprocity is the lower chance of low or noncompliance when the victim has high compliance.

TABLE 4'.10 *Ordered probit analysis predicting noncompliance with the laws of war dropping aerial bombing*

| Variable | Cases unweighted by data quality | Cases weighted by data quality | Only cases without standardized coding |
|---|---|---|---|
| Joint ratification | –.819, .419, .051 | –1.196, .432, .006 | –1.102, .547, .044 |
| Violator ratified | –.025, .175, n.s. | –.040, .184, n.s. | –.216, .220, n.s. |
| Violator democracy | .408, .181, .024 | .450, .182, .013 | .371, .216, .086 |
| Violator democracy times joint ratification | –.078, .301, n.s. | .168, .309, n.s. | .216, .412, n.s. |
| Violator democracy times violator ratified | –.529, .325, n.s. | –.810, .336, .016 | –.783, .442, .076 |
| Power ratio | .327, .283, n.s. | .221, .295, n.s. | –.075, .358, n.s. |
| Power ratio times joint ratification | –.412, .330, n.s. | –.208, .345, n.s. | .175, .421, n.s. |

*Notes*: Each cell gives estimated coefficient, standard error, and significance for a two-tailed test that the coefficient is different from 0 if the statistical significance exceeds the 0.1 level.

The estimations include all of the variables in Table 4'.6. I present only the estimated coefficients for the variables above to focus on how they change when the aerial bombing cases are dropped from the analysis.

The omitted category for the dummy variables of the issue areas is treatment of the wounded.

Constant is set to 0 to identify cutoff parameters.

cases of aerial bombardment. I only report the coefficients for democracy, ratification status, power ratio, and their interactions in the interest of brevity; likewise, I do not report replications of the instrumental variable analyses of Table 4'.7, because they produce the same pattern. The tendency of democracies to commit more violations when they are not legally bound is reduced by about one-third when dropping aerial bombardment from the data. Nevertheless, the pattern that democracies commit more violations when they are not legally bound and fewer violations when they are still holds. Aerial bombing does not completely explain this pattern; it is something deeper about how democracies fight.

### Relative Power
Relative power enters the multivariate analyses in several places, making its full effect complex. Stronger sides are less likely to comply unless they are restrained by legal obligation through joint ratification. The coefficient for power ratio alone is positive and statistically significant. The effect of power when joint ratification exists; the sum of the power ratio and its interaction with joint ratification, is not. Overall, the effects of power on compliance are smaller than those of reciprocity and democracy.

*Issue Area*

Compliance varies significantly across issues in the laws of war. The estimated coefficients for each issue in Table 4'.6 give the difference in average compliance between that issue and treatment of the wounded, which is the omitted category. CBW has the highest average level of compliance. After CBW, a group of issues – armistice/ceasefire, conduct on the high seas, and aerial bombing – have the next highest levels of compliance. The difference between the coefficient for CBW and any of these three issues is statistically significant at the 0.001 level. None of the differences with this group of three issues is statistically significant at the 0.1 level. Protection of cultural property and treatment of the wounded come next in typical levels of compliance. The differences between both of these issues and armistice/cease fire are statistically significant at the 0.054 level or higher, but the differences with conduct on the high seas or aerial bombing are not. POWs has even less average compliance, and the differences between it and aerial bombing and treatment of the wounded are statistically significant at the 0.011 and 0.043 levels, respectively. Treatment of civilians produces the least compliance. The difference between it and every other issue but POWs is statistically significant. There is a ladder of average compliance, with CBW producing the best record, followed by a group of armistice/ceasefire, conduct on the high seas, and aerial bombing, then a pair of protection of cultural property and treatment of the wounded, trailed by POWs and treatment of civilians.

*Initiation and Intensity of War*

To complete this discussion of estimated effects, more intense wars as measured by battle deaths per 1,000 prewar population have more violations. Initiators are also less likely to comply as are losers. The effect of losing is reduced by power ratio, so that weak losers commit more violations than strong ones.

To summarize this section, I pull together the relative magnitude of all the effects already discussed. The relative magnitude can be judged by comparing the products of the estimated coefficients in Tables 4'.6 and 4'.8 with the typical variation in each of the variables. The difference in average compliance between CBW and treatment of civilians is larger than any of the other differences considered here. Next and comparable in magnitude to issue is reciprocity when both parties are legally obligated through joint ratification, and then democracies that have ratified. Their effects on compliance are roughly comparable. From Table 4'.8, a shift of two levels in the compliance of the other side produces a movement of 1.5 to 2.0 in the latent variable underlying the violator's noncompliance under joint ratification. Changing a democracy from not ratifying to doing so lowers that latent variable by about 1.1 to 1.5 in Table 4'.9 depending on whether the victim has also ratified. Shifting from the issue with the best compliance (CBW) to the issue with the worst (treatment of civilians) raises the noncompliance latent variable by about 1.5. All of these effects are much larger than any of the other variables in the analysis. The effects of issue and reciprocity under joint ratification are roughly one level of compliance; changing the issue from CBW to treatment of civilians reduces compliance one level, such as from high to low, and shifting the victim's compliance from full to none has about the same effect. After these two, the unilateral restraint of a democracy which has ratified the relevant treaty has the next biggest effect. Losing the war at hand and increasing the intensity of the war produce similar and lesser reductions in compliance. The strength of reciprocal responses does not vary appreciably with either legal clarity or whether the violations are state policy or the result of individual acts nor does relative power have much effect on compliance.

## MULTIVARIATE ANALYSIS OF RECIPROCITY AND TOTAL COMPLIANCE

The companion chapter presented dyadic analysis of reciprocity (the difference between the two sides' compliance on a given issue) and total compliance (the sum of their compliance scores) using comparisons of average levels of under different conditions to show the patterns there. I subtract these scores from their highest values – 8 for total compliance and 3 for reciprocity – to ensure that higher scores mean stronger reciprocity and more total compliance. This section presents multivariate analysis that extends and supports those results. Because I have already summarized these main conclusions in the companion chapter, I focus here on the details of the analysis.

Because the observation in these analyses is the warring dyad-issue, the variables tested earlier change from directed dyad to dyad. Two variables – joint ratification and only one side ratified – assess ratification status in the dyad. I interacted these variables with whether there is a democracy in the dyad for joint ratification and create another variable for when the only side that has ratified is a democracy. The latter allowed to me test whether unilateral restraint by democracies undermines reciprocity and produces lower levels of total compliance. For the analyses of reciprocity, I included maximum clarity of violations, the greater of the two clarity scores in the dyad, to capture whether reciprocity is stronger in the face of clear, legal violations. I examined whether reciprocity varies with the centralization of violations by creating two variables, one for cases in which both sides commit state violations and the other for when both sides commit individual violations. I interact these with joint ratification to investigate how legal obligation shapes reciprocity at the state level and on the battlefield. I grouped the issues into low noise issues – aerial bombing, armistice/ceasefire, CBW, and conduct on the high seas – and high noise issues, including a dummy variable for the former and an interaction of low noise issue with joint ratification. I tested for the effects of relative power with power differential – the power ratio for the stronger side in the dyad (and so this variable ranges from 0.5 when the sides are equal to 1). I also include the minimum battle deaths per 1,000 prewar population as an indicator of the intensity of the war.

Table 4'.11 presents the results of an ordinal probit analysis of reciprocity. As with the analysis of compliance, I present three analyses that vary on how the issue of the quality of the data is handled. The first column treats all cases equally, the second weights the case by the sum of the quality of data for each side, and the third column excludes any case for which one side has a standardized coding. Ratification has complicated effects. As in the figures in the companion chapter, unilateral ratification by a democracy weakens reciprocity, although the effect is not statistically significant in Table 4'.11 (the appropriate test is for the sum of Only One Side Ratified and Only Democracy Ratified). Joint ratification strengthens reciprocity indirectly by changing how the parties respond in different situations. Dyads without joint ratification respond to state and individual violations similarly; reciprocity is stronger when both commit the same type of violation, and the difference between the two is not statistically significant. Under joint ratification, reciprocity is stronger when both sides commit individual violations than state violations, and this difference has strong statistical significance (better than 0.001). States may respond more strongly to individual than state violations under joint reciprocity because retaliation has already failed to deter the other side when state violations are committed, and they might be sufficient to induce the other side to discipline its soldiers committing violations against state policy. Joint ratification also changes the effect of low noise issues on reciprocity; without it, those issues have lower records of reciprocity, but joint ratification eliminates that difference.

Legal clarity has a strong effect in these analyses, but it is subject to a major qualification. That variable has its lowest score when neither side commits any violations, meaning that reciprocity is perfect. This coefficient may then simply be the result that it also tracks which dyads have any violations. Large differences in power between the two sides do weaken reciprocity in these analyses. Finally, it does not appear that more intense wars have better or worse records of reciprocity.

Table 4'.12 reports parallel analyses for total compliance – the sum of the compliance of both sides. Again, compliance deteriorates as this variable increases, so positive coefficients reflect less total compliance. Reciprocity clearly induces better compliance in Table 4'.12. The positive and highly significant coefficient for reciprocity shows that reciprocity leads to better compliance. Joint ratification produces higher levels of total compliance, as shown by its negative coefficient. Democracy slightly strengthens this effect. Unilateral ratification, with or without a democracy being the ratifying side, produces a small improvement in total compliance. This could result from restraint by the ratifying side. Low noise issues have much better records of total compliance. Power difference has only a weak effect in undermining reciprocity,

TABLE 4'.11 *Ordered probit analysis of reciprocity*

| Variable | Cases unweighted by data quality | Cases weighted by data quality | Only cases without standardized coding |
|---|---|---|---|
| Joint ratification | −.132, .247, n.s. | −.061, .248, n.s. | −.091, .312, n.s. |
| Joint ratification and democracy in dyad | .264, .212, n.s. | .137, .206, n.s. | .325, .257, n.s. |
| Only one side ratified | .010, .174, n.s. | .005, .177, n.s. | .250, .218, n.s. |
| Only democracy ratified | −.221, .194, n.s. | −.202, .182, n.s. | −.373, .232, n.s. |
| Maximum clarity of violations | −.888, .076, <.001 | −.835, .074, <.001 | −.864, .082, <.001 |
| Both sides committed state violations | .922, .260, <.001 | .705, .223, .002 | .742, .268, .006 |
| Both sides committed individual violations | 1.245, .235, <.001 | 1.122, .247, <.001 | 1.331, .313, <.001 |
| Joint ratification times state violations | −.608, .365, .096 | −.460, .309, n.s. | −.555, .376, <.001 |
| Joint ratification times individual violations | .383, .324, n.s. | .266, .348, n.s. | .236, .468, n.s. |
| Low noise issue | −.755, .205, <.001 | −.708, .200, <.001 | −.761, .241, .002 |
| Joint ratification times low noise issue | .792, .273, .004 | .756, .262, .004 | .706, .316, .025 |
| Power difference | −.977, .410, .017 | −.917, .408, .025 | −.471, .490, n.s. |
| Minimum battle deaths per 1,000 population | −.0097, .0069, n.s. | −.0009, .0068, n.s. | .001, .008, n.s. |
| First cutpoint ($\mu_1$) | −6.84 | −6.62 | −4.90 |
| Second cutpoint ($\mu_2$) | −5.41 | −5.03 | −3.11 |
| Third cutpoint ($\mu_3$) | −3.54 | −3.37 | not needed |
| N | 533 | 533 | 399 |
| Log-likelihood | −345.44 | −368.85 | −243.57 |
| $\chi^2$ | 270.3 w/13 d.f. | 236.1 w/13 d.f. | 188.8 w/13 d.f. |
| Significance probability of model | <.0001 | <.0001 | <.0001 |
| Pseudo $R^2$ | .281 | .242 | .279 |

*Notes:* Each cell gives estimated coefficient, standard error, and significance for a two-tailed test that the coefficient is different from 0 if the statistical significance exceeds the .1 level. Constant is set to 0 to identify cutoff parameters.

TABLE 4'.12 *Ordered probit analysis of total compliance*

| Variable | Cases unweighted by data quality | Cases weighted by data quality | Only cases without standardized coding |
|---|---|---|---|
| Reciprocity | .590, .075, <.001 | .532, .073, <.001 | .642, .091, <.001 |
| Joint ratification | .557, .173, .001 | .653, .182, <.001 | .693, .225, .002 |
| Joint ratification and democracy in dyad | .176, .166, n.s. | .111, .166, n.s. | .124, .202, n.s. |
| Only one side ratified | .258, .143, .071 | .221, .146, n.s. | .266, .170, n.s. |
| Only democracy ratified | −.199, .157, n.s. | −.211, .151, n.s. | −.164, .187, n.s. |
| Low noise issue | 1.529, .146, <.001 | 1.477, .148, <.001 | 1.595, .173, <.001 |
| Joint ratification times low noise issue | −.136, .203, n.s. | −.191, .203, n.s. | −.281, .242, n.s. |
| Power difference | .712, .330, .031 | 1.050, .335, .002 | .904, .397, .023 |
| Minimum battle deaths per 1,000 population | −.033, .0056, <.001 | −.038, .0055, <.001 | −.039, .0066, <.001 |
| First cutpoint ($\mu_1$) | 0.04 | 0.36 | 0.54 |
| Second cutpoint ($\mu_2$) | 0.79 | 1.20 | 1.40 |
| Third cutpoint ($\mu_3$) | 1.56 | 1.97 | 2.22 |
| Fourth cutpoint ($\mu_4$) | 2.19 | 2.48 | 2.64 |
| Fifth cutpoint ($\mu_5$) | 3.01 | 3.19 | 3.29 |
| Sixth cutpoint ($\mu_6$) | 3.78 | 3.85 | 3.99 |
| N | 533 | 533 | 399 |
| Log-likelihood | −772.06 | −803.70 | −567.01 |
| $\chi^2$ | 297.8 w/9 d.f. | 298.0 w/9 d.f. | 229.7 w/9 d.f. |
| Significance probability of model | <.0001 | <.0001 | <.0001 |
| Pseudo $R^2$ | .162 | .156 | .168 |

*Notes:* Each cell gives estimated coefficient, standard error, and significance for a two-tailed test that the coefficient is different from 0 if the statistical significance exceeds the 0.1 level. Constant is set to 0 to identify cutoff parameters.

but it noticeably improves total compliance. Reciprocity is weaker and total compliance better in wars between unequal sides, suggesting that the stronger side can deny the weaker the ability to respond in kind to any violations that it commits. Finally, intense wars experience higher levels of violations, which is consistent with the analysis of compliance reported earlier.

## SEARCHING FOR FIREWALLS WITH NUMBERS

Firewalls separate the different issues in the laws of war to prevent a failure on one issue from spreading to other issues. A test for firewalls examines whether compliance by one side on one issue affects the compliance of the other side on a different issue. The ideal test would be to include the other side's compliance on all other issues, using instrumental variables to control for the simultaneity bias discussed earlier. Unfortunately, we lack the information to construct reliable instruments for all these reciprocal variables. The only variables available to identify compliance by issue area are the issue dummies. Given the difficulties of constructing valid instruments for more than one reciprocal variable, the ideal instrumental variable analysis of cross-issue reciprocity cannot be done with this dataset.

The observation in this test is the directed warring dyad, not the warring directed dyad-issue. I took the residuals of the instrumental variables analysis including the compliance of the other side interacted with the legal clarity of its violations weighted by the quality of the data from Table 4′.7 (middle cell of the second row of that table). I collapsed the dataset to determine the residuals on all eight issues for both sides for each directed dyad. Table 4′.13 presents the full set of cross-issue correlations of the residuals. Of the twenty-eight correlations reported there, only five are statistically significant at the 0.1 level and only one at the 0.05 level. The largest correlation, that of protection of cultural property and conduct on the high seas, is negative, contradicting cross-issue retaliation as an unusually high level of violations by one side on one issue is linked to the other side have an unusually high level of compliance on the other. Table 4′.13 does not support cross-issue retaliation generally.

Table 4′.14 provides a parallel analysis of looking at the correlations of residuals across issues for each warring party on its own. Do sides that tend to commit high levels of violations on a given issue consistently commit more violations on another? Here the evidence is much stronger than compliance by warring states is correlated across issues. Of the twenty-eight correlations in Table 4′.14, fifteen are positive and statistically significant at the 0.05 level, and eight are statistically significant at higher than the 0.001 level. These correlations suggest that the residuals do contain determinants of compliance not included in the statistical analysis. The failure to find a pattern of cross-issue correlation across the sides while strong patterns exist in the cross-issue correlations of each side on its own suggests that firewalls do exist across issues in the laws of war.

## DURATION ANALYSIS OF FIRST VIOLATIONS

We collected dates of first violations in the dataset when we could find such dates. The best evidence for such dates are single acts that are violations tied to a specific report with the date of the act. Chronologies of the World Wars

TABLE 4'.13  *Correlations of residuals between warring parties across issues*

| Side A's residual | Aerial bombing | Armistice | Chemical and biological weapons | Treatment of civilians | Cultural property | Conduct on high seas | Prisoners of war |
|---|---|---|---|---|---|---|---|
| | | | | Side B's residual | | | |
| Armistice | .121 n.s. | | | | | | |
| Chemical and biological weapons | .016 n.s. | .155 n.s. | | | | | |
| Treatment of civilians | -.047 n.s. | .173 n.s. | .028 n.s. | | | | |
| Cultural property | -.137 .085 | .045 n.s. | -.011 n.s. | .148 .027 | | | |
| Conduct on high seas | .017 n.s. | .148 n.s. | .100 n.s. | .157 .068 | -.165 .055 | | |
| Prisoners of war | .138 .083 | -.109 n.s. | .109 n.s. | .068 .078 | .078 n.s. | .048 n.s. | |
| Treatment of wounded | .046 n.s. | .069 n.s. | -.018 n.s. | .017 n.s. | -.051 n.s. | -.039 n.s. | .074 n.s. |

*Note:* Each cell lists the bivariate correlation between the residuals of the corresponding issues with its statistical significance below if it is higher than the 0.1 level.

TABLE 4'.14 *Correlations of residuals within warring parties across issues*

| Side A's residual | Side A's residual | | | | | | |
|---|---|---|---|---|---|---|---|
| | Aerial bombing | Armistice | Chemical and biological weapons | Treatment of civilians | Cultural property | Conduct on high seas | Prisoners of war |
| Armistice | -.151 n.s. | | | | | | |
| Chemical and biological weapons | .163 <.001 | .048 n.s. | | | | | |
| Treatment of civilians | .260 <.001 | -.038 n.s. | .142 .043 | | | | |
| Cultural property | .196 .013 | .093 n.s. | .229 .001 | .185 .006 | | | |
| Conduct on high seas | .329 <.001 | .146 n.s. | .313 <.001 | .001 n.s. | .166 .053 | | |
| Prisoners of war | .040 n.s. | .113 n.s. | .221 .002 | .283 <.001 | .164 .015 | .126 n.s. | |
| Treatment of wounded | -.006 n.s. | .103 n.s. | .051 n.s. | .374 <.001 | .369 <.001 | .012 n.s. | .292 <.001 |

*Note:* Each cell lists the bivariate correlation between the residuals of the corresponding issues with its statistical significance below if it is higher than the 0.1 level.

185

(e.g., Gray and Argyle 1990) and detailed military histories are particularly helpful in tracking down these dates. Dates were coded conservatively with the last date of the month used for violations for which we had only the month in which the violation occurred. All the cases of standardized coding of violations are dropped from this analysis because such coding was used only when we had no information on specific violations and so could not place a date.[19]

These dates of first use have the important caveat that the first violation was coded even if it was minor compared to major violations by the same side later in the war. For example, Germany's first use of chemical weapons on the Western Front of World War I is the chlorine gas attack on April 24, 1915 in the Second Battle of Ypres. The Germans claimed that this attack did not violate the 1899 Hague Declaration (IV,2) on the Use of Projectiles the Object of Which is the Diffusion of Asphyxiating or Deleterious Gases because the gas was discharged from cylinders. Like the Western Allies, Germany later used gas shells, a clear legal violation of the standard for the coding of legal clarity. The first use of gas was not the same as the acts underlying Germany's coding on the issue across the entire war.

Survival analysis, also known as event history analysis, is the statistical analysis of durations before an event occurs (see Box-Steffensmeier and Jones [2004] for an introduction to survival analysis as used in political science). It is called survival analysis because it was developed for data on how long medical patients lived. The basic unit of observation here is the warring party for a particular issue, and the dependent variable is time in days from the start of the war until a side commits its first violation on that issue. Those cases for which the side in question fully complies throughout the war are right-censored; the observation is simply that no violation had occurred by the time the war ended. The statistical techniques of survival analysis allow us to use this information in addition to all the cases that resulted in a violation. I focused on hazard rates, the chance that a case ends – here that the party in question commits its first violation – at a given time. Hazard rates can be expressed as a function of time, which tells us how the chance of a first violation changes as a war progresses. If the hazard rate is increasing with time, then first violations become more likely as the war goes on. If it is decreasing, first violations are more likely early in the war. If the hazard rate is flat, the chance of a first violation per time period does not change during the course of the war. We can also see how the hazard rate across cases varies with the variables we have examined earlier in this chapter. Here the analysis tells us whether the chance of a first violation increases (or decreases) with a given variable. Typically, such analysis assumes that an independent variable has the same effect on the hazard rate across time, simply multiplying it by the same amount at every time; this assumption is

---

[19] The exception here is CBW, where the standardized coding is full compliance based on the lack of any report of the use of those weapons. These cases are kept in the analysis as cases without a violation.

known as proportional hazards. Variables may have effects on the hazard rate that are not proportionate, and I test for those exceptions.

As discussed in the companion chapter, duration analysis of first violations tests the hypothesis that violations come early in a war rather than late. The hypothesis to be tested is that the hazard rate of a first violation declines as the war progresses. A side that saw a strategic advantage in violating the laws of war should do so as soon as possible in the war. I tested the shape of the hazard function by fitting a parametric model to the data. Statistical tests on the parameters tell us whether the hazard rate is increasing, decreasing, or constant over time. A variety of parametric models are available, and they make different assumptions about how the hazard rate could vary over time. An exponential model assumes that the hazard rate is fixed; a Weibull model assumes that it is monotonic, always increasing or decreasing with the direction determined by its single parameter; and logistic models, such as the log-logistic or log-normal, allow the hazard rate to be increasing over some time periods and decreasing over others. All of these parametric models are special cases of a generalized gamma distribution that has two parameters. Depending on the values of these two parameters, we can determine which of these special cases seems to best fit the data and then examine how the estimated hazard rate of that distribution changes over time.

Table 4′.15 presents the results of these parametric survival analyses. Time is measured in days until the first violation or the end of the war. I also include the variables examined earlier to control for how the hazard rate varies across cases. I converted the violator's battle deaths per 1,000 prewar population into a death rate per day by dividing it by the length of the war. I did this because the casualties across the entire war are heavily affected by the length of the war, and the conversion to a daily death rate eliminates the possibility of including the duration of the war in the estimation. The first column of Table 4′.15 presents the results of the generalized gamma distribution. The scale parameter shows that a log-normal distribution best fits the data; the generalized gamma distribution reduces to a log-normal distribution when the scale parameter, $\kappa$, equals 0. Here a statistical test for whether the scale parameter differs from 0 does not reject the null hypothesis that a log-normal distribution fits the data. The second column of Table 4′.15 presents the results of an estimation fitting a log-normal distribution to the data; the results are very close to those from the generalized gamma distribution as we would expect from the test. The shape parameter of both models allows us to tell whether the hazard rate is falling or rising across time. When the shape parameter $\sigma$ is greater than one, the hazard rate rises first and then falls with the turnover point coming earlier as $\sigma$ increases.[20]

The models in the first two columns of Table 4′.15 assume proportional risks across the variables. We can test this assumption by running a Cox

---

[20] An estimation fitting a Weibull distribution to the data provides similar results.

TABLE 4′.15 *Results of parametric survival models not including retaliation*

| | Generalized gamma distribution | Log-normal distribution | Log-normal with correction for nonproportional hazards |
|---|---|---|---|
| Scale parameter ($\kappa$) | .213, .158, n.s. | | |
| Shape parameter ($\sigma$) | 2.699, .144, <.001 | 2.840, .094, <.001 | 2.585, .085, <.001 |
| Independent variables | | | |
| Joint ratification | –.392, .637, n.s. | –.433, .638, n.s. | –.674, .584, n.s. |
| Violator ratified | .307, .454, n.s. | .322, .458, n.s. | .196, .416, n.s. |
| Violator democracy | –1.131, .351, .001 | –1.110, .355, .002 | –.820, .323, .011 |
| Violator democracy times joint ratification | –.327, .809, n.s. | –.233, .819, n.s. | –.441, .749, n.s. |
| Violator democracy times violator ratified | 1.404, .813, .084 | 1.289, .820, n.s. | 1.142, .748, n.s. |
| Power ratio | –2.150, .624, .001 | –2.249, .627, <.001 | –1.963, .575, .001 |
| Power ratio times joint ratification | .010, .787, n.s. | .165, .779, n.s. | .169, .716, n.s. |
| Aerial Bombing | .569, .435, n.s. | .511, .429, n.s. | .133, .400, n.s. |
| Armistice | 2.879, .447, <.001 | 2.787, .440, <.001 | –4.495, .758, <.001 |
| Armistice times log(time) | | | 1.483, .151, <.001 |
| Chemical and biological warfare | 3.458, .465, <.001 | 3.467, .461, <.001 | –.786, .984, n.s. |
| CBW times log(time) | | | .737, .168, <.001 |
| Treatment of civilians | –2.232, .400, <.001 | –2.246, .411, <.001 | –2.199, .374, <.001 |
| Protection of cultural property | –1.375, .547, .012 | –1.357, .566, .017 | –1.298, .515, .012 |
| Conduct on the high seas | 1.237, .430, .004 | 1.191, .433, .006 | 1.035, .393, .009 |
| Prisoners of war | –.796, .408, .051 | –.783, .418, .061 | –.805, .380, .034 |
| Violator initiated war? | –.960, .205, <.001 | –.927, .207, <.001 | –.717, .191, <.001 |
| Violator battle death rate | –.370, .109, .001 | –.376, .116, .001 | –.241, .103, .019 |
| Violator lost | .661, .425, n.s. | .670, .430, n.s. | .382, .395, n.s. |
| Violator lost times power ratio | –2.035, .759, .007 | –2.092, .762, .006 | –1.557, .703, .027 |
| Constant | 7.596 | 7.422 | 7.303 |

|  | Generalized gamma distribution | Log-normal distribution | Log-normal with correction for nonproportional hazards |
|---|---|---|---|
| N | 1248 | 1248 | 1248 |
| Log-likelihood | −1564.8 | −1565.7 | −1505.1 |
| $\chi^2$ | 371.5 w/18 d.f.s | 390.7 w/18 d.f.s | 511.8 w 20 d.f.s |
| Significance probability of model | <.0001 | <.0001 | <.0001 |

*Notes*: Each cell gives estimated coefficient, standard error, and significance for a two-tailed test that the coefficient is different from 0 if the statistical significance exceeds the 0.1 level.

The omitted category for the dummy variables of the issue-areas is treatment of the wounded.

proportional hazard model and conducting a nonproportionality test on the Schoenfeld residuals (see Box-Steffensmeier and Jones [2004, chapter 8] for a discussion of such tests). The Cox model does not assume a form of the hazard function as the parametric models do, but instead tests for how the pattern of survival times varies with the included variables. The test shows that the risks associated with two variables, the issues of armistice/ceasefire and CBW, are not proportionate. Visual inspection of the graphs of estimated hazard rates of both reveal that the hazard rate of each rises and then falls with the turnover point coming much later in the war than is the case for the hazard rate overall. This pattern arises for both issues for clear reasons. A side cannot violate an armistice or cease fire until one has been in place, and there has to be a period of fighting before a ceasefire can be agreed to. As seen in the earlier analyses, CBW is one area for which the standard is often observed. Many of the cases of the use of such weapons occur during World War I when such weapons came into use during 1915, almost a year after the main warring parties had been fighting. The observed hazard rate for CBW reflects this observation, rising to its peak hazard about one year into a war. The final column of Table 4'.15 controls for the nonproportional hazards of these two variables by including an interaction of each with the logarithm of the time until first violation or the end of the war (if no violation occurs). There is no substantive change in the hazard rate from these interactive terms, although the fit of the model is noticeably improved.

Reciprocity poses an endogeneity problem in that the first violation of the other side is not independent of the continued compliance of the side in question. As with the ordered probit analyses earlier, the following survival analysis of reciprocal responses should be viewed conservatively. To assess reciprocity, I included whether the other side has committed a violation. Cases in which the

TABLE 4'.16 *Results of parametric survival model including retaliation*

| | Log-normal with correction for nonproportional hazards |
|---|---|
| Shape parameter ($\sigma$) | 2.772, .088, <.001 |
| Reciprocal variables | |
| First violation by other side? | −8.985, .888, <.001 |
| Log(time since first violation by other side) | 1.347, .156, <.001 |
| Independent variables | |
| Joint ratification | −.739, .646, n.s. |
| Violator ratified | .438, .457, n.s. |
| Violator democracy | −.928, .379, .014 |
| Violator democracy times joint ratification | .292, .902, n.s. |
| Violator democracy times violator ratified | .811, .920, n.s. |
| Power ratio | −2.522, .638, <.001 |
| Power ratio times joint ratification | .290, .789, n.s. |
| Aerial bombing | .457, .430, n.s. |
| Armistice | 2.671, .432, <.001 |
| Chemical and biological warfare | .108, .954, n.s. |
| CBW times log(time) | .570, .158, <.001 |
| Treatment of civilians | −2.071, .383, <.001 |
| Protection of cultural property | −1.511, .473, .001 |
| Conduct on the high seas | 1.208, .421, .004 |
| Prisoners of war | −.700, .382, .066 |
| Violator initiated war? | −.909, .208, <.001 |
| Violator battle death rate | −.335, .087, <.001 |
| Violator lost | .608, 431, n.s. |
| Violator lost times power ratio | −1.785, .766, .020 |
| Constant | 7.790 |
| N | 1248 |
| Log-likelihood | −1488.6 |
| $\chi^2$ | 465.2 w 21 d.f.s |
| Significance probability of model | <.0001 |

*Notes*: Each cell gives estimated coefficient, standard error, and significance for a two-tailed test that the coefficient is different from 0 if the statistical significance exceeds the 0.1 level.
The omitted category for the dummy variables of the issue-areas is treatment of the wounded.

other side has committed a violation while the side in question has not yet are then split into two cases at the time of that violation by the other side. Cases in which both sides committed first violations on the same day were not considered as reciprocal responses to one another. I conducted the same steps of the analysis as before, using a generalized gamma distribution to determine the appropriate parametric form and tested the hypothesis that the risks induced by the variables are proportional using the Schoenfeld residuals of a Cox model.

Because the two variables that posed nonproportional risks were whether the other side had committed a violation and CBW, I added interactions of these variables with the natural logarithm of time. Table 4'.16 presents the results of this final analysis estimated with a log-normal distribution as indicated by the generalized gamma distribution.

Finally, I turn to the effects of the variables on the hazard rates of first use in Tables 4'.15, and 4'.16. The coefficients in these tables indicate whether the variable in question makes first use more likely, if the coefficient is negative, or less likely, if the coefficient is positive. The pattern of results is the same as reported earlier; the variables which reduced overall compliance in the earlier analyses made first use more likely here. Again, my interest in the survival analyses lies primarily in the shape of the hazard function, not in how the variables shift those hazards.

## DRY HOLES

As I mentioned at the beginning of this chapter, I conducted many other specifications than those reported here. I explored a large number of other plausible patterns that did not prove fruitful with testing. Some of these other specification may have already occurred to the reader. This section briefly explains the "dry holes" that I prospected in reaching the reported results. The interested reader can find the results of these estimations at my Web site.

First, several plausible arguments about how reciprocity varies receive no support when they are included in the analysis. Some argue that democracies lack the ability to reciprocate, allowing autocracies to violate international law without consequence. However, whether the violator is a democracy has no statistically or substantially significant effect on the violator's response to the victim's compliance, even when including the interaction of joint ratification, democracy, and the victim's compliance. There is some evidence that dyads that are unequal in power have less reciprocity but more total compliance. However, relative power as measured by the power ratio has no effect on the size of reciprocal responses, so it is unclear whether the weaker side cannot retaliate or whether the stronger side is restrained.

Second, signing a treaty but not ratifying it has no significant effect on behavior. Ratification is the key signal of intent.

# 5

## Spoilt Darlings?

### Treatment of Prisoners of War during the World Wars

> To-day the prisoner of war is a spoilt darling; he is treated with a solicitude for his wants and feelings which borders on sentimentalism.... Under present-day conditions, captivity ... is usually a halcyon time, ... a kind of inexpensive rest-cure after the wearisome turmoil of fighting. The wonder is that any soldiers fight at all.
>
> (J. M. Spaight, 1911, 265)

The statistical results of Chapter 4 provide the broad pattern of compliance with the laws of war. This chapter complements those results by looking at the details of compliance with a specific area of the laws of war, the treatment of prisoners of war (POWs). Treatment of POWs is a good candidate for detailed study because there is wide variation in compliance with the treaties, compliance depends on what happens at the state and the individual level, and the clarity of obligations increased from World War I to World War II. POWs then allow a test of the central ideas of compliance discussed in Chapter 3. Additionally, POWs is an issue in the laws of war which has received less attention than others such as the use of chemical weapons.[1] The next chapter provides some brief analysis of the issues which have received more attention in the political science literature. I limit this chapter to the World Wars simply to allow a coherent presentation. Later wars, particularly the Korean War, the Vietnam War, and the Iraq-Iran War, presented interesting issues in the treatment of POWs, but adding them to this discussion would lengthen it substantially without adding new leverage on the hypotheses to be tested.

This chapter begins with a discussion of the relevant treaties and the obligations they impose on state parties. Then I discuss the strategic logic of POWs;

---

[1] See Wallace (2012) for a recent effort to evaluate when states mistreat POWs. Wallace does not consider conduct on the battlefield or whether treaty ratification strengthens reciprocity.

how different states perceived their interests in how they treat POWs. The issue of POWs operates at both the state level – what are state policies toward enemy soldiers who attempt to surrender – and at the individual level – what soldiers do on the battlefield. Furthermore, the two levels are connected; state policy attempts to regulate how their own soldiers act and induce enemy soldiers to act, but the success of those policies depends on the logic of the battlefield. I discuss compliance and reciprocity at both the state and individual levels during the World Wars in chronological order. During World War I, most countries sought to treat prisoners humanely but disagreed about what that required, particularly during the material shortages of wartime. During World War II, there was a clearer agreement of what humane treatment required, but less interest across the warring parties in providing such treatment. I examine statistical evidence of death rates of POWs, judgments by historians concerning behavior on the battlefield, and accounts of individual actions on the battlefield and in POW camps. I end the chapter by pulling together the conclusions in an assessment of why men can surrender and be treated humanely in some wars, while they are routinely slaughtered in others.

## THE POW TREATIES AND THE OBLIGATIONS THEY IMPOSE

Three agreements regulate the treatment of prisoners of war: (1) the 1907 Hague Convention (IV) respecting the Laws and Customs of War on Land (henceforth 1907 Hague Convention [IV]), (2) the 1929 Geneva Convention, and (3) the 1949 Geneva Convention (III) on POWs.[2] The 1907 Hague Convention (IV) applied during World War I and defined the four conditions that identify combatants: (1) that they are commanded by a person responsible for his subordinates, (2) that they have a fixed distinctive emblem recognizable at a distance, (3) that they carry their arms openly, and (4) that they conduct their operations in accordance with the laws and customs of war. It placed the responsibility for proper treatment of POWs on governments, not on individual captors or their commanders. Captor governments were obligated to provide food, lodging, and clothing at the same level as they did to their own troops. The regulations allowed the captor nation to use the labor of prisoners provided that it pays them and that the work is not related to the war effort. The distinction in the latter provision is more easily discerned in theory than in the conditions of total war. Captor nations were also obligated to account for the prisoners they held by establishing an inquiry office and reporting their identity and status to that office, making the information available to the home nation. Furthermore, state parties to the Convention were also obligated to allow relief services to provide aid to POWs. All of the major power combatants – except Italy – were state parties to these regulations through ratification before the war; the

[2] Full texts of each of these treaties can be found at http://www.icrc.org/applic/ihl/ihl.nsf/vwTreatiesByDate.xsp, accessed June 19, 2013.

other combatants who were not – Serbia, Montenegro, Turkey, Bulgaria, and Greece – were signatories.

The 1929 Geneva Convention expanded and qualified the protections of POWs in light of experience during World War I (Howard, Andreopoulos, and Shulman 1994, 127–128). Many of the obligations were made more explicit; for example, the famous right of prisoners to state only their name, rank, and serial number was stated. States had the responsibility to feed POWs at least as well as their own troops, to provide them with a clean living environment and basic health care, not to use POWs as labor in their war efforts although POWs among enlisted mem could be used for labor, and to repatriate them quickly at the end of a war. Limits on discipline of POWs for their conduct while prisoners and the need for judicial processes for more serious offenses were established. The Red Cross was recognized as a nonstate agency that had the right and responsibility to deliver packages and mail to prisoners, inspect POW camps, and report on their condition to the nations whose soldiers were held prisoner. A role of a neutral country, called the protecting power, was established to serve as a liaison and monitor for pairs of warring nations. The obligations of the treaty were made binding on a state party even if the opposing state was not a member of the treaty. Among the major combatants of World War II, Japan attended the negotiations and signed the treaty but did not ratify it, while the Soviet Union neither attended the negotiations nor ratified the treaty (Barker 1975, 16–17; Garrett 1981, 184). Of the minor participants, only Finland did not ratify the 1929 Geneva Convention; they were bound by the 1907 Hague Convention (IV).

The 1949 Geneva Convention on POWs added further detail and clarity to these legal obligations in light of the experience of World War II. As this chapter covers what happened in those wars, the legal obligations of the 1949 Geneva Convention on POWs did not exist, and I will not cover them in detail. Broadly, the protections were extended more clearly to civilians who take up arms in resistance to military occupation, the obligation of the captor state to provide for the welfare of POWs were stated in greater detail, and the requirement for rapid repatriation after the end of a war established. The Convention goes into great detail as far as specific standards for POW treatment, going so far as to specify pay scales in Swiss francs for POW labor according to rank and explicit standards of what disabilities, wounds, and medical conditions qualify a prisoner for repatriation during wartime. In Chapter 7, I return to the development of POW law in when I discuss changes in institutions over time.

THE STRATEGIC LOGIC OF PRISONERS OF WAR

Treatment of prisoners of war poses a range of issues that have led states to differ in what they see as being in their interest. For some issues in the laws of war, the interests of states in complying with their obligations or violating them are clear. For example, Germany had clear strategic incentives pushing it toward unrestricted submarine warfare against Britain in both wars because of the difference in their vulnerabilities to such attacks on merchant shipping. Such cases tend to be clearest when central authorities have the most control over violations. But with POWs, the incentives are mixed, and the interplay between state policy and what happens on the battlefield is complicated. Furthermore, views of how POWs should be treated have changed over the course of the twentieth century, and those changes have altered state policies toward POWs.

## The Logic of the Battlefield

The logic of kill-or-be-killed rules the battlefield. As Richard Holmes describes it, "surrendering during battle is a difficult business" (1985, 381). For an individual to signal his intent to surrender, he must either expose himself to the enemy or find himself at close quarters with the enemy. Both situations are fraught with danger. In the former case, he may be shot because his intent to surrender is not realized by the enemy in time or because an enemy soldier shoots him out of anger, bloodlust, or fear that the signal to surrender is a ruse. In the latter case, the logic of kill-or-be-killed often leads men to shoot, bomb, knife, or club first and ask for surrender later. Niall Ferguson describes the problem as "the captor's dilemma," how can both the soldier attempting to surrender and his prospective captor overcome their mutual mistrust to conclude a surrender where both sides survive unharmed (1999, chapter 13)? Yet in many situations, soldiers can and do surrender in close quarters (Holmes 1985, 382–387; Fritz 1995, 52–57; Linderman 1997, 118–132).

Surrender is further complicated by the danger of being killed at the front once one is a captive of the other side. Pure hatred for the enemy or anger over loss of a buddy often leads to murder of men whose surrender has been accepted. As General Harper insisted during World War I, "no man in the Great War was ever killed by a bayonet unless he had his hands up first" (quoted in Winter 1978, 110). In some occasions, prisoners are executed because the immediate tactical situation has changed and they cannot be held. In general, the risk of execution decreases as the number of prisoners taken at once rises. As one Canadian officer explained after a battle during World War I: "it was impossible to avoid taking so many [prisoners] as they surrendered in batches of from 20 to 50" (Cook 2006, 654). Even in those cases, there are notable massacres of tens to hundreds of prisoners at one time. From World War II, Americans remember the Malmedy massacre, the British the Wormhout massacre, and the Soviets and Germans suffered too many such massacres at one another's hands to remember any one incident specifically.

It is a safe guess that most POWs are taken in groups, not as individuals surrendering on the battlefield, although I do not know of any statistical study of the subject.[3] These groups, whether they number in the tens or the thousands, surrender when they deem that their situation on the battlefield is no longer tenable. They may be surrounded, outnumbered, or outgunned. Whoever is in

---

[3] As a digression, this essential point is the flaw in Niall Ferguson's essay on surrender in World War I, "The Captor's Dilemma" (chapter 13 of his *The Pity of War* [1999]). The difficulties of

command is the judge of whether the unit should continue to fight or to surrender. Regulations against surrender and orders to fight to the end may mean little to those facing a bleak situation on the ground.[4]

These dynamics of the battlefield produce the first two strategic problems that prisoners of war pose to every army at war. First, how can one discourage one's own soldiers from surrendering too readily? Second, how can one encourage enemy soldiers to surrender? Armies seek to deal with these problems through training and doctrine. They also have the additional tool of altering their soldiers' expectations of what the enemy will do to them if they try to surrender. Rumors of the enemy killing fellow soldiers trying to surrender spread fast and often in combat units. Soldiers often retaliate when they believe that atrocities have been committed against their comrades in arms. And both sides understand this bitter reciprocity. As one German soldier put the matter after watching the SS butcher 300 Soviets taken prisoner, "[i]t was already clear to us that it would have repercussions. That our prisoners [in Soviet hands] would be treated the same way" (quoted in Fritz 1995, 57). One way to induce your own soldiers to fight on rather than surrender is to deny quarter to the enemy, forcing the grim reality of kill-or-be-killed on all combatants (Ferguson 2004, 153).

Other countries have sought to encourage enemy soldiers to surrender through humane treatment. As Richard Holmes puts it, "when men have reason to believe that captives will not be mistreated, then surrender is a far more easily-acceptable alternative than we might suppose" (1985, 324). A state that wished to encourage the enemy to surrender must discipline its own soldiers to take prisoners rather than kill them.

surrendering and making it possible for the enemy to surrender in the face of the incentives to kill on both sides are real for individuals and very small units surrendering. But larger units rarely face this problem as their surrenders are typically negotiated, and a majority, if not a vast majority, of prisoners are taken in units, not as individuals. The reason why relatively few prisoners were taken on the Western Front of World War I lies not in the realities of the captor's dilemma aptly described by Ferguson, but rather in the integrity of the front line until spring 1918. Once both sides were able to rupture the front line of the other side, then units became cut off and surrendered. Alon Rachamimov makes this point about how soldiers were captured on the Eastern Front of World War I:

> Of the estimated two million Austro-Hungarian POWs in Russia at least half were taken captive during "big catches," usually in the course of major battles. It should be emphasized that battles on the eastern front during World War I were inherently different from western-front battles. Whereas western-front battles such as Verdun, the Somme or Passchendaele were first and foremost attrition battles with negligible territorial advances, eastern front battles involved often rapid and significant movement of forces....
> In the process of capturing vast areas, the belligerents on the eastern front regularly captured many enemy soldiers as well (Rachamimov 2002, 38).

[4] Watson (2008, 109, 178–179, 224–229) provides examples of groups surrendering and the key role of commanding officers in managing the surrender of groups of their soldiers.

## After Capture and before Imprisonment

Despite the difficulties of surrendering and surviving to pass into captivity, all armies take some prisoners. Once in enemy hands, POWs are sent to collection points behind the lines and then to POW camps. At this stage, prisoners have valuable information that their captors would like to know. Raids are often conducted to seize prisoners as sources of information. Although soldiers need only provide their captors with their name, rank, and serial number to identify themselves for registration as POWs, many prisoners provide the enemy with some information. The interrogation of most POWs occurs close to the front by intelligence officers attached to combat units and seeks to obtain information about the unit's immediate situation. In some cases, coercion is used to extract information, but many prisoners talk willingly. At a minimum, their uniforms typically identify their unit. Field interrogations are rarely lengthy because the information sought has a short half-life (Barker 1975, chapter 5; Vance 2000, 147–149).

Particularly valuable prisoners – high-level officers and those with technical knowledge (such as pilots) – were often separated for extensive interrogation before being placed in a camp (Barker 1975, 60–61; Vance 2000, 147–149). These prisoners receive the full range of techniques that are used in the effort to extract information from uncooperative individuals. Western nations have generally not used torture as a policy against prisoners, finding rewards and trickery as more effective. As was the case in the notorious Abu Gharab prison outside Baghdad, this policy is on occasion stretched and broken. At the other extreme, the Japanese often tortured submariners they took prisoner in an effort to extract technical information about the performance of submarines (Barker 1975, 61). A different form of coercion is brainwashing as practiced by the Chinese during the Korean War. Here the object is to produce a compliant prisoner who can be used for propaganda purposes, rather than forcing him to divulge military secrets. Brainwashing involves a long period of episodes of good and bad treatment to bend the prisoner's mind to what the captor would like him to think. Compliant behavior is rewarded; resistance punished. In one extreme example, twenty-one U.S. POWs and one British refused repatriation and elected to stay in China after the war was over (Vance 2000, 162).

The standards of acceptable forms of interrogation have become stricter over time. The 1907 Hague Convention (IV) simply stated that prisoners "must be humanely treated." In World War I, forcing a prisoner to stand at attention for long periods of questioning or withholding food and water were not seen as inhumane treatment. The 1929 Geneva Convention went further, stating that POWs must "be humanely treated and protected, particularly against acts of violence, from insults and from public curiosity" (Article 2). Pressure to extract information was ruled out (Article 5).

## Treatment while a Prisoner

Eventually most POWs are interned in a camp. POWs in camps must be sheltered, fed, and clothed. The term camp covers a wide range of facilities for holding prisoners for the duration of the war and until they can be repatriated afterward. The archetypical POW camp as depicted in the movies consists of basic barracks for communal living surrounded by a wire fence with guard towers. Treatment in camps is largely in the hands of the camp commander and his guards. Inspections can reveal some deficiencies in camp conditions and treatment, but ultimately the commander and guards are the authority. In one case in which POWs complained about violations of the Geneva Convention to a guard, "he taps his rifle and says 'Here is my Geneva Convention'" (quoted in Garrett 1981, 141). Difficult prisoners such as serial escapees are often moved to more secure facilities in remote locations with more guards; the most famous of these facilities was Colditz Castle used by the Germans to hold high-risk prisoners. Food for prisoners reflects the general food shortages that many societies at war suffer from and the institutional blandness that only a military can produce. Often, prisoners in camps grow vegetables to supplement their diet and help pass the time. POWs typically retain their uniforms as clothing, but over time, the captor state provides them with replacement clothing.

Providing these resources to POWs poses a burden on the captor, a burden that is greater for some states than others. Some captor states, such as the United States during World War II, can provide ample support for POWs because they do not face shortages of food or material. Others, such as Germany during World War I, suffer from a general shortage of food, making feeding prisoners a major burden. In those cases, POWs are generally the last on the list for food. In response to such cases, the Geneva Conventions on POWs have become more specific about the required level and type of food to be provided. Relief packages sent from the home country often plays a critical role in sustaining prisoners when food is scarce. POWs in some situations can also use the pay they earn to purchase more food. Of course, not all captor states deliver the pay that POWs earn from their home country (Vance 2000, 237–240).

POWs are an important source of labor during wartime, and almost every country that has held large numbers of POWs puts some of them to work (Barker 1975, 97–112). Agricultural work is highly prized by POWs because it is outside and they get more to eat, either by scrounging or simply from the greater availability of food on farms. POWs working in agriculture are sometimes lodged at the farm at which they work. Work gangs for construction or industrial work are another common form of POW work. Any form of work relieves some of the monotony of camp life. The extremes of exploitation of POW labor were the coal mines at which Nazi Germany worked Soviet POWs to death and the infamous Death Railway constructed by the Japanese with a combination of POWs and impressed Asian civilians. The death rate of those who were forced to work on Death Railway is estimated as high as 50 percent

(Vance 2000, 37).[5] The combination of criminal neglect of prisoners, starvation diet, and brutal punishment to compel work killed so many prisoners that the cost of improved treatment in these cases would have been more than compensated by greater work accomplished.

Some states have tried to enlist POWs into their own armies or into special units of their own nationality. Because they cannot compel recruitment, such efforts rarely succeed in producing a large number of recruits. The most successful such effort was the large number of captured Soviet soldiers enlisted by the Nazis to fight and to serve in construction battalions during World War II. It is estimated that as many as 1 million Soviet POWs served as Hiwis, short for volunteer in German (Overy 1998, 128). The primary reason for Nazi success where others generally failed was the horrible conditions in German POW camps for Soviet prisoners, although POWs from some nationalities volunteered out of hatred for the Soviet system.

All three of these stages of becoming and being a POW can lead to very different judgments of what policies are in the interest of the state. Some militaries have chosen to uphold the standards of the law because they believe that those standards help encourage enemy soldiers to surrender and they do not wish to provide the enemy with an excuse to mistreat their own soldiers taken prisoner. Other militaries seek to discourage their own soldiers from surrendering by making the battlefield a more brutal place and abuse the prisoners they do take. Furthermore, the dynamics of reciprocity on the battlefield limits how military policies can shape what happens there. Understanding such incentives and dynamics then is necessary to see how treaty law can shape treatment of POWs behind and at the line.

POWS IN WORLD WAR I

As the first general war between modern, industrial nation-states capable of raising mass armies through conscription, World War I was the proving ground of modern weaponry, tactics, and economic mobilization. It was also the first extensive experience with international law regulating the treatment of prisoners of war. The 1907 Hague Convention (IV) began to move the norms for handling POWs from earlier ideas concerning parole and ransom to the modern idea of holding those who surrender out of combat for the duration of the war. All warring parties took substantial numbers of POWs.

## Death Rates and Treatment in POW Camps

Death rates in captivity provide an important summary judgment of the quality of treatment accorded POWs once they reach camps. Prisoners die for many

---

[5] Sibylla Jane Flower estimates that 12,000 out of 64,000 POWs who worked on the railroad died, a bit less than 19 percent (Flower 1996, 240, 247).

TABLE 5.1 *Death rates of POWs in captivity during World War I*

| Captor State | State of POWs | Number of POWs taken | Number of POWs who died in captivity | Death rate of POWs in captivity |
|---|---|---|---|---|
| Germany | Russia | 1,434,000 | 55,000 | 4% |
| Germany | France[a] | 520,579 | 17,000–38,963 | 3.3–7.5% |
| Germany | Great Britain[a] | 175,624 | 5,550–12,425 | 3.1–7.1% |
| Germany | Italy | 133,000 | 5,300 | 4% |
| Austria-Hungary | Russia | 1,269,000 | 63,000 | 5% |
| Austria-Hungary | Italy | 468,000 | 92,451 | 19.8% |
| Turkey | Russia | 15,164 | 2,500 | 16% |
| Turkey | Great Britain | 36,000 | 4,200 | 12.3% |
| Russia | Germany | 167,000 | 16,000–25,000 | 9.5–15% |
| Russia | Austria-Hungary | 2,111,146 | 385,000 | 18% |
| Russia | Turkey | 51,000 | 10,000 | 20% |
| France | Germany | 392,425 | 25,200 | 6.4% |
| Great Britain | Germany | 328,900 | 10,000 | 3% |
| Great Britain | Turkey | 42,500 | 4,500 | 10.5% |
| Italy | Austria-Hungary | 528,154 | 35,000 | 7% |

*Note*: Dominion troops included in Great Britain's totals.
[a] These figures are only POWs held in Germany, not in occupied territory (Jones 2011, 23).
*Source*: Figures taken from Rachamimov 2002, 39–42; Kramer 2010; Jones 2011, 19–24.

reasons: prior wounds, poor living conditions, inadequate diet, overwork, and disease. Higher death rates are a general indicator of worse treatment. Table 5.1 presents figures on total prisoners held, the number who died in captivity, and death rate. The figures are rounded or only available as estimated ranges for some cases. The death rates for prisoners taken on the Eastern Front and in the Middle East were higher than for those taken on the Western Front. Conditions in camps were better in the latter cases. Hygiene was a serious problem in Russian and Austro-Hungarian camps leading to deaths from epidemic diseases such as typhus (Rachamimov 2002, 103–107). Camps at first were improvised, and the larger number of prisoners on the Eastern Front meant more men were held in substandard housing (Vance 2000, 321–322). The initial period after capture and before reaching camps was often difficult for lack of food and the difficulties of transportation to camps (Jones 2011, 42–44). The worst example was the death march of British and Indian troops taken by the Turks after the fall of Kut al-Amara in what is now Iraq. About one-third of the surrendered garrison died in captivity (Millar 1970, 280–285; Gilbert 1994, 247–248).

Lack of sufficient food to preserve health contributed to death rates in camps. The 1907 Hague Convention (IV) obligated captor states to feed their prisoners as well as their own troops. Although this obligation was broadly met, POWs often objected to the military diet of their captors. German soldiers, for example, objected to twice-weekly substitution of codfish for meat in French camps (Speed 1990, 69, 83, 100, 113). As the war progressed, food for everyone became scarcer as agricultural production dropped. In Germany, the British blockade reduced the civilian diet to near-starvation levels. The amount of meat and the overall quality of POW rations dropped as Germany hoarded what food it had for its own soldiers at the front (Jackson 1989, 106–112) German authorities directly compared the meager diet available to civilians to what should be fed to POWs, even those working hard labor (Jones 2011, 131). French, British, and U.S. prisoners in German and Austrian hands fared better than other nationalities, particularly Russians and Italians, because their home countries provided regular parcels of food, clothing, and other goods in short supply (Jackson 1989, 64–67; Speed 1990, 74–75; Jones 2011, 263–269).

Prisoners of war are often put to work by their captors, and the conditions of work for many POWs during World War I contributed to their deaths in captivity. Article 6 of the 1907 Hague Convention (IV) provided only general guidance on the work that POWs could do during captivity. "The tasks shall not be excessive and shall have no connection with the operations of the war" (Article 6, Annex to 1907 Hague Convention IV). But what sort of work qualified as part of "the operations of the war"? Total war created the demand for POW labor to fill just about every task in the war effort. Most able-bodied adult males were conscripted into the military, creating labor shortages which led to the mass employment of women in factories by all belligerents and the recruitment of colonial subjects and Chinese by Britain and France to work behind the Western Front (Stevenson 2004, 188–198). Not all POW work was dangerous, with agricultural work preferable for the better diet and less militarized supervision. The worst was mining or the construction of the Murmansk railway by the Russians. German and Austrian prisoners on the railway suffered from the extreme climate, rudimentary camps, inadequate food, and disease; more than one-third are estimated to have died in the effort to complete the railroad that would allow Russia to import war material through Murmansk (Gatrell 2005, 561–562).

The lack of clarity about what work was allowed and what not led to widespread abuses of POW labor. Germany began using Russian POWs for labor behind the Western Front during 1915. France sent 12,000 German POWs to its North African colonies to work on public works, including railroad construction, and the prisoners suffered heavily from malaria (Jones 2011, 110–115, 130–133). In reprisal, Germany sent 30,000 French and a lesser number of British prisoners to work behind the lines of the Eastern Front in difficult and dangerous conditions (Jones 2011, 136–144). This led to a string of tit-for-tat reprisals that ended with the British, French, and Germans using POWs to dig trenches, repair roads and railroads, and unload ammunition within artillery range of the front lines. Living conditions were appalling, shelter and sanitation were inadequate, and food was limited for those engaged in hard labor. The Germans and Austrians imposed the same physical discipline – flogging and tying to stakes – on POW labor that they did on their own soldiers.[6] Violence was often used to compel prisoners to work, particularly when they objected to work in the war effort or when they organized to stop work. All sides used the violations of the other to justify their own violations as reprisals to enforce the rules. Without clear lines about what sort of work was against the convention, governments and militaries bent the presumption that POW labor should not aid the war effort, ending in widespread use of POW labor in military construction within the shadow of the front line (Speed 1990, 89–91, 101–103, 118–119; Rachamimov 2002, 107–115; Kramer 2010, 77–82; Jones 2011, 169–175, 178–209, 225–248 on POW labor and labor camps).

One group of POWs – officers – fared better than others. In the 1907 Hague Convention (IV), officers were exempted from work and paid the same rate as officers in the captor army. They were separated from enlisted men in better quality quarters or different camps. Officers had access to canteens in which they could purchase food and other items that made their lives in captivity easier (Speed 1990, 83–91; Rachamimov 2002, 55–57, 98–103). The separation of officers from enlisted men and their superior treatment reflect treatment of them in earlier wars as gentlemen rather than prisoners. Officers were often paroled on the promise of not returning to fight or allowed to live freely in the captor country on their own means, whereas common soldiers were held in prison hulks or crowded, substandard housing (Barker 1975, 9–12; Vance 2000, 199–201). The different status of officers and enlisted men also reflected their different status in European armies at that time, a status that the demands of total war for mass conscription broke down.[7]

Several captor states treated different nationalities among their prisoners differently. France offered preferential treatment to German prisoners from Alsace-Lorraine, Schleswig-Holstein, and Prussian Poland and then punished prisoners from these nationalities who continued to state their loyalty to Germany (Kramer 2010, 79–80). Russia sought to encourage prisoners from the multiethnic Austro-Hungarian army to enlist in national units that would fight against the empire. The most successful and famous example was the Czechoslovak Legion of 40,000 which fought as part of the Russian Army in 1917. After the Bolshevik Revolution, the Czech National Committee arranged to ship the Legion to France to continue the fight. The outbreak of the Russian Civil War stranded it halfway across Russia on the Trans-Siberian Railway. The Legion eventually fought its way across Siberia. Even this success at recruiting enemy prisoners was limited; less than one-sixth of the estimated

---

[6] Germany stopped tying to stakes as military discipline of its own troops in 1917 (Watson 2008, 58).

[7] The erosion of the officer class is one of the main themes of the first great POW movie, *Grand Illusion*.

250,000 Czech and Slovak POWs taken by Russia joined the Legion (Vance 2000, 68–69). Efforts by Russia to recruit among the other nationalities of the Austro-Hungarian Empire met with little success. Not surprisingly, soldiers who survived combat to be taken prisoner were generally reluctant to leave captivity to return to combat (Rachamimov 2002, 115–122).

Behind the battle lines, states followed the rules broadly, subject to their gray areas. Lack of clarity led to tit-for-tat reprisals over the use of POW labor. Some of the warring states convened bilateral negotiations to resolve disagreements about how the rules should be interpreted. Britain and Germany concluded agreements in July 1917 and July 1918, including an exchange of disabled prisoners. The second of these agreements clarified issues of diet and accommodations for POWs. France and Germany reached agreements in December 1917 and April 1918. The United States and Germany concluded a similar agreement just as the war ended. The exchange agreements also allowed disabled prisoners to be interned in Switzerland if there was some possibility that they would heal sufficiently to rejoin the military if they were returned to their home country (Speed 1990, 15–42; Kramer 2010, 76–77). Despite these agreements, Germany continued to use POW labor within thirty kilometers of the front, a clear violation of the agreements. Pressure from the British and French governments induced Germany to substitute POWs of other nationalities and French civilian workers for British and French POWs working in this zone (Jones 2011, 182–186).

International monitoring of camp conditions also developed during the war. At first, states learned of the treatment of their men held prisoner through the reports of escaped and repatriated prisoners and mail from POWs. During the period of reprisals, Germany encouraged British and French POWs to write home about the severity of their treatment to create pressure from public opinion for change in how those countries treated German POWs (Jones 2011, 62, 63, 71, 156–161). The United States, Switzerland, the Netherlands, Denmark, and Spain served as Protecting Powers because they were neutral, with the United States ending its role on its entry into the war on April 6, 1917. The International Committee of the Red Cross (ICRC) began to take on the role of monitor of camps and POWs, beginning with the creation of the International POW Agency in Geneva. The Agency complied records of millions of POWs and civilian internees, each on his own index card; some of them are displayed in the International Red Cross and Red Crescent Museum in Geneva. It collected lists of prisoners taken from the warring nations and responded to requests from families about the status and whereabouts of their missing men. Although the ICRC did not have a recognized role in the 1907 Hague Convention (IV), it used its status as a coordinator of national Red Cross agencies to advocate for closer attention to the standards of the treaty and for inspections of camps by representatives of the Protecting Powers and officials of the national Red Cross agencies. As such visits to camps were conducted either by neutrals or nationals of the captor state, they were more acceptable to the captor authorities. The

ICRC took stands against reprisals but was unable to stop them. This was the beginning of the ICRC's role as the monitor for the POW regime (Durand and Boissier 1984, 31–82).

## On the Battlefield

Death rates reflect the treatment of those who reached prison camps and were recorded as POWs; they do not show what conditions were like on the battlefield for those trying to surrender. Official attitudes toward those who surrendered were often suspicious. Canadian military law mandated boards of inquiry for every man taken prisoner to judge whether he had fulfilled his duty before becoming a prisoner (Vance 1994, 26–27). The French High Command ordered that unwounded soldiers taken prisoner would be investigated for court martial (Jones 2011, 79, 328). Orders of "no quarter" and the killing of soldiers trying to surrender were banned by the 1907 Hague Convention (IV), yet both still occurred, even as late as the Battle of the Somme in 1916 (Griffith 1994, 72; Kramer 2007, 63). The Italian Supreme Commander, General Luigi Cadorna, threatened those who surrendered with "the summary justice of the bullet," and Italian authorities interned returning POWs after the war was over to interrogate them on the circumstances of their capture (Thompson 2008, 262, 364). France discriminated against repatriated POWs and the children of POWs who died in captivity after the war was over (Jones 2011, 327)

Perfidy and fear of it undermined the willingness to take prisoners:

> The enemy, having failed to turn our men out by fair means, attempted one of the many ruses peculiar to the children of "Kultur." A party of Germans advanced up a communication trench with their hands up in token of surrender. As they got nearer, we discovered that behind them were machine guns ready to fire on any of our men who might show themselves. This enterprising party met with a suitable reception (quoted in Gilbert 1994, 115).

Concerns about perfidy reached the highest levels of authority in some cases. First Lord of the Admiralty Winston Churchill noted on December 22, 1914 that "Sir John French had ordered 'instant fire' to be made on any German white flag on the Western Front, 'experience having shown that the Germans habitually and systematically abuse that emblem'" (quoted in Gilbert 1994, 117). Rumors also spread rapidly about atrocities by the other side against those who tried to surrender; the rumors were often amplified by government propaganda (Jones 2011, 73–79). The official attitudes against surrender, perfidy, and rumors of atrocities did not contribute to a climate on the battlefield conducive to humanity toward those who surrendered.

It is unclear how common such concerns were on the battlefield. Clearly, fear of perfidy or killing after signaling a desire to surrender did not stop large numbers of men successfully surrendering. Niall Ferguson argues that the fear of perfidy made soldiers unwilling to take prisoners (Ferguson 1999, 367–394).

Joanna Bourke contends that killing prisoners was widespread and motivated by military expediency (Bourke 1999, 182–183, 189). Some military training inculcated the fear of perfidy in U.S. soldiers (Doyle 2010, 161–163). Even in the last months of the war, when large numbers of German soldiers surrendered to the Allies, many German soldiers believed that the risk of being killed while trying to surrender were substantial; and the Allies distributed leaflets to reassure German soldiers that they would be treated well if they surrendered (Watson 2008, 219–221). Tim Cook reviews the difficulties of surrendering in the heat of combat in the Canadian experience with examples both of Germans being killed when they tried to surrender and of those that did surrender successfully (Cook 2006). The Canadians were noted as the shock troops of the British Army and had the reputation for not taking prisoners, nor being taken prisoner. But the Canadian Corps did capture 42,000 German soldiers during the war. In contrast, Alan Kramer concludes that the reports of no quarter and killing of those trying to surrender were exceptional precisely because they were recorded by the participants: "the best conclusion appears to be that such behavior [killing those trying to surrender] was episodic, not routine; opportunist, not systematic; with some well-documented cases and others more like apocryphal stories" (Kramer 2007, 64).

The experience of the 1907 Hague Convention (IV) in protecting POWs during World War I was mixed. All the major powers – except Italy – had ratified the Convention, signaling their willingness to live up to the vague standards of that treaty. And they did, with notable exceptions. Treatment of POWs during World War I are examples of how common acceptance of a norm leads to stronger reciprocity, which can produce either higher or lower compliance. Both sides responded in kind to acts of the other that they saw as breaches of the norm. The lack of clarity of those standards in practice led to disagreements about what was allowable, and reprisals after those disagreements caused the treatment of POWs to deteriorate.

## POWS IN WORLD WAR II

Treatment of POWs during World War II differed from that in World War I. The 1929 Geneva Convention improved the standard of treatment by clarifying key issues. When both sides ratified the Convention, treatment of POWs was better than during World War I. Two nations – Japan and the Soviet Union – rejected the standard of the 1929 Geneva Convention by not ratifying it; and – with these nations – the standard of treatment both on the battlefield and in the camps was much worse for them and their opponents. Furthermore, the dynamics of the battlefield for all cases showed the difficulty of controlling soldiers from killing enemies attempting to surrender. Because conduct was quite different on the various fronts of the war, this section considers each individually after comparing death rates in prison camps across all of them.

The 1929 Geneva Convention sought to address the holes in the POW regime induced by the 1907 Hague Convention (IV), but it was not completely successful. The work that POWs could be required to do was slightly clarified by specifying that detaining powers could not "employ prisoners in the manufacture or transport of arms or munitions of any kind, or on the transport of material destined for combatant units" nor force them to do "unhealthy or dangerous work." Procedures for prisoners to complain to the captor authorities about the conditions of their detentions were introduced. Punishments, particularly after unsuccessful escape attempts, were limited. The ICRC sought to move POW law from the realm of Hague law with its focus on limiting the ways wars are fought in favor of Geneva law which seeks to protect the victims of war. In essence, the ICRC sought to shift the conception of POWs from limiting violence during wartime to treating them as innocent victims of war. States resisted this move in part because they still saw reprisals as necessary for enforcement. One does not take reprisals against innocent victims. The ICRC also failed to achieve a recognized role as the monitor of the agreements as states preferred retaining Protecting Powers as the primary parties to represented their interests on behalf of their soldiers held prisoner by the enemy (Wylie 2010a; 2010b, 44–53).

## Death Rates in Camps

The Soviet Union did not take part in the negotiation of the 1929 Geneva Convention nor did it sign or ratify the treaty. Japan participated in the negotiations and signed the treaty at the end of the conference but did not ratify it. My theory expects that treatment of prisoners of war by Japan and the Soviet Union was likely to be the worst of all powers. Furthermore, the countries at war with those two are likely to have not upheld the standards of the conventions. Failure to ratify the treaty is a signal of intent to violate it, creating expectations of violations should war come. Even given a shared understanding that both sides intend to comply by joint ratification, compliance is not automatic. The practical problems posed by prisoners of war both on the battlefield and in the camps can frustrate the best intentions of the parties. The efforts of military authorities to train their soldiers in the rules and to enforce those rules when their soldiers break them are necessary for compliance. Failure to ratify, on the other hand, creates strategic dynamics that are likely to lead to mistreatment of POWs according to the terms of the conventions. Failure to ratify signals the intent to ignore the conventions in the effort to produce a battlefield where soldiers find it difficult to surrender.

Mutual ratification of the treaty predicts death rates and the mistreatment which kills prisoners. Table 5.2 shows the grim statistics of the numbers of prisoners taken during and after World War II and the percentages who died in captivity. The worst treatment of POWs was between Nazi Germany and the Soviet Union. Both sides used prisoners taken from one another as labor

TABLE 5.2 *Death rates of POWs in captivity during the World War II*

| Captor state | State of POWs | | Number of POWs taken | Number of POWs who died in captivity | Death rate of POWs in captivity |
|---|---|---|---|---|---|
| Germany | Soviet Union[a,b] | | 5,700,000 | 3,300,000 | 57% |
| Germany | United States | | 93,941[c] | 1,121 | 1.2% |
| | | | 96,048[d] | 1,368 | 1.4% |
| Germany | Commonwealth | | 235,473 | 9,348 | 4.0% |
| Germany | France after surrender[e] | | 1,580,000 | 49,200 | 3.1% |
| Germany | Italy after surrender[f] | | 640,000 | 30,000 | 4.7% |
| Japan | United States (not | | 23,281 | 8,288 | 35.6% |
| | including Filipino | | 132,134 | 35,756 | |
| | Scouts taken prisoner)[c] | | 33,587 | 12,526 | |
| Japan | Commonwealth | | 135,800 | | 28.6% |
| Soviet Union | Germany | high[b] | 3,155,000 | 1,185,000 | 37.6% |
| | | low[g] | 2,388,000 | 356,000 | 15% |
| Soviet Union | German Allies[a,g] | | 1,097,000 | 162,000 | 15% |
| Soviet Union | Japan after the war[a,g,h] | | 600,000 | 61,855 (low) 92,053 (high) | 10% |
| Commonwealth | Germany[i] | | 381,632 | | |
| United States | Germany during the war | | 378,898 | | |
| United States | Germany high[j] | | 3,193,747 | 56,285 | 1.8% |
| | after the official | | 3,193,747 | 15,285 | 0.5% |
| | war count[j] | | | | |
| Commonwealth and United States | Japan[k] | | 38,666 | | |

*Sources:* [a] Vance 2000, 329

[b] Bartov 1986, 153

[c] Bird 1992, 141–142; Navy and Marine casualties all treated as POWs of Japan

[d] Kochavi 2005, 303

[e] Fishman 1991, 229, 254

[f] Keefer 1992, 15

[g] Overy 1998, 297

[h] Igarashi 2005, 225

[i] Moore 1996, 19

[j] Bischof and Ambrose 1992, 79, 92

[k] Doyle 2010, 209

in their war effort and failed to provide sufficient food and lodging under the convention. Roughly 3 million Germans were taken prisoner by the Soviet Union; about one-third of them died in captivity. Five to six million Soviet soldiers were taken prisoner by the Nazis and about three out of five died in captivity (Barker 1975, 194; Bartov 1986, 153). These totals do not include men who were killed somewhere between the point of surrender and the formal collection points behind the lines. Anecdotal evidence suggests that the chance of being killed by one's captors on the Eastern Front was quite high (Bartov 1986).

Treatment between the Western Powers and Nazi Germany, on the other hand, generally upheld the convention. Both sides housed and fed prisoners at acceptable levels most of the time. Very few Germans or Italians held prisoner by the United States or Commonwealth powers died in captivity. Most POWs from the Western Powers held by the Germans survived the experience; only about 4 percent died in captivity (Barker 1975, 194; Bartov 1986, 154). Access to POWs and their camps by the Red Cross and protecting powers was generally observed, unlike in other camps. Occasional violations by one side were typically met with reciprocal treatment of prisoners held by the other.

## At the State Level and in the Camps

At the outbreak of war, Britain and Germany drew up regulations within their armies for the handling of prisoners. Both they and the United States relied on the 1929 Geneva Convention for the regulations used by their militaries and the information they distributed to their soldiers (Vourkoutiotis 2003, 26–29). German policy was under the control of the Army High Command (OKW) for most of the war, and it saw the Geneva Convention as being in the interest of its military role. The United States and Switzerland became the protecting powers for both sides. POW issues were not taken seriously during the "Phony War," in part because there were so few prisoners for either side to deal with. That changed with the surrender of tens of thousands of British soldiers at the end of the Dunkirk evacuation and in the following weeks as France fell to the Nazis. The disparate number of POWs held by Germany compared to Britain rendered reciprocity an ineffective tool to secure concessions. Germany allowed the delivery of Red Cross parcels from the Commonwealth nations to their men held as POWs; the food and clothing in these parcels made life in the camps more tolerable. Distribution of parcels in the early years of the war was limited by the disorganization of efforts in Britain to collect, pack, and transmit them to Germany for distribution. The British government faced strong criticism in Commons on behalf of the families of POWs for its failure to produce and deliver sufficient parcels (Kochavi 2005, 18–27). Because Britain held few Germans soldiers prisoner, it made little progress in efforts to exchange disabled and critically ill soldiers and protected personnel – doctors and diplomats. Germany insisted on one-for-one reciprocity, which was not acceptable to Britain who would have give-up its right to the return of all its men who were supposed to be exchanged under the 1929 Geneva Convention (Kochavi

2005, 111–116). The number of British soldiers held as prisoners swelled with those captured during the fall of Greece and Crete in the spring of 1941.

The Shackling Crisis was the most dramatic example of state-to-state reciprocity. On August 19, 1942, Canadian and British commandos conducted a large-scale raid on the port of Dieppe in France. The Germans recovered orders that directed Canadian troops to bind the hands of Germans they took prisoners. They threatened to chain the Canadians taken prisoner at Dieppe but did not do so after the British government mollified them with the claim that any such orders were rescinded. A subsequent commando raid on the island of Sark on October 3, 1942 took five German engineers prisoner and bound their hands. When the prisoners attempted to escape, four of them were shot and killed. The Germans discovered their bodies with their hands still tied, clear evidence that British commandos continued to tie prisoners. They quickly declared that 1,376 Canadian POWs taken at Dieppe would be shackled. Their hands were bound, which was more an inconvenience than punishment. The British government chose to retaliate by binding German POWs. As most POWs were held in Canada, there was some symmetry with German shackling of Canadian prisoners. Germany announced that it would then bind three times more British POWs, leading the British government to do the same. The proposed reprisal opened up differences between the British government in favor of it whereas the Dominion governments were more skeptical. The shackling also provided the prisoners of both sides with an opportunity to frustrate their guards by resisting the measure or untying themselves. Public opinion in Britain turned against the reprisal shackling, and the British government sought to negotiate an end to all shackling. Hitler, however, sought a positive declaration by the British government that its soldiers would no longer bind prisoners. Churchill was unwilling to make such a declaration as he believed that Hitler sought to restrict commando raids on Nazi-occupied Europe. Hitler had secretly ordered that commandos taken prisoner were to be killed, although the British did not learn of this order for another two years. On December 10, 1942, the British government gave into public opinion at home and opposition by the Dominion governments and announced that it would no longer shackle any POWs in the camps, ending its reprisal. Germany did not end its shackling of POWs until November 22, 1943 (MacKenzie 1995; Vance 1995; Kochavi 2005, 40–53; Wylie 2010b, 138–154 on the Shackling Crisis).

This sort of direct reprisal attracted public attention but had little consequence on the health of the prisoners. The other issues of exchanging disabled and severely ill POWs, however, had to wait until after the surrender of Panzer Army Africa in May 1943. The mass surrender in Tunisia brought in approximately 150,000 German POWs, leading to roughly equal numbers of POWs in the control of both sides (Kochavi 2005, 116). Germany became more interested in exchanges, with the first exchange of disabled POWs and protected personnel occurring during October 1943. Three more exchanges followed. These exchanges required negotiations over which soldiers qualified and the numbers involved. Presumably, disabled soldiers could not return to active service once exchanged, but exchanged medical personnel could (Kochavi 2005, 105–147; Wylie 2010b, 162–171).

Britain was also interested in exchanging long-term POWs. By 1944, some British soldiers had been prisoners for four years. The limited diet and strain of detention wore on the physical and mental health of long-term prisoners. These proposed exchanges drove a wedge between the United States and Britain. The United States had few men taken prisoner until after D-Day, meaning it had little to gain from an exchange of long-term prisoners. It was concerned that returned long-term German POWs would be returned to active service as Germany was running short of manpower in 1944. Even if repatriated German POWs were sent to the Eastern Front, their return posed a political issue with the Soviet Union. The U.S. Congress did not pose the same source of criticism of government policy toward POWs that the House of Commons did in Britain. The three-sided negotiations between London, Washington, and Berlin were not completed before the imminent collapse of Germany rendered them moot (Kochavi 2005, 148–168; Wylie 2010b, 243–248).

Monitoring the conditions under which POWs were held posed several problems. Many prisoners were not held in the large POW camps with barracks, but in smaller work camps or even in small detachments working on farms. Inspectors from the protecting powers and the ICRC visited the large POW camps regularly. Their reports led to formal interchanges between the warring governments concerning specific complaints of substandard treatment. Camp commanders and guards had ways of covering some of their worst abuses, particularly if they had advance notice of an inspection. Even with some ability to obscure serious issues, the inspection reports revealed unacceptable conditions in camps. The conditions for those POWs who lived outside the camps, such as on farms, were rarely – if ever – monitored. Although this allowed some German overseers of POW labor to abuse them, conditions for these POWs were generally better than those in large camps because of more exercise and a better diet. Those who worked in salt or coal mines faced the worst conditions overall. The monitoring system of the protecting powers and the ICRC worked because both sides allowed access to the camps and were willing to attempt to rectify substandard treatment (Vourkoutiotis 2003, 6–9, 165–183; Kochavi 2005, 3–4, 58–65, 75–102; Wylie 2010b, 171–175).

The killing of recaptured prisoners after their escape from Stalag Luft III in March 1944 showed how monitoring addresses noise and the deterioration of German conduct as the war turned against them. The mass escape, immortalized in the movie *The Great Escape*, was the largest in a series of escapes. Escaped prisoners posed a serious security problem for the Nazis because of the large number of foreign laborers in Germany. Although a majority of escapees overall were French, Polish, or Russian, Hitler chose to make an example out of the recaptured escapees from the Sagan camp. According to the popular book that made that escape "Great":

> "They [escapees in the Great Escape from Sagan POW camp] are all to be shot on recapture," he [Hitler] said flatly.
>
> As tactfully as he could, Goering protested – not, be it said, on grounds of humanity, but of practical politics.
>
> To shoot them all, he explained, would make it quite obvious that it was murder. Besides, there might be reprisals taken on German prisoners in Allied hands.
>
> Hitler apparently saw the logic of this.
>
> "In that case," he said, "more than half of them are to be shot" (Brickhill 1950, 209–210).

The 1929 Geneva Convention allowed the punishment of recaptured escapees with a short period of confinement. Prisoners attempting to escape or on the run were sometimes shot and killed in the effort to stop them; half of the fatalities among British POWs during the first half of 1943 were shot during escape attempts. Seventy-six prisoners broke out in the Great Escape on March 25; three of them reached neutral countries, and fifty of the recaptured escapees were killed. The Swiss official representing British interests in Berlin, Gabriel Naville, received the report of the death of forty-seven of the escapees during his visit to the camp on April 17. The camp commandant, Colonel Friedrich-Wilhelm von Lindeiner-Wildau, reported that the forty-seven had died resisting recapture. Discussions with senior British officers in the camp discredited the possibility that such a large proportion of the escapees could have been killed while trying to avoid recapture. Although Hitler backed off his demand that all recaptured escapees should be killed to disguise the killings, it did not fool the British government. Naville did not report the deaths to London until May along with his discussions with the other prisoners that cast doubt on the German claim that all fifty were killed resisting arrest (Kochavi 2005, 175–182; Wylie 2010b, 176–178, 218–222).

As the war turned against Germany, new problems arose. The Allied bombing campaigns took a heavy toll on German cities and killed tens of thousands of German civilians during the summer of 1943. Reichsfuhrer Heinrich Himmler declared that the German police should not interfere if civilians took out their rage on shot-down Allied airmen. This abandonment of their responsibility to protect those entitled to POW protection led to lynchings of shot-down aircrew. An estimated 700 to 800 Allied airmen were killed by German civilians (Schrijvers 1998, 254; Wylie 2010b, 234); this suggests that such killings were neither rare nor universal. Hitler ordered that only Allied airmen who had committed war crimes of their own, including those who attacked downed German pilots or hospitals, should be killed. At different times, the Nazis threatened to kill POWs in retaliation for Allied bombing of German cities, particularly after the firebombing of Dresden, but they did not do so directly. Nazi leaders encouraged lynching in part to avoid responsibility for themselves and any

possible reprisal against their own POWs. They could claim they had not broken the 1929 Geneva Convention. The former failed as one of the charges
against Foreign Minister Joachim von Ribbentrop at the Nuremberg trials
concerned his role in encouraging the lynching of downed Allied airmen (Foy
1984, 23–26, 37–43; Vourkoutiotis 2003, 187–119; Kochavi 2005, 171–175;
Wylie 2010b, 229–236, 255).

The German High Command controlled POWs and policy on them for most
of the war. Although Hitler occasionally interfered with direct orders, such as
the order to kill recaptured escapees after the Great Escape, he took little interest in POW affairs. He never visited a POW camp during the war (Kochavi
2005, 10). OKW lost complete control of the camps in October 1944 when the
SS gained authority over them. Hitler shifted command authority to the SS out
of fear of continued disruption in the Reich from escapes. Security was tight-
ened at the camps, but army officers retained an important role in running the
camps. Still, the shift of authority alarmed the British and U.S. governments.
The United States and Britain announced that POWs no longer had a duty to
escape their imprisonment as a result of the shift of control to the SS (Kochavi
2005, 186–189; Wylie 2010b, 232–234).

The combination of the killing of the Sagan escapees, the shift of control of
camps to the SS, the Western Allies finally learning of Hitler's order to kill all
commandos taken prisoner, and the approach of the defeat of Nazi Germany
raised concerns in the Western Allies that their soldiers held prisoner would
be killed or used as hostages at the end of the war. In October 1944, the
British government began to push for a joint declaration with the United
States and the Soviet Union that German officers would be held responsible in postwar trials for any deliberate killing of POWs. Long negotiations
between the three governments delayed a joint declaration until April 23,
1945 when leaflets were dropped over Germany with that declaration and
followed up with a radio broadcast the next day (Kochavi 2005, 188–201;
Wylie 2010b, 260).

Conditions for POWs held by the Germans declined dramatically with the
military decline of Germany in late 1944 and early 1945. Most Allied POWs
were held in camps in eastern Germany and Poland to make it more difficult
for escapees to reach the Allied front line. As the Soviet Army descended on
these regions, the Germans began forced marches of POWs westward. These
marches were horrific because of the winter weather and a lack of sufficient
food. Even within camps, the amount and quality of food provided declined,
and parcel deliveries became irregular. The last months of the war were the
most difficult for POWs held by Germany (Kochavi 2005, 203–221; Wylie
2010b, 237–248).

The Allied concern that their POWs would be killed at the end of the war
was misplaced, however. German officers wanted to surrender to the Western
Allies rather than the Soviets and did not therefore want to take any measure
that would alarm them. Gottlob Berger, the SS General placed in command

of the camps in October 1944, actually sought to protect Allied POWs in the last months of the war. Berger attempted to use the *Prominente*, POWs who were from prominent families such as British aristocrats, as hostages to secure his own surrender to the Western Allies, but he disobeyed Hitler's order to kill them. Gabriel Naville, the same Swiss diplomat who relayed the information about the killing of the Sagan escapees, saw no evidence that the Germans were preparing for a mass slaughter of Allied POWs (Kochavi 2005, 199, 201–202; Wylie 2010b, 248–264).

Treatment in U.S. and British camps was typically quite good (Springer 2010, 151–153). One German POW held in a camp in Canada titled his auto-biography *Thank You, Canada* (Priebe 1990). When problems in British camps were reported through inspections, OKW understood British violations arose from "the overzealous or irresponsible actions of the men on the spot rather than officials in Whitehall" (quoted in Wylie 2010b, 134). Treatment in POW camps in the United States provoked complaints from U.S. citizens and politi-cians that the Army was being too lenient on German POWs (Krammer 1979, 77–78; Foy 1984, 154–155).

Reciprocity posed a problem for the prosecution of crimes committed by pro-Nazi German POWs against anti-Nazi ones. Ardent Nazis among the pris-oners, particularly those from U-Boat crews and the Africa Korps, imposed discipline inside camps and encouraged the use of the Nazi salute. Camp com-manders typically worked through the leadership of the prisoners of the camp, which placed them in the awkward position of encouraging discipline imposed by pro-Nazi POWs. In the eyes of U.S. camp commanders, the Nazi POWs intimidated other prisoners who they considered to be anti-Nazi. In extreme cases, Nazi POWs held kangaroo courts and killed other prisoners who they considered to be traitors. U.S. authorities prosecuted the perpetrators of these murders and sentenced some of them to death. They did not carry out the death sentences until after the war was over out of concern that Germany would execute an identical number of U.S. POWs they held (Krammer 1979, 147–188; Doyle 2010, 223–224, but see Robin 1995, 34–42 for a more benign view of the use of Nazi discipline in POW camps).

In summary, both sides followed the 1929 Geneva Convention in the broad-est terms in the war in the west. It is notable that Nazi Germany, not a regime one typically thinks of as enlightened, generally lived up to its treaty obliga-tions to treat prisoners acceptably with respect to its Western opponents. The common and public acceptance of the 1929 Geneva Convention by both sides backed by reciprocity contributed to compliance with its standards. Vasilis Vourkoutiotis attributes the treaty to limiting the worst violations:

> What at first seems like simply a capricious policy of near-starvation with regard to American and British prisoners was, in fact, part of the general German pol-icy of avoiding as much of their treaty obligations as possible without provok-ing a direct reprisal against their own prisoners in British-American captivity (Vourkoutiotis 2003, 5).

Reciprocity, in this view, placed a floor under German poor treatment of Allied POWs. Neville Wylie, on the other hand, believes the 1929 Geneva Convention played a more positive role in helping parties comply and understand that the other side was as well.

> There was nothing incongruous, then, at a time when mortality among Soviet prisoners were running at more than sixty per cent, for officials in the OKW to feel fully bound by the POW convention in their dealings with British prisoners (Wylie 2010b, 82):

> What is perhaps more surprising, however, is the extent to which the rules set out in the 1929 POW convention actually constrained German behavior. Clearly the presence of neutral diplomats and inspectors inside Germany played an important part in this process by providing the system of oversight essential for the functioning of reciprocal relations.... It was, however, the very clarity of the convention's provisions that made it difficult for the German authorities, or British for that matter, to openly flout the agreed rules.... [T]he existence of the regulations required Berlin to adopt procedures and routines that proved remarkably resilient, despite radical changes in the environment.... Equally importantly, the convention provided the common language and set of understandings and expectations needed to promote dialogue between the two sides (Wylie 2010b, 272–273).

## On the Battlefield

The efforts to comply once soldiers became prisoners were matched by a general willingness of those at the front to take prisoners. The war in the North African desert was described as *The War without Hate* in a documentary produced by a German television network (Linderman 1997, 91). Although soldiers from both sides committed violations against enemy soldiers trying to surrender, these violations were not widespread. Wylie summarizes conditions on the battlefield: "Prisoners on both sides were occasionally shot out of hand, employed on war-related tasks, or ill-treated, but both sides recognized these incidents as exceptions, violations of accepted norms, rather than setting a new standard for the conduct of military operations" (Wylie 2010b, 72).

Even with a climate conducive to compliance, surrender to the enemy was not easy or risk-free. John Ellis claims that those surrendering at the front had a 50-50 chance of being killed then and there, although this estimate excludes the surrender of groups of soldiers (Ellis 1980, 318). The range of reasons why soldiers killed those who had surrendered or were trying to surrender ran the gamut from malice and revenge for fallen comrades to anger with the attitude of those who surrendered and the inconvenience of taking and guarding prisoners in exposed positions to callous weariness from being in combat too long (Linderman 1997, 109–114, 122–126; McManus 1998, 194). Social control, in the form of fellow soldiers, officers, and the command structure, did reign in some of the impulse to kill enemies who surrendered (Linderman 1997,

126–136). In the balance, killing of prisoners at the front happened, more often that we might think, but hundreds of thousands entered captivity alive. Many were taken prisoner, and we will never know how many were not.

Cultural factors, in the sense of military practices and beliefs, complicated the act of surrender. U.S. GIs learned to dispose of any captured German items before the moment of surrender. German soldiers assumed that a soldier with a German pistol had killed its original owner and so forfeited any protection of the law. Looting of the dead or of those captured violated the Geneva Convention. On the other hand, German army regulations dictated that soldiers could not surrender until they had fired all of their ammunition. German soldiers would continue to fire when under attack until their ammunition was gone and the attackers close. U.S. soldiers often failed to see why they should take someone prisoner who moments before was doing everything in his power to kill them until he was at risk. As one Canadian soldier put the matter concerning house-to-house combat, where combat was sudden and at close quarters: "Not many prisoners were taken, as if they did not surrender before we started on a house, they never had the opportunity afterwards" (quoted in Ellis 1980, 91). In both of these examples, beliefs about proper conduct on the battlefield – beliefs not common across the soldiers of the two sides – led to the killing of some trying to surrender (Linderman 1997, 108–114, McManus 1998, 192–194; Schrijvers 1998, 70, 76).

Retaliation for dead comrades motivated many killings of those trying to surrender. Blind rage at the recent death of a buddy (soldiers at the front do not have friends, only buddies) often led to revenge against the nearest defenseless German prisoner. For some men, the long, steady stress of combat and the toll of lost comrades produced a callous attitude toward killing enemy prisoners. In other cases, the retaliation was specific to enemy units believed to have recently killed U.S. soldiers who surrendered. As one soldier responded to a request to identify prisoners at the front to serve as stretcher bearers: "Haven't taken many lately. We're not fighting that kind of war *right now*" (quoted in Linderman 1997, 137, italics in original). Elite units of both sides, the U.S. airborne troops and SS troops in the German army, fought harder, took fewer prisoners, and were rarely taken prisoner. The killing of SS men and paratroopers was in part revenge for their reputation for not taking prisoners and in part because of their reputation for ferocity in combat (Linderman 1997, 119–121, 124–126, 136–139; McManus 1998, 186–189, 194–196; Schrijvers 1998, 73, 77–80; Kindsvatter 2003, 200–201)

Perfidy led to reciprocity in both directions; violations provoked retaliation, but generous treatment led to further goodwill. After an incident in which U.S. troops provided a German medical unit with gasoline to enable them to return to their own lines, a German soldier in the same unit alerted a U.S. medical jeep of a minefield up the road (Linderman 1997, 104–105). During the Battle of the Bulge, a German machine gunner fired on U.S. medical personnel trying to evacuate the wounded of both sides from the battlefield. In response, one soldier suggested using German prisoners as human shields to stop the fire and protect the medics. His commanding officer pointed out that this act would violate the Geneva Convention, provoking the reply "Geneva Convention shit, sir. What do you suppose that bastard over there is doing to the Geneva Conventions when he shoots at medics and wounded?" (quoted in Linderman 1997, 141). His lieutenant found his logic compelling. Violations of using a white flag to cover attacks also provoked responses of no prisoners taken (Linderman 1997, 103–112; Schrijvers 1998, 75–76).

Strategic expectations – what soldiers thought the enemy would do – determined how soldiers acted. When they believed they faced an enemy who would follow the Geneva Conventions, they were more willing to take prisoners and treat them kindly. When they believed the enemy would break the rules, they were less willing to take prisoners.

> Revenge seems justifiable when troops are regularly told that their enemy will not take them captive.... A Canadian intelligence officer reported that captured Germans understood that they would be executed and their first question was usually, "Will we be shot?" Because so many thought that the other side obeyed no rules, it seemed appropriate to reciprocate (Brode 1997, 221).

Many factors contributed to these strategic expectations: unit reputations, local conditions, and notorious atrocities. They often hardened with the experience of battle and knowledge of what the enemy had done. By November 1943, when U.S. troops had been on the line only a year, more than one-third of them claimed to know of examples of Germans abusing prisoners (Schrijvers 1998, 75–77). German soldiers, on the other hand, knew of good treatment of prisoners by the United States (McManus 1998, 198–200). Creating and sustaining a shared belief in following the rules was difficult. Although that belief broke down in some situations, it was often sustained.

Allied leaders tried to encourage a belief that the rules would be followed, both among their own troops but particularly in the armies of the enemy. Encouraging surrender saved soldiers' lives. U.S. officials had a calculation of how many GIs lives were lost per 25,000 German prisoners (Kochavi 2005, 165). Italian soldiers during the Sicily campaign asked U.S. troops to come and take them prisoner (Schrijvers 1998, 51–52); encouraging surrender by German soldiers could reduce losses and end the war earlier. Operation Sauerkraut dropped leaflets on the Italian front for ten months to encourage German soldiers to surrender (Doyle 2010, 190). General Eisenhower, the Supreme Commander in Europe, dropped millions of safe passes over German lines in 1945 promising proper treatment under the Geneva Convention and reported to Congress that it was "causing a considerable number to surrender" (quoted in Krammer 1979, 256). Churchill threatened that Germans continuing to fight after the official end of hostilities would lose the protection of the laws of war. Some Germans were prosecuted after the war for continuing to fight (Barker 1975, 26).

In balance, the rules often held on the battlefield despite the complications described earlier. Hundreds of thousands surrendered, entered captivity, and survived the war on both sides. Sustaining a common belief that rules would be followed was not easy, and it did often break down. The full consequences of these failures are incalculable. Conduct between the Germans and the Western Allies showed that the law on prisoners of war improves conditions on the battlefield, but that perfection does not occur even when both sides seek to follow the rules. Individual soldiers commit violations, and compliance with the law is measured not in those failures but in the many successes.

THE EASTERN FRONT

The war on the Eastern Front between Nazi Germany and the Soviet Union was brutal in every way imaginable. The Nazi armies killed millions of Soviet citizens, and the descent of the Red Army on eastern Germany in 1945, with mass rapes, looting, and wanton destruction and killing, is often compared to that of the Huns on the Roman Empire. The Soviet Union had neither signed nor ratified the 1929 Geneva Convention, and Hitler used its refusal as a justification of the Nazis ignoring the standards of that treaty on the Eastern Front. Harsh and inadequate camp conditions led to high death rates among those prisoners who reached one. Summary execution of those trying to surrender was common on the battlefield. The knowledge of the likely fate of those who surrendered led soldiers on both sides to fight to the death and refuse to take prisoners. The leadership of both sides adopted policies to punish those who surrendered. Out of the 9 million soldiers of all armies taken prisoner on the Eastern Front, 4 million died in captivity (Overmans 2010, 127).

**Between Totalitarian Governments**

The Soviet Union did not sign nor ratify the 1929 Geneva Convention perhaps because it considered inspection of POW camps to open an avenue to spying. It justified its non-ratification on the basis that the Convention called for the racial segregation of prisoners which violated the Soviet Constitution. In contrast, it ratified the 1929 Geneva Convention for the Amelioration of the Condition of the Wounded and Sick in Armies in the Field, which did not call for inspections behind the line. The Soviet government had renounced most of the treaties ratified by the Tsarist government before the Revolution. The Soviet Union did recognize that it would observe 1907 Hague Conventions as one of the few Tsarist treaties that it did accept (Bellamy 2007, 20–21; Overmans 2010, 127).

Nazi Germany, on the other hand, had ratified the 1929 Geneva Convention, but Hitler had no intention of following its standards during the war in the East. On March 30, 1941, he gave his infamous "War of Extermination" speech to his military leaders that the upcoming war with the Soviet Union would be different from the other wars they had fought. Hitler ordered that commissars attached to Soviet military units were to be executed on capture by regular soldiers. Soldiers taking Soviet prisoners were to hand them over to the Special Detachments (Sonderkommandos) of the Security Service (SD), who would separate them into favored nationalities – Baltics, Finns, Ukrainians and ethnic Germans – to be released, Russians to be imprisoned, and those to be killed, in particular Jews and communists. There was some resistance from the military intelligence service (*Abwehr*) after the war began, but it was brushed aside. Although the army published its own orders for the proper treatment of Soviet prisoners, these were overruled by the central army command (OKW). The contrast with the Western Front is clear; Hitler interfered little with Army policy and control of POWs there but directly controlled policy on the Eastern Front (Bellamy 2007, 24–27; Overmans 2010, 132–134).

Shortly after the German surprise attack on June 22, 1941, the Soviet Union communicated its willingness to follow the standards of the 1907 Hague Conventions through the Swedish and Japanese governments. Hitler brushed aside these overtures, claiming Soviet violations of the laws of war from the onset of fighting. Neither side seemed seriously interested in these efforts. The Soviet Union did not take the formal step of accepting the applicability of the Hague Conventions by filing a note with the Dutch government. That would have created a public signal of intent to comply, unlike the communications it made through private diplomatic channels. The latter can be denied afterward (Streim 1997; Overmans 2010, 128–129).

The steps taken by both sides that appear to seek to comply with the treaty standards sought only propaganda advantages with others. The ICRC sought to create the regular institutions of the compilation and exchange of lists of prisoners, camp inspections, and relief parcels. The Soviet Union created a prisoner bureau at the request of the ICRC but then did not collect any names. Germany submitted one list of 300 names of Soviet soldiers taken prisoner. Both sides blocked ICRC inspections of camps, with the Soviet Union failing to accept any ICRC representative. Neither country provided relief packages for their soldiers held prisoners and blocked most relief efforts from other countries to those they held prisoner (ICRC 1948, 1:404–437, 3:53–62; Durand and Boissier 1984, 503–521; Overmans 2010, 129). At the state level, neither side was interested in protecting the rights of enemy soldiers taken prisoner.

### In the Camps

As mentioned earlier, German orders for the treatment of Soviet soldiers specified that "undesirable" prisoners would be killed outright after being separated from other prisoners. These executions account for at most 200,000 of the millions of Soviet soldiers who died during the war after surrendering (Overmans 2010, 134). The remainder died in the camps. Germany took vast numbers of Soviet soldiers prisoner in the opening months of the invasion. Massive encirclements at Bialystok, Minsk, Smolensk, Uman, Kiev, Briansk, and Vyazma each captured hundreds of thousands of Soviet soldiers, and many others surrendered in smaller groups. These men were herded into barbed wire enclosures close to the front without food, shelter, water, or sanitation or force marched to camps in the rear. Starvation, exposure, and then epidemics killed more than a million. Although the numbers taking prisoner vastly exceeded what the German Army expected, it made no real effort to accommodate the influx (Bellamy 2007, 22–23). Prisoners were forced to eat tree bark and grass; Reichsmarschall Goering joked about their condition to Count Ciano, the Italian Foreign Minister: "… after having eaten everything possible, including the soles of their boots, they have begun to eat each other and, what is more serious, have eaten a German sentry" (quoted in Clark 1965, 207). Christian Streit estimates that close to two-thirds of the prisoners taken by the Nazis during 1941 were dead by early 1942 (Streit 2000, 80–84; Mawdsley 2005, 102–104; Overmans 2010, 134–137).

Self-interest changed Nazi policy toward Soviet prisoners. By late 1941, it was clear that the Soviet Union would not be defeated quickly. Labor shortages were a critical issue for war production in Germany as many able-bodied men were in the military. By February 1942, the Nazi leadership decided to improve the conditions of Soviet prisoners to exploit their labor in mining, construction, and agriculture. Some were even used as laborers in the death camps. Although diet and living conditions of prisoners were raised, the "improved" conditions were those of concentration camp prisoners, enough to keep them alive to work. Food rations were not raised to the level of the German civilian population or Western prisoners until near the end of the war. Death rates remained high among Soviet prisoners, higher than among prisoners from the Western powers (MacKenzie 1994, 509–510; Streit 2000, 87–89; Mawdsley 2005, 104–105; Overmans 2010, 135–137).

The Germans also recruited Soviet prisoners into their military effort. Initially, these efforts were directed at nationalities favored under the initial orders for the treatment of Soviet soldiers taken prisoner. As with the improved treatment for prisoners, efforts to recruit more POWs into the German Army expanded in late 1941 and early 1942. Non-Russian nationalities, such as those from the Caucasus and Central Asia, were singled out because the Nazis believed they were less loyal to the Communist system. Some of these soldiers were added to combat units, particularly anti-partisan units, but most were put in transportation or construction units to work on roads, airfields, and fortifications behind the front line. For many prisoners, regular meals and a way out of the camps or forced labor was enough incentive to join. As the commander of the German Ninth Army put the matter: "No prisoners at all would make their way to service in the German Wehrmacht for intellectual reasons; the reason why they will be ready is terror of the prison camps, and the prospect of a better life with the German troops" (quoted in Bellamy 2007, 337). As many as a million Soviet prisoners joined the German army during the war (Overy 1998, 126–130; Mawdsley 2005, 229–230).

The Soviets took few Germans soldiers prisoner before Stalingrad. It is suspected that most German soldiers who attempted to surrender in the first year of the war were executed on the battlefield. The surrender of the Sixth Army at Stalingrad in early 1943 created the first large number of German soldiers held prisoner, 91,000. They were marched off in the depth of the Russian winter to collection camps behind the lines and later sent off to points around the Soviet Union, packed into boxcars without food, water, or sanitation. Half of them were dead by spring. As the war turned, the Red Army began to surround and capture large numbers of German soldiers. Conditions in the camps were comparable to the Gulag prison camps, enough to sustain life so that the prisoners could continue to work. Soviet policy and internal orders on the treatment of prisoners laid out the goal of humane treatment, but the resources were not made available to ensure the health of the prisoners. Furthermore, the Soviet leadership viewed POWs as another source of forced labor to be deployed in the remote and difficult areas of the country where others would not work willingly. The NKVD (abbreviated from the Russian spelling of People's Commissariat for Internal Affairs, the internal security service of the Soviet Union at the time) ran the prison camps; tellingly, Minister of Internal Affairs Lavrenti Beria threatened to transfer those prisons to the control of the Gulag system if the treatment of prisoners did not improve. Death rates were higher than for either side in the war in the west, but not as bad as those in German camps holding Soviet POWs. More than one-half of the Italian prisoners taken by the Red Army died in captivity, a sign of the initial lack of resources available to house and feed prisoners when large numbers were taken for the first time in and near Stalingrad (Barker 1975, 104–106; Beevor 1998, 406–417, 420–431; Overy 1998, 297–299; Hilger 2005, 61–65; Mawdsley 2005, 237–240; Bellamy 2007, 27–30).

To the extent that either side cared about the condition of prisoners in their camps, that concern was driven solely by the desire to exploit the men held there as slave labor.


## On the Battlefield

Large numbers of Soviet soldiers surrendered readily in the first month of the war. Some of them hated Stalin's regime and had no interest in fighting for it, whereas others found themselves in impossible military positions, cut off by fast-moving German formations. German conduct on the battlefield and in the camps ended the mass surrenders. The order to kill commissars was enforced from the first day of the war, but German soldiers were also killing many Soviet soldiers at the front after they surrendered. German divisional commanders in the first weeks of the war issued orders for their men to stop killing ordinary Soviet soldiers, suggesting such killings were a problem from the beginning

(Bartov 1986; Boll and Safran 2000, 243–245). Rumors of the mistreatment in German POW camps and the mass deaths there steeled the resolve of Soviet soldiers. A Soviet colonel interviewed by Alexander Werth during the siege of Sevastopol in 1942 stated:

> Not every man in our army is a hero. So let him die, rather than surrender.... Listen, this is a terrible war, more terrible than anything you have seen. It's an agonizing thought that our prisoners are starved to death in German camps. But, politically, the Germans are making a colossal blunder. If the Germans treated our prisoners well, it would soon be known. It's a horrible thing to say; but by ill-treating and starving our prisoners to death, the Germans are *helping* us (quoted in Werth 1964, 422, italics in original text).

Surrounded Soviet soldiers no longer surrendered en masse; instead, they disappeared into the woods and wastes of Russia to join partisan groups. The Germans saw the change in the willingness of Soviet soldiers to surrender:

> In February 1942 the 18th Panzer admitted that "Red Army soldiers ... are more afraid of falling prisoner than of the possibility of dying on the battlefield," and maintained that this was manifested by the fact that "since November last year ... only a few deserters have come over to us and that during the battles fierce resistance was put up and only a few POWs were taken" (Bartov 1991, 87).

More Soviet soldiers surrendered during the first six months of fighting than the remaining forty months (Bartov 1986, 118; Bartov 1991, 84–89; Fritz 1995, 51–58; Overy 1998, 147; Bellamy 2007, 21–23).

As mentioned earlier, few German soldiers were taken prisoner until the surrender of the Sixth Army at Stalingrad. Soviet soldiers retaliated brutally against those who tried to surrender, mutilating corpses in some cases. Furthermore, German soldiers believed their own crimes against Russians who tried to surrender would rebound against them in turn. After watching the SS kill 300 Soviet prisoners, one soldier observed:

> It was already clear to us that it would have repercussions. That our prisoners [in Russian hands] would be treated in the same way (quoted in Fritz 1995, 57).

Once formed, these expectations did not change. During the battle of the Korsun Pocket at which Soviet forces surrounded approximately 50,000 Germans, the Russian commander sent a delegation to offer the German commander favorable terms if he surrendered. The terms were communicated in letters signed by three of the highest Soviet commanders of the war, Zhukov, Konev, and Vatutin. The German commanders rejected the terms, although the staff officer who met the Soviet delegation did offer a toast to his counterpart delivering the offer (Zetterling and Frankson 2008, 1–3). One young Alsatian sent to the Russian Front (Alsatians were drafted into the German Army after Hitler annexed Alsace-Lorraine after the fall of France) put the matter bluntly: "Surrender was never an option. We knew what they did to Germans they captured" (quoted in Kladstrup and Kladstrup 2001, 133; Bartov 1991, 34–36;

Fritz 1995, 47; Overy 1998, 123; Mawdsley 2005, 237; Bellamy 2007, 28–30 for remainder of paragraph).

We will never know precisely how many men were killed on the Eastern Front in the act of trying to surrender. Omar Bartov estimates that 600,000 Soviet soldiers were summarily executed after surrendering during 1941 (Bartov 1991, 83). Those killed on the battlefield do not enter into the statistics as prisoners of war. Sometimes the statistics give us a glimpse at the magnitude of the killing. After the war, Soviet Foreign Minister Molotov claimed that the Soviet Union had repatriated 1 million German prisoners and held another 900,000, with 356,000 dying in captivity. German sources claimed that 3 to 4 million German soldiers were still missing, implying that an additional million or more had been captured and then died in Soviet hands. Table 5.2 reflects this difference in the high and low estimate of Germans held by the Soviet Union as some sources continue to report the higher figures. When the Soviet archives were opened after the end of the Cold War, Molotov was proved to have been telling the truth for once. This difference implies that approximately 1 million or more German soldiers were missing on the Eastern Front; that is, missing from German army rolls yet never registered as captured by the Soviet Union. Not all of these men were killed on the battlefield, of course, as soldiers become Missing in Action (MIA) for many reasons, including desertion and being killed in a way that does not allow for a report of their death. But this figure is surely expanded by the killing of those trying to surrender; the U.S. Army, in contrast, reported only 23,514 MIA for the European theater of World War II (Clodfelter 2002, 587). Even if only a fraction of the million German MIAs were killed while trying to surrender, hundreds of thousands died that way. To be careful, this conclusion is a surmise from the figures we have (Overy 1998, 297; Mawdsley 2005, 238–239 defends the higher figures for Germans captured by the Soviets).

The efforts that both Nazi Germany and the Soviet Union undertook to discourage their own soldiers from surrendering are not a matter of speculation, however. Both sides played up the violations of the other and the instruments of military discipline to force their soldiers to fight rather than surrender. The Nazis created a war crimes unit that documented and publicized violations committed by Soviet troops (De Zayas 1989). Soviet executions of Germans who surrendered were publicized to discourage others from surrendering and justify bad treatment of surrendered Soviet soldiers. This propaganda played on historical memories of poor treatment of German POWs by Russia during and after World War I. The war ground down the numbers and morale of the Wehrmacht. German officers turned to summary executions to encourage their men to continue fighting rather than desert or surrender. Stephen Fritz estimates that 20,000 soldiers were summarily executed by their own officers on the Eastern Front (Fritz 1995, 90), but Bartov puts the number at 13,000 to 15,000 (Bartov 1991, 96). In contrast, the U.S. Army executed only 102 men for all crimes and only one for desertion during World War II (see Ellis 1980, 243–246 on desertion and its handling in the U.S. and British armies).[8] "Disciplinary" battalions of those thought to lower morale were given the most dangerous tasks on the battlefield, such as clearing minefields. Hitler authorized and encouraged the use of the most severe discipline, including summary executions, at the front. But discipline was focused on forcing the troops to fight, not controlling their own violations. When the army did convict an officer of mistreatment of POWs, Hitler quashed the verdicts and released the officers in question (Streim 1997, 307–308). Nazi policy focused on ensuring that German soldiers fought regardless of the circumstances by making surrender difficult, playing up the atrocities of Soviet soldiers, and using the mechanisms of military discipline only against those who did not fight (Bartov 1991, 61, 77–79, 95–105; Fritz 1995, 89–97; Overmans 2010, 130–131).

The Soviet Union used the full range of levers to get its soldiers to fight rather than surrender. Red Army propaganda used Nazi crimes to incite raw hatred of the Germans. Stalin originally urged the killing of all Germans in all conditions in August 1941, although he backed off this position publicly in February 1942. The Soviet military code prescribed death by firing squad for "premeditated surrender." The disorder after the surprise attack led to the first use of "blocking detachments," soldiers – often from NKVD divisions – delegated to shoot deserters from the front. In August 1941, Stalin issued Order 270 which labeled all Soviet soldiers who surrendered as "traitors to the motherland" and authorized the imprisonment of their families. Stalin's daughter-in-law was sent to the Gulag under Order 270 after his son was captured. Stalin refused a German offer to exchange him, and he was later shot by a camp guard when he deliberately walked into a forbidden zone in his POW camp. Order 227 in July 1942 strengthened these measures by threatening death sentences to those who retreated without orders to do so. It is estimated that the Red Army executed at least 158,000 of its own soldiers during the war (Mawdsley 2005, 215). *Shraftbaty*, penal battalions, were formed out of those suspected of cowardice or desertion. With manpower short, the Red Army could not afford to execute them, but they could force them to lead suicidal assaults on German positions. If one in the *shraftbaty* was wounded, he could rejoin a regular unit, having "[a]toned [for his cowardice] with his own blood" (Overy 1998, 160). The number of men assigned to the penal battalions increased during the war. Like the Nazis, the Communists used all measures possible to force their men, and some women, to fight. Both sides wanted and got a battlefield on which no quarter was offered or expected (Overy 1998, 80–81, 158–164, 213, 301; Mawdsley 2005, 167–169, 215–217; Polian 2005, 124–128; Bellamy 2007, 20–31, 203–205, 260, 477–478).

Chris Bellamy accurately summarizes the conduct of both sides on the Eastern Front:

> Reciprocity is crucial, and it was so in the Great Patriotic War. Horrific brutality by one side was met by horrific brutality on the other (Bellamy 2007, 30).

---

[8] For contrast, during World War I, Germany executed 48 soldiers and Britain executed 346.

One German soldier described the dynamics exactly after seeing German corpses mutilated by Soviet soldiers: "Unfortunately it was really like that: what you do to me, I do to you" (quoted in Bartov 1991, 184). Law is powerless in the face of those who want lawlessness.

## THE WAR IN THE PACIFIC: NO GAME OF CRICKET

In *The Bridge over the River Kwai*, Colonel Saito, the Japanese commander, answers the demands of Lt. Colonel Nicholson that he follow the rules of the Geneva Convention: "You will not speak to me of rules. This is war! This is not a game of cricket." Japan signed but did not ratify the 1929 Geneva Convention. The Western powers arrayed against her had ratified the treaty. Behind the lines, Japanese treatment of prisoners was abusive; more than one-quarter of those they held died in captivity. The POW camps of the Allies met the standards of the 1929 Geneva Convention, but few Japanese were taken prisoner until the end of the war was in sight. Furthermore, the Allied countries found it difficult to determine which of their men were prisoners and the conditions under which they were held. On the battlefield, the soldiers of both sides regularly killed those who might have surrendered. Japanese perfidy reinforced the willingness of Allied soldiers to kill all Japanese on the battlefield. Japanese army policy strongly discouraged surrender, and strong social pressures were used to enforce those rules. Additionally, most Japanese soldiers expected to be tortured to death if they surrendered. The battlefields of the South Pacific and East Asia were brutal, perhaps even more brutal than those of the Eastern Front in Europe.

### Between the Warring Parties

After the Japanese attacks at Pearl Harbor and throughout Southeast Asia, the ICRC, the United States, Canada, and Britain asked the Japanese government if it would honor the terms of the 1929 Geneva Convention. The Japanese government replied:

> Since the Japanese government has not ratified the Convention relating to the treatment of prisoners of war, signed in Geneva on July 27, 1929, it is not in fact bound by the said Convention. Nevertheless, as far as is possible, it intends to apply the Convention, *mutatis mutandis*, to all prisoners falling into its hands, while at the same time respecting the customs of each nation and people in relation to the food and clothing of prisoners (quoted in Durand and Boissier 1984, 521, italics in original).

This reply reflects the two realities of Japanese policy on POWs; Japan would apply its own customs to enemy soldiers taken prisoner, and its central authorities were evasive about the actions of their military and their responsibility for those actions. Japan had not ratified the 1929 Geneva Convention because it conflicted with the views of the military concerning POWs at that time; that is, Japanese leaders feared that the Convention would impose a unilateral obligation on Japan because Japanese soldiers would never surrender (Fujita 2000, 99; Kibata 2000, 140–141; Straus 2003, 21–22). Philip Towle summarizes the Japanese attitude toward the men they took prisoner:

> Japanese military doctrine suggested that POWs were both despicable and responsible for their own fate. They should not have surrendered and, if they survived subsequently, this was due to the generosity of their captors. They expected the POWs in their hands to appreciate this generosity (Towle, Kosuge, and Kibata 2000, xv).

The list of abuses in Japanese POW camps is extensive and gruesome. To save the reader's stomach, I will not dwell on the gruesome cases. The Bataan Death March in 1942 was the most infamous atrocity committed by Japanese forces on men who were prisoners, but there were many more. Diet was substandard to sustain the health of Westerners accustomed to more calories and meat than was provided in the camps. Most liberated prisoners in 1945 were skeletal because of their loss of weight during captivity. Many also suffered and died from nutritional deficiencies such as scurvy, pellagra, and beri-beri. Guards routinely executed escapees who were caught; almost all escapees were caught because Westerners were easily identified among the Asian populations under occupation. Some camp commandants punished other prisoners, including some executions, after escape attempts. Many prisoners were used as forced labor, particularly on the Burma-Thailand railway. Backbreaking labor, insufficient diet, extreme conditions, and brutal punishments by guards and supervisors led to the deaths of about one-fifth of all prisoners who worked on the railway, although treatment was not universally bad, depending on the local commander. The movie *The Bridge on the River Kwai* sanitized Japanese treatment of those who worked on the railway, including large number of Asian civilians pressed into forced labor, one-half of whom died during its construction (Flower 1996; Kinvig 2000). As mentioned in the anecdote at the beginning of this book, the Japanese also executed Allied airmen as war criminals. This is a partial and restrained list of the abuse of prisoners by the Japanese (Garrett 1981, 184–201; Vance 1994, 191–194, 206–207; Waterford 1994, 178–181, 236–245; Vance 2000, 36–37; see Daws 1994 for gruesome stories).

Japan blocked the activities of the ICRC. It rarely provided lists of men taken prisoner, only occasionally forwarding numbers of prisoners. This step made communication between POWs and their families difficult. Most requests to inspect camps were denied, and when the ICRC was allowed to visit a POW camp, Japanese authorities improved camp conditions solely for the visit. ICRC representatives were not allowed to interview prisoners without one of the camp authorities present. Camp commandants retaliated against prisoners who complained about camp conditions during ICRC visits. Afterward, the Japanese government censored ICRC reports when they did allow camp inspections. It also blocked efforts by the ICRC to send relief packages to the POWs they held, with only a trickle getting through (ICRC 1948, 1:229, 437–509; Durand and Boissier 1984, 521–537; Vance 1994, 183–138).

The difficulties of determining the treatment of Allied POWs complicated the responses of their home governments. Because Japan controlled inspections by the ICRC, those reports did not reveal camp conditions or other atrocities. Reports did trickle out from Asian eyewitnesses and the rare successful escapee, so that the story of Japanese atrocities against prisoners and the wounded when Hong Kong fell reached British and Canadian newspapers about three months later. The Canadian government was reluctant to respond to these reports out of the fear that Japan would further punish Canadians held prisoner if it pressed Japan on its misconduct. Reciprocity was one tool open to it. Similarly, the British government was reluctant to publicize the details of Japanese treatment of POWs during the war out of fear of the consequences for POWs still held. The Canadian government recognized reciprocity between Japanese internees in Canada and Canadian POWs held by Japan on January 14, 1942. It used the threat of withholding lists of Japanese nationals it interned to extract a list of all Canadian POWs held by Japan, but the threat took more than a year to extract that list. Later in the war, the Canadian government responded to public pressure on behalf of their men held prisoner by publicizing the deceptive ICRC reports of camp conditions, in the hope of allaying concern (Garrett 1981, 186–187; Vance 1994, 185–191).

The abuse of prisoners was not centrally directed by the Japanese government. It publicly held to the position that it would treat POWs properly subject to its own judgment and military codes of "proper treatment." The formal orders for the treatment of prisoners issued in April 1942 drew on the codes used during the Russo-Japanese War when Japan's treatment of Russian prisoners was exemplary. But neither the resources needed to provide adequate conditions nor the supervision to ensure that local commanders followed those instructions was provided. In practice, conditions depended on local, often low-level, commanders and guards in charge of camps. Some were brutal, whereas others were merely strict. Occasionally, some commandants and guards were generous and humane. Camp guards were recruited from those the army considered would make poor front-line troops, including Koreans and drunkards (Flower 1996, 236–239; Towle 2000, 12). The harsh military discipline and contempt of those who surrendered shaped the attitudes of local commanders and guards toward their prisoners. The lack of central control allowed abuses to foster and fester. One Korean guard explained his training during his trial after the war, "it was not actually taught at the school that we could beat prisoners of war, but we were told that we should not be too soft with them as otherwise they would not respect us" (Flower 1996, 238). Publicly, however, the government of Japan tried to retain a proper image. During the Shackling Crisis, Japan refused German requests to shackle prisoners because that reprisal would be public and open it up to retaliation by the British. The Japanese government claimed that it treated POWs humanely to its own people and played up violations by the Allied powers (Kosuge 2000, 159). Appearances of propriety mattered more to Japan than humane treatment of those they held (Waterford 1994, 36–37, 353–358; MacKenzie 1995, 88; Towle, Kosuge, and Kibata 2000, xvii on the central orders of Japanese authorities and their disconnect with actual treatment).

Noise also contributed to the deaths of POWs in transit. As the war progressed, Japan sought to move prisoners from camps in Southeast Asia to others closer to the home islands of Japan to use them as slave labor in the war effort. The men to be transferred were packed by the thousands into the hulls of merchant ships. Many, already weakened by their detention, succumbed to the unsanitary conditions of these ships. At least nineteen of these ships were sunk by U.S. submarines or aircraft conducting anti-shipping patrols in the sea lanes between Southeast Asia and Japan. Of course, the submarine captains and aircrew did not know the unfortunate cargo of prisoners these ships carried when they attacked them. The Allied powers rejected a proposal by the ICRC to publicize sailings of vessels carrying POWs out of a concern that Japan would exploit the opportunity to provide cover for other merchant shipping. It is estimated that 22,000 POWs died in the sinkings of these prison ships (Garrett 1981, 197; Waterford 1994, 149–170; Vance 2000, 294–295).

Allied POWs camps in New Zealand, Australia, Hawaii, the South Pacific, and the mainland of the United States met the standards of the 1929 Geneva Convention. Few Japanese prisoners died in captivity, with the mass escape attempt at Camps Cowra in Australia and the riot at Camp Featherston in New Zealand being the prime causes of deaths. The ICRC regularly inspected camps, and the Allied governments provided lists of prisoners they held, subject to the limit that many Japanese soldiers refused to provide their names to their captors (Hata 1996, 270; Vance 2000, 64–65, 97–8; Straus 2003, 176–225; Doyle 2010, 214–215).

## On the Battlefield

But few Japanese soldiers were taken prisoner. This is surprising given the conditions of island combat common in the Pacific theater. Once the U.S. forces decided to invade a small island, the defenders could not evacuate; death or surrender was the only option. (The larger islands, such as the Philippines, offered the chance for defenders to disappear into the jungle.) Some committed suicide, including some grievously wounded soldiers blowing themselves up with hand grenades. Many others died in banzai charges – pointless, mass attacks on U.S. positions – rather than surrender when further resistance was futile. Others simply stayed in their fortified positions while U.S. forces either entombed them with explosives or killed them with flamethrowers. More than one-half of Japanese taken prisoner were sailors plucked from the ocean where they could not kill themselves, only one-third surrendered willingly (Straus 2003, 46; Springer 2010, 149). Furthermore, U.S. soldiers and marines routinely killed all Japanese wounded they found on the battlefield, reducing the number of incapacitated men taken prisoner (Ellis 1980,78; Dower 1986, 45–46; Bergerud 1996, 131, 408–425; Linderman 1997, 143–184; McManus 1998, 175; Schrijvers 2010, 177–179).

Outrage at Japanese perfidy and atrocities motivated the murderous rage of U.S. soldiers on the battlefield. Japanese soldiers routinely fired on U.S. medics and hospitals. The contrast with the war against the Germans is striking; medics in Europe occasionally armed themselves, whereas those in the Pacific did so routinely. When clearing a battlefield, Japanese soldiers who seemed dead would spring up to attack U.S. personnel off guard. Even the most grievously wounded would attempt to take a U.S. soldier or medic with them by detonating a grenade when approached closely. White flags and offers to surrender were used as ruses to get U.S. marines and soldiers to expose themselves to Japanese fire. It was not unusual for U.S. soldiers to find the mutilated bodies of others who had surrendered (Dower 1986, 41–46, 48–52; Linderman 1997, 147–159; McManus 1998, 136–137, 152).

The evidence for Japanese perfidy is anecdotal, so it is unclear how often it occurred, whether it was rampant or merely frequent. Stories about Japanese perfidy and atrocities were widespread among U.S. soldiers and marines and the belief in Japanese treachery and the inability to trust any signal of intent to surrender commonly held. Rumors of Japanese brutality and deceit spread rapidly, whether or not they were based on truth. The most famous story of treachery occurred early in the Guadalcanal campaign. A Japanese sailor described a group of Japanese ready to surrender if a group of Americans came out to get them. The landing party led by Lieutenant Colonel Frank Goettge was massacred after they waded ashore at the beach at the meeting point. The story of the Goettge patrol spread widely and quickly and became part of the common lore of U.S. troops sent to fight the island war (Dower 1986, 52; Linderman 1997, 157–158; McManus 1998, 98, 173–174, 176–179; Kindsvatter 2003, 206–209, 213, 215; Schrijvers 2010, 176–177, 189–190, 221–223).

With these beliefs, it is hardly surprising that U.S. marines and soldiers did not want to take Japanese prisoners. Close to one-half of U.S. soldiers surveyed really wanted to kill a Japanese soldier (McManus 1998, 172). A common account is U.S. soldiers shooting every Japanese corpse on a battlefield to make sure they were dead before approaching them. Why take the risk that one might be playing dead and attack you unawares? The perception of Japanese treachery and brutal close combat of the war in the Pacific also led to brutality by U.S. soldiers. Body parts of dead Japanese were collected as souvenirs and trophies. Some U.S. soldiers knocked out and collected the gold teeth from Japanese corpses to sell later. Officers did not always encourage their troops to take prisoners; one regimental commander told his men: "Don't bother to take prisoners; shoot the sons of bitches" (quoted in Straus 2003, 117). By all accounts, the island war was vicious and cruel (Dower 1986, 62–71; Linderman 1997, 173–184; McManus 1998, 95–96, 175–176, 180–181; Schrijvers 2010, 207–210).

The reluctance of Japanese soldiers to surrender arose from their military training reinforced by social pressure within their units. In one survey of Japanese soldiers taken prisoner, 84 percent expected to be tortured or killed if they were captured (Dower 1986, 68). Japanese taken prisoner during the New Guinea campaign were surprised not to be shot after capture. Officers fostered these rumors that U.S. soldiers would torture and kill all they took prisoner. Furthermore, there were cases in which U.S. soldiers did kill Japanese who tried to surrender; the rumors had some basis in fact. One Japanese soldier told an Australian POW that "the ill-treatment and torturing of Australian troops was done by the order of their officers so that the Japanese soldiers would fight and not surrender, because the same things would be done to them now that these atrocities had been committed on the Australians" (quoted in Russell of Liverpool 1958, 107). These atrocities made it harder for both sides to surrender (Dower 1986, 61–62, 68–71; Linderman 1997, 153–154; Fedorowich 2000, 76).

Japanese military training emphasized that the disgrace of capture was worse than death. The Japanese Military Field Code (*Senjinkun*) in 1941 stated:

> Those who know shame are weak. Always think of [preserving] the honor of your community and be a credit to yourself and your family. Redouble your efforts and respond to their expectations. Never live to experience shame as a prisoner. By dying you will avoid leaving behind the crime of a stain on your honor (quoted in Straus 2003, 39).

The government of Japan further wished to know nothing about its men taken prisoner: "our Army maintains the position that Japanese prisoners of war do not exist" (Vance 1994, 208). Many Japanese prisoners gave false names when asked to identify themselves after capture. At one point, more than 1 percent of the Japanese held prisoner at the camp in Hawaii identified themselves as Hasegawa Kazuo, the leading Japanese film star of the time (Straus 2003, 123). When captured, most Japanese POWs preferred that their name and status as a prisoner not be sent to the government of Japan as required by the 1929 Geneva Convention. The Allied governments also realized that Japanese military training would induce Japanese soldiers to fight to the death. A report by the Australian government in 1942 stated the following:

> Such a contingency as capture by the enemy is not recognized by the Japanese military authorities. It is carefully inculcated into the Japanese soldier that to allow himself to be captured is a disgrace worse than death. Indeed, to some extent, he even welcomes the chance to die for his country.... The Japanese is therefore a difficult fish to catch. He will resist to the last, and under the circumstances our forces can scarcely be blamed for helping him to achieve his ambition to die for his country (quoted in Fedorowich 2000, 62).

The policy that surrender was worse than death was adopted to make Japanese soldiers fight harder in combat.

Japanese military training was also more brutal than that of the Allied nations. It sought to toughen Japanese soldiers for the rigors of combat. Absolute obedience to orders and the central role of unit cohesion were the central tenets of Japanese military training. Discipline was strict and beatings by officers were common, including the use of baseball bats in some of those beatings (Harries and Harries 1991, 411–412; Straus 2003, 34–8). The brutality of training contributed to the brutal treatment of Allied POWs as superiors – in this case, guards – were encouraged to use physical violence against those under their charge. On the battlefield, military discipline and social pressure were used to encourage self-destruction over surrender. Banzai charges, the suicidal attacks that were almost always ineffective (*gyokusai*), were a form of social control to ensure that all died. As one U.S. Marine officer put it, a banzai charge was "a sure sign of American victory" (quoted in Linderman 1997, 165). Even the seriously wounded were forced to participate just to ensure they did not survive to surrender. This suicidal gesture ensured their honor. The social pressure from their training not to surrender made it difficult for soldiers to consider discussing surrender in their units, and many soldiers went to their deaths or killed themselves to preserve family honor (Linderman 1997, 164–167; Towle 2000, 7–8; Straus 2003, 50–54; Schrijvers 2010, 181–182).

The Japanese policy of stigmatizing surrender had an unexpected benefit for its enemies. Those Japanese taken prisoner, expecting death or torture but receiving humane treatment, began to identify more with their captors than their homeland. After all, they no longer existed in the eyes of Japan. Because their training had not covered their rights under the 1929 Geneva Convention, they did not know that they did not have to answer questions in an interrogation. Many of them talked freely, providing key details of Japanese technology in addition to operational intelligence. Some drew detailed diagrams of warships on which they had served. Both Australia and the United States created elaborate programs to interrogate POWs, with the United States moving those prisoners to camps in the continental United States. They found that lenient treatment led to more prisoners talking than harsher methods, such as trickery or threats of coercion. The intelligence value of prisoners led the U.S. leadership to encourage their troops to take more prisoners. Even with these orders, U.S. soldiers took few additional prisoners until they were offered additional leave for each prisoner taken, a sign of the hatred they held for the Japanese. Capturing Japanese soldiers continued to be difficult. Leaflet campaigns were attempted, and although many Japanese soldiers knew of them, they scorned the offer of good treatment if they surrendered (Fedorowich 2000, 76–82; Straus 2003, 54–55, 85–87). Not all Japanese cooperated with their captors; the riot at Camp Cowra was in part a mass suicide out of shame at being taken prisoner (Fedorowich 2000; Straus 2003, 116–149, 173–195; Hayashi 2005, 51).

Large numbers of Japanese soldiers were taken prisoner only during the battles on Okinawa, the last large island battle of the war. More than 10,000 prisoners were taken, but this change reflects the special conditions of Okinawa more than the imminent defeat of Japan. Large numbers of Okinawans had been impressed into second-line militia units (*Boeitai*) before the U.S. invasion. Regular Japanese officers and soldiers discriminated against these units and treated them poorly. Many of these soldiers deserted as they could blend into the local population. Furthermore, they had not received the same military training that regular Japanese troops did. They did not receive the same instructions about the disgrace of being taken prisoner. Only the threat by Japanese units to kill their families if they surrendered deterred them from giving themselves up. Still, 13,000 of the *Boeitai* died during the battle (Hayashi 2005).

The treatment of prisoners of war during the war in the Pacific was asymmetric in all ways. One side was democratic and sought to protect prisoners, whereas authoritarian Japan discouraged its soldiers from surrendering and did nothing to ensure proper treatment of U.S. and Commonwealth soldiers it took prisoner. In the statistical results in Chapter 4, these asymmetric cases had the least reciprocity and the worst overall compliance. The war in the Pacific exemplifies this pattern. Atrocious treatment and perfidy by the Japanese both on the battlefield and in POW camps led the soldiers of the Western powers to respond in kind on the battlefield. Military authorities of the Western powers could ensure good treatment once prisoners reached collection points and moved into camps, but their efforts to encourage the taking of prisoners were rarely successful. Reciprocity of the most brutal kind led to the war in the Pacific being the most difficult for soldiers to surrender and survive the war in captivity.

## AFTER THE SHOOTING STOPPED

Reciprocity requires two sides that view one another as equals and possess the ability to respond in kind. The latter disappears when one side loses a war. The treatment of prisoners after countries left the war shows how reciprocity fails when one side cannot retaliate. Conditions for those held prisoners deteriorated once their country was defeated.

The United States and its Western allies took millions of German soldiers into captivity as the war in Europe ended in the spring of 1945. German soldiers and civilians desperately fled westward to surrender to the Western allies than suffer the wrath of the Red Army's descent on Eastern Europe. The United States captured more than 7 million German soldiers during 1945, including those detained after the war had ended. The numbers, together with displaced persons and German civilians, overwhelmed the ability of the Allied forces to provide for them. Those detained after V-E Day were labeled DEFs (Disarmed Enemy Forces) and herded into barbed wire camps. At first, food and shelter were insufficient for the large numbers of men held; the average diet in some camps was as low as 1,000 calories a day. Although U.S. authorities processed and released DEFs within a few months, about 50,000 of these men died in U.S. custody. This death rate is higher than that of German POWs held during the war, particularly given the short time of their detention. Those DEFs turned over to French authorities suffered worse than those held by the United States. The French also recruited some of these men into the Foreign Legion. France used German POWs to clear mines, which is against the 1929 Geneva Convention, during the summer of 1945. Two thousand POWs died each month doing this work (ICRC 1948, 3:334). The Dutch also used German prisoners to clear mines, leading to the deaths of 210 of them (Garrett 1981, 177). Coupled with the executions of German POWs who committed crimes while prisoners, the Allied commitment to protect and provide for prisoners declined once the war was over (Bischof and Ambrose 1992; Doyle 2010, 230–233; Moore 2010, 120–121).

Allied treatment of other nationalities also declined after their countries surrendered. U.S. treatment of Japanese prisoners deteriorated after Japan surrendered. Those held on the mainland were sent to California to pick cotton, the hardest work they did during their time in U.S. custody (Straus 2003, 225–119). Great Britain and the United States held approximately 450,000 Italians as prisoners when Italy surrendered to them in September 1943. German forces moved into Italy in response to Italy's surrender and occupied the country north of Naples. They seized prisoners held by Italy and transferred them back to camps in Germany. The Germans also disarmed and seized 640,000 Italian soldiers as prisoners and sent them back to Germany as well. Britain and the United States did not repatriate the Italian prisoners they held after Italy's surrender until the war in Europe was over. Instead, they formed the men into Italian Service Units (ISUs) to take advantage of their labor. As ISUs were essentially the same as work details for POWs, the status and rights of the prisoners changed little. Participation in the ISUs was voluntary, and a majority of prisoners volunteered because the alternative was remaining in a POW camp. ISUs provided valuable agricultural labor that compensated for the labor shortages during the war. Repatriating all Italian prisoners would have been impossible as the Germans occupied Northern Italy until the end of the war. Still, few Italian prisoners from Southern Italy were repatriated; their labor was too valuable (Keefer 1992; Moore 1996, 32–34).

Germany also exploited prisoners it held during the war after their countries surrendered. Approximately 1,850,000 French soldiers were taken prisoner during the six-week campaign that ended with the fall of France in June 1940. The successor Vichy government pressed for these men to be released as part of its policy to collaborate with Nazi Germany. Instead, the Nazis used the French prisoners, and the pressure from their families to release them, as leverage to secure the movement of French skilled labor into industry in Germany. In June 1942, French Prime Minister Pierre Laval announced the *relève*, a policy by which Germany agreed to release one prisoner for every three skilled laborers who agreed to work in Germany. These workers often found that the conditions of their work, pay, and hours, changed once they were in Germany and had no real option to leave. Vichy France had no leverage on Nazi Germany, and could therefore do little to free its men held there (Calvocoressi, Wint, and Pritchard 1989, 330–331; Thomas 1996, 87; Vance 2000, 302–303).

The Soviet Union held roughly 2 million Germans prisoner at the end of the war and then captured about 600,000 Japanese when the Red Army overran Manchuria in August 1945. These men were sent to the labor camps where they helped build a railway in Siberia. Japanese prisoners went into long-term captivity in Siberia and the Far East where they worked on reconstruction of the Soviet economy. Like German prisoners, camp conditions matched those of the Gulag. The death rates were high in the months after the end of the war, but then conditions improved to keep the prisoners alive to work. Roughly 10 percent of the Japanese prisoners died during their imprisonment. The Soviet Union only began releasing large numbers of prisoners in 1949 and did not release the last German and Japanese prisoners until 1956 when the Federal Republic of Germany opened diplomatic relations with the Soviet Union (Glantz and House 1995, 378; Overy 1998, 297–298; Igarashi 2005, 105, 108–112; Overmans 2005, 17–18; Overmans 2010, 132).

The Soviet Union treated its own soldiers who had been taken prisoner harshly after their return. Those who had enlisted in the German Army faced the worst fate. Many of them were killed; their leaders were killed after being tortured. Others who had been taken prisoner and then survived the ordeal of German POW camps also fell under suspicion. Some were tried in courts martial for violations of orders against surrendering. Most were sent to labor camps in the Gulag, including those who were not tried for any crime. Pavel Polian summarizes the Soviet approach to repatriated prisoners:

> All you rascals deserve only shooting with expropriation as patricides. But following the victory, the Motherland shows great leniency to you, the skunks, and instead of 'extreme penalty' sends you to the special settlement for six years (Polian 2005, 131).

The soldiers send to the Gulag had their military service expunged from their record and were restricted as to where they could live after release from the camps. The Western Allies repatriated many Soviet soldiers taken prisoner, handing them over to their fate. Soviet citizens who the Germans had impressed to work in German industry suffered the same fate (Overy 1998, 298–304; Polian 2005, 123–134).

Treatment of prisoners by all countries deteriorated once they had won and the other side lost the ability to retaliate in kind to their soldiers taken prisoner. It is one of the clearest pieces of evidence of the critical role of reciprocity in the protection of prisoners of war during the World Wars.

## AN ALTERNATIVE EXPLANATION: CULTURE

Variation in conduct toward prisoners of war during World War II is often ascribed to culture in the sense of societal attitudes toward the enemy and the act of surrendering. For example, Arieh Kochavi ascribes the difference in German conduct toward prisoners on the Western and Eastern Fronts to the Nazi view of German racial ideology:

> In the racial ideology of the Nazis, both the British and American peoples were, of course, inferior to the Aryan German Volk but as Anglo-Saxons nevertheless ranked high in the hierarchy of races.... This was part of the reason why, where British and U.S. prisoners of war were concerned, Berlin adhered throughout the war to the 1929 Geneva Convention.... The contrast with the Soviet troops the Nazis captured could not be starker: these were *Untermenschen* (subhumans) who did not deserve to live in the first place (Kochavi 2005, 280–281).

Reciprocity could not function when one side did not view the other as racially equal. Nazi Germany was not the only country where racist views drove brutality on the battlefield. John Dower (1986) describes the racial attitudes and propaganda espoused by the United States and Japan during the war in the Pacific, arguing that these racist attitudes contributed to that war becoming a "war without mercy." Japanese historical attitudes about the disgrace of surrender – that suicide was preferable to capture and that captives could be tortured – also contributed the self-destructive behavior of its soldiers and their brutality toward the prisoners they held (Straus 2003, 17–19; Towle 2010). What role can law play in the face of these cultural attitudes of the inferiority of captives, an inferiority that denies them their humanity?

First, culture and law are complementary, not contradictory, explanations of how states act during war. State preferences about the willingness to protect prisoners are a key element of the model in Chapter 3 about how and when law limits violence. Law, and political institutions more generally, do not produce outcomes directly by forcing actors to behave in one way; they shape how those actors pursue what they believe to be their self-interest. Cultural attitudes toward surrender and prisoners – in some cases, stigmatizing surrendering, while emphasizing the humanitarian treatment of those out of combat in others – play a role in these preferences. Nazi racial theories contributed to the "war of extermination" on the Eastern Front, but the need for a legal justification of German policies and conduct in that war led Hitler to grasp the Soviet Union's public rejection of the 1929 Geneva Convention. Against the Western Allies, the 1929 Geneva Convention and the need to avoid the most blatant breaches of it restricted the worse impulses of the Nazi regime against prisoners, such as Hitler's desire to kill all the Sagan escapees. In the Pacific, racist attitudes and atrocities on the battlefield fed on one another in a reinforcing spiral of hatred, as Dower describes the process. Law and culture work together in some cases, and against one another in others, in part because states adopt law to help them realize the values embedded in their culture.

Second, conduct on the battlefield may play a larger role than culture in forming expectations of what will happen on the battlefield. Dower accurately describes the racial indoctrination of U.S. soldiers and marines during World War II. But those who fought against the Japanese invasion in the Philippines in 1941 and 1942 had not been indoctrinated with these racist attitudes. They entered combat believing that the Japanese would follow the Geneva Convention on the battlefield. Experience disabused them of these beliefs (Linderman 1997, 143–148, 151–153). Similarly, the Americans and Australians who fought on Guadalcanal and in New Guinea in 1942 had not been indoctrinated as the racist element of training came later. Yet they too quickly learned of examples of Japanese atrocities such as the Goettge patrol and took very few Japanese prisoners (Bergerud 1996, 403–425).

Third, the interplay of law and culture is more subtle than arguments that culture drives POW policy allow. Law limits the worst impulses of racist culture in some cases, while the strategic logic of compliance with law opens up opportunities for abuse even when the state committing the abuses is not driven by ideas of cultural superiority. The Nazis had a racial hierarchy for prisoners they held, with British and Americans at the top, French and Dutch in the middle, and "Slavs" – Poles and Russians – at the bottom (MacKenzie 1994, 504). Treatment of the POWs they held followed this hierarchy, but there were important exceptions. During the Polish campaign in 1939, German soldiers often executed Polish soldiers after they surrendered (Rossino 2003, 179–185). Conditions in camps holding Polish prisoners taken in 1939 were worse than those holding British POWs (MacKenzie 1994, 499–500). A substantial number of Polish soldiers fled across the borders of neutral Hungary and Romania in 1939 and joined the forces of the Western Allies. The Soviets also released to Britain a large number of the Polish prisoners they took when they invaded and occupied the eastern half of the country in 1939. By 1944, the British Army reformed these men into Polish divisions that operated under the Polish flag in Italy and France; they were not just Polish soldiers enlisted in British units (Keegan 1982, 262–264).[9] The Germans segregated Polish soldiers they took prisoner by the army to which their formation was attached when captured (ICRC 1948, 3:251–256; Wylie 2010b, 125). Reciprocity required that Germany treated these prisoners based on the army they fought with, not their ethnic origin. Law limited cultural prejudice here.

Fourth, culture changes, but it does slowly; yet policy on prisoners can change dramatically without such cultural change. Surrender has been disgraceful in Japanese culture for centuries. Few Japanese soldiers were taken prisoner during its earlier wars – the Sino-Japanese War, the Russo-Japanese War, and World War I. Repatriated prisoners faced Courts of Inquiry after their return to determine the circumstances of their capture. Many officers were forced out of the army as a result of these proceedings, whereas some

[9] A division is roughly 10,000 soldiers and the main organizational unit of modern armies.

received commendations if they had performed heroically. Some were ostra-
cized when they returned to their civilian homes; social disapproval of former
prisoners was more common in rural villages, which led some to move to
large cities to avoid the social stigma of their captivity. Japanese treatment
of the prisoners they captured was exemplary during these wars (Hata 1996,
256–260; Straus 2003, 20–21; Drea 2009, 119–120, 137). Lieutenant General
Mikio Uemura, head of the POW Information Bureau and POW Management
Division during World War II stated, "we gave them [the Russians during the
Russo-Japanese War and the Germans during World War I] excellent treatment in order to gain recognition as a civilized country" (quoted in Kinvig
2000, 47). This attitude changed during the interwar period. The Japanese
military saw the Western Powers as their potential enemy and saw no reason to curry favor with them by following their rules. Instead, they saw the
1929 Geneva Convention as imposing obligations on Japan alone as Japanese
soldiers would not surrender. The Japanese military saw fighting spirit as one
military advantage they had over the Western Powers. Training emphasized
the need to uphold honor by fighting to the death or committing suicide rather
than suffering the disgrace of capture. Recruits were taught to hold those who
surrendered in contempt, including enemies taken prisoner. Treatment of prisoners was largely left to camp commanders and guards, and while they did
not have orders to abuse prisoners, their treatment of their prisoners reflected
the contempt for those who had surrendered instilled during their training.
But the disdain for those who were captured in Japanese culture could support
lenient or brutal treatment of enemies taken prisoner while still emphasizing
that Japanese soldiers should never allow themselves to be taken prisoner. As
the head of the POW information bureau during World War I stated at a conference in 1916:

> It is agreeable with *Bushido* to treat enemy braves leniently, and it is necessary
> for us, as a great nation, to demonstrate our behavior on behalf of our national
> pride. At the same time, as nations in this empire, we should fight harder, should
> be honored with death, and never be shamed by being taken prisoner (quoted in
> Kosuge 2000, 156).

Japanese training against surrender and the social control used in military units
to ensure that soldiers fought to the death or committed suicide rather than be
captured was a deliberate choice by the Japanese military during the interwar
period. Culture did not dictate the outcome (Drea 2009, 176, 257–260).

Let me reiterate the central conclusion of this section. Cultural attitudes
toward surrender and prisoners are an important element in the treatment
of prisoners because they influence whether state leaders believe that taking
prisoners is in their interest, and so their willingness to adhere to treaties that
seek to protect prisoners of war. Culture, however, does not determine when
states comply; law has some power to shape how states treat the men they take
prisoner during war.

Treatment of prisoners of war during World War II varied with the willingness of states to protect enemy soldiers who surrendered. Those countries that wished to follow the terms of the 1929 Geneva Convention, and signaled their interest in doing so by ratifying the treaty, broadly complied with those standards when fighting another country that had also ratified. Compliance even in these cases faced challenges both between states on prisoner exchanges and between soldiers on the battlefield. Those states who believed they would gain from harsh treatment of prisoners broke the standard. Their camps failed to meet any standard of humane treatment, and large numbers of men died in captivity. Conduct on these battlefields deteriorated into brutality because the governments that sought to make it difficult for their soldiers to surrender ordered and encouraged their men to not take prisoners, and the soldiers of the other side responded in kind. Only the countries that wished to take prisoners tried to control their soldiers through military discipline; the others instead used military discipline to force their soldiers to fight rather than surrender. Conditions for prisoners deteriorated once their country surrendered because the captors no longer had to worry about reciprocal responses to their own men held prisoner. During World War I, most countries sought to treat prisoners humanely but disagreed about what that required, particularly during the material shortages of wartime. During World War II, there was a clearer agreement of what humane treatment required, but less interest across the warring parties in providing such treatment.

## TESTING THE CONCLUSIONS OF THE MODEL WITH THE CASES

The model led to seven testable hypotheses about the laws of war. How do those hypotheses hold up against the record of these historical cases? More importantly, do the cases provide evidence of the causal processes underlying them as elaborated in the model in Chapter 3? The cases provide a closer look at the traces of evidence left by these causal processes. By checking for these traces, we complement the comparison of the statistical patterns with the hypotheses.

The first three hypotheses concern reciprocity, joint ratification, and compliance. In the model, states ratify the relevant treaty standard when they wish to comply with it. Joint ratification creates a common conjecture that both sides will follow the treaty standard to the best of their ability. This strengthens reciprocity and increases compliance, subject to reciprocal retaliation if one side systematically violates the standard. The shared belief in following the standard does not exist when one or both sides do not ratify the relevant treaty. The presence or absence of a shared understanding to follow the standard creates expectations of how the other side, both the political and military authorities and the soldiers who carry out the dirty work of war, will act during wartime.

The record on prisoners of war during the World Wars fits this logic well. Both governments and soldiers entered wars with expectations that the other

side would or would not follow the rules. Military authorities sought to culti-
vate those expectations in their soldiers through training, which reflected the
state's desire to follow the treaty standard or to ignore it. In some cases, such
as U.S. soldiers in the Pacific, expectations of good conduct were shattered by
how Japanese soldiers abused those who surrendered. They retaliated by rarely
taking Japanese soldiers prisoner, contributing to the brutality of the island
war. At the state level, some lack of clarity in the treaty standard complicated
compliance during World War I. The legal standards, when clear, also helped
limit isolated violations – such as the execution of the recaptured Sagan escapees in 1944 – that might have triggered reciprocal sanctions. By limiting such
violations, retaliatory spirals never started.

The fourth and fifth hypotheses concern individual violations and whether
states try to control them. Individual soldiers can and do violate the laws of
war on their own against state policy. These violations pose agency and noise
problems for states that wish to comply with the laws of war. Military discipline and training are necessary to limit these individual violations. When
a state does not wish to comply with the standard, it will not discipline its
soldiers, instead trying to encourage violations on the battlefield. The scope
for individual violations varies across issues with greater scope increasing individual violations and making compliance more difficult. A test of the logic
behind the latter can be done only by comparing across issues, which the next
chapter does.

The record of prisoners of war during the World Wars fits this logic well.
Individual soldiers killed men who tried to surrender or had surrendered in
all armies. Even the strongest efforts of military authorities to encourage their
troops to take prisoners did not stop these killings. Conduct on the battlefield,
such as the British binding of prisoners at Dieppe and Sark, complicated state-
to-state compliance. Still, military discipline and training did reduce individual
violations in some armies. In others, military discipline and training focused
on discouraging surrender, which caused individual violations to rise with the
brutality of a war with no quarter given or asked. Attitudes toward surrender
also changed across the time period, with greater emphasis on taking prisoners
and less on discouraging surrender, except in the armies that sought to discourage their soldiers from surrendering.

The last two hypotheses concern the timing of violations. When a state
believes it can gain from violations, its forces will commit violations from the
earliest days of the war. Why wait to gain the advantage? If the first violations
come late in the war, the winning side is more likely to do so than the losing
side. Raising the costs of war may force the loser out of the war.

When states broke the treaty standards, they did so from the first opportunities they had. The Nazi armies were killing Soviet soldiers who surrendered
from the first day of Operation Barbarossa. The Japanese also tortured and
killed prisoners in their first opportunity, the fall of Hong Kong and Wake
Island in December, 1941. The seventh hypothesis on late violations cannot

be tested with the prisoner of war issue as all warring parties committed some violations, even if only by individuals.

Although Spaight saw prisoners of war as "spoilt darlings," they suffered greatly. Many were killed in the act of surrender or shortly thereafter. Even those who reached POW camps suffered when their captors did not see any value in providing for their sustenance. Some armies shared Spaight's view and sought to stigmatize or punish those who surrendered to the enemy. Others saw that humane treatment was in their interest as it encouraged enemy soldiers to surrender, shortening the war and saving the lives of their own soldiers. The Hague and Geneva Conventions helped states treat prisoners humanely when they sought to do so by clarifying expectations of good treatment and defining what was such treatment. Those conventions could not force those who saw advantage in brutality to comply with even a minimal standard of humane treatment. The measure of international law lies not in its failures, but in its successes.

# 6

## Assessing Variation across Issues

*Aerial Bombing, Chemical Weapons, Treatment of Civilians, and Conduct on the High Seas*

Chapter 5 explored the detail of how international treaties shaped conduct on the battlefield and in the camps. A single issue, however, does not allow us to understand how the practice of the laws of war varies with the characteristics of those issues. From the statistical analyses in Chapter 4, issues with less scope for individual violations produce better records of compliance. How does the logic of compliance vary with this scope? This chapter provides brief case studies of four issues other than prisoners of war – aerial bombing, chemical weapons, treatment of civilians, and conduct on the high seas – that vary in the scope for individual violations. Chemical weapons have the most centralized control and the least scope because individual soldiers can use chemical weapons only when their commanding authorities provide them. All soldiers in a combat zone have the power and opportunity to commit violations against civilians (except for the rare cases in which the armies fight in sparsely populated areas such as the Western Desert of Egypt and Libya). The other two issues fall between these two because individual soldiers do not have the opportunity to commit violations but lower-level officers, such as ship captains, do. Violations as a matter of state policy can and have happened on all four issues. The cases also examine the interplay of state policy and what happens on the battlefield on these issues. As with the chapter on prisoners of war, I focus on the experiences during the World Wars.

These four issues have also been the focus of other analyses in political science. Jeffrey Legro (1995) argues that military culture – the organizational practices of a military that inculcate how battles will be fought and weapons used – predicts whether states will act with restraint during wartime. He examines aerial bombing, chemical weapons, and submarine warfare during World War II in detail. As we will see, his argument corresponds to key elements of mine, but a broader view of events suggests that law shapes how these military practices arise and play out during wartime. Richard Price (1997) contends that a taboo against the use of chemical weapons has arisen from our fears of poisoning and grown over time as a way of civilizing war. Again, important elements of his argument are correct, but law and the ratification of treaties shape whether the taboo holds. Benjamin Valentino, Paul Huth, and their coauthors (Valentino, Huth, and Balch-Lindsay 2004; Valentino, Huth, and Croco 2006) examine the killing of civilians during interstate and civil wars. Alexander Downes (Downes 2008) concludes that states, including democracies, deliberately kill enemy civilians when they find themselves in a protracted war or when they seek to conquer enemy territory. Again, there are important elements of truth in Downes's argument, but the legal status of the policies that lead to civilian victimization cloud responsibility for those policies. Legality constrains and enables action in different circumstances. Failing to understand those circumstances – and whether the parties are legally obligated – obscures how international law shapes what states do during wartime.

These case studies are shorter than those in Chapter 5. Each explains what the law was, how the major powers complied with their legal commitments if any, and how noise – in the form of individual violations and the uncertainty of the battlefield – made compliance more or less likely. The centralized control of chemical weapons made compliance easier to verify; it also led to widespread use when one side used chemical weapons and the other side could respond in kind. A clear legal prohibition on the use of chemical weapons reinforced the commitment not to use those weapons by creating the anticipation of retaliation if they were used. There was no binding legal restraint on aerial bombing, and the inaccuracy of bombing during the World Wars made restraint impossible short of banning all bombing, something no power would accept. Conduct on the high seas foundered on the issue of blockades enforced either by surface ships or submarines. The countries most vulnerable to submarine warfare wished to ban it, but their possible opponents would not accept such a ban. The law on the treatment of civilians primarily concerns conduct on the battlefield during this period. The 1949 Geneva Convention (IV) relative to the Protection of Civilian Persons in Time of War (henceforth 1949 Geneva Convention on civilians) added stronger and more precise commitments limiting military occupation, but that was after the World Wars. The critical issue here was the spread of irregular violence by civilians and retaliatory violence by armies. The worst cases of abuse of civilians in war zones were conducted by authoritarian states that made no effort to control their troops. The chapter ends with a reconsideration of the other arguments described previously.

## CHEMICAL WEAPONS

The 1899 and 1907 Hague Conventions addressed chemical weapons even though they had not been developed for military use at that time. The 1899 Hague Declaration (IV,2) on the Use of Projectiles the Object of Which is the Diffusion of Asphyxiating or Deleterious Gases (henceforth 1899 Hague

Declaration on Gas) stated the agreement to "to abstain from the use of projectiles the sole object of which is the diffusion of asphyxiating or deleterious
gases." Article 23 of the Annex to 1907 Hague Convention (IV) respecting the
Laws and Customs of War on Land (henceforth 1907 Hague Convention (IV))
reinforced this prohibition with provisions against the use of "poison or poi-
soned weapons" and "arms, projectiles, or material calculated to cause unnecessary suffering." But these provisions would prove to be vague when countries
developed chemical weapons during World War I.

Germany launched the first successful chemical attack on April 22, 1915
during the Second Battle of Ypres. More than 5,000 cylinders containing chlorine gas were mounted in the German front line and opened to allow the green
gas to float over Allied lines. The French troops in the path of the cloud fled,
coughing and hacking as the corrosive gas ate away their lungs. A gap of five
miles opened in the Allied lines on the north side of the Ypres salient. Eventually,
the Allies rushed troops to fill the gap in their line. Five subsequent chemical
attacks during the battle produced less dramatic results as soldiers adopted ad
hoc protection against the gas, such as urinating on cloths which they then held
over their mouth and nose (Haber 1986, 34–36; Richter 1992, 10; Harris and
Paxman 2002, 5). These first chemical attacks did not produce dramatic results
because they were experiments with the technology.

The Allies condemned these chemical attacks as another example of German
"frightfulness." The Germans justified their chemical attacks as legal because
the gas was dispersed from cylinders; they did not employ projectiles that
released the gas (Herwig 1996, 169–170). As one German newspaper claimed,
"the letting loose of smoke clouds, which, in a gentle wind, move quite slowly
toward the enemy, is not only permissible by international law, but it is an
extraordinarily mild method of war" (quoted in Harris and Paxman 2002,
7). This justification rested on the treaty language because it violated norms
against the use of poison in war (Price 1997, 47–51, 58–60). The Allies gained
an advantage in the ongoing propaganda war to convince their populations
and those of neutral countries that Germany broke the spirit, if not the letter,
of the rules (Brown 1968, 13–14 for Allied propaganda about German use of
gas; Spiers 1986, 18; Hammond 1999, 12; Spiers 2010, 40).

The Allies later responded with their own chemical attacks, the British in
September 1915 at Loos and the French in February 1916 at Verdun. The
need to produce chemical agents and to deploy the means of delivering the
agents slowed retaliation against initial German use. This delay accounts
for the time dependence in the survival analysis of retaliation after first use
reported in Table 4'.16. The French escalated the chemical war by the first use
of chemical shells fired from artillery. These shells clearly violated the Hague
standard. They were also much more effective than gas clouds released from
cylinders because they could deliver chemical agents behind the lines in higher
concentrations than gas clouds. Gas clouds required a favorable wind to float
over enemy lines, but if that wind was too strong, the cloud would disperse,

lowering the concentration of the chemical agent and rendering it ineffective. All sides adopted gas shells as the preferred way to deliver chemical agents despite their illegal status. The short supply of shell casings, rather than concern about the Hague Convention, slowed the adoption of gas shells (Haber 1986, 63–66). Other mechanisms of delivering gas, such as the Livens projector used by the British, were also developed. New, more deadly agents – phosgene, cyanide, and mustard to name the most infamous ones – replaced chlorine. From 1916 on, chemical warfare was common on the Western Front. Soldiers kept their gas masks and other protective gear at hand (Spiers 1986, 18–30; Spiers 2010, 33–39).

Chemical warfare also spread to other fronts, although it was not as common there as on the Western Front. Germany launched successful chemical attacks against Russia beginning in May 1915, causing tens of thousands of casualties (Haber 1986, 36–39). Russia suffered the most of all countries from chemical warfare, largely because it was not able to provide the level of protection that Germany, France, and Britain could to their own troops (Spiers 1986, 19, 32; Spiers 2010, 44).

Although the chlorine cloud at Second Ypres began the escalation to widespread chemical warfare, it was not the first attempted chemical attack in World War I. Germany launched an attack using xylyl bromide against Russia on January 31, 1915, but it failed because the gas did not vaporize in the cold temperatures. France and Germany both experimented with the use of tear gas – an irritating agent that rarely kills – delivered by rifle cartridges and shells during 1914 and 1915 before the chlorine attack at Ypres (Trumpener 1975, 462–469; Spiers 2010, 30). Tear gas raises the issue of what constitutes a chemical weapon and an attack. The French argued that the use of tear gas in combat was allowed under the Hague Convention because it did not asphyxiate (Trumpener 1975, 462). Governments commonly use tear gas as a riot control measure in extreme cases. It is rarely fatal; is it a chemical weapon or not? Similarly, were the defoliants used by the United States during the Vietnam War chemical weapons (see Harris and Paxman 2002, 193–198 on United States use of riot control agents and defoliants during the Vietnam War)? The United States publicly declared in 1969 that it considered riot control agents as banned as it began the process of finally ratifying the 1925 Geneva Protocol on CBW (Hammond 1999, 26). Debates rage over both of these cases in the absence of clear legal agreement on which agents are chemical weapons.

The extensive use of chemical weapons during World War I led to movements to outlaw their use after the war. There was not unanimous support for a ban. Important military interests in the major powers argued against one, contending that chemical weapons were humane because they killed a smaller proportion of their victims than other weapons. Yet a ban was adopted in two measures. The Washington Conference of 1922 included a ban on the use of chemical weapons in the treaty negotiated there, but this treaty did not enter into force. The 1925 Geneva Protocol on CBW banned the use of chemical weapons and expanded that ban to include biological weapons. Forty-three countries ratified the protocol, although the United States did not, nor did Japan. The protocol bound ratifying states not to use gas only when both sides had ratified. The protocol only addressed the use of the banned weapons, not their manufacture (Brown 1968, 61–72, 98–110; Spiers 1986, 40–47; Price 1997, 74–86; Spiers 2010, 48–52).

The slow collapse of the interwar system led to the string of wars we associate with World War II. Chemical weapons were used extensively in two, the Italo-Ethiopian War and the Sino-Japanese War. Although Italy had ratified the 1925 Geneva Protocol on CBW and Ethiopia did so three days after the outbreak of war, Italy used mustard gas extensively, and Ethiopia lacked the means to respond in kind. Italy used aerial spraying to deliver chemical weapons for the first time in combat (Spiers 1986, 89–97; Sbacchi 1997, 58–63). Japan had signed but not ratified the protocol, and China had not even signed it. Japan used chemical weapons and experimented with biological weapons as well. China, like Ethiopia, lacked the ability to respond fully in kind, although it did use chemical weapons against the Japanese a few times during their eight-year war (Spiers 1986, 97–104; Harris and Paxman 2002, 50–52). Similarly, Spain used a variety of chemical weapons against the Rif revolt in Morocco (Spiers 2010, 72–79).

The ban almost always held on the main fronts of World War II. Germany used choking agents to force Soviet soldiers out of deep caves during the siege of Sevastopol in Spring 1942, but the use of chemical weapons did not spread beyond these circumstances (Bellamy 2007, 461–463). These rare uses were unlikely to be reported to Soviet authorities because the garrison was cut off from Soviet lines. During 1944, Churchill argued for the use of gas on cities in the Ruhr in retaliation for German attacks with the V-weapons, which were early cruise and ballistic missiles; his proposal received no support from either British military or civilian officials. Fear of German retaliation played a large role in the minds of British leaders, including the possibility that Germany would use Allied prisoners to clean up contaminated areas. The long-term consequences of having to fight a chemical war outweighed the short-run gains from first use (Spiers 1986, 80–84; Price 1997, 122–124; Harris and Paxman 2002, 127–137).[1] Even though the United States was not legally bound because it did not ratify the 1925 Geneva Protocol on CBW, proposals to use chemical weapons against heavily fortified Japanese positions during the later stages of the island war received little support within the government and military. Japan stopped using chemical weapons against China once it was at war with

---

[1] Churchill often argued for the use of chemical weapons throughout his career. He was interested in using sulfur dioxide in 1914 (Spiers 1986, 14) and advocated for the use of chemical weapons in colonial conflicts in the Middle East in the aftermath of World War I. He pushed for increases in British production of chemical agents in 1940 (Harris and Paxman 2002, 113–115). The British military was always much cooler toward their use than he was (Spiers 2010, 70–72).

the Western Powers and reduced its capacity to produce chemical weapons (Brown 1968, 253–261; Spiers 1986, 66; Price 1997, 113–114; Hammond 1999, 14; Harris and Paxman 2002, 120–121; Spiers 2010, 76–77).

The nonuse of chemical weapons during World War II was backed up by extensive preparation for chemical warfare. The major powers feared that their opponents would use chemical weapons when the war broke out, and Britain, France, and Germany reaffirmed their commitments not to use gas in the first days of the war (Legro 1995, 149; Harris and Paxman 2002, 109–110). The major powers produced stockpiles of chemical agents and deployed them close to the front (Harris and Paxman 2002, 121). As the British General Staff put it, "no nation can take the risk of abandoning it [gas warfare] without the absolute certainty – which will be impossible to attain – that it will never be used by an adversary" (quoted in Spiers 2010, 47–48). The United States, like the other major powers, began the war with small stockpiles that would not last long in sustained chemical combat. It produced more than 135,000 tons of poison gas during the war (Spiers 2010, 59), more than the 125,000 tons estimated to be used by all countries during World War I (Spiers 2010, 27).[2] Other major powers also produced substantial stocks of chemical weapons. Germany developed nerve gases that were far more deadly than either asphyxiants or vesicants. Depots of chemical shells and other means of delivery were built behind the front lines. The stockpiles led to accidental releases of gas clouds when they were bombed. On December 2, 1943, a German air attack on the port of Bari, Italy sank a U.S. ship carrying 2,000 mustard gas bombs. Six hundred and thirty servicemen suffered burns from exposure to the chemicals in the water and the vapors they released. The cloud released by the mixture of burning oil and mustard gas in the water killed more than 1,000 civilians. The Allied leaders suspected that Germany had launched a chemical attack in addition to the aerial bombing. General Eisenhower tried to keep the accident secret, but the spread of the casualties to hospitals outside Bari made this impossible. From then on, Allied commanders were informed of when chemical stocks were in their rear areas (Harris and Paxman 2002, 121–125). A similar attack at Anzio a few months later led the U.S. local commander to inform his German counterpart of the drifting gas cloud to avoid any misunderstanding of the accidental nature of its release (Legro 1995, 200). Combat troops were issued gas masks and resistant clothing in case of chemical attack, although many discarded them after experience at the front taught them they were not needed (see Ambrose 1992, 60 on gas protection for paratroopers on D-Day). Mistaken alarms of gas attacks occurred when troops mistook smoke screens or phosphorus shells for gas, but these were quickly corrected and did not lead to retaliation (McManus 1998, 33; Schrijvers 1998, 61–62).

---

[2] Spiers (2010, 33) estimates that 150,000 tons of chemical weapons were produced during World War I.

The D-Day invasion provided tempting targets for Germany to use chemical weapons first. As General Omar Bradley said: "When D-Day finally ended without a whiff of gas, I was vastly relieved. For even a light sprinkling of persistent gas on Omaha Beach would have cost us our footing there" (quoted in Harris and Paxman 2002, 66). But the Germans passed on the opportunity, a decision that reflects the dynamic nature of the decision to violate a convention first. The short-run gain from first use was large, but the long-run vulnerability of Germany in a war in which both sides would use chemical weapons was large in the summer of 1944. The British and U.S. air forces dominated the skies over Western Europe, allowing them to target almost all German cities. First use on the battlefield would have opened up German cities to retaliatory chemical bombings. Unlike Britain in 1940, Germany had not distributed gas masks widely among their civilian population, making them vulnerable to chemical attack. The long-run loss outweighed the short-run gain (Spiers 1986, 78–79; Price 1997, 120).

Germany had also synthesized and produced the first nerve gases, which are substantially more lethal than other agents. Production started late and faced many difficulties with large enough stocks for use available only at the end of 1944. Josef Goebbels, Martin Bormann, and Robert Ley urged Hitler to use nerve gas, either against British cities or the approaching Soviet armies. He refused, fearing Allied retaliation. Other German leaders, including Albert Speer and the top military leaders, were prepared to take steps to prevent the use of gas if authorized by Hitler (Harris and Paxman 2002, 64–67).

The 1925 Geneva Protocol on CBW held during World War II because it created a shared expectation that no one would use chemical weapons. Those expectations did not rely on blind optimism that the other side would follow the rules; they were backed up by deterrent capabilities. Although few wished to use chemical weapons, they were prepared to retaliate in kind. Although the United States had not ratified the protocol, President Roosevelt made public pledges in 1942 and 1943 not to use chemical weapons first while forcefully stating that the United States would retaliate against any use by the Axis (Brown 1968, 264–265; Price 1997, 118). Noise posed little problem for reciprocal enforcement because inadvertent violations were rare. Widespread violations, such as those of Italy against Ethiopia and Japan against China, were obviously state policy. In both cases, the victim state lacked the ability to retaliate fully. Furthermore, Japan could use gas legally because it had not ratified the 1925 Geneva Protocol on CBW. The combination of a shared understanding that chemical weapons were prohibited, stockpiles for retaliation, and the ability to determine that violations were the result of state policy made the ban hold.

An alternative explanation is that states did not use chemical weapons because they were ineffective on the battlefield. The widespread use of gas during World War I gave neither side a clear military advantage nor broke the stalemate of the trenches. According to this explanation, states simply abjured the use of weapons they would not have used in any case. The utility of chemical weapons cannot be judged from the evidence of World War II because nonuse could result from either their military inefficacy or the shared understanding that they would not be used. The value of gas as a weapon can only be judged when the latter broke down, namely during World War I. The lack of legal clarity led to a breakdown of the 1899 Hague Declaration on Gas that could have limited the use of chemical weapons. The record of the use of chemical weapons during World War I does not support the position that the warring states saw them as ineffective on the battlefield. If they had, they would have used less gas as the war progressed and they learned that these were not useful weapons. To the contrary, the use of chemical weapons increased as the war progressed (Spiers 2010, 42). Amounts used roughly doubled every year after their introduction in 1915 (Spiers 1986, 13). Once both Germany and the Western Allies had used gas on the Western Front, all of them used gases more often and in new ways. The advent of mustard gas in June 1917 accelerated the use of gas and the casualties it produced (Harris and Paxman 2002, 26–30). Mustard gas proved superior to asphyxiants such as chlorine and phosgene on the battlefield, both increasing the use of gas and the casualties. According to Victor Lefebure, "mustard gas ... was the war gas *par excellence* for the purpose of causing casualties" (1923, 68). Asphyxiants required strong concentrations of volatile gas to kill, concentrations that often dispersed quickly. Mustard and other vesicants were persistent; their boiling point was low enough that they retained dangerous concentrations on the battlefield, including pools of liquid. They could create contaminated zones that could last for days, making them effective offensively by creating zones on the flank of an attack or hindering enemy artillery or defensively by making the ground the attackers had to cover poisonous. The innovation of mustard also made other gases more effective. During 1918, it is estimated that one-third to one-half of all shells fired by the German army on the Western Front were gas shells. Armies used gas during World War I because it was valuable and effective (Price 1997, 81).[3] The argument that chemical weapons were ineffective fails to note that none of the other military innovations of World War I – indirect fire heavy artillery, tanks, close air support, superior open order infantry tactics, among others – were decisive just by being used. All of these innovations added useful capabilities on the battlefield, yet required understanding how they could contribute to successful attacks.

AERIAL BOMBING

"[A] question of accuracy and not a question of intent(Colby 1925, 710)."

Airplanes had not been invented by the time of the first Hague Conference in 1899, and they were still a novelty during the second in 1907. Balloons had

---

[3] See Haber 1986, 176–238 and Spiers 2010, 36–39, 42–44 on gas tactics and the effectiveness of chemical weapons during World War I. Haber 1986, 259–282 argues that gas was a failure as a weapon during World War I, but he does not compare gas to other innovations of the war.

been used during war as observation posts but not as manned platforms to deliver bombs.[4] The 1899 Conference considered whether to ban the discharge of projectiles from powered lighter-than-air craft, such as Zeppelins, and similar methods. This effort to head off the militarization of the air foundered because the British and U.S. representatives were unwilling to ban possible methods of war when there was little idea how they would develop. Instead, a five-year ban was adopted, a ban that lapsed with time. It was renewed during the 1907 Hague conference but the continental European powers did not ratify that provision because they now sought to develop aerial capabilities with dirigibles and opposed a ban on air warfare (Watt 1979, 60–61; Parks 1990, 10–12, 16–17; Biddle 1994, 141–144).

The Hague Conventions did lay out principles for bombardment of cities and town, which many drew on when thinking about how aerial bombardment should be limited. Articles 25 through 27 of the 1899 Hague Convention (II) with respect to the Laws and Customs of War on Land prohibited attacks on undefended towns and buildings, required military authorities to inform civilian authorities before beginning the bombardment of a town, and required them to avoid targeting cultural sites and hospitals. These rules drew on the traditions of siege warfare in which an army would bombard an enemy-held city to breach its defenses and compel the defenders to surrender it. They sought to limit such bombardments to cases in which they were necessary to take the city and to limit their damage to the defenses where possible. The 1907 Hague Convention (IV) reaffirmed these three principles of bombardment. It also laid out more specific conditions for naval bombardments, allowing the bombardment of naval bases and facilities that could be used for "the needs of the hostile fleet or army" (1907 Hague Convention [IX] concerning Bombardment by Naval Forces in Time of War, Article 2). As many industrial facilities could fall into this category, it opened up gray areas for what buildings could be targeted. By this article, commanders of a bombardment were not held responsible for collateral damage (that is, the destruction of other property hit by mistake during a bombardment). These principles sought to limit artillery bombardments with their inaccuracies to the destruction of military targets and in the abstract could have been extended to cover bombardment from the air. But these principles were more difficult to apply to aerial bombing than artillery bombardments. If undefended towns could not be bombed, how could the aircrew of a bomber verify whether a town was defended? Would any military presence of any sort constitute a defense, making the city eligible for bombardment? Unlike a land force which could take control of an undefended town, air forces could not (Parks 1990, 10–12, 16–19; Biddle 1994, 141–144).

Inaccuracy complicates the legal regulation of aerial bombing. In an era of precision-guided munitions, many have come to believe that every bomb hits

---

[4] The Austrians tried to use unmanned balloons to float bombs to land on Venice in 1849 (Parks 1990, 10).

its target and so every nonmilitary target hit breaches humanitarian norms to protect civilians and protected sites. Nevertheless, there are many reasons why a side seeking to follow the rules might bomb protected sites and people. First, intelligence about what sites are targets could be incorrect. Second, the aircrew might incorrectly identify the target during their mission, possibly because of weather conditions or camouflage. Third, the bombing aircraft could be under attack, leading the aircrew to drop their munitions to save themselves. Attack here includes electronic jamming by the defender that throws off the guidance of a bomb. Fourth, even guided munitions go ballistic and fall unguided sometimes. Fifth, ballistic munitions, such as the bombs used during the World Wars, are inherently difficult to target in the best circumstances. Sixth, the crew may disobey orders and attack other targets on their own initiative. Finally, the skill of the crews influences all of these concerns (Parks 1990, 184–202). Inaccuracy creates noise in the terms of the model in Chapter 3; the bomber may hit targets that the military and civilian authorities never intended to target. Those bombed may interpret those mistakes as deliberate.

All forms of aerial bombing face these issues of hitting the wrong targets, but they loom larger in strategic bombing. Broadly speaking, tactical bombing supports ground or naval forces by attacking enemy forces from the air, while strategic bombing aims at destroying targets behind the lines that support the troops at the front, such as transportation networks or factories producing war material. Planes conducting tactical missions can hit protected targets, such as hospitals or civilian sites near the front line. Their intent to identify and target enemy forces reduces the risk of attacks on protected sites. In strategic bombing, it is often difficult to identify which sites constitute acceptable military targets. Is any factory in an enemy city an acceptable target because the country's industry supports its war effort? Most strategic targets have both civilian and military value. Bombing rail yards hurts both military and civilian transportation. Because strategic targets are often located in cities, inaccurate bombing means that nonmilitary sites are likely to be hit. For these reasons, strategic bombing has posed greater challenges for the control of aerial bombing than tactical bombing.

Military aviation advanced greatly during World War I. At the beginning, the major combatants had small numbers of airplanes used for scouting and reconnaissance. A German zeppelin carried out the first aerial bombing on Antwerp on August 25, 1914, killing ten Belgians (Gilbert 1994, 42). Germany launched its first zeppelin raid on Britain on the night of January 19/20, 1915 (Raleigh and Jones 1922, 3:90). Zeppelin raids on Britain continued sporadically throughout the war. They were conducted at night as the airships were vulnerable to fighter aircraft and antiaircraft guns. Bad weather also broke up missions as the zeppelins either could not find their targets or were blown off course. The Germans turned to building airplanes large enough to fly from bases in Belgium to Britain while carrying bomb loads. These early strategic bombers, the Gotha and the Giant, conducted multiple raids on Paris and cities in Britain during 1917. These raids were more effective because they were conducted at daytime, making it easier for the bombers to find British cities. All told, German strategic bombing killed 1,413 British civilians during World War I (Banks and Palmer 1989, 296; Corum 1997, 34–36). Although these raids alarmed and enraged the British public, they had little effect on the war. The British sought to retaliate against these German raids. Major General Hugh Trenchard formed the Independent Air Force, the first strategic bombing force in history. It conducted daily raids on targets in German cities from April 1918 until the end of the war.[5] These raids were not appreciably more successful than the German ones on Britain (Cooper 1986, 134–136). At this time, the technology of aerial bombing limited strategic bombing. Early bomb racks were crude; one of the first British raids on Germany ended up dropping a bomb on Rotterdam in the Netherlands when it fell out of its rack as it flew over the city (Grey 1942, 15). The range and bomb loads of planes were limited, and navigation to find the cities in which the targets were located was primitive. Although all sides tried to hit industrial targets that supported the other side's war effort, very few of the bombs dropped did so. Strategic bombing was a curiosity that awaited further development in airplane and targeting technology (Corum 1997, 40–43; Biddle 2002, 20–48).

During the interwar period, the potential of strategic bombing excited military minds in many countries. Here might be a way to avoid the slaughter in the trenches by knocking out the enemy with a massive and decisive blow from the skies. General Billy Mitchell in the United States advocated for an independent air force to conduct strategic bombing through public speeches and popular books, but his efforts were unsuccessful and he was eventually court-martialed for insubordination (Murray 1985, 308–311; Biddle 2002, 136–138; Budiansky 2004, 150–151). Trenchard urged Britain to create its own bomber force as a deterrent in the belief that defense of cities against enemy bombers was not possible (Watt 1979, 65, 67, 71–72; Murray 1985, 301–302; Legro 1995, 129–131; Biddle 2002, 69–102). The most famous theorist of air war was the Italian Guilio Douhet. *The Command of the Air* (1942), his apocalyptic tract on the potential of air power, foresaw wars in the future ending quickly with massive strategic bombing of enemy cities with high explosive and poison gas. Like many others of the time, Douhet saw civilian morale as the weak point at which national will could be broken and wars won. Better thousands of dead civilians in a war of a week than millions dead in a struggle of years. The expectation that the next war would see mass bombing of cities spread across the public (Corum 1997, 89–107).[6]

---

[5] See Raleigh 1922, Appendices, 42–84 for a table of these raids.

[6] Douhet's theory of strategic bombing assumed that chemical weapons would constitute an important part of terror bombing of civilians. In a sense, Douhet's theory was never tested during World War II, or since.

The limited strategic bombing of World War I also led to increasing efforts to legally restrict aerial bombing. The victorious Allied powers sought to deprive Germany of all military aircraft through the Versailles Treaty, a restriction that postwar German leaders did all they could to subvert (Legro 1995, 103–104; Corum 1997, 49, 55–78, 115–118). The 1922 Washington conference briefly considered and then passed on setting rules for the new ways of war, including aerial bombing. A panel of jurists drafted rules restricting aerial bombing to military targets and banning terror bombings of civilians, cultural monuments, and other nonmilitary targets, but no nation signed them, much less ratified them. These rules describe what jurists of the time thought that rules regulating aerial bombardment should be. They codified norms restricting aerial bombardment to military targets, while recognizing that some targets would be located within cities. Stronger visions, such as restricting aerial bombing to the support of ground troops in active combat zones or limiting the range of aircraft, were rejected. These rules also recognized that the defender bore some responsibility to ensure that protected sites were not used for military purposes of any kind. Although the draft rules were never adopted, they provide legal language spelling out what a legal standard would look like. No country, however, accepted this standard (Watt 1979, 66–67; Parks 1990, 24–44; Biddle 1994, 148–151; Legro 1995, 97–99; Lippman 2002, 9–12).

The outbreak of war brought dread of death from the skies. The British Ministry of Health distributed 1,000,000 death forms in April 1939 in anticipation of the expected civilian casualties from aerial bombing (Parks 1990, 48). This dread did not immediately come to pass. The first British air raids on Germany dropped leaflets rather than bombs. President Roosevelt called on the warring powers to foreswear bombing civilians, and Britain, France, and Germany affirmed they would do so while reserving their right to respond in kind if their opponents did not (Legro 1995, 99). These public affirmations were not legally binding nor did they specify how one might judge when a violation had occurred. As J. M. Spaight wrote at the time: "It [the law of bombardment] is indeed in a state of baffling chaos and confusion which makes it almost impossible to say what in any given situation the rule really is" (quoted in Biddle 1994, 151).

Even though these three nations restricted their air war against one another at first, escalation to general city bombing unfolded over time. A bombing of military targets in Warsaw coordinated with the German attack on September 1, 1939 was cancelled by inclement weather. Later that month, the Luftwaffe bombed military targets in support of German ground forces in the assault on Warsaw. Rotterdam suffered from a heavy air raid the day before the Netherlands surrendered to Germany. The intent of these bombings was tactical rather than terror, but the Allies – particularly the British – did not interpret them as purely military bombardments, even though German leaders defended them as such (Legro 1995, 115–116). The British launched air raids on the

Ruhr cities on May 15, using the Rotterdam bombing as justification that their bombing was retaliation (Legro 1995, 135). The Battle of Britain accelerated the escalation to general city bombing. The Germans began the battle to gain air superiority over Britain by attacking the bases of the Royal Air Force (RAF). The British used errant bombing on August 24 as an excuse to launch an air raid on Berlin the following night (Legro 1995, 137–140; Biddle 2002, 188). The resulting aerial battle of attrition favored the RAF over the Luftwaffe, leading Hitler and Goering to order a bombing raid on the docks of London on September 7. Although this raid caused substantial damage in the dock-lands, the RAF broke up the following attack on London a week later, scattering the German bombers and the bomb loads they dropped over London. The failure of this raid led the Luftwaffe to move to night bombing of British cities, in what became known as the Blitz. These raids continued into Spring 1941. In response, Bomber Command of the RAF expanded its own nighttime raids on German cities, adopting indiscriminate city bombing with an attack on Mannheim on the night of December 16, 1940 (Legro 1995, 140–141). Night bombing was much less accurate than day bombing because pilots were fortunate to locate the city they were sent to attack, much less identify a specific military target within that city. Both sides considered themselves to be retaliating against the indiscriminate city bombing of the other. Of the two, the British pushed the escalation of city bombing more than the Germans did (Legro 1995, 136–141).

The campaign of night bombing of German cities increased as Bomber Command built up its strength in long-range bombers. These raids were very inaccurate; "only one in three got within five miles [of their target]" (quoted in Biddle 1994, 152). In early 1942, Bomber Command adopted the strategy of "de-housing," the decision to target cities with no effort made to hit specific targets within them. These raids were popular with the British public as they were a way to strike at Germany (Budiansky 2004, 285). Sir Arthur "Bomber" Harris was appointed the head of Bomber Command and became linked forever with the nighttime city busting bombing. Harris believed that city bombing would combine the physical destruction of German cities with the morale effect, and so cripple German production and society. The pinnacles of this campaign were the firebombing of Hamburg in July 1943 and the bombing of Dresden in February 1945. Both cities were destroyed over the course of several nights and days of bombing, killing tens of thousands of civilians (Biddle 2002, 197–203, 219–222).

The United States entered strategic bombing with the buildup of the Eighth Air Force in Britain. Unlike RAF's Bomber Command, the U.S. Army Air Corps believed it could accurately hit military targets in the midst of cities, such as factories supporting the German war effort, through daylight bombing (Biddle 2002, 208–213). Tests of the Norden bomb sight indicated that industrial targets could be hit accurately, but unfortunately, the skies over Europe were not the cloudless target ranges of the American Southwest where the tests were conducted (Neillands 2001, 168–170; Budiansky 2004, 173–176). A joint U.S.-British study in 1945 revealed that 42 percent of bombs dropped by the U.S. Eighth Air Force under heavy cloud cover fell more than five miles from their intended targets; even in good weather, almost one-third of bombs missed their targets by at least 3,000 feet (Biddle 2002, 223–224, 243–244). Unescorted bomber missions deep into Germany during 1943 proved too costly to sustain. The air war over Germany turned with the advent of the P-51 Mustang fighter equipped with drop tanks that allowed it to escort bombing missions to Berlin and back. The Western Allies gained control of the skies over Europe through the resulting war of attrition (Murray 1985, 223–232; Biddle 2002, 227). German cities were pounded from the air, night and day, as the British and U.S. bomber forces sought to knock out Germany. The culmination of the bombing campaign included massive raids on Berlin in February 1945 that sought to break German morale. When no surrender was forthcoming, British leaders chose Dresden as the second target. U.S. leaders, in contrast, concluded from the Berlin bombing that bombing could not end the war by breaking German morale and so participated in the Dresden bombing solely to disable the rail yards and links in the city (Biddle 1994, 259; Biddle 2002, 253–256). These final bombings are an example of a winning side breaking the rules in an effort to compel the loser to surrender.

German air raids on Britain continued fitfully after the Blitz, but the majority of the Luftwaffe was moved east for the invasion of the Soviet Union. The V-weapons – the first cruise (V-1) and ballistic (V-2) missiles used in war – provided the final efforts at aerial bombing by the Germans against Britain. These weapons were quite inaccurate and were targeted at the greater London area rather than individual military targets.[7] As noted in the section on chemical weapons, the V-weapons attacks enraged Churchill to the point that he advocated chemical attacks on German cities in response.

In the Pacific theater, Japanese air forces terror bombed Chinese cities soon after the outbreak of war in 1937. Japan itself was invulnerable as China had few aircraft and none that could reach the Japanese islands. The Doolittle Raid on April 18, 1942 shattered Japan's sense of invulnerability. The raid used sixteen B-25 bombers launched from the deck of the aircraft carrier *Hornet* to bomb Tokyo, doing minor damage, and then flying onto the landing strips in China if they could make it. The Japanese tried the air crews who were forced to land in Japanese-held territory as war criminals for their indiscriminate bombing, executing three of them (Calvocoressi et al. 1989, 1032–1036). Strategic bombing of Japan had to wait for bases that could support regular raids. Raids staged from bases in China triggered Japanese offensives aimed at seizing the airfields, offensives that led to the deaths of thousands of Chinese soldiers and civilians (Sherry 1987, 122–123, 169). The fall of the Marianas in the summer of 1944 provided the bases

---

[7] Some V-weapons were launched against military targets in support of German ground troops.

for the B-29 Superfortresses to begin routine bombing raids on the cities of
Japan. The raids initially targeted Japanese industry, flying at high altitude
and trying to bomb precisely. These raids were not producing the desired
effect, and General Curtis LeMay changed tactics after he was promoted to
command. Because Japanese industry was spread out in small workshops
rather than large factories, LeMay shifted from high explosives to incendiary
bombs, a strategy that the United States had tested on its proving grounds.
He also stripped out the defensive armament of his B-29s to maximize bomb
loads and bombed at low altitude at night. The first raid hit Tokyo on the
night of March 9/10, 1945; the resulting firestorm killed an estimated 78,000
Japanese civilians. The relentless tide of firebombing burned out the centers of
almost every Japanese city in the following months; Hiroshima and Nagasaki
were chosen as targets for the first atomic bombings in August 1945 in part
because they were two of the few Japanese cities that had not been devastated
by the fire bombings. These fire bombings were justified as strategic bombing
of the decentralized workshops that supported Japan's war effort, but their
practical effect was the indiscriminate killing of civilians. In response, Japan
treated downed airmen as war criminals, conducting show trials followed
by executions in some cases such as the one that opened this book (Russell
of Liverpool 1958, 70–71; Piccigallo 1979, 69–73; Sherry 1987, 169; Biddle
2002, 261–270).

World War II saw little restraint in aerial bombing. Although there were
ideas about what restrained bombing would look like and some efforts to limit
bombing to military targets, the inaccuracy of aerial bombing technology made
limits impossible. Even when one side sought to bomb within limits, the other
side could not tell that from the results. Efforts to bomb military targets within
cities, which most accepted as legitimate targets, led to widespread bomb damage in the target cities. Furthermore, all sides used the results of their enemy's
bombing as justification for their own aerial bombing of enemy cities. Churchill
used errant German bombing of London as an excuse to escalate British night
raids on German cities. Germany, in contrast, sought to avoid escalation of the
air war during the first years of the war. As Legro (1995) describes, German
officials offered explanations for the bombings of Rotterdam and London in
an effort to justify them as acceptable and so forestall British escalation. But
there was no consensus on what the rules to limit bombing should be, meaning
that all sides interpreted the attacks of the other as indiscriminate. The combination of inaccuracy of bombing and the lack of a publicly accepted standard to limit bombing offered the opportunity for those who wished to bomb
indiscriminately.

Legro argues that military culture – the practices of doctrine about how
a military should fight – determine whether they follow conventions during
wartime. In aerial bombing, the RAF prepared for strategic bombing, whereas
the Luftwaffe trained for close support of the Wehrmacht, explaining in his
view why the British escalated to city bombing while the Germans were more

circumspect.[8] There is an important element of truth in this view. Britain and the United States built heavy bombers needed for long-distance strategic bombing, whereas Germany invested in medium bombers. In the words for former Secretary of Defense Donald Rumsfeld: "you go to war with the Army you have, not the Army you might want or wish to have at a later time."[9] As Legro recognizes, the composition of the forces influences what strategy a country adopts during war, and so the lack of heavy bombers inclined Germany to avoid strategic bombing against enemies like Britain that could hit German cities in response (Legro 1995, 113–115). Germany abandoned the development of heavy bombers in the mid-1930s when it focused aircraft development on medium bombers and fighters; German industry was incapable of producing the larger, more powerful engines required by heavy bombers at that time (Murray 1985, 8–10; Corum 1997, 170–173). Aircraft had long development times from impetus to design to production at a level from which they could be deployed into battle. The Heinkel 177 bomber project began in 1937 but had not yielded planes in sufficient quantity to deploy en masse by 1944 (Murray 1985, 10, 236; Corum 1997, 268–269).[10] The lack of heavy bombers meant that Germany could not respond in kind to the strategic air offensives of Britain and the United States.[11] German doctrine that focused on tactical close air support did not prevent the Luftwaffe from engaging in terror bombing against opponents who lacked the ability to retaliate in kind. The German invasion of Yugoslavia began with a bombing of Belgrade that deliberately sought to kill civilians as punishment and killed 17,000. The Luftwaffe's objective was "*the city of Belgrade* will be destroyed from the air by continual day and night attacks" (quoted in Murray 1985, 78, emphasis in text). The Luftwaffe's bombings of Moscow and Leningrad during 1941 were limited only by the need to have aircraft support ground attacks (Murray 1985, 87). The battle of Stalingrad was fought in ruins because the Germans bombed the city heavily before their forces reached it, killing 40,000 out of a population of 525,000 (Beevor 1998, 104–106; Overy 1998, 165–166; Bellamy 2007, 507–510). Richard Overy (1998, 89) estimates that 500,000 Soviet citizens died from German aerial bombing during the war. Even though the Luftwaffe's doctrine favored close support over strategic bombings, this military culture did not stop it from bombing the civilians of countries who could not retaliate. Their restraint came only when those who could, particularly the

---

[8] John Corum (1997, 233–249) presents a more nuanced view of German air doctrine before World War II, one in which strategic bombing played an important role, contrary to Legro's position.

[9] Quoted in http://www.cnn.com/2004/US/12/08/rumsfeld.kuwait/index.html, accessed on June 20, 2013.

[10] Normally, the full cycle from initial design to deployment of an aircraft was about three years in the Luftwaffe during the 1930s (Corum 1997, 166 for examples).

[11] Corum (1997, 282–284) argues that the lack of an effective escort fighter rather than the lack of a heavy bomber compromised German efforts to win the Battle of Britain.

British, might use any such bombing as justification for their own strategic bombing of Germany.

## CONDUCT ON THE HIGH SEAS

War at sea brings to mind the great sea battles that decide the command of the seas – Jutland, Midway, and Leyte Gulf, to name three of the most famous naval battles of the World Wars. For the laws of war, however, the action lies in the day-to-day struggle to interrupt enemy commerce on the oceans and seas. The great battles were fought at a distance at which the obligations to aid sailors whose ships have sunk and to allow the free passage of neutral ships not carrying contraband do not bind. These obligations arise when a warship intercepts a merchant ship that may or may not be carrying cargo which could aid the war effort of the enemy. This is the mundane and daily business of blockade which is allowed during war.

Ideas of what is allowed and what is not in a blockade had evolved over centuries of experience (Hattendorf 1994, 104–108). The Declaration Respecting Maritime Law signed with the Treaty of Paris in 1856 stated four basic principles of the laws of war on the high seas:

1.  Privateering is, and remains, abolished;
2.  The neutral flag covers enemy's goods, with the exception of contraband of war;
3.  Neutral goods, with the exception of contraband of war, are not liable to capture under enemy's flag;
4.  Blockades, in order to be binding, must be effective, that is to say, maintained by a force sufficient really to prevent access to the coast of the enemy (Treaty of Paris, 1856).

These principles sought to create a system by which countries at war could conduct blockades that cut off war materials while allowing trade in other goods to move freely. Neutral countries could gain by trading military and other goods with those at war. The other side wished to restrict that trade to hurt the enemy's war effort. The protection of the lives of merchant sailors was secondary at this time because blockades seized merchant ships or discouraged them from entering the blockade zone rather than sinking them (Ranft 1979, 40–45).

The Hague Conventions sought to add detail to these principles and adapt them to changes in naval technology. The 1899 Hague Convention (III) for the Adaptation to Maritime Warfare of the Principles of the Geneva Convention of 1864 protected hospital ships from attack and restrictions on their movement and obligated ships to pick up and care for shipwrecked sailors, extending humanitarian protections on the land to the sea. The 1907 Hague Convention (X) for the Adaptation to Maritime Warfare of the Principles of the Geneva Convention reaffirmed these humanitarian protections. The technology of naval combat changed rapidly in the decades before World War I. Ranges of guns increased, and mines and torpedoes provided new ways to sink ships. Together, these three made close blockade of harbors untenable. The expansion of trade and the national merchant fleets that carried that trade led to the legal protection of merchant ships in enemy harbors on the outbreak of war; the 1907 Hague Convention (VI) relating to the Status of Enemy Merchant Ships at the Start of Hostilities gave them the right to leave and sail home without the threat of confiscation. The 1907 Hague Convention (VII) relating to the Conversion of Merchant Ships into War-ships required warships, including converted merchantmen, to carry distinctive markings to distinguish them from merchant ships at a distance. Naval mines were required to be secured to the ocean floor and could not be used to interrupt shipping (1907 Hague Convention [VIII] relative to the Laying of Automatic Submarine Contact Mines). Other conventions within the 1907 Hague Convention protected non-warships and their crews (XI), detailed the rights of neutral shipping (XIII), forbade warships from seeking indefinite protection in neutral ports (XIII), allowed for the creation of national prize courts for ships seized while limiting what those courts could do (XIII), and banned neutrals from providing "war-ships, ammunition, or war material of any kind whatever" to parties at war (XIII). The London Declaration of 1909 added further detail to these provisions, including lists of what could be considered contraband and what could not. These rules were not binding, although all the major powers signed the declaration. Most of the major combatants in World War I had ratified the naval provisions of the 1907 Hague Conventions in advance of the war, with the exceptions of Russia, Italy, and the United States, all of which ratified some but not all of separate conventions. Great Britain ratified all except those conventions on the rights of neutral shipping.

These provisions floundered during World War I. Britain and France declared naval blockades of Germany and Austria-Hungary on August 12, 1914 (Gilbert 1994, 46–47). The British maintained their blockade across the English Channel and the north end of the North Sea, intercepting almost all merchant shipping along these routes. This distant blockade violated the rules for close blockade but was adopted to avoid the risks of mines and sorties against a blockade close to the German ports and naval bases. At first, the list of contraband focused on war material broadly, including food, that was bound for Germany. The blockade angered neutrals, particularly the United States, that sought to do business with both sides. Cut off from most of their seaborne trade, the Germans traded heavily with the neutrals on their borders. The Netherlands became a main transit port for goods bound for Germany. The British pressed the Dutch to end this trade by declaring that any contraband, now expanded to cover raw materials that might conceivably be used in the war effort, headed for the Dutch ports would be intercepted under the presumption that the goods were ultimately bound for Germany. The British blockade cut off the majority of German trade, which dropped two-thirds in volume in the first two years of the war. It led to shortages of most goods in Germany, helped to create widespread hunger and malnutrition among the civilian population as food was hoarded for the army, and hundreds of thousands died as a result (Stevenson 2004, 200–204, 228–229).

The Germans sought to disrupt British trade as well. The first year of the war saw German cruisers originally based in their colonies in Africa and the Pacific raid the sea lanes, but the British Navy tracked down these raiders and sunk them (Stevenson 2004, 66–69). With the Kaiser unwilling to commit the High Seas Fleet to a decisive battle and surface raiders unable to evade the British blockade, German leaders turned to the U-boats, their submarine force. Submarines pose problems for the rules on the interception of merchant shipping. Blockading ships are supposed to intercept ships so they can inspect them for contraband. Ships carrying contraband cargoes to the enemy can be seized as prizes and brought into port. In extreme conditions, the ship can be sunk at sea, provided that the crew is allowed to evacuate first; surface vessels commonly take the crew on board and release them once back in port. These prize rules, so called because captured merchant ships and their cargos were prizes of wars, sought to protect neutral shipping and sailors from harm, provided that they were not carrying contraband. Searching a stopped ship and then seizing it or evacuating the crew if it had to be sunk take time. Submarines are vulnerable to almost all warships and airplanes when on the surface. They submerge to avoid combat with surface warships. When a submarine follows the prize rules by surfacing, stopping the merchant vessel, and searching it, it is vulnerable if the ship radios for help and a warship responds. Furthermore, submarines cannot take captured ships back to port nor do they have the space to take on the crews of ships they intercept and sink. In practice, submarines attack merchant ships without warning using either their guns on the surface or torpedoes if they are submerged. Blockades enforced by submarines often break the prize rules and put the crews of merchant ships, including neutrals, at risk (Blair 1996, 7–9; Detter Delupis 2000, 308–314).

On February 4, 1915, Germany declared the waters around the British Isles to be a war zone in which all merchant shipping, British and neutral, was liable to be sunk without warning by submarines (Gilbert 1994, 127–128). These attacks, most famously the sinking of the *Lusitania*, enraged neutral countries whose citizens drowned when the ships they were traveling on were sunk. President Woodrow Wilson of the United States pressed Germany to pay compensation for the victims and stop the unrestricted attacks. The pressure worked, and, on May 4, 1916, the German Navy reverted to the prize rules for submarine attacks on shipping. These restrictions reduced the effectiveness of the submarine blockade of the British Isles. As the German position in the war became more difficult and particularly as the British blockade imposed severe hardships on the German population, pressure to resume unrestricted submarine warfare grew within the German political and military leaders. The politics inside the German government turned against Chancellor Theobald von

Bethmann-Hollweg, who argued against unrestricted submarine war because of the fear that it would provoke the United States to join the war. Even respecting the prize rules, increases in the number of U-boats had led to more sinkings of merchant ships. This progress convinced Hindenburg and Ludendorff to push for unrestricted submarine warfare in the hope of knocking out Britain before the United States could mobilize its military, if it chose to intervene. At the Pless conference on January 9, 1917, German leaders agreed to begin unrestricted submarine war on February 1 of that year. The resulting loss of U.S. citizens in sinkings, the disruption of trade, and the Zimmermann telegram combined to drive the United States into the war against Germany. Sinkings of merchant ships in the waters around Britain rose, leading the British to adopt convoys, which reduced the U-boat threat greatly (Terraine 1989, 8–16; Halpern 1994, 335–344; Stevenson 2004, 208–214, 254–261, 365–368).

Before the height of unrestricted submarine warfare in 1917, Britain adopted other means of fighting the U-boats that violated the existing rules. Q-ships, armed merchantmen which concealed their armament until a U-boat attacked them on the surface, broke the distinction between unarmed merchantmen and warships. Their tactics were perfidious as they attempted to lure submarines into attacking them on the surface. Smaller merchant ships were used so that the submarine commander would surface to use his deck gun rather than waste a torpedo to sink it. Although Q-ships were not used widely, their threat led U-boat commanders to sink merchant ships without warning to avoid the risk that the target was a Q-ship (Corbett 1923, 50–53; Halpern 1994, 343).

Submarine warfare also posed problems for the protection of hospital ships, particularly in the Mediterranean where submarines were rare. The Germans charged that the British used hospital ships as military transports, making them fair game for having abused the protection of the Red Cross symbol. The French retaliated by loading German officers held as prisoners on their hospital ships and informed the Germans of this practice; the Germans responded by relocating French prisoners to sections of the front line in France within the range of Allied guns. The British began protecting hospital ships in convoys escorted by warships. The Austrians, on the other hand, announced that they would not attack hospital ships and asked the Germans to reflag any of their submarines operating in the Adriatic under the Austrian flag. Eventually, the issue was solved by having the neutral Spanish provide officers to inspect hospital ships to confirm that they were carrying only the wounded and ill and then accompany the ship on its voyage. The Germans were unwilling to extend this agreement beyond the Mediterranean. The most infamous sinking of a hospital ship was the *Llandovery Castle*, sunk off Ireland on June 27, 1918. Captain Patzig of *U-86* may have sunk it in error, but he compounded the atrocity by machine gunning the survivors in the lifeboats afterward (Newbolt 1928, 809–811; Halpern 1987, 309, 316–324; Brode 1997, 132).

Both sides pointed to what the other was doing as justification for their own acts that violated the principles of the Hague Conventions and the London

Declaration. Great Britain could claim that it was not bound to follow the conventions with respect to its treatment of neutral ships because it had not ratified the relevant conventions (1907 Hague Convention XIII). The London Declaration was not binding because no state ratified it, which allowed the British to claim that their blockade was legal. Germany justified its submarine war as a blockade of British waters equivalent to the British blockade (Gilbert 1994, 127–128; Blair 1996, 11; see Corbett 1921, 261–265, 282–284 for an overheated defense of the British position). In turn, Britain justified Q-ships as a response to sinkings on sight of merchant ships even though those ships violated Hague Convention (VII) relating to the Conversion of Merchant Ships into War-ships, which Britain had ratified. The sinkings of hospital ships gave rise to similar charges and countercharges as did the laying of underwater mines as part of blockades. Both sides were quite willing to use the lack of specific, binding law to justify the acts they undertook on the high seas. They used the law to justify their claims when they could, and when they could not, they justified their acts as retaliation against the illegal acts of the other side.

Great Britain made repeated efforts during the interwar period to outlaw submarines, or failing that, legally obligate them to follow prize rules when they attacked merchant ships. These rules, if put into action, would limit greatly commerce raiding by submarines. The treaty negotiated at the Washington Conference in 1922, the same one that first banned poison gas, included such provisions and urged that submarine captains who violated it should be treated as pirates. The treaty did not mention keelhauling or walking the plank as possible punishments, however. France was hesitant; not wishing to outlaw submarines, it signed but did not ratify the treaty. The 1930 London Treaty for the Limitation and Reduction of Naval Armaments also included similar language. When these provisions were set to expire at the end of 1936, Britain pushed to reaffirm the specific language of these rules in the 1930 London Treaty. This effort was successful in that all the major powers either reaffirmed their ratification of the 1930 London Treaty or ratified the 1936 London Treaty for the Limitation of Naval Armament. Their primary legal defect was a lack of clarity about whether armed merchantmen or those guarded in convoys were legitimate targets to sink without warning (Burns 1971, 57–60; Ranft 1979, 53–54; Legro 1995, 36–38; Blair 1996, 26–29).

Despite these legal efforts, few countries followed these rules during World War II. Germany announced that it would follow the prize rules at the outbreak of war, but the *Athenia* was sunk without warning on September 4, 1939, one day after Britain declared war (Blair 1996, 64–69).[12] Hitler denied that the *Athenia* had been torpedoed by a U-boat and had Goebbels invent an elaborate deception that Britain had sunk the ship herself. This deception misled

---

[12] Legro (1995, 56–59) speculates that the practices of the U-boat service in favor of commerce raiding and unrestricted submarine warfare led the captain to torpedo the *Athenia*.

world opinion to the extent that the U.S. government did not formally accept the British account for a year (Van der Vat 1988, 4–6). The sinking led the British government to believe that the German declaration was an outright lie, and it began to arm its merchantmen. The British also directed merchant ships attacked by a U-boat to resist if capable and evade if not. Similarly, Britain organized convoys beginning on September 2, before it had declared war (Terraine 1989, 243–245; Legro 1995, 66–67; Blair 1996, 70–78). These measures violated the agreements and reflected British anticipations that Germany would use unrestricted submarine warfare regardless of what Britain did. Germany lacked enough U-boats to blockade British waters or to sink enough ships to threaten British trade at the start of the war. Despite this, Admiral Raeder, head of the Kriegsmarine, pushed for unrestricted submarine war using the British responses as justification (Legro 1995, 59–60). Hitler agreed to drop the prize rules and move to unrestricted submarine warfare on September 30, 1939, with all restrictions lifted by November 17, 1939 (Burns 1971, 59–60; Terraine 1989, 215–218; Padfield 1995, 481 for date).

The Battle of the Atlantic developed slowly as Germany built more U-boats and Britain moved all shipping into convoys. Germany also used surface raiders, airplanes, and armed merchantmen (sort of their own Q-ships) to raid commerce. The fall of France opened up ports on its Atlantic coast as U-boat bases. With these ports and more U-boats, Germany turned to "wolf pack" tactics where groups of submarines coordinated the detection of and attacks on convoys, typically on the surface at night. The sinkings of merchant ships slowly involved the United States more deeply into the convoy system, with President Roosevelt announcing that the U.S. Navy would assist with convoy duties on September 11, 1941 (Kershaw 2007, 320–322). Germany had little chance of winning the Battle of the Atlantic, and the tide turned decisively against it in the first half of 1943. Britain, the United States, and Canada were able to provide air cover and escort over all of the North Atlantic, including escort carriers to accompany convoys. Losses of U-boats rose, and sinkings of merchant ships remained below the rate at which they were being built.

There were few places where Britain could respond in kind. Britain imposed a blockade to cut off contraband imports to Germany. Hitler's autarkic economic policies meant that Germany, unlike in World War I, had little seaborne trade to interrupt. Sweden shipped iron ore to Germany via the Baltic Sea, but Germany could close the Kaggegat and Skagerrak, the straits between the Baltic and North Seas, to protect that trade. The British government considered using its submarines in the Baltic to attack iron ore shipments, but decided not to out of the fear of alienating neutral Sweden and Norway (Legro 1995, 71–73). When the war expanded to North Africa, the British used their submarines to attack the supply convoys from Europe to Libya. The prize rules were dropped for British submarines operating with thirty miles of the coasts of Italy and Libya during July 1940, the zone expanded in February 1941, and all restrictions removed in November 1942 (Padfield 1995, 483, 485, 495). Given the opportunity to hit a vulnerable target, the British did not hesitate to break the rules they had promoted during the interwar period.

The United States, however, conducted the one effective campaign of unrestricted submarine warfare against Japan. Being an island with few resources of its own, Japan, like Britain, relied on imports of raw materials. Before Pearl Harbor, the Navy began to consider a submarine campaign against Japan's merchant fleet. Some pointed to Germany's use of unrestricted submarine warfare and its alliance with Japan to justify an U.S. submarine campaign as retaliation rather than unilateral escalation (Legro 1995, 90–91). Within hours after Pearl Harbor, the U.S. Navy began sending submarines to attack Japanese shipping, even though this was contrary to prewar doctrine that limited submarines to supporting the battle fleet (Andrade 1971, 55–56; Burns 1971, 60; Blair 1975, 106–107; Padfield 1995, 183–185). The greatest problem the submarine campaign faced was the distances in the Pacific. Until bases nearer the sea lanes south of Japan could be seized, submarines would spend much of their time sailing from Pearl Harbor or Australia to their stations and little time on patrol (Holmes 1966, 92). As the number of submarines increased, the United States attacked the sea lanes between southeast Asia, where the Japanese had seized the natural resources they needed for their war effort, and the home islands of Japan. This campaign reduced the Japanese merchant marine to one-third its prewar size, at which point it could no longer carry the resources needed for the war effort (Keegan 1989, 194–195). U.S. submarines attacked without warning once they found a target; as noted in Chapter 5, U.S. submarines accidentally sunk Japanese freighters carrying POWs back to Japan.

Almost all naval powers violated the agreements that sought to outlaw unrestricted submarine war. The exception was Japan, who used its submarines to support its combat fleets by scouting and attacking enemy warships. Japanese doctrine (rather than restraint) explained why Japanese submarines sunk so few merchant ships (Burns 1971, 60). The Imperial Japanese Navy saw submarines as a way to wear down the U.S. Navy before a decisive naval battle and so compensate for their smaller surface fleet (Boyd and Yoshida 1995, 3–7). Some Japanese submarines attacked shipping in the Indian Ocean and off Australia, but the Japanese Navy made little effort to attack U.S. merchant shipping (cf. Holmes 1966, 95; Padfield 1995, 182 for examples of such attacks). Nine submarines were posted on the west coast of the United States after Pearl Harbor, but they sank only five merchant ships because their primary mission was scouting for U.S. warships headed west into the Pacific (Boyd and Yoshida 1995, 65–69). In the early years of war, results supported the Japanese doctrine as their support of the fleet produced more important results than those of the U.S. submarines that targeted merchant shipping (Blair 1975, 359–362, 551–554). Japanese submarines played less of a role as the war progressed as many were converted to running supplies to isolated island garrisons. With an increase in available submarines, better torpedoes, and closer bases, the U.S.

Navy's submarines inflicted serious damage on both Japanese Navy and merchant marine starting in 1944 (Blair 1975, 816–819).

The Soviet Navy used its submarines in the Baltic and Black Seas to attack German naval traffic. Hospital ships were attacked from the first months of the war in retribution for claims of German attacks on Soviet hospitals on land (De Zayas 1989, 261). The opportunities for the Soviet Navy were limited, however. The Black Sea Fleet dominated the waters there, but there was no substantial merchant traffic to attack. The Baltic Sea Fleet was cooped up in Leningrad during the long, horrible siege of that city. The surrender of Finland in August 1944 opened up access to the Baltic, and Soviet submarines began to attack German ships. A Soviet submarine sunk the sealiner *Wilhelm Gustloff* which was crammed with perhaps as many as 10,600 refugees on the night of January 30, 1945; only 996 survived, making it the worst maritime disaster in history. The Soviet Union would have honored the submarine captain as a Hero of the Soviet Union except for the fact he had an affair with a foreigner (Beevor 2002, 51; Bellamy 2007, 263, 624–626).

Because national leaders choose to engage in unrestricted submarine warfare, noise plays less of a role on conduct on the high seas. Individual ship captains on the high seas retain the ability to order their crew to commit violations on their own and against national policy. Incidents such as attacking sailors from the sunken ship in their lifeboats do occur. During World War I, the crew of the *Baralong*, a British Q-ship, murdered eleven members of the crew of the *U-27* they pulled from the sea after sinking it. The British submarine *Torbay* shot German survivors in the Mediterranean in 1941, and the *U-852* hunted down and killed the survivors of the *Peleus* in the South Atlantic. Ironically, the crew of the *U-852* was in turn attacked by British fighter planes after it was sunk off the coast of Somaliland two months later (De Zayas 1989, 259). In these examples of individual violations, only the German government punished the responsible parties (Hattendorf 1994, 113). The captain of the *U-30*, which sank the *Athenia*, was reprimanded and confined to quarters for his act (Burns 1971, 59). Hitler was dissuaded from carrying out reprisals against reports of the British killing shipwrecked U-boat crews because those cases were the exception rather than the policy (De Zayas 1989, 107–108, 245–260). Although the Japanese did not attack many merchant ships, their submarine captains had standing orders to capture a few prisoners from the crew for interrogation and then attack the survivors in the life boats (Russell of Liverpool 1958, 215–232). They also attacked shipwrecked survivors of warships they had sunk in some but not all cases (Michno 2001, 8–15). All sides pointed out the cases in which they thought their opponents had attacked shipwrecked sailors or hospital ships and offered excuses when they were accused of the same.

Conduct on the high seas was successfully limited in some areas, but failed in those areas in which the principles of the system conflicted with the realities of combat on the high seas. Although there were instances of attacks on shipwrecked sailors, these were the exception rather than the rule. Blockade in both of its main forms caused the primary problems. The surface blockades practiced by the British did not give rise to the losses of neutral shipping and deaths of passengers than submarine blockades did, but they expanded to cover a much wider range of goods than was anticipated in the law before the world wars. Modern industrial economies did not allow for a clear separation between goods that supported the war effort and those that did not. Submarines put themselves at exceptional risk if they tried to follow the prize rules, leading to the abandonment of those rules in unrestricted submarine warfare. British responses to the U-boat threat led to tactics like arming merchant ships in clear violation of the prewar rules. Between the wars, British efforts to ban submarines, or at least unrestricted submarine warfare, failed. Even though the major combatants ratified the 1936 London Treaty that restricted submarine warfare, the British anticipated that the Germans would adopt unrestricted submarine warfare when war broke out. These treaties failed to create a shared expectation that all sides would follow the rules in key areas, and so those agreements broke down in the face of the difficulties of submarine warfare.

TREATMENT OF CIVILIANS

The modern battlefield spreads over a continuous front that moves. Civilians are trapped in war zones, exposing them to both collateral damage and deliberate crimes by soldiers. The Hague Conventions focused on the latter and ignored the former. The deliberate destruction of undefended civilian sites and structures was banned, but this did not speak to collateral damage or the destruction of buildings used as defensive positions. Wanton destruction of property was forbidden, and cultural, religious, and scientific buildings were protected if they were demilitarized and clearly marked. Military forces were not allowed to coerce contributions from civilian populations and any requisitions had to be paid for. Pillage was proscribed. Troops were to respect civilians, their property, and their "family honor and rights." Historical practices of armies ravaging civilian populations were outlawed (1907 Hague Convention IV). All the major powers except Italy ratified the convention; Germany, Austria-Hungary and Russia expressed reservations about Article 44 which forbade coercing civilians for information about the enemy.

Military occupation poses significant challenges for these rules. The forces of the occupying power replace the authority of the state and the agencies that enforce that authority and its rules on the population. Additionally, occupied populations, being from the enemy country, are hostile to the occupier, sometimes covertly, sometimes openly, and sometimes violently. Opposition to occupation can lead to oppression by the occupier. If enemy forces are still in the field, occupied populations could be treated as hostages to coerce their government's submission. Finally, occupying soldiers may abuse their position for personal advantage. The ideal of military occupation holds the civilian populations in abeyance until the war is over, at which point they are restored to their prewar state (allowing for possible cession of territory in the peace settlement). The Hague Conventions sought to put this ideal in action by limiting the power of the occupier to change the domestic institutions and laws during the period of occupation (Benvenisti 1993, 7–29). Although changes in institutions and laws can have large political effects on state sovereignty, how the occupying force treats civilians directly has a bigger impact on them. This section focuses on how armies treat civilians in the area of operations as well as those under occupation, because that treatment poses the greatest threat to their life and property. To parallel the data analyzed in Chapter 4, this section considers treatment of civilians during the period in which their country is still actively at war with the opponent. Cases of military occupation after a government has surrendered, such as the French resistance during World War II, are excluded.

The Hague Conventions did not clarify how armies could address the possibility of armed resistance by citizens. Article 2 recognized citizens "who, on the approach of the enemy, spontaneously take up arms to resist the invading troops" as legal combatants entitled to the protections of regular troops. Article 43 empowered the occupier to "take all the measures in his power to restore, and ensure, as far as possible, public order and safety."[13] The key issues are whether irregular combatants lose their protections once occupation commences and what steps the occupier is allowed to take to enforce order in the face of irregular resistance.

The German Army entered World War I with the experience of fighting *franctireurs* during the latter stages of the Franco-Prussian War, expecting irregular resistance as their forces moved westward (Horne and Kramer 2001, 94–113, 140–144; Ousby 2002, 150–151). The Belgian town of Hervé was burned to the ground and many of its residents killed in retribution for nighttime sniping at German troops. The Germans claimed the snipers were illegal civilian resistance, the Belgians claimed that they were uniformed troops. This and other killings of Belgian civilians began with the first fighting on August 4, 1914 (Horne and Kramer 2001, 13–17). Belgium used the Garde Civique, a volunteer militia, as part of its defense of the country. The Belgian government first ordered that all members of the Garde must follow the Hague regulations, that is, wear a distinctive badge, follow a responsible officer, and carry their arms openly (Horne and Kramer 2001, 19, 125–129). Even with these restrictions, German killings led the Belgian government to order its people not to resist German forces after the initial atrocities (Best 1980, 236; Gilbert 1994, 36). Many incidents occurred where German commanders and soldiers concluded that Belgian and French civilians attacked them, and they responded with harsh measures. German soldiers even killed some German citizens in Alsace whom they suspected of French loyalties (Horne and Kramer 2001, 22, 159–161).

---

[13] Both the 1899 and 1907 Conventions use identical language in these provisions.

Hostages were taken from local leaders of places where the Germans thought attacks had taken place, and many of these hostages – including women, children and the elderly – were executed as examples (see Gilbert 1994, 41–43, 52, 65–66, 75, and 90 for examples of these attacks). The Germans saw these as necessary steps to deter civilian resistance to occupation by setting examples. Field Marshall Baron Colmar Von der Goltz, the military governor of Belgium, declared in a public statement:

> It is the stern necessity of war that the punishment for hostile acts falls not only on the guilty, but on the innocent as well (quoted in Gilbert 1994, 65–66).

The Allies publicized these reprisals as German "frightfulness," the primary example of the horrors of the "Huns" (cf. Marshall 1915; Horne and Kramer 2001, 229–261).

Using official documentation by the Allied governments after the war, German military reports, and recollections by German soldiers, John Horne and Alan Kramer documented 129 killings of ten or more civilians in Belgium and France from August through October 1914; 5,146 civilians were killed in these incidents. Buildings were also destroyed in most of the incidents, and there were numerous uses of civilians as shields to protect targets like bridges after capture (Horne and Kramer 2001, 74–78, 435–443).

The Germans were not alone in their atrocities against enemy civilians. The Austrian army killed and raped when it entered Serbia in August 1914 (Gilbert 1994, 41, 111). Losses numbered in the thousands (Horne and Kramer 2001, 84–85). The Russians engaged in isolated instances of killing of civilians during their invasions of East Prussia and Galicia in 1914, mainly after looting by Russian troops (Showalter 1991, 159–161; Horne and Kramer 2001, 82–83).[14] When they moved into Russian Poland the next year, the German conduct was more restrained that it had been in Belgium and France, although incidents did occur (Horne and Kramer 2001, 81–82).

Sometimes civilians suffered at the hands of their own soldiers. The massacre of Armenians by the Turks is well-known; these killings triggered the Armenian revolt, which was then used to justify mass killings (Gilbert 1994, 142–143, 166–167, 177; Slim 2007, 42–43). The people of Russian Poland suffered during the Great Retreat after the Austro-German breakthrough at Gorlice-Tarnow in May 1915. Jews were particularly targeted by marauding Russian soldiers; as one observer noted: "Even the most extreme anti-Semites have been moved to complain at treatment of the Jews" (Stone 1975, 183–184, quote at 184; Gilbert 1994, 139; Horne and Kramer 2001, 83–84). The Russian army plundered Romania when it moved into the country to assist

---

[14] Gilbert (1994, 49) and Herwig (1996, 128–129) provide the propaganda story of extensive killing and plunder by the Russian Army during 1914. The official German investigation in 1915 found only 101 such deaths; the Austrian report 69 civilian deaths (Horne and Kramer 2001, 79–83).

its ally (Stone 1975, 277). Italian soldiers killed Slovene civilians in retaliation against purported killings of Italian wounded (Schindler 2001, 49).

Civilians living in enemy countries at the outbreak of war were interned. The Hague Conventions provided no guidance on how enemy civilians should be handled during wartime. As young men commonly had military reserve obligations to their homeland, allowing them to leave strengthened the enemy. There were also the concerns that enemy nationals would carry out hostile acts, even if there was little to no evidence of such (cf. Panayi 1993, 57–58 on the case of Britain). France demanded that enemy nationals leave the country on August 2, 1914 and then forbade any who did not from leaving the country later. Britain did not intern enemy nationals until May 13, 1915. The German imprisoned Japanese as well as British and French (Gilbert 1994, 46). At least 400,000 civilians were interned during the war under conditions comparable to those of prisoners of war (Speed 1990, 141–153).

The victorious Allies pushed Germany to establish war crimes trials after Versailles. The Leipzig trials were a fiasco. Belgium, Britain, and France submitted lists of German war criminals for trial, including some in other areas such as the sinking of the *Llandovery Castle*. Broad opposition grew against these trials in Germany because they focused only on German crimes and were seen as victor's justice. In the end, the one case in which a German officer was brought to trial for atrocities against Belgian civilians was thrown out on a technicality. Out of the cases that went to trial, only one German, an officer who had testified in the trial of his superior for killing French prisoners, was convicted (Bass 2000, 58–105; Horne and Kramer 2001, 345–355; Lipkes 2007, 588–594).

The interwar period did not clarify the ambiguities about the treatment of civilians. The Red Cross conference in Tokyo in 1934 drafted a treaty that sought to deal with both military occupation and internment of enemy aliens during war. It allowed enemy aliens to leave unless they could be drafted within a year if they returned home or posed a security threat. It recognized but limited the taking of hostages and the deportation of civilians from a combat zone by an occupying power. The main humanitarian innovation in the treaty required belligerents to provide access to areas under occupation for relief efforts of the ICRC. No state signed the draft treaty, much less ratified it. Substantial changes in the legal regime for the treatment of civilians would wait until the Geneva Conventions in 1949 (Slim 2007, 19).

The atrocities of World War II motivated these changes. The numbers of civilians killed on the battlefield or under occupation during World War I numbered in the tens of thousands; those in World War II numbered in the millions. The killing began with the outbreak of the war. German soldiers killed at least 16,000 and maybe as many as 27,000 Polish citizens during the month of September 1939 when they overran Poland (Rossino 2003, 263). Their policies against civilians included taking hostages, reprisal killings, and shooting militia soldiers who followed the Hague rules rather than taking them as prisoners of war (Horne and Kramer 2001, 406; Rossino 2003, 86–86, 128–130, 142, 175–179). The German Army was careful not to repeat the widespread atrocities of 1914 when in 1940 they invaded France and the Low Countries. Hitler ordered discipline and warned that violators would be prosecuted, even threatening the death penalty. Suspected *franc-tireurs* were to be tried by court-martial rather than summary execution backed by reprisals. These measures could not prevent all killings, but they did control them (Bartov 1991, 61–69; Horne and Kramer 2001, 401–403). Restraint disappeared when the Wehrmacht invaded the Soviet Union. Even though some Soviet citizens greeted the Germans as liberators, killings of civilians spread quickly. The Einsatzgruppen, the genocidal death squads that operated behind German lines, began their grisly business of liquidating "Bolshevik agitators, guerrillas, saboteurs, and Jews" (quoted in Bellamy 2007, 25) in the first days of the war. Front line troops also engaged in the killing from the beginning of the war. The countryside was plundered to help feed the troops (Bartov 1991, 76–79, 93; Fritz 1995, 54, 58–59).

Partisan warfare provoked killing by the German army on a larger scale. Violence was often indiscriminate as villages suspected of supporting partisan groups were destroyed. This includes countries such as France, Yugoslavia and Greece where national resistance movements grew after their governments surrendered (Calvocoressi et al. 1989, 307–308). These cases fall outside of this discussion because the Germans occupied these countries during the time that the resistance movements became active, but German killings of civilians to repress partisan activity behind their lines continued after Allied forces invaded France and Italy. The Soviet population suffered the most from brutal anti-partisan measures (De Zayas 1989, 105–107). Irregular warfare, such as the partisans conducted, puts civilians at risk from both sides. Partisans often threaten civilians to secure food and other support and to prevent them from informing on them. Anti-partisan forces use violence to secure information and to retaliate against those who support partisan bands. In 1941, the German army adopted the rule that 50 to 100 Soviet citizens should be executed for every German soldier killed by partisans. Anti-partisan campaigns by the Germans devastated and depopulated areas of the Soviet Union. Estimates of the number of Soviet citizens killed by the Nazis range from 17 to 20 million (Overy 1998, 288 for the low estimate; Haynes 2003, 306 for the high estimate). These figures include those who died indirectly from German action, such as those who starved to death during the siege of Leningrad, as well as those directly killed (Glantz and House 1995, 56–57; Overy 1998, 142–153; Horne and Kramer 2001, 406–408; Mawdsley 2005, 232–237).

The Red Army carried out its revenge against German civilians when it invaded Germany. Soviet soldiers committed widespread looting and rape in addition to killings of German civilians. Antony Beevor estimates that 2 million German women were raped (2002, 410). Attacks were not limited to German civilians; Red Army soldiers raped Russian women prisoners of the Nazis after their liberation (Beevor 2002, 65, 67). The top leadership, including

Stalin, knew of the complete breakdown of discipline, intervening only when it reduced combat performance (Beevor 2002, 104–105, 412–414). Stalin thought it was a trivial matter: "And what is so awful in his having fun with a woman, after such horrors?" (quoted in Overy 1998, 262). The death toll of German civilians killed during the descent of the Red Army numbered in the hundreds of thousands (Overy 1998, 261–262; Beevor 2002, 29–31, 107–109; Mawdsley 2005, 215–217, 393–394; Bellamy 2007, 660).

The Japanese army also killed and brutalized enemy civilians. The Rape of Nanking was a six-week orgy of rape, plunder, and murder conducted against the Chinese population of that unfortunate city. An estimated 200,000 to 377,400 civilians and prisoners of war were killed (Chang 1997, 99–104). The Japanese population was aware of this as it happened; a contest between two Japanese officers to see who could first behead 100 Chinese received extensive newspaper coverage (Chang 1997, 56). This was not an isolated incident; the Japanese military killed millions of Chinese civilians during their eight years of war (Russell of Liverpool 1958, 48–51; Dower 1986, 295–301; Yin, Shi, and Dorfman 1997, 9–10, 56). It adopted the Three All policy against the Communists in North China: take all, kill all, burn all (Li 1975, 13). European and Asian civilians alike were killed when the Japanese conquered them (Dower 1986, 46–47; Calvocoressi et al. 1989, 998). Even defeat did not stop the atrocities; as U.S. forces closed in on Manila in March 1945, the Japanese garrison conducted a four-week bout of rape, mutilation, and killing of the local population, all fueled by drunken binges (Piccigallo 1979, 50–55; Lael 1982, 79–95; Dower 1986, 43–45; Brackman 1987, 244–246). Contempt for the defeated enemy people along with ordered brutality fostered these atrocities. The expectations of abuse for civilians also led to the tragic episodes in which Japanese civilians on Saipan and Okinawa killed themselves and their children rather than face the tortures they expected from U.S. soldiers and marines (Dower 1986, 45).

The soldiers of the Western armies generally treated enemy civilians with restraint. Soldiers of all armies commit some crimes, but in the Allied armies, the major offenses were often prosecuted. Looting was the only widespread crime, in part because few soldiers faced a court-martial for it (Ellis 1980, 233; Ambrose 1992, 143, 250–251, 260–261; Brode 1997, 217–221; Beevor 2002, 192–193).

The desire to limit atrocities and an effective system of military justice are the keys to protecting enemy civilians. When militaries adopted policies in which civilians were seen as enemies who might kill you, their soldiers killed in response and in anticipation. When armies did not discipline their own soldiers, many of them abused their power against civilians. Treatment of civilians on and near the battlefield faces the challenge that every soldier has the ability to abuse civilians, to kill, and to loot. Irregular warfare increases the challenge by breaking down the clear distinction between civilians and combatants. The legal system of the Hague Conventions was vague and weak for the protection of civilians, which compounded these difficulties. The atrocities of World War II, particularly those under Nazi and Japanese occupation, led to the 1949 Geneva Convention (IV) relative to the Protection of Civilian Persons in Time of War which created detailed standards to limit what occupying powers could do.

OTHER EXPLANATIONS

This chapter focuses on how variation in the legal clarity of the current treaty standard, its public acceptance through ratification, and the scope for individual violations drive compliance across these four issues. Other explanations have been proposed to account for why states follow or break the laws of war; this section considers two of them. Military culture, the ideas about how a military should fight, could determine their conduct during wartime. The drive to win protracted wars could lead states to break the rules, specifically to target enemy civilians, in their effort to end the war at an acceptable cost. Both of these alternative explanations have elements of truth within them, but the strategic logic of compliance through the creation of a common conjecture explains these cases better.

Military culture is the organizational culture of a military. Organizations have cultures that explain how they are run inside and how they deal with outside forces. Culture is a set of shared beliefs across the members of the organization that defines what an organization should do and how it should do it. Although these beliefs help the organization coordinate the efforts of their members, they may not be efficient in the sense that organizations facing the same external environment could have different cultures and some of those cultures may deal with that external environment more effectively than others. Militaries as organizations need these beliefs about how they should fight to prepare for combat through training and planning. Military culture persists in part because it is valuable to the organization and in part because even war produces mixed signals about the most effective ways to fight (Legro 1995, 17–29).

Military culture, in this view, determines whether states comply with norms of restraint in combat. When those norms accord with their culture, a military will follow the prescriptions of the norms to the best of their ability. When they clash, a military will follow their culture and violate the norms. Legro (1995) examines the issues of submarine warfare, strategic bombing, and chemical weapons and concludes that military culture accounts for compliance or the lack thereof between Germany and Great Britain on these three issues. Germany, for example, was reluctant to escalate to strategic bombing against Britain because the military culture of the Luftwaffe emphasized close support rather than strategic bombing; Britain escalated because the RAF saw strategic bombing as the way it could contribute to winning the war (Legro 1995, 94–143).

How militaries prepare for war influences how they fight. Because large organizations do not change quickly, prewar judgments about how to organize and fight persist during wartime. The Japanese military, as discussed in the previous chapter, sought to instill fighting spirit in its troops so they would fight harder than the enemy and endure more difficult conditions. Its training that surrender was disgraceful and worse than death, backed up with mechanisms of social control at the unit level to ensure soldiers fought to the death, explains some of Japanese treatment of the prisoners they took. Military culture affects compliance because it favors some strategies over others. Countries that invested in heavy bombers or submarines were in a better position to use those weapons, and break the norms that sought to limit them, than those that did not.

A broader view, however, reveals a more complex picture. As mentioned earlier, the Luftwaffe engaged in terror bombing of the cities of countries that could not retaliate against German cities. Its culture of close tactical support did not foreclose this option. The British Navy may not have had a doctrine of unrestricted submarine war, but it was willing to breach the rules of conduct on the high seas after Germany unleashed its U-boats. The U.S. Army Air Corps' doctrine emphasized precision daylight strategic bombing, but it abandoned it in favor of night firebomb attacks on Japan's cities. Military culture shapes how militaries fight, but it does not dictate how they must fight.

Military culture is a product of decisions about how a military should fight. Prewar commitments to restraint can alter those decisions. States accept limitations on how they fight because they think they will benefit from them, particularly when they induce restraint from their opponents. They incorporate them into military doctrine and culture in part to meet those commitments. Germany rejected limits on submarines and adopted a doctrine of unrestricted submarine warfare even though Hitler preferred restraint at the outbreak of the war. Britain wanted submarines outlawed, but failed in that effort; it adopted a doctrine which used submarines in support of the battle fleet rather than attacking merchant shipping.

Once fighting begins, these commitments can shift. Violations by the other side, even those outside the control of central military authorities, provoke responses. The absence of clear legal agreement on what the standard is and the mutual public acceptance of it make misunderstandings and misinterpretations of what the other side is doing, and therefore how to respond, more likely. When military culture incorporates restraint and backs it up with military discipline, compliance by that military is more likely. Military culture matters for compliance because it reflects the commitment of a state and its military to follow the rules. Even with institutional restraints, compliance is not guaranteed in the face of an unrestrained opponent and an unclear standard.

Protracted wars could provide the reason to break the rules. Increase the costs of continuing to fight for the other side, and you may be able to break their will. Alexander Downes (2008) argues that states adopt policies that kill enemy civilians either to end a protracted war or to clear territory which the state wishes to annex. The costs of protracted war encourage the killing of enemy civilians to limit one's own losses. Provocatively, Downes argues that democracies are more likely to adopt policies that deliberate kill enemy civilians than autocracies. The human costs of war weigh more heavily in a democracy because their leaders must eventually answer to their voters whose sons, brothers, and husbands may be dying in an endless, bloody war. Downes collected data on numbers of civilians killed during interstate wars, showing that democracies on average kill more enemy civilians, particularly when they are fighting a war of attrition. He supports these statistical results with case studies of the British blockade of Germany during World War I and the Allied bombings of Germany and Japan as well as shorter studies of cases where civilians were not victimized, particularly the Gulf War in 1991.[15] Benjamin Valentino, Paul Huth, and Sarah Croco (2006) similarly argue and find that the strategic conditions of the war drives levels of deliberate killing of civilians. They also find that neither democracy, ratification of the Hague or Geneva Conventions, depending on time period, nor the combination of the two have a statistically discernable effect on the numbers of civilians killed.

There is an important element of truth here; democracies have done some horrible things during their wars. They have used a variety of strategies in their efforts to win that have killed hundreds of thousands of enemy civilians. Democratic leaders answer to their own people, and their primary responsibility is to preserve the lives of their own citizens, including those inducted into the army as soldiers. Put bluntly, enemy civilians do not vote in their elections. The statistical results in Chapter 4' showed that more intense wars have lower levels of compliance, which matches the results of both Downes (2008) and Valentino et al. (2006). Desperate wars call for desperate measures.

The picture is more complicated once we look closer, however. Both Downes (2008) and Valentino et al. (2006) treat all policies which kill civilians the same, even when they fall under different portions of the law of war. The British blockade during World War I may have violated the naval rules in the Hague Conventions, but it did not violate the provisions to protect civilians. The aerial bombing campaigns of World War II probably violated the provisions of the Hague Conventions concerning bombardment, but there was no treaty regulating aerial bombardment directly. Relatively few of these cases fall into the issue of treatment of civilians used here. Legal compliance has to be assessed against the relevant treaty standard, not just a general norm not to kill enemy civilians. Actions that violate a norm to avoid killing civilians are not necessarily legal violations.

---

[15] Downes (2008) also has longer studies of the Boer War and the Arab-Israeli War of 1948. Because these are cases of civilian victimization in a guerrilla war and a war fought to add territory, I do not discuss them here.

The designs of both the Downes (2008) and the Valentino et al. (2006) analyses focus on the country at war as the unit of analysis, making it difficult to test for dyadic relationships such as reciprocity and joint ratification. Both include the character of the fighting as both contend that wars of attrition lead to the killing of enemy civilians. Both sides face the same character of war, making it dyadic.[16] Downes includes whether the other side is killing your civilians, finding inconsistent results with incidences of civilian victimization increasing in it, while total deaths and incidence of mass killing decline (Downes 2008, 65, 71, 74–75). Valentino et al. assess legal obligations under the Hague Conventions as joint ratification because those treaties bind only when both sides had ratified, while the 1949 Geneva Conventions are unilaterally binding, obligating ratifying states regardless of what the other side does.[17] These designs do not directly test for reciprocity or how reciprocity varies with legal obligation. If warring parties engage in reciprocal responses to each other's violations, variables that are correlated across both members of the warring dyads will soak up the effect of reciprocity and have inflated coefficients.[18]

Even though democracies adopt policies that kill civilians, they do not do so as openly as autocracies do. They seek to obscure the consequences of their policies for enemy civilians. The British government denied in the House of Commons that it was intercepting food shipments bound for Germany in February 1915, even though it had begun to do so (Downes 2008, 93). The blockade was also popular with the British public; the primary constraint was the possible reactions of neutral countries (Downes 2008, 96–98). Autocratic Germany, in contrast, was open about its use of unrestricted submarine war, again only constrained by the reactions of neutrals. Similarly, the aerial bombing campaigns of the United States and Britain during World War II were publicly justified as precision bombing of military targets, regardless of the real effects of those missions. The harshness of German occupation policy during the war, in contrast, was explicit and public.

---

[16] In Valentino et al. (2006), the strategy variables are coded separately for each side and are not identical. They are correlated.

[17] Valentino et al.'s (2006) coefficients for treaty status and regime type are not statistically significant, but their estimated substantive effects are large. Because their model is multiplicative, the effect of treaty status is to shrink civilian deaths to a percentage of the base. From their Table 1 (2006, 366), the estimated effects are as follows:

Treaty status (joint ratification for the Hague Convention and unilateral ratification for the Geneva Convention) alone (from Model 1) = 41.6% of base rate (i.e. a 60% reduction in civilian casualties).

Treaty status and democracy (from Model 3) = 28.6% of base rate (almost a three-quarters reduction).

Treaty status and democracy and maneuver strategy (from Model 4) = 10.4% of base rate (90% reduction!).

The variables on which they focus – strategy, war aims, and duration of the war – have larger substantive effects than treaty status and regime type.

[18] This is the problem of simultaneity bias discussed in Chapter 4'.

Democratic leaders often invoke retaliation to the violations of the other side and point to legal ambiguities to justify these acts. "Bomber" Harris quoted the Bible dramatically in justifying the British bombing of Germany in a newsreel: "They [the Germans] have sown the wind; and now they are going to reap the whirlwind."[19] Churchill privately had doubts about the efficacy and morality of the bombing of Germany, but he did not express them publicly, instead claiming that the bombing sought to destroy the industrial sinews of Germany (Slim 2007, 152–155). U.S. leaders persisted in describing their strategic bombing of Germany as precision when it was anything but that. The British defended their blockade during World War I as allowed under the law, including its expansion to cover food. All of these acts were popular with British and U.S. citizens, in part because they were seen as retribution against an enemy that committed its own atrocities. When democracies kill civilians, their leaders describe it as a response justified by the violations of the enemy.

Protracted wars may provide the motivation to break the rules, but law and regime type shape how they do so. This is how law differs from norms. Norms prescribe broad standards of conduct without the detail necessary to judge which specific acts violate those standards. Law sets such standards subject to interpretation and application of those standards to specific cases. Furthermore, law both renders some acts as legal and rules some out as illegal. Strategic bombing that targeted the war industry could be argued to be legal even when its effect was indiscriminate city bombing. Parties can also interpret law in their own favor to justify their own acts. For the gas attack at Ypres, Germany interpreted the standards in the 1899 Hague Declaration on Gas opportunistically to claim that attack was allowed within the law. Finally, law cannot prevent those who will violate, no matter what the sanction is. The law of war limits violations in some cases, but it cannot prevent all of them, much as the law of murder does not ensure a society free from homicide.

CONCLUSION

The short case studies of the four issues in this chapter show how ratification, legal clarity, and noise influence compliance. Ratification creates a shared expectation that the ratifying state intends to uphold standards of the treaty in question to the best of its ability during wartime. Reciprocity backs up this shared understanding. The general nonuse of chemical weapons during World War II is the clearest example of this logic. Most countries ratified the 1925 Geneva Protocol on CBW, and the standard was clear and easy to apply. Chemical weapons were used widely only when the attacked state could not retaliate in kind. When a norm was not codified into a treaty, this shared understanding may not have existed. There were vague ideas that it was wrong to

---

[19] See the wartime newsreel, "On the Chin!" for Harris' address, http://www.britishpathe.com/record.php?id=22954, accessed June 28, 2011.

target civilians through aerial bombing, but that understanding was insufficient to prevent the spread of city bombing and the deaths of hundreds of thousands of Germans and Japanese.

Lack of clarity in the standard opened space for states to interpret the rules in their own favor. The German justification of the gas attack at Ypres is the clearest example of a self-interested interpretation of a treaty standard. Treatment of civilians floundered during both World Wars because the Hague Conventions did not spell out how armies could respond to attacks by civilians. The conventions recognized such attacks as legal if the civilians took up arms and operated as soldiers, but failed to specify what measures were not allowed in response to irregular attacks. The Germans believed that reprisals were allowed against civilian attacks, whereas others did not. The lack of specificity in legal standards led to new treaties, both during the interwar period and after World War II.

Noise in all its forms made the enforcement of any standard more difficult. Acts of the enemy were taken to be deliberate violations regardless of the intent behind them. Violations by individual soldiers were the primary source of noise. Chemical weapons were clearly deliberate acts of state policy and so provoked the strongest responses when they were used. Conduct on the high seas or against civilians presented more opportunities for lower-level officers and individual soldiers to violate on their own. Military discipline is necessary to limit such violations, and the worst cases – such as the crimes committed against civilians by Japanese, Germans, and Soviet soldiers during World War II – occurred when their militaries did nothing to discipline them. Noise could also arise from the confusion of the battlefield and the inability to attack with discrimination. The inaccuracy of aerial bombing ensured that civilian targets would be hit if military targets in cities were attacked and that the targets would believe that those attacks were deliberate. Noise led to strings of tit-for-tat retaliations, opportunistically using those unintended violations as justification for their own deliberate violations in response, as the British used the bombing of London during the Battle of Britain as a justification to expand their own bombing of German cities.

There is an irony in these cases; strategic warfare that caused civilians to suffer may have been counterproductive. Naval blockades, whether carried out by submarines or surface ships, and aerial bombing of strategic targets killed directly or indirectly hundreds of thousands of civilians during the World Wars. Of these efforts, only the British blockade in World War I and the U.S. submarine war against Japan in World War II clearly contributed victory in those wars. The blockade did so by slowly strangling Germany and its army, undermining morale by 1918. The U.S. submarine campaign sunk most of the Japanese merchant marine, cutting Japan off from the raw materials it needed. The primary contribution of the Allied air offensive against Germany was indirect. It created a war of attrition in the skies over Germany which allowed Britain and the U.S. to achieve air superiority by March 1944, air superiority that greatly aided the D-Day invasion (Murray 1985, 223–232, 242, 264–268). The irony is that strategic warfare was extremely costly. Bomber and submarine crews were all volunteers, often from the best recruits, the same men who would have made excellent low-level officers (McManus 1998, 10–11). These strategic forces also suffered grievous losses; half of the aircrew who served in Bomber Command during World War II were killed (Biddle 2002, 197). Sixty-three percent of German U-boats crew in World War II died during the war (Van der Vat 1988, 382; Terraine 1989, 669 gives the casualty rate as 85 percent). These human costs do not include the lesser costs of the expense of building, maintaining, and using the bomber and submarine fleets used in strategic warfare. Strategic warfare was costly for its targets and those who carried it out.

# 7

## Dynamics of Common Conjectures
### *The Rational Evolution of Norms*

Having established that the laws of war guide state action during wartime and how international norms codified into law shape strategic calculations, I turn to the question of change in expectations and the role of law in such changes. The analysis so far has assumed the law is fixed to focus on how law shapes what states and soldiers do during wartime. But the law of war has evolved over time with experience of it in practice. How can we understand these changes? States drew up the laws of war to create an effective system of limiting violence during war. Some of these changes eliminated points of ambiguity in the law; others expanded the coverage of the law to new issues and novel problems.

The central question of constructivism is how norms and identities change over time; the answer is they are (surprise!) socially constructed. At least eight mechanisms of normative change – natural selection, cultural selection, social learning, persuasion, coercion, imitation, socialization, the evolution of empathy and other universal values – operate through at least five vectors of change – international negotiations, social movements, epistemic communities, international bodies, and shared senses of community and its purpose (Wendt 1999, 318–366; Finnemore 2003, 146–161). The common claim across all of these mechanisms and vectors is that change is not efficient; it is not directed with the conscious aim of realizing mutual benefit. In the words of Peter Katzenstein, "institutions do not merely create efficiencies" (1996, 518). Social construction leads to a world not of our own choosing or design. It results from a social process outside the control of either any one actor or all of them together. Institutions are not optimal; indeed, they may be pathological, acting in ways to subvert their own purposes (Barnett and Finnemore 1999). Explanations of social institutions that center on rational design are "driving with the rearview mirror" because they can only explain what has been, not what can be (Wendt 2001).

Optimal design, however, does not require intent to produce such a design. If actors seek to change institutions that produce undesirable results, the process can produce optimally designed institutions over the long run, even though no one consciously designed the result. Inefficient institutions lead to efforts to change them, while efficient ones are retained. The resulting evolution leads to efficient institutions. The laws of war evolve over time, but not all normative limits are enforceable during wartime, and therefore not all norms are the basis of effective law. This chapter uses evolutionary game theory as a model of that process to show that even actors with limited rationality may adopt efficient institutions in the absence of explicit and conscious design of those institutions.

If treaties help to create the shared strategic expectations that bring order to social life, we need to understand how such expectations are formed. In game theory, the common conjecture asserts that players have such shared expectations, but why do they have a common conjecture? Common conjectures can arise from preplay negotiation, shared cultural assumptions, a history of interaction, or a focal point among the set of equilibria (see Morrow 1994a, 94–98, 305–311 for a brief, nontechnical discussion of common conjectures). After discussing constructivist views of institutional change, I discuss these alternative sources of common conjectures and how they correspond to the sources of international law. I expand my discussion on the third alternative by exploring the literature on evolutionary game theory to explain how common conjectures evolve over time from a common history of play among players. Evolutionary game theory seeks to explain how players' understandings of which strategies to use evolve in response to their play. The players learn over time about how to play the game, which strategy combinations are good moves, allowing them to revise what they do as they learn how others will play. Some patterns of play are stable over time, meaning the players have arrived at a common understanding of how to play. Even though these patterns are stable, they are not impervious to change over time. If the players can evolve toward a stable pattern of play, that pattern has to be a Nash equilibrium of the stage game. In the long run, they move toward the risk-dominant Nash equilibrium. Although the evolutionary theory that results cannot predict that a particular change will happen at a given time, it predicts which patterns can be stable over time and the likely direction of movement when it occurs.

Evolutionary game theory concludes that players will play a Nash equilibrium over time if their behavior settles into a stable pattern. If Nash equilibria are the only patterns that can be stable over long periods of interaction, this result justifies treating such equilibria as the only norm-driven behavior that can persist and so shape and structure social interaction. Stable institutions must be Nash equilibria even under a selection process with weak rationality and no conscious design to seek equilibrium.

States have negotiated the laws of war over time, adding conscious design to evolutionary selection. I examine the evolution of the norms and law on prisoners of war as an example of institutional change that combines design and evolution. Concerns with the system in force led states to seek to change the law on prisoners of war; they have negotiated to seek a single standard that most view as superior to the prior law. Not all accepted those changes, leading to the divergence in adherence to that system seen in Chapter 5. Underlying these divergences are different ideas held by states about how to generate military power during wartime and their responsibility to their own citizen-soldiers. This case shows that the laws of war evolve through negotiations impelled by concerns about the inadequacies of the existing law. Institutions change through a process of rational evolution.

If actors can always change institutions through negotiations, how can political institutions persist? They might all be better off by agreeing to change institutions. Political institutions are constellations of equilibria of interconnected strategic problems, as argued in Chapter 3. We cannot change one without considering its effect on the others. Furthermore, different actors play in these different but linked games, and while those in one game may agree to change, those in other games may not go along. Whether states can restrain violence on the battlefield depends on how their enemies train their soldiers, something outside their control. Efficiency, in the form of Pareto optimality of equilibria, is a weak test because many equilibria can be Pareto optimal. In contrast to the claim that institutions cannot be optimal because of their wide variety, rational evolution could lead to a wide range of sustainable political institutions. Furthermore, the process that leads to the adoption of one institution over another appears arbitrary rather than designed. Nonetheless, the resulting institutions still follow the dynamics of equilibrium, self-interest married to a shared understanding of how others will act. Nor does rational evolution imply that any only arrangement is possible; not all combinations of strategies are equilibria. Rational evolution limits, but does not determine, the character of political institutions.

## THE SOURCES AND WAYS OF CHANGE IN NORMS ACCORDING TO CONSTRUCTIVISTS

Constructivism places priority on the question of changes in norms over how they operate in practice. Constructivists identify numerous mechanisms that lead to change in norms. Multiple mechanisms may operate at the same time, reinforcing one another, so they should not be thought of as competing paths to change. Natural and cultural selection produce change by replacing some elements with others through a process of selection. In natural selection, those units that fail to incorporate new norms are eliminated; in cultural selection, new norms and identities supplant older ones as time passes. Social learning and socialization are two ways that cultural selection can occur. In social learning, actors adopt new norms because they come to believe they are superior. In socialization, actors adopt norms to fit into the system. An actor becomes fully socialized when it internalizes its identity and the norms attached to that identity (Checkel 2005). Imitation resembles social learning and socialization but requires less of the actor in question as it need not learn that norms are superior or internalize them. Persuasion convinces actors that they should adhere to norms because doing so advances their own interests or shared values. Appeals to universal values, such as justice or equality, could also persuade actors to adhere to norms. Finally, coercion could support the spread of norms by punishing those who do not adhere to them. Reducing defection could lead others to be more willing to comply. These mechanisms can complement one another.

These mechanisms can work through different paths to change. International negotiations provide venues for states to persuade one another what norms should be, allowing for social learning. International organizations can socialize their members to their principles and provide positive incentives for those who wish to adhere to those principles. Social movements and epistemic communities allow society to spread ideas of proper conduct and shared values transnationally even in opposition to state governments. A shared sense of community and purpose can help actors identify how to pursue that purpose and who is entitled to join that community. As with the mechanisms, these paths can support one another. Human rights as a program of normative change has advanced through international negotiation of treaties, through the creation of nongovernmental organizations that advocate for those rights, and through a shared sense that human rights are universal, particularly for those states that wish to join the developed world. Norm cascades, for example, combine several of these paths and mechanisms, where norm entrepreneurs first elaborate and advocate for a norm which leads to the building cascade of acceptance and adherence to it (Finnemore and Sikkink 1998).

The constructivist view of normative change exhibits several key properties. Change is not controlled and directed. Even when norm entrepreneurs seek to promulgate a norm, they cannot control its spread, the timing of its adoption, or whether it succeeds in cascading into unquestioned acceptance. Although actors are strategic in their efforts to advance or retard norms, those strategies are limited by the complexity and uncertainty of the process. Change is unpredictable; norm cascades cannot be anticipated by those who seek to launch them. This unpredictability means that change may hinge on factors that seem arbitrary rather than deliberate and designed. Institutions are not efficient and could be pathological because their spread depends on whether they can be propagated through one or more of the mechanisms sketched previously. How could such a process lead to optimal institutions?

## THE SOURCES OF COMMON CONJECTURES

Game theory solves the problem of strategic expectations by assuming the players share a common conjecture, but where does it come from? When a game has multiple equilibria, the common conjecture allows the players to know that their strategies in a particular equilibrium are best replies. But its existence and why the players hold it lie outside typical equilibrium analysis. Instead, theorists point to three possible sources of such a shared understanding: preplay negotiation, culture, and shared experience playing the game. Additionally, each of these three views also implies a way to select among multiple equilibria (Schelling 1960; Kreps 1990).

Preplay negotiation is the approach to common conjectures most amenable to formal analysis. If the players have the opportunity to discuss how they will play the game before they do so, they may be able to negotiate which equilibrium they should play. Figure 2.2 is a simple coordination game between two players; it has two pure-strategy equilibria and a mixed strategy. If they are allowed to discuss which strategies they intend to play in advance, they will agree to play a pure-strategy equilibrium and that those promises will be convincing and self-enforcing. This outcome is better than if they enter the game with no idea of how the other will play and both play the mixed strategy equilibrium. In general, preplay negotiation allows the players to agree to play an equilibrium that makes both better off and selects a Pareto optimal equilibrium.

Many games, however, have multiple equilibria that are Pareto optimal. Figure 2.7 gives the Battle of the Sexes game, where both (A;a) and (B;b) are Pareto optimal equilibria. If the players are allowed to negotiate before they play, it is not clear which equilibrium they will play. Indeed, the preplay negotiation creates a whole new game of its own.[1]

Bargaining games generally have many Pareto optimal equilibria because they concern the division of a surplus that the players can only obtain through agreement. The canonical version of the bargaining game has two players divide a unit that they can only obtain if they agree on its division. This game has a continuum of Nash equilibria because any division of the unit that provides both players with some portion of it, no matter how small, is better for both than failing to agree and getting nothing.

Schelling (1960) argued that this multiplicity was inherent to bargaining and not solvable through equilibrium.[2] Instead, he suggested that elements outside the game, such as culture, would determine which equilibrium players would adopt. Fairness could be a cultural rule that would direct players to an even division of the unit. But culture could also dictate other splits, such as a higher-status player receiving a larger share of any division. David Kreps (1990, 102) speculates that Korean students from his business school classes play bargaining games differently from American students, such as deferring to

---

[1] Cheap talk can aid in addressing the coordination issue even here (Farrell and Gibbons 1989; Morrow 1994b).

[2] Assuming a specific protocol and subgame perfection can, however, as most famously discussed by Rubinstein (1982).

a perceived social superior. Cultural rules could also determine the bargaining protocol, such as whether the seller or buyer makes the first offer. Those rules could go as far as banning bargaining totally (ever tried to bargain the price of your grocery bill in a supermarket?). Schelling went so far as to argue that cultural rules were more important than strategic dynamics in determining the outcomes of bargaining.

Common culture could provide common conjectures on how to play a game with multiple equilibria. It could solve the multiplicity problem that pre-play negotiation cannot. Norms of equality direct us to symmetric equilibria of a game, where players with the same moves and payoffs must act and be rewarded identically. Culture, however, does not explain why the players hold the common conjecture that they do; it pushes the question back to the level of why they have a common culture and what is its content. Culture might account for why the players share expectations of appropriate conduct; it does not say why they hold that conduct to be proper. Similarly, Schelling's famous idea of focal points, particular strategy combinations that all understand are different and so should coordinate on, does not explain why those strategy combinations are focal. It just asserts that they are.

Culture is often thought of as the accumulation of social knowledge from past experiences, which brings us to the third explanation of where common conjectures come from – that is, shared experience playing the game. Through trial and error, the players could learn what are reasonable expectations for how one another will play. Vincent Crawford and Hans Haller (1990) examine a case of learning to play an equilibrium in a coordination game in which the players lack even a common language for describing the game. Preplay negotiation is pointless because they do not know how to describe the actions they could agree to. The players' strategies look for moves that will help them identify when they have successfully coordinated. Depending on the value of the different ways to coordinate and what each player knows, these strategies can involve the use of dominated strategies in the stage game or lead the players to play a Pareto dominated equilibrium.[3] In these examples, the players lock into strategies that coordinate their behavior; the players have learned how to coordinate. Once there, they hold a common conjecture on how to continue to play the game.

This example is illustrative, but it leaves important questions open. How do players develop a common conjecture in games with divergent as well as identical interests? Can such understandings be transmitted to others who lack the history of play but will enter into play in the future? Culture by definition transcends the individuals who hold it. Evolutionary game theory expands on the idea of equilibrium arising from a shared history of play.

---

[3] The latter occurs when the short-term loss from searching for a Pareto superior coordination point exceeds the long-term gain from achieving that outcome.

Before describing evolutionary game theory, its central results, and its insights for the development and change in common conjectures, I note a parallel between these three sources of common conjectures and three sources of international law. Morton Kaplan and Nicholas Katzenbach identify three sources of international law; negotiated agreement, custom, and precedent (1961, 236–264). Preplay negotiation parallels negotiated agreement; culture parallels custom; and a shared history of play parallels precedent. All three sources are important in explaining how international law develops. Custom and precedent emerge from politics over time. The understandings of appropriate conduct come from prior interaction where the consequences of inappropriate conduct can be seen and alternative measures for controlling such conduct tested over time. Such understandings alone rarely suffice to create binding law; customary international law unsupported by a treaty lacks both explicit rules and public acceptance of its principles. Negotiation of a formal treaty creates those rules, and public ratification creates the common knowledge of which states accept those obligations. International law aids the players in their expectations about how one another will act, and so helps to bring order to international politics. Again, however, assuming that such understandings exist, as game theory commonly assumes that the players hold a common conjecture, does not explain how we arrived at that understanding. To do that, I turn to evolutionary game theory.

## WHAT IS EVOLUTIONARY GAME THEORY?

Game theory examines how rational players should play a game with one another. Calculation of best replies based in part on anticipation of the other player's moves is the focus of the analysis. As I have argued, common conjectures are central to this strategic analysis.

Evolutionary game theory approaches the same interest in strategic interaction using similar definition of a game with very different assumptions about strategic decision making and a different array of analytic tools. These tools arose from applications of game theory to evolutionary biology (the seminal contribution is Maynard Smith 1982). A large number of players, or more accurately animals, play fixed strategies in a competitive environment of a game that is played repeatedly, say a competition over territories containing food. Each animal begins with a fixed strategy with a range of different strategies across the entire population. In each round, the players are matched against one another, perhaps two animals competing to control the same territory. A player's fixed strategy can be thought of as a characteristic of the individual that influences its ability to survive and propagate – its phenotype – that is linked to its genetic makeup – its genotype. Over time, the players are replaced as they reproduce and die out, with the relatively successful individuals in the game reproducing more than others. The strategies that prove successful in competition with the other strategies in the population become more common in the next generation and on. Because the mix of strategies in the population changes over time, so does the selection environment facing the players and their strategies. The question is what distributions of population characteristics are stable in the long run? The introduction of novel strategies through mutation or invasion by outsiders raises the possibility that a distribution of strategies could be upset and change dramatically. An evolutionary stable strategy is a distribution of strategies across the population which resists any such mutations or invasions and returns to its mix afterwards.

In social settings, the focus shifts from propagation of phenotypes through competitive selection to learning by bounded, rational actors through imitation and innovation.[4] A player's strategy represents its routine for dealing with the situation in the game, and those strategies are generally restricted to simple rules. Players lack sufficient knowledge of the situation to calculate optimal strategies or lack the cognitive ability to do so, explaining why they play fixed strategies in the short run. Players learn by changing these strategies periodically, keeping their strategy when it is successful or adopting another strategy which has been successful for other players. When a player evaluates her strategy, she compares the results she has achieved with it to those achieved by other players using other strategies. The worse her strategy does (compared to others in the population), the more likely she is to adopt one of those better strategies. A player might also experiment after evaluating her strategy by randomly adopting another strategy, paralleling mutation in the biological version. The social setup assumes a large number of players playing a symmetric game, so they can learn about what strategy would be best for themselves by observing the success of others. Learning by imitation in a symmetric game reaches the same conclusion as calculating best replies against the existing pattern of plays of the other players. Players learn to play the strategies that have been best against the mix of strategies being played in the immediate past. The question is whether this process converges to a set of strategies that are resistant to further change. There are several definitions of what constitutes this stability, with the central idea being that once at a stable set of strategies, the players will return there as the rate of experimentation goes to zero.[5] Such set is a prediction of the long-run outcome of the process.

Two questions dominate the use of evolutionary game theory in economics: Do players play Nash equilibria, and if so, which one (Mailath 1998, 1348)? The first question concerns whether conscious rational calculation is necessary

---

[4] My discussion of the application of evolutionary game theory to social institutions draws heavily on Young (1998) because I find his results the most useful in thinking through these issues and his book-length presentation is more accessible to the reader than the articles in economics that I cite in this section.

[5] I remind the reader that the error rate going to zero means it never equals zero. We are examining stability when the players experiment, provided that the experiments are rare and learning from those experiments dominates as a source of social change. Obviously, nothing would be stable if the rate of experimentation was high.

for Nash equilibrium. These players have very limited rationality; they use fixed strategies rather than calculate best replies, learn by imitation rather than logical reasoning, and experiment randomly rather than thoughtfully. If these players eventually reach a Nash equilibrium, then actors who reason game theoretically, even if that reasoning is partial rather than fully rational, should as well. The second question concerns whether evolutionary game theory helps us choose among multiple equilibria of a game. Knowing that the players will eventually reach a Nash equilibrium is nice; it would be better if we could say which one they play. The latter would then have a strong claim on being the solution of the game in settings in which the players would play long enough to allow the process to converge to it.

The general result is that if play converges on a set of strategies, it must be a Nash equilibrium of the stage game. The intuition behind this result is simple. Imagine that a stable set of strategies did not form a Nash equilibrium. Then at least one player would have an alternate strategy that was better for him than the strategy he was using in the candidate stable set. Given the dynamics of experimentation, eventually he would try that superior alternate strategy, and, having done so, would prefer to stay there rather than migrate back to his original strategy. Then the original set of strategies cannot be stable. Eventually, the processes of learning and experimentation will lead the players away from it. This result answers the first question only partially because it does not say that the process must reach stability, only that Nash equilibria are the only candidates for stability.

Evolutionary game theory does not directly address my interest in the source of common conjectures because the players do not hold conjectures about one another's strategies. Ideally, one would like to have an evolutionary model in which the players hold individual conjectures about one another's likely behavior, which they then adjust as they play the game. Fictitious play for which the players' conjectures are the frequency with which the other has played each strategy in the past plays of the game is an attempt to directly model the evolution of conjectures (see Young 1998, 30–41 on fictitious play). The players play best replies against their conjectures, and – over time – fictitious play converges to a Nash equilibrium in some games; and one can say that both conjectures and strategies converge together when that happens. However, it has been long known that not all games converge to any strategy under fictitious play (Shapley 1964), and which equilibrium fictitious play converges to depends on the initial beliefs when there are multiple Nash equilibria. Models of rational learning to play (e.g., Fudenberg and Levine 1993b; Kalai and Lehrer 1993), where the players infer which strategy one another is playing by updating from their observed moves, also lead to the general result that the players should eventually play a Nash equilibrium. These results, however, face the issue that the set of strategies a player could use is uncountably infinite (for example, consider all mixed strategies of just two pure strategies), and a finite history of play cannot definitively judge among that uncountable set in some games

(Nachbar 1997). Other versions of rational learning (Sanchirico 1996) avoid this issue by having the players improve their predictions of the future plays of the game using the history of the game to date. In any case, these approaches to learning how to play an equilibrium produce generally similar dynamics to evolutionary game theory (Hofbauer and Sandholm 2002; Hopkins 2002; Benaim and Weibull 2003). I examine the patterns found by evolutionary game theory because they are likely to hold with more cognitively complex actors and the dynamics of those games are understood better.[6]

## THE DYNAMICS OF CONVENTIONS

As I noted in the prior section, the central result of evolutionary game theory is *if* the process converges over time, the result is a Nash equilibrium. Strategy combinations that do not form an equilibrium cannot sustain themselves over time in the face of individual incentives to adopt better strategies whether through imitation or experimentation. This result does not imply, however, that the process necessarily moves to an equilibrium and stays there forever.

First, the process may not converge at all. Although the process reaches a stationary state, that state could include different strategy combinations, none of which is a Nash equilibrium either by itself or with the combinations in the state. Glenn Ellison (2000) has an example with a stationary state in which the players cycle between suboptimal moves rather than coordinate on a Pareto superior outcome.

Second, the process may converge on a class of strategy combinations that produce the same behavior on the equilibrium path – the moves that happen when the players use those strategies – while diverging off the path. Because the players learn by experience and respond to the moves of other players that they observe, they cannot learn about how to play in moves that are not reached in their experience. They converge to a class of Nash equilibria whose strategies differ only off the path. This observation has an important implication for the incomplete nature of law.

Third, experimentation implies that the players will not rest forever, even at a stable equilibrium. If the players never experimented, then they would remain at a Nash equilibrium if they reached one, because all of them would be playing best replies. The introduction of random experiments creates the possibility that enough players experiment at the same time that all now see other moves as better than their Nash strategy. This movement could lead the

---

[6] There are other issues that could cause convergence to a common conjecture to differ from convergence in evolutionary games. The number of players is small compared to evolutionary games, making it more useful to predict what individual other players will do. The source of experimentation could also vary from random to systematic. It could be that random experimentation is more effective than designed experimentation because it searches a wider set of strategies over time, so that the not-very-bright players of evolutionary game theory do better in the long run than calculating Bayesian maximizers. Maybe it is smart to play dumb.

players away from a stable equilibrium for some time, but they are likely to return more quickly than they departed. Unstable strategy configurations are more likely to be overturned by experimentation than stable ones; that is the definition of stability. Many of the results of evolutionary game theory identify stable sets as the rate of experimentation goes to zero. Obviously, players will shift out of a stable set as the rate of experimentation increases simply because the chance of having sufficient simultaneous experiments to induce the players to shift away increases as the chance of any individual player experimenting rises. By examining stability as the rate of experimentation goes to zero, we can characterize stable sets. When players actually experiment, we should expect that some experiments lead them astray, and so the stable set is not a prediction that the players must always play that combination of strategies.

This last point brings us to the key for thinking about what makes a strategy combination stable. A strategy combination is stable if it takes a larger amount of experimentation to move away from it than toward it. Because the players play best replies when they respond to experiments, the payoffs of the game play a critical role in determining when experimentation leads the players away from the configuration of strategies they are currently playing.

The fraction of experimenters needed to induce a change in a stable set depends on all the payoffs of the game, not just those at the outcomes of the stable set, because the payoffs of outcomes outside the stable set help determine the value of adopting a change. This result allows us to draw some conclusions about equilibrium selection. First, the evolutionary process will choose the efficient outcome, the one with the greatest payoff to the players, in a game of pure coordination (Young 1998, 140–141).[7] Such games reward the players identically for playing the same strategy, although the reward can vary based on which strategy they all play, with all receiving zero if they fail to coordinate. The strategic problem among the players is pure coordination to figure out which strategy to play. Any strategy which rewards the players for coordinating is a Nash equilibrium. Second, the evolutionary process selects the risk-dominant equilibrium (Harsanyi and Selten 1988) of two-by-two coordination games (which need not be symmetric). This result, however, does not easily generalize to more complicated games.

If the evolutionary process converges, the result is a Nash equilibrium. Viewing the process as a whole, what are its dynamics? Because experimentation will induce the players to move from one stable strategic combination to another, it is difficult to determine the long-run distribution among those combinations over time. Instead, results examine the distribution in the long run as the rate of experimentation goes to zero. The rate of experimentation has two effects on the persistence of a given strategic combination. First, higher rates increase the chance of leaving the state for another, implying less stability. This

---

[7] This result does not hold for other coordination games in which the players may have different payoffs over the different ways to coordinate, as in Battle of the Sexes (Young 1998, 101–106).

higher chance of leaving also increases the chance that the players will adopt the most stable strategic combination earlier by increasing the chance that they shift into it from an inferior combination. Because the players will stay in the most stable configuration longer than others, a higher rate of experimentation could lead to more stability in the long run, the second effect. The general result is that as the rate of experimentation goes to zero and the number of time periods increases without bound, the probability that the players are playing the most stable strategic configuration goes to one. They may not always play that configuration, but eventually, they spend almost all their time there.

But this is a conclusion about the very long run, and we live in the short to medium run. The persistence of any strategy combination depends how easy it is to convince players to move away from it, the overall rate of experimentation, and the number of players. Over time, the players will move from one stable configuration to another. If the only stable configurations are Nash equilibria of the stage game, they will move from one to another over time. As stated previously, they will spend the overwhelming proportion of the time in the very long run in the most stable equilibrium. In a game of pure coordination, the players will eventually reach the best way to coordinate. But before then, they may persist for long periods in Pareto-dominated forms of coordination before experimentation leads them to the superior alternative. We can think of these periods as short-run equilibria which eventually change when a superior alternative is found through experimentation. The periods of transition from one short-run equilibrium to another are brief because the learning dynamic takes the players immediately to the best reply against the current collection of strategies including experiments. Most experiments fail because they are not extensive enough to induce a change in equilibrium. The dynamics have the players playing a Nash equilibrium almost all the time, and particular ones over long stretches of the game. These conventions change dramatically and unpredictably from the view of both the players and us as observers. The difference between a successful and an unsuccessful experiment can be small. Over time, the players will eventually reach the most stable collection of strategies and can then expect to stay there longer than any other equilibrium. If they leave, it will generally take less time to return to it than it did to leave it.

These conclusions, however, should be qualified. The speed of transition from one equilibrium to another depends on how quickly actors learn from experiments with new strategies. When they update their strategies, they use the most successful strategy they observe from the most recent period. The spread of a new equilibrium could be slowed if the players interact and learn only locally. Small groups might adopt a new equilibrium among themselves, which would then spread slowly to others through the diffusion of contact. It might also be that different players require different levels of success to be convinced to switch strategies. Some might be convinced by success over a short period of plays while others require a longer record of success before switching. Real institutional innovations might take longer than they do in the evolutionary setup. Institutional interregna might persist over noticeable periods of time.

The change in conventions limiting war in Ancient Greece illustrates these dynamics. During the period of hoplite warfare (700–450 BCE), conventions limited wars between Greek city-states to direct battles between the hoplite phalanxes of the two sides, composed of heavily armored infantry. Battles ended when one side conceded the field, and wars ended after one battle. Violence against the surrendered and defeated was proscribed, and the bodies of the dead returned to the defeated for proper burial. Most important, combat was limited to hoplites, drawn from the upper quarter to half of free men in each city-state, commonly farmers who worked their own land. This system helped to preserve the political dominance of the hoplites within their own city-state by denying a military role to lesser freed men and slaves and keeping wars short to allow the hoplites to return to their farms in their city-state. These restraints collapsed in the Peloponnesian War when Athens refused to contest Sparta's invasion of Attica, instead protecting its population within its fortified walls and harrying Sparta and its allies using Athenian naval power. Pericles chose this innovative strategy of refusing to fight a hoplite battle as the conventions prescribed. But this strategy foundered when the plague struck Athens, and the conduct of both sides eroded the restraint of the conventions of hoplite warfare. Both sides began to raid and encourage revolt in the non-hoplite classes of their opponent. Both began to arm light troops for this new war, undermining the military dominance of the hoplite class. Both sides committed atrocities, the most famous being the destruction of Melos by the Athenians. The responses to the strategic innovation of Pericles was a shift to a different way of war, a new equilibrium in which mercenaries replaced citizen soldiers, sieges and subversion were common, and war became more destructive (Ober 1991, 187–192; Ober 1994; Hanson 2005, 26–30 on Pericles's strategy).

Evolutionary game theory also suggests three ways in which an evolved shared understanding could be incomplete. First, evolutionary processes only produce expectations of equilibrium behavior for those actions that occur in that equilibrium. The players may diverge in their expectations for behavior off the equilibrium path, or in more common terms, they can differ in the expectations of the consequences of counterfactual acts. Equilibria in which the players can hold different beliefs off the path are called self-confirming equilibria (Fudenberg and Levine 1993a). Second, the players might be uncertain whether a particular player will follow its equilibrium strategies, either because of incomplete information about its type or the possibility of experimentation with a new strategy. Behavior in those cases would diverge from equilibrium expectations. Third, actors might play mixed strategies in equilibrium so that they could not predict one another's strategy in a given play. One might get noncompliance that is anticipated in general but not predictable specifically. We anticipate that some violations will occur but cannot predict who will commit them.

Each of these three sources of incomplete expectations implies certain features of international law as shared understanding. Divergence of expectations off the equilibrium path reflects the incomplete nature of law. Ideally, law could anticipate all possibilities and prescribe how every possibility should be handled. Practically, law cannot anticipate all possibilities, and instead, relies on general principles and procedures for applying those principles to specific cases that arise in the future. Abstract principles in law provide one way to deal with cases that cannot be anticipated from what has already happened – that is, those that lie off the equilibrium path. Uncertainty about whether another player intends to follow the equilibrium in path leads to the role of acceptance of law as a signal of intent. Public acceptance of international law through ratification aids the parties in dealing with this second incompleteness of expectation. Law deals with the third issue through sanctions and enforcement. The evolutionary approach to understanding the sources of common conjectures leads directly to three important properties of international law.

Constructivists often argue that rational approaches to understanding institutions cannot explain actual institutions that emerge from historical processes. Actors cannot anticipate the full effects of institutions and so cannot design them to fulfill a function (Wendt 2001). Instead, they claim that one must examine the historical process by which institutions are created and evolve to understand why they take the form they do. The central result of evolutionary game theory – evolutionary processes lead to the same set of stable institutional equilibria as rational design through negotiation – invalidates this criticism. Goal-seeking actors, even those with very limited understanding of their situation, will eventually adopt institutionalized behavior from a Nash equilibria of the underlying game. Institutions will be consistent with rational design even if the process of their development is not consciously designed. Evolutionary selection pressure leads actors toward the same solutions as conscious design, even in the absence of intent to design institutions to be efficient.

Additionally, the evolutionary process could lead to institutions commonly characterized as inefficient. Many games have numerous Nash equilibria that are Pareto optimal, the definition of efficiency from economics. For example, the iterated Prisoners' Dilemma game discussed in Chapter 2 has an infinite number of Pareto optimal asymmetric equilibria, where one player exploits the other a fixed percentage of the plays. These equilibria are Pareto optimal because any change to another equilibrium that makes one player better off makes the other worse off. Even if the sum of their payoffs would be increased by shifting to the equilibrium in which both play Cooperate in every round, the player doing the exploiting would see a reduction in its payoff, and so presumably block that change. Although the all-Cooperate equilibrium (backed by reciprocity) produces a higher total payoff, it is more efficient only when the players have a mechanism to redistribute that higher total to make both better off. In the absence of such a mechanism, an unequal, exploitative equilibrium is efficient in the sense of being Pareto optimal. The evolutionary process can lead to institutions that appear inefficient to some.

In summary, evolutionary game theory provides a reason to believe that stable institutions must be Nash equilibria. It also provides an account of how such institutions change over time, only rarely shifting from one to another as the players experiment with new strategies. The dynamics of institutions fall somewhere between the extremes of preplay negotiations among fully rational actors and the groping toward a solution by the cognitively limited actors of evolutionary game theory. Actors may learn how to anticipate one another's play through the evolutionary pressure of repeated interaction, but they also sharpen those anticipations through negotiations to design explicit institutions that capture and reflect them. Both paths work together in the dynamics of institutional change. Blending the evolutionary and the rational negotiations approaches also holds the promise of a richer model of institutional development and change than either alone.

## RATIONAL EVOLUTION OF POLITICAL INSTITUTIONS

This discussion of institutional change has been general and generic; it could address the evolution of norms of etiquette. Political institutions change through a combination of both evolution in response to the strategic dynamics of the situation and public negotiation to hone the understandings that have evolved. The blend of these two approaches provides a way to think about how international institutions have changed over time.

Political institutions often encompass multiple strategic problems, all of which must be addressed for the institution to function. The strategic problems facing effective laws of war as developed in Chapter 3 include state-to-state signaling of intentions and deterrence of deliberate violations by policy, soldier-versus-soldier on the battlefield, and the control of soldiers by each state to ensure that they follow state policy. A solution to each of these individual problems can be thought of as an equilibrium to a game reflecting that strategic problem. Each equilibrium that addresses one of these strategic problems relies on the equilibria that solve the other problems, so they are linked together in the resulting institution. A state can control its soldiers through summary executions on the battlefield by officers or through a legal system of military justice, but the latter requires solving the strategic problems of courts while the former does not. Instead, summary discipline faces the different issues of the control of officers to prevent abuse of their arbitrary power and maintaining the morale of line soldiers in the face of such discipline. We can think of each of these equilibria separately, assuming that the supporting equilibria that address other strategic problems are in place and fixed for the analysis of any one of them. Political institutions encompass a constellation of equilibria, dependent on one another and interrelated.

Kathleen Thelen's (2004) book, *How Institutions Evolve*, provides an example of a constellation of equilibria within the institutions that regulate the training of skilled workers in Germany, Britain, the United States, and Japan. Historical forces – the particular political coalitions and the existing laws and arrangements for training through apprenticeships – have led to two distinct styles of vocational training. On-the-job-training by firms faces the problem that workers may leave the firm for a higher wage once they have obtained the skills. Firms then may be unwilling to invest in general skills because they will pay the cost of training while other firms receive the benefit of skilled workers. Germany and Japan have high-skill training for which firms provide extensive skill training to their employees and apprentices because the broadly negotiated wages – which are tied to seniority in Germany and lifetime employment in Japan – both give firms an incentive to broadly train their workers and give workers an incentive not to jump for a higher wage once trained. That is, inefficient labor markets can help create an incentive for both firms and workers to commit to high-skills training. Britain and the United States have open labor markets, meaning that firms lack the incentive to broadly train their workers and instead rely on workers acquiring skills either in public schools or by paying for the training at technical schools themselves. Because these forms of vocational training are not as effective, Britain and the United States can be thought of as having low-skills among their factory workers. Thelen deftly traces the evolution of all four systems of vocational training from the late 1800s to examine how the politics of these issues among firms, workers, labor unions, and politicians led to high- or low-skills systems in each country.[8]

Skills training, conceived of broadly as Thelen does, fits well with my definition of an institution as an interdependent collection of equilibria that address related strategic problems. The strategic logic of skills training involves solving at least three interrelated strategic problems: (1) the mutual assurance problem between trainees and firms where the firm promises to provide costly training and the trainee promises not to change jobs quickly for a higher wage; (2) a public goods problem among firms to avoid poaching one another's trained

---

[8] Thelen, like much of the literature on different varieties of capitalism, veers into claims that the high-skills systems are better than the low-skills systems. As a student of war, this conclusion strikes me as odd. The low-skills mass production systems of the United States, Great Britain, and the Soviet Union greatly out-produced the high-skills systems of Germany and Japan during World War II, which was a crucial component of their victory over the Axis. Germany, in particular, faced two difficult issues because of their high-skills system. First, the need for manpower in the army faced the difficult issue of whether skilled labor should be exempted because those men were needed both at the front and in the factories. This was a major reason why Germany placed high demands on the occupied countries to provide skilled workers for the German economy that I discussed in Chapter 5, in the context of the Nazis' use of French POWs as bargaining chips for French skilled labor. Second, production based on skilled labor is difficult to expand rapidly. Consequently, the mass production systems greatly out-produced the skilled labor system, with Germany only making substantial gains in its production of war material when Albert Speer introduced mass production using unskilled labor. High and low-skill systems are different with important consequences for a state's economy, but it strikes me that neither is clearly superior to the other.

workers to maintain the incentive to train; and (3) a bargaining problem between unions and firms concerning whether wages are negotiated broadly across the economy – corporatism – or narrowly by open labor markets and firm specific collective bargaining (Thelen 2004, 8–20).[9] Furthermore, each strategic problem can be thought of as separate from the others in the sense that firms think about the provision of training separately from labor negotiations with unions. There are at least two institutions possible here: (1) the high-skills institution in which control of wages through corporatism or lifetime employment solves the assurance problem by eliminating poaching of skilled workers, and (2) a low-skills institution in which this does not happen. There are multiple institutions, and which one occurs in each country depends on the history of their development. A change in the equilibrium that addresses one of the strategic problems – such as changes in the labor market produced by the growth of unions – leads to adjustments in the equilibria that address the other strategic problems.

This mutual dependence of the equilibria explains a key role of explicit negotiation in the establishment and change of political institutions. Evolutionary processes may lead to change within one equilibrium that undermines another equilibrium within the institution. Unchecked, that change could cause a number of the rules, norms, and procedures of the institution to fail. Negotiation among actors provides a way for them to adjust the rules and norms of the now-destabilized equilibrium to restore predictability for the actors and prevent failure of the institution. This way, evolution and negotiation are twin drivers of institutional change; evolution explains why more actors adopt new strategies over time than can improve or threaten institutional orders, and negotiation gives actors a change to adapt existing institutions in the face of evolutionary change.

The interdependence of equilibria in an institution also explains why abstract principles often lie at the heart of an institution, suffusing the common conjectures of the different equilibria. The evolution of behavior under one equilibrium in an institution can undermine the stability of other equilibria – that is, render current non-equilibrium strategies into best replies. Renegotiation of these destabilized equilibria requires some consensus on the outlines of the resulting negotiation. Abstract principles provide those outlines. They limit the range of possibilities in the renegotiation and focus the parties on certain new equilibria over others. The principles have to be broad and abstract because the specific ways in which they are implemented in the equilibria of the institution will vary over time. These abstract principles form part of the core of the institution because they are the elements of the institution that do not change as the constituent equilibria evolve and are renegotiated over time.

---

[9] One of the great strengths of Thelen's argument is that she is very clear about the strategic dynamics underlying the two different institutions of high- and low-skills training.

Rational evolution of institutions reflects the interplay of evolutionary change in behavior through experimentation and adaption and renegotiation in response to such changes. This approach to evolutionary change requires us to specify the different games the actors play and how the equilibria of these games support one another. We have to explain how actors change their behavior over time to produce the evolutionary dynamic between explicit negotiations over the institutions. Moments of institutional change occur when the actors realize the difficulties of sustaining some of the current set of equilibria and seek to adjust the features of the institution to the new incentives presented by the evolving behavior under the institution. Accounts of how institutions have rationally evolved must be historical because the evolutionary process does not make specific predictions about its future path. Furthermore, renegotiation often presents several alternatives to change the institution in ways to preserve it. Which new forms the actors choose at those moments of change are the results of political bargaining, which also rarely predicts a single outcome.

Rational evolution also suggests why institutional change often requires a period of consolidation before we can be certain that the new institution will hold or what its precise features will be. A change in one equilibrium of an institution may provoke changes in the equilibria addresses the other bundled strategic problems. Resolving the consequences of the change in those other strategic situations may take time. If the change entails the creation of new social roles – that is, new identities – it may take time to train people to fill those roles. It may also be that the incentives needed for those individuals to carry out their roles properly are unclear when those roles are created. Systems that appear to address problems when viewed in the abstract may fail in practice because the pattern of behavior that results fails to create the proper incentives for actors to carry out their necessary roles. The creation of third-party law enforcement is an example of these issues. In principle, third-party enforcement is preferable to personal enforcement through revenge because it controls the consequences of a violation more effectively by removing the judgment of when a crime has occurred to a legal process based on the merits of the case and relocating the punishment to a third-party. This movement reduces the chance of mistaken retaliation and of reciprocal feuds. Such a system, however, requires new social roles, such as police, attorneys, and judges, all which require training that takes time and the creation of the proper incentives for them to carry out their proper roles for third-party enforcement. Getting any one set of incentives wrong can undermine the whole system as corruption can spread from police to the judiciary or the other way. It is often difficult to tell whether a set of changes to an institution will prove to create the proper incentives when those changes are designed and implemented. For these reasons, political institutions require a period of consolidation before we can be certain that an effective change has occurred.

Rational evolution of institutions is closely connected to the two central concepts in Avner Greif's analysis of institutional change (Greif and Laitin

2004; Greif 2006). He sees behavior under an institution as an equilibrium in which the game is characterized by parameters, some of which he calls "quasi-parameters," vary over time. His paradigmatic example is how the governing institutions of medieval Genoa at first stabilized violent conflict among family factions. With the conflict controlled, Genoese merchants could then devote their efforts to trade instead of fighting over control of the city. Many became wealthy as a result, but the new wealth made fighting over political control of the city more valuable, which caused renewed conflict. Wealth is a quasi-parameter on which the political equilibrium that controlled factional conflict depended. In terms of my argument, there are two interdependent equilibria, one that is political among Genoese factions, and another that is economic on how incentives to invest in trading relationships changes with the political stability of Genoa. "Self-reinforcement" occurs in Greif's argument when changes in the quasi-parameters reinforce equilibrium behavior under the institution. An example is how stable democracy enhances economic growth through the provision of the public goods that support it (B. Bueno de Mesquita et al. 2003), and in turn a wealthier society makes democracy more stable. In my argument, self-reinforcement occurs when evolutionary change in one equilibrium in an institution strengthens the stability of the others, making them less susceptible to evolutionary experiments. Rational evolution expands on Greif's view of institutional change by stating that institutions are composed of several interrelated games whose equilibria support one another, by providing the evolutionary dynamic to explain pressures for change over time, and by allowing the actors to renegotiate the institution in response to those evolutionary changes. Now I turn to an example of the rational evolution of institutions in international politics, and specifically the laws of war.

## THE EVOLUTION OF HOW PRISONERS OF WAR SHOULD BE TREATED

Ideas about how prisoners should be treated have changed greatly over time. General attitudes toward those who have surrendered have changed, and treaty law has specified these understandings in greater detail in response to the experiences with less developed law. In ancient times, prisoners were often treated with contempt: enslaved, killed, or treated as hostages; Rome returned those who surrendered after the battle of Cannae to slavery in Carthage because the Senate held them to be cowards who had disgraced the Republic (Livy 1948, XXII: chapters 58–61).[10] In the late Medieval Period, the ransoming of those taken prisoner during battle was a primary source of income and motivation for the warrior class, and a substantial body of law grew to regulate capture,

---

[10] I would like to thank Steve Krasner for bringing this example to my attention.

ensure the payment of ransom, and resolve disputes over them (Keen 1965). European armies in the early modern period often recruited captives after a battle into the victorious army (Vance 2000, 290; Wilson 2010, 51–52). By the Age of Enlightenment, treatment of prisoners of war varied with class. Noble officers were paroled, released to their home country under a pledge not to rejoin the army, or allowed to establish themselves on an estate by paying their own expenses while a captive. Common soldiers, in contrast, were housed roughly and given little support, leading to high death rates in captivity.

The demise of the *ancien régime* and the rise of governments based on popular support slowly changed ideas about how prisoners of war should be handled. The French Republic in 1792 declared that – in an effort to identify foreign monarchs as their enemy rather than their common soldiers – it would protect prisoners from abuse and provide for them at a level comparable to their own soldiers. In practice, French armies varied in their treatment of enemy prisoners, with guerrilla warfare in Spain and Russia triggering the worst abuses (Best 1980, 77–84, 112–121, 125–126; Vance 2000, 200). The Lieber Code, adopted by U.S. forces during its Civil War, laid out the initial concepts of humane treatment of prisoners of war: prisoners may not be punished except for any crimes they may have committed in service or detention, their property is their own and not subject to seizure, soldiers who resort to perfidy lose POW status, and the captor nation cannot refuse to take prisoners and must take care of them during detention. The Lieber Code sought to create consistent treatment of prisoners across an army expanded rapidly through the influx of civilian recruits with few professional officers. It also embodied President Lincoln's desire that the conduct of the war be limited to that which was necessary to win militarily rather than punishing Southerners for their rebellion (Carnahan 1998). The desire to restore the Union after the war impelled restraint against those who would once again be U.S. citizens. The Brussels Declaration of 1874 sought to create some protections for prisoners of war, but it languished unratified (Vance 2000, 34).

Prisoners of war were a central concern of the Hague Conferences of 1899 and 1907 that produced the Hague Conventions. Before then, treatment of the wounded took precedence as an issue of humanitarian concern (Moorehead 1998, 126–128). These Conventions resulted from the push for humanitarianism, pacifism, and disarmament from activists that we would now call "global civil society," a push resisted and limited by state representatives often drawn from the military and who wanted to ensure that their armed forces could fight as their generals and admirals saw fit. Their desire to block binding arbitration and disarmament combined with the need to produce something tangible contributed to the drafting, signing, and ratification of the Hague Conventions. Of the various limitations on war considered, prisoners of war were not controversial, and the Conventions passed with little discussion (Tuchman 1966, 229–267, 277–288; Moorehead 1998, 169–170).

The experience of World War I with the Hague Conventions – the misunderstandings created by a lack of clarity, the failings of clear provisions to protect prisoners and others, and the many atrocities of the war – led to broad demands to revisit treaty law and improve it. The ICRC, after its new role in prisoner affairs during the war, called for a new treaty to regulate the treatment of prisoners, what would become the 1929 Geneva Convention on POWs, matched by a convention on the treatment of the wounded in the field. It took the leading role in pushing states toward a new treaty by calling for an international conference in 1918 and drawing up a draft treaty by 1923. The ICRC used the Swiss government to call the 1929 Geneva Conference. Great Britain also took a leading role in laying out the principles that should underlie a new treaty on prisoners. It succeeded in keeping a right to escape, an issue more pressing for the countries on the continent where escaping prisoners had a better chance of returning home than the prisoners held in Britain or Canada for whom escape and return required a sea voyage rather than just crossing a land border. The United States favored adding just some guidelines for the application of the Hague Convention instead of a detailed new treaty, trusting parties to treat the prisoners they held well. This position failed as the 1929 Convention has ninety-seven articles – compared to the twenty articles in the 1907 Hague Convention – that address some aspect of prisoners of war. The ICRC's main triumph lay in outlawing reprisals despite opposition of states that were more concerned with preventing spirals of retaliation under the guise of reprisals. The treaty also recognized the roles of protecting powers and the ICRC as intermediaries between warring parties. Japan participated and signed, but not did not ratify, the convention; the Soviet Union boycotted the conference, later blaming their refusal to sign the treaty to Article 9, which prescribes segregation of the races into different camps (Durand and Boissier 1984, 250–252, 255–259; Bellamy 2007, 20–21; Wylie 2010a, 44–53; Wylie 2010b, 94–104).

The abuse of prisoners during World War II led to another round of negotiation to improve the treaty standard, culminating in the 1949 Geneva Convention. The four treaties of the Convention are best known for the creation of explicit and detailed standards governing military occupation, a weak feature of the Hague Conventions as demonstrated during the war. The POW treaty was not as controversial, and the 1949 Geneva Convention (III) on POWs is even more detailed than the 1929 Geneva Convention on POWs, with 143 articles in total. The primary innovations of the 1949 Convention are that it binds unilaterally on member states, that it allows captor nations to try prisoners for violations of the laws of war, and extends some protections to irregulars if they meet the conditions to be considered active combatants. It also adds further detail to the conditions under which prisoners of war are held to address some of the shortcomings experienced during World War II. The allowance for criminal trials of prisoners for their conduct on the battlefield grew in part out of the postwar war crimes trials that established that individual soldiers bore criminal responsibility if their conduct breached treaties ratified by their countries.[11] The treaties did not, however, move the power to try war criminals to an international body. Politically, the primary concern for the Western Powers was whether the Soviet Union would participate and do so constructively in their view. France served as an important go-between for the United States and Great Britain on one hand, and the Soviet Union on the other. The 1949 Convention also marked the end of differences in the handling of officers and enlisted men from centuries earlier, with the exceptions that an officer cannot be compelled to work and they receive a higher rate of pay while in captivity (Best 1994, 80–114, 135–142, 158–168; Moorehead 1998, 553–554).

The 1949 Geneva Convention on POWs is now ratified by all member states of the UN. Despite the widespread ratification of the treaty, wars in the post-1945 period had often had substantial problems with compliance. In some cases, like the Korean War, one side had not ratified the 1949 Geneva Convention at the outbreak of the war. In others, such as the Vietnam War and the Iraq-Iran War, autocracies committed abuses despite their ratification of the treaty. Compliance remains problematic, even given almost universal ratification of a more detailed standard.

The process of change in ideas about how prisoners of war should be treated has been incremental in the short run, but substantial in the long run. Humanitarian attitudes concerned with the protection of prisoners have supplanted earlier attitudes that surrender is disgraceful. Experience with initial treaty law led to efforts to expand that law to remedy its shortcomings in practice. These changes represent a rational evolution in response to practical experience; ideas changed in response to the incentives and strategic problems of protecting prisoners of war.

The prisoners of war system evolved over time to produce a system that protects prisoners in the face of the three different strategic problems in the laws of war. Although states had ideas about the system they desired when negotiating POW treaties, those principles faced the challenges of working during wartime. When they failed, states sought to change them to remedy those failures. Although no one state had a complete rational design for the institutions for POWs, the resulting system embodied rational design (Morrow 2001). Rational design of institutions arises from actors who seek to adjust them in response to their results; it does not require conscious design.

[11] Some Japanese were tried for violations of the Hague Conventions that Japan had ratified, rather than the 1929 Geneva Convention that it had not.

# 8

## Conclusion

### *Current Issues and Policy Insights*

The laws of war shape but do not determine how states fight. States have created these laws to limit the violence and destruction of war, but those efforts face the reality of the strategic incentives of states and soldiers at war. Not all states see the limits of the laws of war as in their interest during war; not all soldiers will follow those rules, even in the best-disciplined armies. Even those who wish to follow the rules may breach them to protect themselves. An effective legal system to limit violence during war must adapt itself to the strategic logics of war and combat. Such a system can shape how states and their militaries act during war by creating shared expectations about what acts are inappropriate conduct and what are proper responses to such conduct. Treaty law creates both a universal standard and the means for public acceptance of that standard. Rejection of a treaty standard signals the desire for an unrestrained battlefield and the likelihood of state policy to create one should war come. Treaty law aids the parties in resolving the uncertainty created by different views of appropriate conduct among states and different willingness to follow any rules among soldiers on the battlefield. Joint ratification entails the belief that both sides will seek to control their own soldiers' behaviors through training and discipline. It also creates strategic expectations of restraint between soldiers of the warring sides. Despite its failures, the law of war has restrained the destruction of war.

The successes and failures of the laws of war arise from differences in wars and the issues faced. Joint ratification leads to more restraint and stronger reciprocal responses when restraint fails. Democracies are more restrained, except when they are not legally bound either through the absence of a treaty, the failure to ratify one, a lack of clarity in what restraint means, or an issue in which noise overwhelms any effort to comply. Autocracies can only be restrained by the threat of retaliation, and unfortunately they do not often fear that retaliation (and they may even welcome it). Unilateral restraint can weaken deterrence through reciprocity. Those issues in which control of violations can be held closely by military authorities have less noise and better records of restraint; those in which every soldier possesses the power to violate have the worst records of compliance. When a state believes it benefits from an unrestrained battlefield, it breaks the treaty standard early in the war; retaliation by the other side also comes swiftly.

Even when states wish to observe the restraints of the laws of war, producing a restrained battlefield requires that soldiers be trained in their rights and responsibilities under law and then disciplined when they violate those responsibilities. Combat is a kill-or-be-killed world, and soldiers are empowered with the right to kill and armed to exercise that right. Acting within the limits of the law can put soldiers at risk. Acts of perfidy provoke retaliation and undermine the belief that the enemy will observe the limits that save soldiers' lives. A limited battlefield is created through training and sustained through discipline against those who break the rules. These measures rarely succeed fully because soldiers can act on their own and detecting their violations is difficult for the military authorities, making punishment sporadic when the authorities seek to control their soldiers. This system for controlling violations on the battlefield is most successful for the issues in which the military authorities have the greatest control over whether the rules are broken, such as chemical and biological weapons. The issues in which they have the least control – prisoners of war and treatment of civilians – have the worst records of compliance. But soldiers can also benefit from their own restraint, enemy soldiers who believe they will be treated well as prisoners are more likely to surrender. Limiting violence through law must work on the battlefield as well as between governments at war, and a commitment within those states to build the law into a military helps to limit violence.

The laws of war limit the destruction of war because they clarify expectations for how the sides will fight and support the parties in their efforts to comply and enforce those obligations. States have created this law, revised it, and publicly accepted it because they seek to limit the destruction of war to the degree that it can be limited. The record of these legal limits has been mixed, which reflects the practical difficulties of limiting violence. The successes are not just the result of the parties' intents to comply no matter what; the law aids them in creating the limited battlefield. The body of the law has expanded and deepened over time as those parties that favor restraint revised treaty law in light of their experiences of applying it during wars. Through this evolutionary process, the laws of war have improved and now limit the battlefield more than in their early days.

## DOES THE PRESENT LOOK LIKE THE PAST?

These lessons from the past mean little if they do not generalize to current and future wars. Recent conflicts differ in several ways from the historic record of interstate wars used as evidence on the laws of war. First, many current and recent conflicts are internal wars rather than interstate wars. Second, even the interstate conflicts in Kosovo, Afghanistan, and Iraq are asymmetric where those who oppose the United States are much weaker than it. Third, news coverage of these conflicts is more detailed, immediate, and willing to report atrocities than in past wars. Fourth, the U.S. military is suffused with legality by which military lawyers approve lists of targets and review rules of engagement and officers follow their advice. Fifth, the technology of war is now so accurate that it is possible to imagine the elimination of collateral damage. Do these differences render the results from earlier wars irrelevant?

I test for these differences using statistical tools for judging how close the data for particular cases are to another set of cases (King and Zeng 2006, 2007). These tools were designed to help us judge whether specific counterfactuals (that is, the recent wars) are close to the data we have (that is, the interstate wars of the twentieth century), meaning that our inferences are based on solid evidence. When a counterfactual is far from existing cases, those inferences require projections beyond what the data can support. The problem is complicated because the values of a counterfactual might all appear in our data but not the specific combination of those values in the counterfactual. For instance, there are democracies and autocracies and states with a free press and those without, but very few autocracies with a free press. Consequently, inferences about how autocracies with a free press might operate are based on almost no data. In this sense, I can judge whether recent interstate conflicts are close or far from the data used to reach the conclusions I report here.

Not all of these differences can be captured easily in variables for either the historical cases or the recent wars. For the wars in Kosovo in 1999, Afghanistan in 2001, and Iraq in 2003, I calculated six of the independent variables – whether the side was the initiator, battle deaths per 1,000 population, power ratio, joint ratification, whether it lost, and whether it was a democracy. Because allied forces operated under joint command in all three wars, there are six directed dyads, each direction of the following pairs of warring sides: NATO-Yugoslavia(Serbia) in Kosovo, United States-Afghanistan, and United States/United Kingdom-Iraq. The Correlates of War coding covers just the interstate war portion of the Afghan and Iraq wars for casualties, excluding all battle deaths during the insurgencies that followed. The power ratio is calculated from the Correlates of War composite capabilities adjusted for distance to the country where the war was fought and summed for those states that fought under unified command; it ranges from 0 to 1 and gives the percentage of the total capabilities of the two sides that each possesses.

These methods ask first whether each counterfactual case – here, the recent wars – fit inside the existing dataset.[1] When cases fall outside the data, we

---

[1] The careful way to say this, for those who know some math, is whether the counterfactual fits in the convex hull of the data.

generalize beyond the data when we apply the results of the data analysis to such cases. Of the six cases, only one – conduct of Iraq toward the United States/United Kingdom in 2003 – falls within the dataset. Judgments about the other five cases require extrapolation away from the interstate wars used in the statistical analysis in this book. The second step is to ask how far away these cases are from the data; is the extrapolation small or great? These methods assess this distance by measuring the variation within the dataset and then asking what fraction of that data falls within that distance of the cases in question. There is a pronounced difference in this based on which side of these directed dyads we look at. For the weaker state (Serbia, Afghanistan, and Iraq), more than 17 percent and up to 20 percent of the data fall within this variation within the data. There are many cases in the data similar to these cases. For the stronger side (NATO, United States, and United States/United Kingdom), only 6 to 8 percent of the cases in the data are that similar. The main difference between these cases and the dataset is the casualties suffered by the stronger side; for Kosovo and Afghanistan, the casualty rates of the coalitions led by United States are minuscule and much lower than any of the interstate wars in the data. There is only one other war in which one side suffered fewer battle fatalities per 1,000 population than the United States and Great Britain did in the Iraq War – France and Britain in the Suez War in 1956. These recent wars then differ from the data in that the stronger side suffered much lower losses. Because compliance in the historical data decreases as losses mount, the prediction is that these low losses should be matched by greater compliance by these stronger warring parties.

The second difference is the great differences in power in these conflicts. The power ratio in the Iraq War is not unusual for the data; twenty-three other warring dyads have power ratios greater than that of the Iraq War. Only one other warring dyad in the data is as unequal as Kosovo was, and none are as unequal as Afghanistan. This inequality poses less of a problem for making projections about compliance in these cases because the power ratio has little effect on compliance when both parties are bound by joint ratification.

Recent wars differ from the historical record of interstate wars because of their asymmetry in capabilities and casualties. This difference should lead us to be careful from generalizing in both directions, especially on the other differences that we did not quantify. These recent wars have been characterized by efforts by the U.S. and its allies to restrict their war efforts to comply with their legal obligations regardless of the conduct of the other side and with greater public scrutiny of their conduct.[2] Three of the differences described

---

[2] I remind the reader here that I am referring to the interstate portion of these wars, not the aftermath with the resulting controversies about U.S. policies for detainees in both Afghanistan and Iraq. Historically, standards of treatment for prisoners goes down after a war ends, one of the clearest pieces of evidence for reciprocity because the loser is not in a position to retaliate against the victor.

previously – greater news scrutiny, greater legal restraint on military operations, and greater precision in targeting reducing collateral damage – seem to have bound military policy to scrupulous compliance with the law of war. The great asymmetry of the recent wars may account for greater attention paid to compliance with the laws of war publicly if not always in the field. These wars were fought over interests that were noticeably less important to the United States than the containment of Communism fought for in Korea and Vietnam, not to mention those fought for in the World Wars. This difference in interest led to the efforts to control casualties and to control and limit violations by U.S. forces through restrained targeting and rules of engagement. We should also be careful, however, not to assume that any recent record of restraint is a historical trend that will continue into the future. More costly wars are likely to see less compliance according to the historical record. Democracies during the twentieth century abandoned restraint when they thought restraint harmed their pursuit of victory and they could justify those actions as legally allowed. We should not assume that the democracies of the twenty-first century will always be automatically restrained by law, particularly when they can justify their violent conduct through gaps in the law.

## CHALLENGES FOR THE LAWS OF WAR IN THE TWENTY-FIRST CENTURY

The end of the Cold War renewed an expansion of the laws of war. The Chemical Weapons Convention sought to end not just the use of chemical weapons but their production on a large scale. The Ottawa Treaty banned the manufacture and use of land mines by ratifying states. Other conventions were negotiated to increase protection for cultural property, ban the use of child soldiers, and ban a variety of weapons, including cluster munitions. This period also introduced new institutions to enforce the laws of war. The UN Security Council created special tribunals to try perpetrators of war crimes and crimes against humanity in the former Yugoslavia, Rwanda, and Sierra Leone. The Rome Statute created the International Criminal Court (ICC).

The end of the Cold War also led to new challenges for the restraint of violence across national borders. As interstate conflict receded, civil wars rose in prominence as the main concern for international security, including the prevention of atrocities. Large-scale atrocities in the former Yugoslavia and Rwanda posed the problem of how to enforce the laws of war in chaotic conditions of civil war. The growth of transnational terrorism conducted by non-state groups linked to the ideological program of Islamic fundamentalism became the central concern after the 9/11 attacks. The response of the United States, the invasions and occupations of Afghanistan and Iraq mentioned earlier, triggered insurgencies in those countries, insurgencies answered by tactics and policies that many saw as deliberate and systematic violations of the laws of war that the United States had pledged to protect.

These issues deserve a book of their own and have received many. Here I have some observations about the ICC and concerning terrorism in light of the arguments of this book. I cannot do full justice to either topic in this space, and so limit myself to the most important observations.

The ICC aims to strengthen the enforcement of the laws of war by creating an international court with the power to accuse and try war criminals above national military and civilian courts. Unlike national systems of military justice that focus on crimes committed by individual soldiers, the ICC seeks to hold national and rebel leaders responsible for the actions of their soldiers. It hopes to deter future systematic and centralized violations by creating credible prosecution and punishment for those who order them. The argument and results presented in this book raise doubts about this program. The leaders of states who see advantages in encouraging violations by their own soldiers have shown little restraint in seizing those advantages. Prosecution is primarily a threat to leaders who lose a war or to those in law-bound states that are willing to turn the accused leader over to the ICC. The former are unlikely to be deterred from violations that they think will help them win, thereby insulating themselves from the threat of prosecution. The latter are leaders of democracies that have been willing to comply with their treaty obligations even unilaterally. The prosecutions then are likely to be autocratic losers and democratic leaders who engage in legally questionable behavior, acts that some would not consider violations and so could justify under their treaty obligations. Both of these types of cases can be seen as politically motivated rather than the pursuit of neutral law; the former because the losers but not the winners are brought to court, the latter because some will accept those leaders' public justifications of their acts as legal.

Turning to the deterrence of individual atrocities, is the ICC in a good position to collect the information needed to prosecute these cases? Armies with the capability and intent of disciplining their own soldiers bring only a selection of cases to trial. Given that fellow soldiers are often the only living witnesses to atrocities, it is often difficult to get eyewitness testimony for trials because they are reluctant to report their comrades who commit crimes or may be intimidated from doing so. Why should we believe that an outside agency would do better in collecting the evidence necessary for successful prosecution of individual violators? The trials of lower-level war criminals after World War II had the advantage that the victors occupied the defeated countries and therefore had complete control of suspects, local witnesses, and records of the defeated militaries. Witnesses from their own armies were more than willing to testify against enemy soldiers who had committed violations against them in POW camps. Individual violations should be left to militaries to discipline their own.

Encouraging internal discipline is the great strength of the ICC system. Under the principle of complementarity, the ICC can only try a case if the national court system with jurisdiction is "unwilling or unable genuinely" to prosecute the case. Indirectly then, the ICC encourages states to develop their own systems of military justice and training to ensure that their soldiers accused of atrocities will be tried by those courts instead of the ICC. The first Chief Prosecutor of the ICC, Luis Moreno-Ocampo, put this indirect effect clearly:

> The second idea that is working well is armies. Armies all over the world are adjusting their standards, their training and the rules of engagement to the ICC. And that, for me, is the perfect impact, because that's a way to ensure that the use of the force will be in accordance with the rules. And that is a way to change the use of violence. This is happening (CFR 2010).

## TERRORISM AND THE CONTROL OF VIOLENCE: THE CRIMINAL MODEL VERSUS THE COMBAT MODEL

> The captured terrorists of the 21st century do not fit easily into traditional systems of criminal or military justice, which were designed for different needs.
> – Secretary of State Condoleeza Rice[3]

Society has two approaches to controlling violence within and across states: criminal law and the laws of war. Criminal law aims at the reduction of violence inside states; laws of war attempt to regulate the use of violence between states. These two systems of law rely on different underlying rationales and address fundamentally different strategic problems in the control of violence in society. The proper form of law depends on the strategic problems it is meant to remedy.

How legal systems work in practice, rather than legal theory, govern how law limits violence. A successful system of criminal law, for example, depends as much on the conduct of the police as on the laws they enforce. The rationale of a legal system addresses an idea of what problem violence poses, how one could control that problem, and the practical issues of making those methods of control work without creating another problem worse than the original one. Once in place, a legal system creates incentives for government agents – police, prosecutors, or soldiers – and other individuals in society, whether or not those incentives have been consciously designed. A successful legal system creates the incentives for people to follow and enforce the law.

I discuss idealized rationales for criminal law and the law of war; the purest form of the logic of each system. Neither system is as clear as its idealization. However, presenting the two systems as idealized types helps to draw out the differences in how they should operate as systems, and therefore how a confusion between the two could alter behavior. I then discuss applying these two models to terrorism, which deliberately strikes at the gray area between the two.

---

[3] December 5, 2005, quoted by The New York Times, http://www.nytimes.com/aponline/national/AP-Rice-Text.html, accessed that day.

There are important similarities between systems of criminal law and the laws of war. Both try to reduce violence by restricting its legitimate use to government agents, police in criminal law and the military in combat. Both prescribe how and when force can be used legitimately by those agents and what acts constitute illegitimate use of force. Both provide ways to enforce those limitations on individual agents and on states.

In the modern world, criminal law and law of war govern separate worlds, inside states versus among states. This separation of the two has not always existed. In late medieval Europe, the kings of England and France relied on local magnates to establish local order and to provide the troops for their armies. The magnates did so because they taxed their local populations and were free to keep what they took – loot, ransoms of prisoners, and payments to forestall attack – during wartime. The legal state of war was key to this system because it separated legal seizure of property during wartime from criminal theft during peace. Needless to say, there were often disputes about exactly whether a state of war existed. Furthermore, the magnates were tied to the kings through a series of contracts that laid out the magnate's responsibilities to the King and his rights to use force. This legal system had no separation between domestic and international law; the two were intermingled in one system that strove to regulate the use of violence by the military class against each other. There were courts that could be used to adjudicate disputes about whether a particular seizure of property or a hostage was legal. Magnates did not always respect such decisions, but they did sometimes (Keen 1965).

## The Criminal Model

The criminal model is the basis of domestic law. The state has a monopoly on the legitimate use of force, and use of force by citizens is criminal. The problem to be addressed is the use of violence by individuals to advance their own ends, primarily economic ends through robbery, extortion, and intimidation. The state can use its monopoly on force against citizens in response to the threat or use of force by criminals.

The criminal model is reactive and relies on deterrence of use of violence through punishment of offenders. State agents do not seek to use violence on criminals before they act; they do so only after a crime or once it is clear that a crime is about to be committed, using force to apprehend the suspected criminal for trial and punishment. Furthermore, their use of force is limited to that necessary to apprehend the suspect. Punishment exists to deter those considering criminal acts. The deterrent of punishment applies only to the criminal in question, not to others the criminal values but who are not involved in the crime in question.

Criminals operate surreptitiously before and after their crimes to avoid arrest. They also typically limit their use of violence to their targets, as opposed to attacking indiscriminately. The essential strategic problem from the view of the state is the detection and arrest of criminals, given the efforts of criminals to hide among the general population. Because state agents cannot be everywhere, they rely on the assistance of the general population in the identification of criminals and their activities.

The essential strategic problem from the view of the citizens is the constraint of state power. Given the state's monopoly on the legitimate use of force and the surreptitious nature of criminal activity, state agents – police and prosecutors – are constrained to prevent abuse of their position. Law is the primary constraint; the set of crimes is defined and limited. Each citizen is assumed to be safe from the use of violence until state agents identify them as a suspected criminal, at which time force can be used to arrest a suspect but not to punish him or her. Before force can be used to punish a criminal, state agents are obligated to prove in a court of law that the suspect did commit the crimes with which he or she is charged. Effective legal systems require the delicate act of the creation and sustenance of an independent judiciary within the context of politics. Trials provide public evidence that state agents had cause in their use of force against the accused, and that the accused should now be punished. Training of police in the appropriate use of force is also an important constraint on the use of force by the state to avoid the ever present problem of abuse of position by police.

The criminal model never works this cleanly. The police make mistakes; they fail to arrest some criminals and, at other times, arrest and convict innocents. No system is free of individual abuses by both police and prosecutors. In a broader sense, the political leadership can subvert the rule of law, so that the use of force by the state against citizens, particularly the opponents of the leadership, is unconstrained. In the abstract, nevertheless, the criminal model produces the incentives for state agents, citizens, and criminals laid out previously. When it works properly, it can reduce crime through deterrence.

### The Combat Model

The logic of the control of international violence is quite different. Little effective constraint is placed on the use of force by state leaders; the focus is instead on the control of violence on the battlefield. State agents, here the military, have the right to use violence freely in combat against soldiers of the opposing side, even when some forms of violence are not permitted. Soldiers are absolved of the moral responsibility for their use of deadly violence because the state sanctions that use.

The limits on violence in war focus on protecting classes of people and property deemed to be out of combat; civilians, medical personnel, the wounded, prisoners of war, and cultural property. In turn, all of these protected classes are supposed to remain out of combat. All of these can lose their protected status if they fail to observe the limits of their status as protected persons and property. Perfidy, the abuse of protected status to gain an advantage in combat, poses an important problem for the law of war because it strikes at the observable and necessary distinction between combatants and protected persons and property.

Soldiers identify themselves on the battlefield by uniforms and by carrying their arms openly. This self-identification of combatants has two important effects. First, it allows soldiers to identify enemy combatants by sight rather than by action, allowing them to attack the other side after identification. Unlike the criminal model, the use of violence is preemptive, not reactive; force is used to destroy threats on the battlefield, not to deter them. The presumption is that any enemy soldier constitutes a threat, and therefore is a legitimate target, unless he identifies himself as surrendering.

Second, clear identification of combatants makes it clear which state is responsible for acts of violence. The open use of violence makes it possible to enforce protection of persons and property that lie outside the bounds of combat. Although the specific perpetrator of an atrocity may not be clear, the side he fights for is clear when the rules for identification of combatants are followed. The question here is of state responsibility for the use of violence, rather than individual responsibility.

The practical limit on the use of violence is the power of each side to protect its targets of value from the battlefield. A state whose forces fight far from home or that are victorious in battle can shield its civilians from both the depredations of the other side and collateral damage from the battlefield. Unlike domestic law in which the power of government is overwhelming, the power of states at war is limited by each other's military forces. This practical limit also matters because military force unconstrained by an opponent or the law of war is capable of vastly greater destruction than that caused by even the most powerful criminal gang.[4] In the combat model, security takes precedence over discrimination.

In practice, the laws of war rarely work this elegantly. Individual soldiers in even the best-disciplined armies commit violations on their own against state policy. These individual violations can make it difficult for a side to determine whether or not the violations of its opponent's forces are state policy. Identifying what side has engaged in a particular act of violence may be difficult because of the lack of witnesses to the act who are willing to attest to what happened. Irregulars blur the distinction between combatants and civilians, and states often turn to a deliberate strategy of atrocity against civilians they believe support a guerrilla movement. Military action rarely has the scalpel-like precision one might like it to have. Bombs and other projectiles do not always hit the target. Even when the bombs can be placed exactly on the target, sometimes the choice of target is in error.

---

[4] Schelling (1966, 1–18) argues that victory on the battlefield matters because it allows the victor to engage in unlimited coercive violence against the opponent.

Enforcement of the laws of war depend on a combination of reciprocity, training of soldiers in their rights and responsibilities, punishment of individuals who commit violations on their own by their own military, and self-restraint. Just as a system of criminal justice addresses how the agents of the state act in pursuit of suspects, so does a system of lawful use of force constrain the conduct of individual soldiers. Historically, the punishment of violations by individual soldiers has been the responsibility of their own military. It has access to the suspects and possible witnesses of their acts. To the extent that it wishes to prevent retaliatory spirals on the battlefield and preserve discipline among its own soldiers, it has a motivation to prosecute them for their violations. The laws of war, like criminal justice, is as much about the control of the actions of individual soldiers as their governments. When they work properly, they ameliorate, even though they cannot eliminate, the wanton destruction of war.

### Terrorism: The Gray Space between Criminality and Combat

Terrorism attacks in the gray area between these two models of law. Terrorists operate as criminals, yet seek to do damage comparable to that of armies. They engage in indiscriminate violence (both in magnitude and in selection of target), recognizing neither the laws of war nor the selective targeting of violence used by criminals. They use the cover of civilian garb to avoid detection and apprehension and the sanctuary of far-off nations where the power of the target government to apprehend them is weak. They employ the weapons of war to engage in violence beyond that of the ordinary criminal.

Both the criminal model and the war model have the strengths and weaknesses in addressing terrorist acts and campaigns. These advantages and disadvantages help us see what features and principles an alternate system should possess.

Terrorist acts are crimes first and foremost. Addressing them with the criminal model focuses on police work to apprehend the full range of perpetrators including those who support the attackers themselves and normal security measures to stop attacks before they happen. The first and most significant advantage of the criminal model is that it clearly distinguishes terrorist acts as illegitimate uses of force, separating their indiscriminate nature from the restrained use of force by government agents in the criminal model. Open trials establish that the perpetrators carried out the attacks, which is useful in countering rumors that suggest otherwise. Criminal punishments also open the possibility of lengthy imprisonment for those convicted.

Restraint by government can aid in separating those who carry out attacks from the broader population sympathetic with their cause which forms the pool for recruits and financial support. This makes the recruitment of informants easier as well as helping to reduce the support terrorist organizations receive. Legal restraint on the acts of government agents can also help retain support from the target population and foreign governments. Both of these sources of support can make anti-terrorist policy easier to sustain over time. A sustained effort is needed to counter terrorist campaigns that may go on for decades at the extreme.

The main weakness of the criminal model is that it reacts after crimes are committed, using only deterrence and passive measures to prevent crimes from occurring. In the face of typical criminal behavior, this caution reflects the judgment that the evil of suffering some crime is preferable to the evils produced by an overly aggressive police force. Faced with attacks that seek to kills tens, hundreds, or even thousands at once, this calculation may change. Sustained terrorist campaigns create political pressure on target governments through repeated attacks whose toll may mount over time. Political leverage on a government comes from the attacks that will come in the future, not those that have already occurred.

Deterrence of terrorism suffers from the twin problems of apprehending those who carry out attacks and then punishing them after a trial.[5] In the extreme case of suicide bombing, there is no perpetrator to punish or use as a lever to unravel the secret support organization for that attack. Because support organizations often lie outside the target country, the cooperation of other states is necessary to apprehend the members of those networks. The links between the attackers and the support network may be difficult to prove in a court of law even after an arrest. The common mechanism of unraveling criminal conspiracies by convicting lower-level operatives and using them as sources to identify, arrest, and convict the high-level operatives may also be difficult to carry out because many of the low-level operatives are not criminals until they conduct an attack. In some cases, it is not clear what crime suspects could be charged with, particularly those detained outside the United States.

The criminal model limits the power of government agents to check the overwhelming power of the government inside its borders. Transnationally, however, the power of a government is limited by the ability of its agents to operate in other countries. Their freedom of action is generally limited by the cooperation of the governments of the states in which they would like to operate. In areas in which no effective government exists, those agents may be able to move and act freely, with the risks of a lawless region limiting their pursuit of terrorists in those regions.

The criminal model also uses passive measures to prevent attacks by making them difficult to carry out. We are all too familiar with airport screening. Passive measures face the problem that terrorists can design their attacks around such measures; the use of box cutters in the hijackings of the 9/11 attacks are a salient example. Furthermore, terrorists can change what targets they attack, moving from well-protected targets to more vulnerable ones

---

[5] But see Trager and Zagorcheva 2005; they focus on the political deterrence of terrorist movements rather than the deterrence of individual terrorists.

(Enders and Sandler 1993). The biggest advantage of passive measures may be the ability to use them to channel attacks toward less valuable targets and into situations in which police and security forces have a higher chance of stopping an attack and apprehending the attackers.

The strengths and weaknesses of the combat model are often the reverse of those of the criminal model. Attacking terrorist organizations as if they are armed forces opens up a wider variety of tactics for security forces and raises the possibility of preventing attacks by destroying the organization needed to support attacks. Once we can identify targets, they can be attacked by the full force of the military. This forces the terrorists to respond to us, rather than allowing them the leisure to plan future attacks.

The combat model also avoids the difficulties involved in prosecuting the full range of those involved in terrorist activities. Assuming that they are identified, security forces do not face the same issue of establishing a legal case to detain or attack terrorists.

The weaknesses of the combat model stem from its assumption that the other side is a well-organized military that has some prospect of following the laws of war. Terrorist movements are typically loose networks in which operatives come together only for particular operations. They often generate a bewildering range of small groups that do as they please even when the movement also has an open political wing (like Fatah has been for the Palestinians). These smaller groups do not answer to a central command either in their choice of tactics or in their overall strategic direction. The lack of clear authority and strong control over the smaller groups that carry out violence is a general principle that the political movements underlying terrorist violence use in part for political leverage.[6] Even if the broader political movement wishes to restrict itself to legal uses of violence (such as only attacking military targets), it is unlikely that the splinter groups that carry out violent attacks will heed their directives.

The combat model assumes that the enemy will operate openly to create the possibility that our forces can readily identify who is and who is not an enemy to allow for the protection of the latter. This distinction is difficult to make when faced with an enemy whose strategy is based on perfidy and atrocity. Because terrorists do not identify themselves publicly and are willing to use protected persons as cover and protected sites as bases, the risk of collateral damage and mistaken attacks on protected persons and sites is substantial. Such attacks can increase support for terrorist groups from the sympathetic population from which they recruit and raise resources. In the extreme, such mistaken attacks create a moral equivalence between the two sides – that is,

---

[6] See E. Bueno de Mesquita 2005 for an analysis of the political consequences of the lack of control that moderates in such movements have over violent extremists. Although Al-Qaeda does not appear to have an affiliated political movement, this absence appears to be the exception rather than rule for such movements.

all attacks on civilians are wrong, no matter which side carries them out. This blurs the distinction in intention between inadvertent government attacks on civilians with deliberate and calculated attacks carried out by terrorists. This blurring can also undermine support for the government carrying out the military in its own population and supportive foreign governments. Loss of support from both of these groups can undermine a government's ability to sustain and prevail in its military effort.

The combat model also implies that the enemy's use of force is legitimate in the sense that the laws of war generally address conduct during wartime rather than the legitimacy of the use of force. Terrorist violence by definition violates the laws of war, but if government responses also harm protected persons and places, it may be easier for terrorist groups to claim an equivalence in actions. This equivalence is likely to appeal most strongly to populations sympathetic to the aims of terrorist groups, when the latter can claim that some of their attacks fall within legal resistance to unjust governments. But this equivalence undermines the distinction of intent that it is critical for the law of war. Law of war recognizes that even parties that strive to follow the law will damage some protected people and sites in the course of conduct. Intent separates collateral damage and proportionate attacks on protected people and sites from deliberate efforts to target the latter, the sort of attacks that undermine any system that seeks to limit violence during war.

The combat model assumes that enemy forces can be brought to battle and defeated through combat, making warfare limited in time if unpredictable in length. That is, the rules define how combat is to be conducted with the idea that combat is a contest in which the defeated will give up once beaten. Because terrorists operate surreptitiously, it is difficult to bring them to combat except at a time of their choosing. Irregular movements have prevailed in some conflicts because they can prolong the state of war, rendering their opponents incapable of bringing the war to a decisive end. Terrorist groups rarely seek combat under any circumstances, although affiliated irregular combatants may do so. This refusal of combat denies the objective of the combat model, a clear victory on a limited battlefield. Even if the central leadership of a terrorist movement could be convinced to cease the use of violence, they rarely have the ability to enforce that will on the small groups that carry out the violence.

As the reader may have noticed, I have detailed the weaknesses of each model at greater length than their strengths. Neither model fits the conditions produced by terrorism. A third model for the control of violence in response to terrorism falls somewhere between the criminal model and the combat model. What principles should guide the design of such a system?

The first principle is that this third model should be arrived at through an open political process ending in domestic legislation and an international treaty. The argument made against such a process and in favor of establishing such rules through secret executive action is that an open process reveals what actions government agents are allowed to take under what circumstances. The targets of terrorist investigations could then avoid the use of communications that may be monitored and design around security measures generally. The advantages of openness outweigh this weakness. First, an open process increases the chance that the measures and laws in question will be sustained longer because there must be a broad domestic agreement in favor of those measures. Otherwise, they would not pass. Terrorist attacks motivated by Islamic extremism are likely to continue for a long period of time around the world; the legal response has to persist over decades to succeed. Only those measures that are supported by a broad consensus across U.S. political opinion have that chance. These measures will have to stand across a series of presidents and alternation of power between the Republicans and Democrats, and therefore must have broad bipartisan support.

Second, the process used to reach such a third model must also be open internationally because the cooperation of other states is an essential part of the U.S. strategy to counter transnational terrorism. International law shapes how states interact by creating shared expectations about appropriate behavior and responses to inappropriate behavior. Failure to make explicit the legal standing and justification of the international response can lead to a failure to coordinate state actions, undermining a common international effort against transnational terrorism. Limits imposed by the need for international agreement could prevent the U.S. government from acting as it wished, but that cost has to be assessed against the benefit of having an international policy that could be sustained over time.

Legal standards and policies arrived at openly and explicitly at the domestic and international levels also face the issue that increasing the precision of international law and agreements could limit the flexibility necessary for political accommodation of policy. This cost should not be underestimated. At the same time, that loss of flexibility of policy has to be measured against greater ability to sustain a system reached through an open process. In my mind, the latter outweighs the former simply because the threat of terrorist attacks is unlikely to disappear in the near future. The ability to sustain policy over the long run trumps the need for short-run flexibility.

There are arguments in favor of either the combat model or the criminal model over any third model. They begin with the settled nature of both of these models; we have a good idea of the principles behind each of them, the institutions used in both, and their consequences. None of those are clear for a third model. How might we choose among the three models? The restraint of government power by law, whether international or domestic, strengthens government by establishing the legitimacy of its use of force and violence. The legitimate use of force by a government will receive greater domestic support over time, will secure continued support from our democratic allies, and may convince those sympathetic to our enemies that there is a difference between how the two sides use violence. If this struggle against transnational terrorist violence will go on for decades, and I believe it will, legitimacy is necessary to sustain our effort and so must be part of our long-term strategy. Democracies are good at sustaining political effort over time, provided that effort is based on a view of what must be done that stretches across the political spectrum.[7] Law is one source of such a consensus. If I have argued that a third model may be appropriate to replace the criminal and combat models as ways to address terrorism, it is because a legal response must be part of our overall strategy. The design of that legal response needs to consider the incentives of the resulting system for government agents and terrorists and the willingness of the public to support that system over time.

The rise of transnational terrorism reflects a misstep in the growth of the laws of war, the legitimation of irregular violence. At the outbreak of World War I, states disagreed about what steps militaries could take against civilians who took up arms in resistance to them. The Hague Conventions recognized irregular combatants as legitimate if they organized into units and took up their arms openly before the enemy established authority over their territory. This left open questions about when effective authority had been established and what occupying powers could do in response to irregular resistance after authority was established. This lack of clarity led to the disagreements about whether German reprisals against Belgian and French citizens in 1914 were legal. The German model of occupation, where the occupying power has the right to take any and all measures to ensure order, was superseded by the system eventually recognized in the 1949 Geneva Convention (IV) on civilians, by which the powers of an occupying power were restricted. This model, adopted in response to the horrors of occupation, partisan warfare, and reprisals against populations in which partisans were active and then extended to non-international armed conflicts in the 1977 Geneva Protocol (II), effectively legitimated irregular warfare during occupation. By placing irregulars not identified with a recognized sovereign state on the same plane as soldiers who answered to a state, irregular warfare received the same protections as soldiers. This legitimacy allowed non-state armed groups to claim the right to use force parallel to that reserved to states, particularly among populations that sympathize with their political causes. Because irregular warfare often leads to violence against civilians by both sides, terrorist groups could claim that their violence against civilians was justified by violence against civilians by the states they targeted. Once irregular warfare became common during the World Wars, it is hard to see how the legitimation of irregular warfare could have been stopped in favor of the German model of occupation. But claims by terrorist groups to be justified in their attacks on civilians arise from this same logic, even if the main body of thought on the law of war rejects such claims.

---

[7] Schultz and Weingast 2003 show that, over decades, democracies can sustain financial effort better than other types of systems.

## THE PERILS OF UNIVERSALISM AND UNILATERALISM

The law of war aspires to universal acceptance and observance. Ratification of the Geneva Conventions is universal. More recent treaties are not universally accepted. The Rome Statute creating the International Criminal Court has not been ratified by seventy-three members of the UN, including the United States, China, and Russia, all permanent members of the Security Council.[8] Universal acceptance is partial and incomplete as of this time.

Universalism – the idea that all states must adhere to international law – would seem to be a great achievement, the universal acceptance that the violence of war must be limited. It would mark the advance of humanitarianism as an essential principle of world politics. But we do not know that all states have embraced and internalized these values, we only know that they have ratified treaties that codify these values. Ratification, however, has not been a signal of intent to comply; failure to ratify is the signal of intent to violate. Universal ratification may create the illusion of universal acceptance while masking those states that would violate them if they find themselves at war. Such violations may not be the open abandonment of restraint but acts justified by tenuous legal justifications. Formal, legalistic evasion could be more damaging to standards of restraint than open rejection by failing to ratify. The creation of a shared understanding of how states should act and their intent to do so to the best of their abilities creates a restrained battlefield, which universal ratification may mask rather than create.

Arguments that the laws of war are customary law and so bind even the states that have not ratified is one form of universalism (cf. Henckaerts, Doswald-Beck, and Cross 2005). In this view, these treaties are accepted widely enough and have been observed sufficiently often that they have entered into the customary practices of world politics. They bind as law even though some states have not formally accepted them. But this view claims that regular application of the law suffices to establish expectations of compliance under all circumstances in the future. The assertion of universalism will only be tested and will perhaps fail when war occurs. Would such violations undermine the customary status of this law, and perhaps lead to less confidence in the law and lower expectations of compliance by all parties?

The push for universalism also undercuts the possibility of using in-group versus out-group logic to enforce compliance. The Chemical Weapons Convention outlaws exports of chemical agents and precursor chemicals from member states to states that have not ratified the treaty.[9] This measure both enforces the Convention by making it difficult for non-member states to produce chemical

---

[8] Ratifications as of June 25, 2013, data found at icrc.org/ihl.

[9] These are the Schedule I and II chemicals; Schedule III chemicals can be exported to states that are not members of the Convention if the recipient certifies how they will be used. Cf. http://www.opcw.org/our-work/non-proliferation/international-transfer-of-scheduled-chemicals/, accessed October 8, 2012.

weapons and provides a positive incentive – access to the international market in restricted chemicals for non-weapons purposes – for states to join the regime. Universalism undercuts this logic if it leads states to ratify even if they will not comply. In-group versus out-group logic requires a clear and public separation between the two groups.

Only the core treaties of the laws of war have achieved universal acceptance. Another peril of universalism lurks in the treaties that are not universally ratified. Universalism seeks to establish the law as legitimate and so require compliance by all states. But the lack of universal ratification for several of the most prominent treaties shows that major powers do not accept that law as legitimate. As mentioned earlier, the United States, China, and Russia have not ratified the Rome Statute and therefore are not members of the International Criminal Court. Is the Court legitimate and so obligatory, as its proponents and advocates argue, or is it a sham of justice and unrestrained legalism, as its opponents contend? Because the law has pushed into areas beyond the consensus of the major powers, its legitimacy is contested. If the Court solely sought to aid state parties in their efforts to police their own agents, the lack of universal acceptance would not be problematic. But the Court aspires to universal jurisdiction, a jurisdiction that will necessarily be ineffective when key states refuse to accept the Court.

Unilateralism – the idea that states are bound by the laws of war even if their opponents are not – complements universalism. The 1949 Geneva Conventions are unilaterally binding on member states, which reflects the belief of some states that restraint during war conveys advantages rather than shackling their forces efforts to win. Earlier, we saw some of the ways restraint could pay – a more effective fighting force through greater discipline, more enemy soldiers surrendering instead of fighting to the death, and greater public support of the war effort. But the cases in which unilateral restraint was strongest – one side ratified when their opponents had not – produced the least reciprocity and worst compliance on average. A restrained battlefield is a product of what both sides do; unilateral restraint may not produce it, even when the restrained party prefers restraint to retaliation.

Universalism depends on the view that universal acceptance of law will lead to compliance. This view is at odds with the argument and results presented in this book. If international law exists to aid states in their efforts to realize cooperative relations (a limited battlefield within the world of war), then it must address the issues that make cooperation difficult. Universalism assumes that public acceptance of law means that all fully accept the law and wish to live within it. But a difference in the desire to limit violence has been a fundamental issue facing the implementation of the law of war; some states that have ratified the treaties have failed to comply during war. Unilateral restraint has not led to a less violent battlefield as it eliminates the ability to respond in kind. Violations by state agents against state policy undermine the legitimacy presumably produced by universalism. Because the law will never eliminate all of these violations nor punish all violators, why should others obey restraints that may put their lives at risk? The law of war has been most successful when it aids states in determining when and how one another is limiting violence during war in their efforts to control violence.

## THE LIMITS OF INTERNATIONAL LAW

International law is an important but fragile tool in world politics. It can help states and their agents form expectations about one another's behavior that make conflict less likely and cooperation more likely. Treaties set standards that allow all to understand what behavior is unacceptable and what consequences will follow from such acts. Ratification of those treaties signals that a state intends to follow the standard, particularly for democracies. When both sides in a war have ratified a treaty, both expect reciprocal enforcement and are therefore more likely to comply with that treaty. Ratification also cues in-group-out-group logic in which those actors who do not accept a treaty may suffer from exclusion from other benefits. It creates actors, like the ICRC, with new interests in upholding the law, changing the strategic dynamics. Law can create dispute resolution procedures that change how states negotiate their disputes, like how the dispute resolution procedure of the World Trade Organization (WTO) changes how states negotiate their trade disputes.

There are also important limits on the order created by the shadow of international law. States, particularly powerful ones, can defy international law if they are willing to accept the consequences of doing so. There is no external form of enforcement, only the responses of other actors. There is no form of international legislation that can bind states to laws against their will. International law is created through consensus rather than the implied consent underlying domestic law. There is no judicial apparatus whose judgments can authoritatively resolve disputes about what the law means, allowing disagreements about what the law is and how it should be applied to fester. All of these differences between international and domestic law make the former weaker and more fragile than the latter, and all are well-understood in international relations.

The nature of law as making decisions based on rules poses another reason for the limits of international law. Frederick Schauer describes law as applying entrenched general rules to specific situations, opposing rule-based decisions with those made on the grounds particular to the decision at hand.[10] Rules of law provide a reason for their being followed even when the application of the rule might be contrary to the spirit of the justification underlying that rule (Schauer 1991, 52, 76). Law will make incorrect decisions, in the sense that those using the rules will make some decisions contrary to the reasons

---

[10] To be careful, Schauer (1991) sees law as just one form of rules-based decision making. For the argument I make, the consequences of using rules to make decisions is the key element of law.

underlying those rules out of their obligation to follow those rules. A judgment on an individual case based on discretion could lead to a decision that reflects the values that justify the rule rather than blindly applying the rules to the case. Regulating decisions by legal rules introduces a tradeoff compared to discretionary decision making; the latter will get more decisions right in terms of underlying values, but at what cost? Law will get more cases "wrong," but it compensates for this loss of efficiency by: (1) creating a regular environment that allows actors to predict one another's behavior and so adjust their actions, and (2) reducing the cost involved in making decisions. Applying a legal rule simplifies making decisions and renders those decisions more predictable at the cost of getting some wrong. The choice of whether issues should be addressed by rules must compare the costs and benefits of doing so with the alternative. As Schauer puts the matter:

> [W]here decisional resources are not scarce, or where there are few attractive alternatives for the use of those resources, then it is less likely that the benefits of efficiency will outweigh the costs necessarily involved in any decision-making procedure that disables itself from seeking the optimal resolution on every decisional occasion (Schauer 1991, 149).

Law generally, and international law specifically, is more likely to be superior to principled discretion when the expected number of cases is large and the consequences of an incorrect decision are small compared to the stakes in the area. In the area of trade, disputes between trading partners are common, and the consequences of resolving a dispute in favor of an industry engaged in practices that restrict free trade is small compared to the value of freer trade generally. A legalized procedure – such as the WTO dispute resolution procedure – makes sense; the benefits of regular and expeditious decisions outweighs the costs of some errors through the application of rules. In the laws of war, the enforcement of the obligations individuals have under the treaties also makes sense to be legalized because the number of cases is often large and the consequences of one individual's acts are small. It does not matter whether the resulting legal process is conducted by states for their own soldiers or by an international body like the International Criminal Court, although I believe that the former is a more effective form of enforcement. In the case of state decisions on whether and how to fight, however, principled discretion should be superior to a legal procedure. The issues are rare, states devote substantial resources to setting such policies, and the consequences of a decision that follows the rules but violates the principles underlying those rules are large. Consequently, international law must be interpreted flexibly for state decisions, and a legal process that applies fixed and entrenched rules to judge state conduct is inferior.

Both the critics and the defenders of international law often assume that international law can only be effective (which they view as either bad or good) if it creates absolute obligations. The critics view these legal obligations as limiting state action so as to prevent the effective functioning of the international system; the defenders see these obligations as imperatives whose moral status is undermined by any violations. Both these views are wrong because breach is essential to the proper role of international law. When a state breaches international law, it signals the importance of the issue to the actor, which in turn may lead other actors to change their stance toward it. Typically, breaking international law should and does provoke a hostile response to the state in breach. In-group-out-group logic leads states that adhere to the law to push that state into the out-group, costing it the benefits of membership. In other cases, however, breach signals the importance of the issue at hand, not an attempt to either subvert the system of law or depart from it. In trade, for instance, all states engage in some practices that are illegal barriers to trade under WTO law and do so because the domestic political benefits of those policies are large enough. The question is how such practices can be controlled to sustain a system of generally open and free trade. The WTO dispute procedure provides a way to discipline such politically opportunistic barriers to trade to keep the system open (Rosendorff 2005). Breach is essential to the proper functioning of the system. Similarly, the UN Security Council system of authorizing military intervention does not preclude states from intervening without an authorizing resolution, but those who do will lose the support of other states (Voeten 2001).

## POWER AND LEGITIMACY

Power and legitimacy have often been seen as competing sources for international order. Power rules in the law of the jungle, and law creates bounds that civilize the international jungle. Deterrence and treaties have been seen as opposite ways to control military rivalry from exploding into war. Law is the tool the weak use to constrain the strong from working their will against them. The moral force of legitimacy provides a way beyond the cruel rule of power politics.

This is a false dichotomy. Power and legitimacy are complements, not competing ways of creating order. Each reinforces the other. Power undergirds law and legitimate purpose, helping to make lawful order a reality. International politics has never been the jungle, although the conventions that rule it respect the role of power. Treaties and deterrence go hand in hand. A treaty clarifies how the parties will deter one another; deterrence enforces that legal agreement. Law helps the strong by restricting their use of force, thereby rallying the weak to support them when the strong use force for legitimate purpose.

Realists and constructivists alike often miss how power and legitimacy complement one another because they focus on one at the expense of the other. Realists emphasize power and so fail to realize that legitimacy is a "force multiplier." Power is most effective when it is exercised with clear, accepted moral purpose. Constructivists address the conventions of legitimacy and so miss the role of power in establishing and enforcing those principles. Power helps establish legitimate rules by enforcing them against violators.

The central theme of this book, the complementary nature of power and legitimacy, is not novel. It is the central theme of one of the classics of international relations, E.H. Carr's *The Twenty Years Crisis* (1946).[11] Carr saw any international order as the fusing of power and purpose, of principles that explain how the international order advances the interests of states and the individuals that compose them and so justified the use of power to protect that order. International law embodies the agreements on what the international system seeks to achieve and how states might realize those ends. This is a practical business of producing international cooperation rather than an idealistic enterprise of binding states by law. It must be practical because the degree of common purpose is less in international politics than within states and because of the difficulties in getting states and their agents to act to produce those common goals in the face of their individual incentives to diverge from them. That practical business must produce the mechanisms that allow the actors to signal their intent to comply, that create consensus on what is allowable and what is not, and that binds them together to enforce their legal obligations on one another when intent to follow the publicly accepted rules fails.

Because law has consequences for who gets what from world politics, the legitimacy of international law will always be in question. Principles of right and wrong advantage some over others. Those who believe they suffer from the international legal order work against it, sometimes with violence unconstrained by the standards of that law. World politics further suffers from the lack of an authoritative interpretation of what the law means, leaving the application of the law to individual states in the light of the shared understanding of what the law means. Treaty law addresses some of this concern by producing identifiable public standards accepted publicly by states. Shared understandings are tenuous and contested in world politics, but law clarifies them, their applicability, and their acceptance. International law provides states with the principles and procedures that aid them in their efforts to create order within anarchy.

---

[11] It is strange that many scholars of international relations read Carr as a realist (e.g., Doyle 1997, 31; Wendt 1999, 30; in contrast, Finnemore and Sikkink 1998 have Carr right). Admittedly, Carr's attack on the idealists is more spirited than his criticism of the realist position, but he summarizes his general view as follows: "If, however, it is utopian to ignore the element of power, it is an unreal kind of realism which ignores the element of morality in any world order" (Carr 1946, 235).

# References

Abreu, Dilip, David Pearce, and Ennio Stacchetti. 1990. Toward a Theory of Discounted Repeated Games with Imperfect Monitoring. *Econometrica* 58 (5): 1041–1063.

Ambrose, Stephen E. 1992. *Band of Brothers: E Company, 506th Regiment, 101st Airborne: from Normandy to Hitler's Eagle's Nest*. New York: Simon & Schuster.

Andrade, Jr., Ernest. 1971. Submarine Policy in the United States Navy, 1919–1941. *Military Affairs* 35 (2): 50–56.

Aumann, Robert and Adam Brandenburger. 1995. Epistemic Conditions for Nash Equilibrium. *Econometrica* 63 (5): 1161–1180.

Axelrod, Robert. 1986. An Evolutionary Approach to Norms. *American Political Science Review* 80 (4): 1095–1111.

Banks, Arthur and Alan Warwick Palmer. 1989. *A Military Atlas of the First World War*. Barnsley: Leo Cooper.

Barker, A. J. 1975. *Prisoners of War*. New York: Universe Books.

1980. *Arab-Israeli Wars*. London: I. Allan.

Barnett, Michael N. and Martha Finnemore. 1999. The Politics, Power, and Pathologies of International Organizations. *International Organization* 53 (4): 699–732.

Bartov, Omer. 1986. *The Eastern Front, 1941–45: German Troops and the Barbarisation of Warfare*. New York: St. Martin's Press.

1991. *Hitler's Army: Soldiers, Nazis, and War in the Third Reich*. New York: Oxford University Press.

Bass, Gary Jonathan. 2000. *Stay the Hand of Vengeance: The Politics of War Crimes Tribunals*. Princeton, NJ: Princeton University Press.

Beevor, Antony. 1998. *Stalingrad*. New York: Viking.

2002. *The Fall of Berlin, 1945*. New York: Viking.

Bellamy, Chris. 2007. *Absolute War: Soviet Russia in the Second World War*. London: Macmillan.

Benaim, Michel and Jorgen W. Weibull. 2003. Deterministic Approximation of Stochastic Evolution in Games. *Econometrica* 71 (3): 873–903.

Bennett, D. Scott and Allan C. Stam. 2000. EUGene: A Conceptual Manual. *International Interactions* 26: 179–204.

Benvenisti, Eyal. 1993. *The International Law of Occupation*. Princeton, NJ: Princeton University Press.

Bergerud, Eric M. 1996. *Touched with Fire: The Land Warfare in the South Pacific*. New York: Viking.

Best, Geoffrey. 1980. *Humanity in Warfare*. New York: Columbia University Press.

1994. *War and Law since 1945*. New York: Oxford University Press.

Biddle, Tami Davis. 1994. "Air Power." In *The Laws of War: Constraints on Warfare in the Western World*, eds. Michael Eliot Howard, George J. Andreopoulos, and Mark R. Shulman, 140–159. New Haven, CT: Yale University Press.

2002. *Rhetoric and Reality in Air Warfare: The Evolution of British and American Ideas about Strategic Bombing, 1914–1945*. Princeton, NJ: Princeton University Press.

Bird, Tom. 1992. *American POWs of World War II: Forgotten Men Tell Their Stories*. Westport, CT: Praeger.

Bischof, Günter and Stephen E. Ambrose. 1992. *Eisenhower and the German POWs: Facts against Falsehood*. Baton Rouge: Louisiana State University Press.

Blair, Clay. 1975. *Silent Victory: The U. S. Submarine War against Japan*. Philadelphia: Lippincott.

1996. *Hitler's U-boat War*. New York: Random House.

Boll, Bernd and Hans Safran. 2000. "On the Way to Stalingrad: The 6th Army in 1941–42." In *War of Extermination: The German Military in World War II, 1941–1944*, eds. Hannes Heer and Klaus Naumann, 237–271. New York: Berghahn Books.

Bourke, Joanna. 1999. *An Intimate History of Killing: Face-to-Face Killing in Twentieth-Century Warfare*. New York: Basic Books.

Box-Steffensmeier, Janet M., and Bradford S. Jones. 2004. *Event History Modeling: A Guide for Social Scientists*. New York: Cambridge University Press.

Boyd, Carl and Akihiko Yoshida. 1995. *The Japanese Submarine Force and World War II*. Annapolis, MD: Naval Institute Press.

Brackman, Arnold C. 1987. *The Other Nuremberg: The Untold Story of the Tokyo War Crimes Trials*. 1st ed. New York: Morrow.

Brandenburger, Adam. 1992. Knowledge and Equilibrium in Games. *The Journal of Economic Perspectives* 6 (4): 83–101.

Brickhill, Paul. 1950. *The Great Escape*. New York: Norton.

Brode, Patrick. 1997. *Casual Slaughters and Accidental Judgments: Canadian War Crimes Prosecutions, 1944–1948*. Toronto: University of Toronto Press.

Brown, Frederic Joseph. 1968. *Chemical Warfare: A Study in Restraints*. Princeton, NJ: Princeton University Press.

Budiansky, Stephen. 2004. *Air Power: The Men, Machines, and Ideas That Revolutionized War, from Kitty Hawk to Gulf War II*. New York: Viking.

Bueno de Mesquita, Bruce. 1981. *The War Trap*. New Haven, CT: Yale University Press.

Bueno de Mesquita, Bruce, James D. Morrow, Randolph M. Siverson, and Alastair Smith. 1999. An Institutional Explanation of the Democratic Peace. *American Political Science Review* 93 (4): 791–807.

Bueno de Mesquita, Bruce, Alastair Smith, Randolph M. Siverson, and James D. Morrow. 2003. *The Logic of Political Survival*. Cambridge, MA: MIT Press.

Bueno de Mesquita, Ethan. 2005. Conciliation, Counterterrorism, and Patterns of Terrorist Violence. *International Organization* 59 (1): 145–176.

Bukovansky, Mlada. 1997. American Identity and Neutral Rights from Independence to the War of 1812. *International Organization* 51 (2): 209–243.

Bull, Hedley. 1977. *The Anarchical Society: A Study of Order in World Politics*. New York: Columbia University Press.

Burns, Richard Dean. 1971. Regulating Submarine Warfare, 1921–41: A Case Study in Arms Control and Limited War. *Military Affairs* 35 (2): 56–63.

Calvert, Randall L. 1994. "Rational Actors, Equilibrium, and Social Institutions." In *Explaining Social Institutions*, eds. Jack Knight and Itai Sened, 57–93. Ann Arbor: University of Michigan Press.

1995. "The Rational Choice Theory of Social Institutions: Cooperation, Coordination, and Communication." In *Modern Political Economy: Old Topics, New Directions*, eds. Jeffrey S. Banks and Eric A. Hanushek, 216–267. New York: Cambridge University Press.

Calvocoressi, Peter, Guy Wint, and John Pritchard. 1989. *Total War: Causes and Courses of the Second World War*. London: Viking.

Camerer, Colin F. 1997. Progress in Behavioral Game Theory. *The Journal of Economic Perspectives* 11 (4): 167–188.

Carnahan, Burrus M. 1998. Lincoln, Lieber and the Laws of War: The Origins and Limits of the Principle of Military Necessity. *American Journal of International Law* 92 (2): 213–231.

Carr, Edward Hallett. 1946. *The Twenty Years' Crisis, 1919–1939*. London: Macmillan.

Chang, Iris. 1997. *The Rape of Nanking: The Forgotten Holocaust of World War II*. 1st ed. New York: Basic Books.

Chayes, Abram and Antonia Handler Chayes. 1993. On Compliance. *International Organization* 47 (2): 175–205.

Checkel, Jeffrey T. 2005. International Institutions and Socialization in Europe: Introduction and Framework. *International Organization* 59 (4): 801–826.

Chwe, Michael Suk-Young. 2001. *Rational Ritual: Culture, Coordination, and Common Knowledge*. Princeton, NJ: Princeton University Press.

Clark, Alan. 1965. *Barbarossa: The Russian-German Conflict, 1941–45*. New York: W. Morrow.

Clodfelter, Micheal. 2002. *Warfare and Armed Conflicts: A Statistical Reference to Casualty and Other Figures, 1500–2000*. Jefferson, NC: McFarland.

Colby, Elbridge. 1925. Aerial Law and War Targets. *American Journal of International Law* 19 (4): 702–715.

Coll, Alberto R. and Anthony C. Arend, eds. 1985. *The Falklands War: Lessons for Strategy, Diplomacy, and International Law*. Boston: G. Allen & Unwin.

Cook, Tim. 2006. The Politics of Surrender: Canadian Soldiers and the Killing of Prisoners in the Great War. *Journal of Military History* 70 (3): 637–665.

Cooper, Malcolm. 1986. *The Birth of Independent Air Power: British Air Policy in the First World War*. London: Allen & Unwin.

Corbett, Julian Stafford Sir. 1921. *Naval Operations, Vol. II*. London: Longmans, Green, and Co.

1923. *Naval Operations, Vol. III*. London: Longman, Green, and Co.

Corum, James S. 1997. *The Luftwaffe: Creating the Operational Air War, 1918–1940.* Lawrence: University Press of Kansas.

Council on Foreign Relations. 2010. "Pursuing International Justice: A Conversation with Luis Moreno-Ocampo." http://www.cfr.org/human-rights/pursuing-international-justice-conversation-luis-moreno-ocampo/p21418?cid=ACCinvite-MorenoOcampo_transcript-100711

Crawford, Neta. 2002. *Argument and Change in World Politics: Ethics, Decolonization, and Humanitarian Intervention.* New York: Cambridge University Press.

Crawford, Vincent P. and Hans Haller. 1990. Learning How to Cooperate: Optimal Play in Repeated Coordination Games. *Econometrica* 58 (3): 571–595.

Daws, Gavan. 1994. *Prisoners of the Japanese: POWs of World War II in the Pacific.* New York: W. Morrow.

Detter Delupis, Ingrid. 2000. *The Law of War.* 2nd ed. New York: Cambridge University Press.

De Zayas, Alfred M. 1989. *The Wehrmacht War Crimes Bureau, 1939–1945.* Lincoln, NE: University of Nebraska Press.

Douhet, Giulio. 1942. *The Command of the Air.* New York: Coward-McCann, Inc.

Dower, John W. 1986. *War without Mercy: Race and Power in the Pacific War.* New York: Pantheon Books.

Downes, Alexander B. 2008. *Targeting Civilians in War.* Ithaca, NY: Cornell University Press.

Downs, George W., David M. Rocke, and Peter N. Barsoom. 1996. Is the Good News about Compliance Good News about Cooperation? *International Organization* 50 (3): 379–406.

Doyle, Michael W. 1997. *Ways of War and Peace: Realism, Liberalism, and Socialism.* New York: W. W. Norton.

Doyle, Robert C. 2010. *The Enemy in Our Hands: America's Treatment of Enemy Prisoners of War from the Revolution to the War on Terror.* Lexington: University Press of Kentucky.

Drea, Edward J. 2009. *Japan's Imperial Army: Its Rise and Fall, 1853–1945.* Lawrence: University Press of Kansas.

Durand, Andre and Pierre Boissier. 1984. *From Sarajevo to Hiroshima: History of the International Committee of the Red Cross.* Geneva: Henry Dunant Institute.

Eekelen, W. F. van. 1964. *Indian Foreign Policy and the Border Dispute with China.* 's-Gravenhage: M. Nijhoff.

Elaydi, Saber. 2005. *An Introduction to Difference Equations.* New York: Springer.

Ellis, John. 1980. *The Sharp End of War: The Fighting Man in World War II.* Newton Abbot: David & Charles.

Ellison, Glenn. 1993. Learning, Local Interaction, and Coordination. *Econometrica* 61 (5): 1047–1071.

   2000. Basins of Attraction, Long-Run Stochastic Stability, and the Speed of Step- by-Step Evolution. *Review of Economic Studies* 67 (1): 17–45.

Enders, Walter and Todd Sandler. 1993. The Effectiveness of Antiterrorism Policies: A Vector-Autoregression- Intervention Analysis. *American Political Science Review* 87 (4): 829–844.

Farber, Henry S. and Joanne Gowa. 1995. Polities and Peace. *International Security* 20 (2): 123–146.

Farrell, Joseph. 1987. Cheap Talk, Coordination, and Entry. *RAND Journal of Economics* 18 (1): 34–39.

Farrell, Joseph and Robert Gibbons. 1989. Cheap Talk Can Matter in Bargaining. *Journal of Economic Theory* 48: 221–237.

Fearon, James D. 1994. Domestic Political Audiences and the Escalation of International Disputes. *American Political Science Review* 88 (3): 577–592.

Fedorowich, Kent. 2000. "Understanding the Enemy: Military Intelligence, Political Warfare and Japanese Prisoners of War in Australia, 1942–45." In *Japanese Prisoners of War*, eds. Philip Towle, Margaret Kosuge, and Yoichi Kibata, 59–86. London: Hambleton and London.

Ferejohn, John. 1993. "Structure and Ideology: Change in Parliament in Early Stuart England." In *Ideas and Foreign Policy: Beliefs, Institutions, and Political Change*, eds. Judith Goldstein and Robert O. Keohane, 207–235. Ithaca, NY: Cornell University Press.

Ferguson, Niall. 1999. *The Pity of War*. New York: Basic Books.

2004. Prisoner Taking and Prisoner Killing in the Age of Total War: Towards a Political Economy of Military Defeat. *War in History* 11 (2): 148–192.

Finnemore, Martha. 1996. *National Interests in International Society*. Ithaca, NY: Cornell University Press.

2003. *The Purpose of Intervention: Changing Beliefs about the Use of Force*. Ithaca, NY: Cornell University Press.

Finnemore, Martha and Kathryn Sikkink. 1998. International Norm Dynamics and Political Change. *International Organization* 52 (4): 887–917.

Fishman, Sarah. 1991. Grand Delusions: The Unintended Consequences of Vichy France's Prisoner of War Propaganda. *Journal of Contemporary History* 26 (2): 229–254.

Flower, Sibylla Jane. 1996. "Captors and Captives on the Burma-Thailand Railway." In *Prisoners of War and their Captor in World War II*, eds. Bob Moore and Kent Fedorowich, 227–252. Washington, DC: Berg.

Foy, David A. 1984. *For You the War is Over: American Prisoners of War in Nazi Germany*. New York: Stein and Day.

Francis, Timothy Lang. 1997. "To Dispose of the Prisoners": The Japanese Executions of American Aircrew at Fukuoka, Japan, during 1945. *Pacific Historical Review* 66 (4): 469–501.

Franck, Thomas M. 1990. *The Power of Legitimacy among Nations*. New York: Oxford University Press.

Freedman, Lawrence and Virginia Gamba-Stonehouse. 1990. *Signals of War: The Falklands Conflict of 1982*. London: Faber and Faber.

Fritz, Stephen G. 1995. *Frontsoldaten: The German Soldier in World War II*. Lexington: University Press of Kentucky.

Fryer, Charles. 1997. *The Destruction of Serbia in 1915*. New York: Columbia University Press.

Fudenberg, Drew and David K. Levine. 1993a. Self-Confirming Equilibrium. *Econometrica* 61 (3): 523–545.

1993b. Steady State Learning and Nash Equilibrium. *Econometrica* 61 (3): 547–573.

1998. *The Theory of Learning in Games*. Cambridge, MA: MIT Press.

Fudenberg, Drew, David Levine, and Eric Maskin. 1994. The Folk Theorem with Imperfect Public Information. *Econometrica* 62 (5): 997–1039.

Fudenberg, Drew and Eric Maskin. 1986. The Folk Theorem in Repeated Games with Discounting or with Incomplete Information. *Econometrica* 54 (3): 533–554.

Fujita, Hisakazu. 2000. "POWs and International Law." In *Japanese Prisoners of War*, eds. Philip Towle, Margaret Kosuge, and Yoichi Kibata, 87–102. London: Hambleton and London.

Garner, James Wilford. 1920. *International Law and the World War*. New York: Longmans Green.

Garrett, Richard. 1981. *P. O. W.* Newton Abbot: David & Charles.

Gatrell, Peter. 2005. Prisoners of War on the Eastern Front during World War I. *Kritika: Explorations in Russian and Eurasian History* 6 (3): 557–566.

Gilbert, Martin. 1994. *The First World War: A Complete History*. New York: H. Holt.

Glantz, David M. and Jonathan M. House. 1995. *When Titans Clashed: How the Red Army Stopped Hitler*. Lawrence: University Press of Kansas.

Glaser, Charles L. 2010. *Rational Theory of International Politics: The Logic of Competition and Cooperation*. Princeton, NJ: Princeton University Press.

Goldsmith, Jack and Daryl Levinson. 2009. Law for States: International Law, Constitutional Law, Public Law. *Harvard Law Review* 122 (7): 1791–1868.

Goldsmith, Jack L. and Eric A. Posner. 2005. *The Limits of International Law*. New York: Oxford University Press.

Gray, Randal and Christopher Argyle. 1990. *Chronicle of the First World War*. New York: Facts on File.

Greif, Avner. 2006. *Institutions and the Path to the Modern Economy: Lessons from Medieval Trade*. New York: Cambridge University Press.

Greif, Avner and David D. Laitin. 2004. A Theory of Endogenous Institutional Change. *American Political Science Review* 98 (4): 633–652.

Grey, C. G. 1942. *Bombers*. London: Faber and Faber.

Griffith, Paddy. 1994. *Battle Tactics of the Western Front: The British Army's Art of Attack, 1916–18*. New Haven, CT: Yale University Press.

Haber, L. F. 1986. *The Poisonous Cloud: Chemical Warfare in the First World War*. New York: Oxford University Press.

Halpern, Paul G. 1987. *The Naval War in the Mediterranean, 1914–1918*. Annapolis, MD: Naval Institute Press.

    1994. *A Naval History of World War I*. Annapolis, MD: Naval Institute Press.

Hammond, James W. 1999. *Poison Gas: The Myths versus Reality*. Westport, CT: Greenwood Press.

Hanson, Victor Davis. 2005. *A War Like No Other: How the Athenians and Spartans Fought the Peloponnesian War*. New York: Random House.

Harff, Barbara. 2003. No Lessons Learned from the Holocaust? Assessing Risks of Genocide and Political Mass Murder since 1955. *American Political Science Review* 97 (1): 57–73.

Harries, Meirion and Susie Harries. 1991. *Soldiers of the Sun: The Rise and Fall of the Imperial Japanese Army, 1868–1945*. London: Heinemann.

Harris, Robert and Jeremy Paxman. 2002. *A Higher Form of Killing*. New York: Random House.

Harsanyi, John C. and Reinhard Selten. 1988. *A General Theory of Equilibrium Selection in Games*. Cambridge, MA: MIT Press.

Hart, Oliver and John Moore. 1988. Incomplete Contracts and Renegotiation. *Econometrica* 56 (4): 755–785.

Hata, Ikuhiko. 1996. "From Consideration to Contempt: The Changing Nature of Japanese Military and Popular Perceptions of Prisoners of War through the Ages." In *Prisoners of War and their Captors in World War II*, eds. Bob Moore and Kent Fedorowich, 253–276. Washington, DC: Berg.

Hathaway, Oona A. 2002. Do Human Rights Treaties Make a Difference? *Yale Law Journal* 111 (June): 1935–2042.

——— 2005. Between Power and Principle: An Integrated Theory of International Law. *University of Chicago Law Review* 72 (Spring): 469–536.

Hattendorf, John B. 1994. "Maritime Conflict." In *The Laws of War: Constraints on Warfare in the Western world*, eds. Michael Eliot Howard, George J. Andreopoulos, and Mark R. Shulman, 98–115. New Haven, CT: Yale University Press.

Hayashi, Hirofumi. 2005. "Japanese Deserters and Prisoners of War in the Battle of Okinawa." In *Prisoners of War, Prisoners of Peace*, eds. Bob Moore and Barbara Hately-Broad, 49–58. New York: Berg.

Haynes, Michael. 2003. Counting Soviet Deaths in the Great Patriotic War: A Note. *Europe-Asia Studies* 55 (2): 303–309.

Heath, Joseph. 2001. *Communicative Action and Rational Choice*. Cambridge, MA: MIT Press.

Henckaerts, Jean-Marie, Louise Doswald-Beck, and International Committee of the Red Cross, eds. 2005. *Customary International Humanitarian Law*. New York: Cambridge University Press.

Henkin, Louis. 1979. *How Nations Behave: Law and Foreign Policy*. New York: Columbia University Press.

Herwig, Holger H. 1996. *The First World War: Germany and Austria-Hungary, 1914–1918*. London: Arnold.

Hilger, Andreas. 2005. "Re-educating the German Prisoners of War: Aims, Methods, Results and Memory in East and West Germany." In *Prisoners of War, Prisoners of Peace*, eds. Bob Moore and Barbara Hately-Broad, 61–75. New York: Berg.

Hofbauer, Josef and William H. Sandholm. 2002. On the Global Convergence of Stochastic Fictitious Play. *Econometrica* 70 (6): 2265–2294.

Holmes, Richard. 1985. *Acts of War: The Behavior of Men in Battle*. New York: Free Press.

Holmes, W. J. 1966. *Undersea Victory: The Influence of Submarine Operations on the War in the Pacific*. Garden City, NY: Doubleday.

Hopkins, Ed. 2002. Two Competing Models of How People Learn in Games. *Econometrica* 70 (6): 2141–2166.

Horne, John N. and Alan Kramer. 2001. *German Atrocities, 1914: A History of Denial*. New Haven, CT: Yale University Press.

Howard, Michael Eliot, George J. Andreopoulos, and Mark R. Shulman, eds. 1994. *The Laws of War: Constraints on Warfare in the Western World*. New Haven, CT: Yale University Press.

Hsèu, Lang-hsèuan and Ha-hsiung Wen. 1972. *History of the Sino-Japanese War, 1937–1945*. Taipei: Chung Wu Publishing Co.

Hurd, Ian. 2007. *After Anarchy: Legitimacy and Power in the United Nations Security Council*. Princeton, NJ: Princeton University Press.

Igarashi, Yoshikuni. 2005. "Belated Homecomings: Japanese Prisoners of War in Siberia and their Return to Post-War Japan." In *Prisoners of War, Prisoners of Peace*, eds. Bob Moore and Barbara Hately-Broad, 105–121. New York: Berg.

International Committee of the Red Cross. 1948. *Report of the International Committee of the Red Cross on its Activities during the Second World War, September 1, 1939-June 30, 1947.* Geneva: International Committee of the Red Cross.

Jackson, Robert. 1989. *The Prisoners, 1914–18.* London: Routledge.

Jepperson, Ronald L., Alexander Wendt, and Peter J. Katzenstein. 1996. "Norms, Identity, and Culture in National Security." In *The Culture of National Security: Norms and Identity in World Politics,* ed. Peter J. Katzenstein, 33–75. New York: Columbia University Press.

Jones, Heather. 2011. *Violence against Prisoners of War in the First World War.* Cambridge: Cambridge University Press.

Kalai, Ehud and Ehud Lehrer. 1993. Rational Learning Leads to Nash Equilibrium. *Econometrica* 61 (5): 1019–1045.

Kandori, Michihiro. 2003. Randomization, Communication, and Efficiency in Repeated Games with Imperfect Public Monitoring. *Econometrica* 71 (1): 345–353.

Kaplan, Morton A. and Nicholas deBelleville Katzenbach. 1961. *The Political Foundations of International Law.* New York: Wiley.

Katzenstein, Peter J. 1996. "Conclusion: National Security in a Changing World." In *The Culture of National Security: Norms and Identity in World Politics,* ed. Peter J. Katzenstein, 498–537. New York: Columbia University Press.

Keefer, Louis E. 1992. *Italian Prisoners of War in America, 1942–1946: Captives or Allies?* New York: Praeger.

Keegan, John. 1982. *Six Armies in Normandy: From D-Day to the Liberation of Paris, June 6th-August 25th, 1944.* London: Cape.

Keegan, John, ed. 1989. *The Times Atlas of the Second World War.* London: Times Books.

Keen, Maurice Hugh. 1965. *The Laws of War in the Late Middle Ages.* London: Routledge & K. Paul.

Keohane, Robert O. 1986. Reciprocity in International Relations. *International Organization* 40 (1): 1–27.

Kershaw, Ian. 2007. *Fateful Choices: Ten Decisions that Changed the World, 1940–1941.* New York: Penguin Press.

Kibata, Yoichi. 2000. "Japanese Treatment of British Prisoners of War: The Historical Context." In *Japanese Prisoners of War,* eds. Philip Towle, Margaret Kosuge, and Yoichi Kibata, 135–147. London: Hambleton and London.

Kindsvatter, Peter S. 2003. *American Soldiers: Ground Combat in the World Wars, Korea, and Vietnam.* Lawrence: University Press of Kansas.

King, Gary and Langche Zeng. 2006. The Dangers of Extreme Counterfactuals. *Political Analysis* 14 (2): 131–159.

2007. When Can History Be Our Guide? The Pitfalls of Counterfactual Inference. *International Studies Quarterly* 51 (1): 183–210.

Kinvig, Clifford. 2000. "Allied POWs and the Burma-Thailand Railway." In *Japanese Prisoners of War,* eds. Philip Towle, Margaret Kosuge, and Yoichi Kibata, 37–57. London: Hambleton and London.

Kladstrup, Don and Petie Kladstrup. 2001. *Wine and War: The French, the Nazis, and the Battle for France's Greatest Treasure.* New York: Broadway Books.

Kochavi, Arieh J. 2005. *Confronting Captivity: Britain and the United States and their POWs in Nazi Germany.* Chapel Hill: University of North Carolina Press.

Kostiner, Joseph. 1993. *The Making of Saudi Arabia, 1916–1936: From Chieftancy to Monarchical State.* New York: Oxford University Press.

Kosuge, Margaret. 2000. "Religion, the Red Cross and the Japanese Treatment of POWs." In *Japanese Prisoners of War*, eds. Philip Towle, Margaret Kosuge, and Yoichi Kibata, 149–161. London: Hambleton and London.

Kramer, Alan. 2007. *Dynamic of Destruction: Culture and Mass Killing in the First World War.* Oxford: Oxford University Press.

Kramer, Alan R. 2010. "Prisoners in the First World War." In *Prisoners in War*, ed. Sibylle Scheipers, 75–90. New York: Oxford University Press.

Krammer, Arnold. 1979. *Nazi Prisoners of War in America.* New York: Stein and Day.

Krasner, Stephen D. 1999. *Sovereignty: Organized Hypocrisy.* Princeton, NJ: Princeton University Press.

Kratochwil, Friedrich V. 1989. *Rules, Norms, and Decisions: On the Conditions of Practical and Legal Reasoning in International Relations and Domestic Affairs.* New York: Cambridge University Press.

Kreps, David M. 1990. *Game Theory and Economic Modelling.* New York: Oxford University Press.

Kreps, David M., Paul Milgrom, John Roberts, and Robert Wilson. 1982. Rational Cooperation in the Finitely Repeated Prisoners' Dilemma. *Journal of Economic Theory* 27 (2): 245–252.

Kydd, Andrew. 1997. Game Theory and the Spiral Model. *World Politics* 49 (3): 371–400.

——— 2000a. Arms Races and Arms Control: Modeling the Hawk Perspective. *American Journal of Political Science* 44 (2): 228–244.

——— 2000b. Trust, Reassurance, and Cooperation. *International Organization* 54 (2): 325–357.

Lael, Richard L. 1982. *The Yamashita Precedent: War Crimes and Command Responsibility.* Wilmington, DE: Scholarly Resources.

Leeds, Brett Ashley. 2003. Alliance Reliability in Times of War: Explaining State Decisions to Violate Treaties. *International Organization* 57 (4): 801–827.

Lefebure, Victor. 1923. *The Riddle of the Rhine: Chemical Strategy in Peace and War.* New York: E. P. Dutton & Co.

Legro, Jeffrey. 1995. *Cooperation under Fire: Anglo-German Restraint during World War II.* Ithaca, NY: Cornell University Press.

Levie, Howard S. 1986. *The Code of International Armed Conflict.* London: Oceana Publications.

Lewis, Michael W. 2003. The Law of Aerial Bombardment in the 1991 Gulf War. *American Journal of International Law* 97 (3): 481–509.

Li, Lincoln. 1975. *The Japanese Army in North China, 1937–1941: Problems of Political and Economic Control.* New York: Oxford University Press.

Linderman, Gerald F. 1997. *The World within War: America's Combat Experience in World War II.* New York: Free Press.

Lipkes, Jeff. 2007. *Rehearsals: The German Army in Belgium, August 1914.* Leuven: Leuven University Press.

Lippman, Matthew. 2002. Aerial Attacks on Civilians and the Humanitarian Law of War: Technology and Terror from World War I to Afghanistan. *California Western International Law Journal* 33 (1): 1–67.

Livy. 1948. *The History of Rome.* Trans. Benjamin Oliver Foster. Cambridge, MA: Harvard University Press.

MacKenzie, S. P. 1994. The Treatment of Prisoners of War in World War II. *Journal of Modern History* 66: 487–520.

1995. The Shackling Crisis: A Case-Study in the Dynamics of Prisoner-of-War Diplomacy in the Second World War. *International History Review* 17 (1): 78–98.

Mailath, George J. 1998. Do People Play Nash Equilibrium? Lessons from Evolutionary Game Theory. *Journal of Economic Literature* 36 (3): 1347–1374.

Maoz, Zeev and Bruce Russett. 1993. Normative and Structural Causes of Democratic Peace, 1946–1986. *American Political Science Review* 87 (3): 624–638.

Marshall, Logan. 1915. *Horrors and Atrocities of the Great War*. Philadelphia, PA: Lasher.

Marshall, Monty G. and Keith Jaggers. 2002. "Polity IV Dataset." Center for International Development and Conflict Management, University of Maryland.

Mawdsley, Evan. 2005. *Thunder in the East: The Nazi-Soviet War, 1941–1945*. London: Hodder Arnold.

Maynard Smith, John. 1982. *Evolution and the Theory of Games*. New York: Cambridge University Press.

McGinnis, Michael D. 1986. Issue Linkage and the Evolution of International Cooperation. *Journal of Conflict Resolution* 30 (1): 141–170.

McManus, John C. 1998. *The Deadly Brotherhood: The American Combat Soldier in World War II*. Novato, CA: Presidio.

Mearsheimer, John J. 1995a. The False Promise of International Institutions. *International Security* 19 (3): 5–49.

1995b. A Realist Reply. *International Security* 20 (1): 82–93.

2001. *The Tragedy of Great Power Politics*. 1st ed. New York: Norton.

Michno, Gregory. 2001. *Death on the Hellships: Prisoners at Sea in the Pacific War*. Annapolis, MD: Naval Institute Press.

Mikes, George. 1957. *The Hungarian Revolution*. London: A. Deutsch.

Milgrom, Paul, Douglass C. North, and Barry R. Weingast. 1990. The Role of Institutions in the Revival of Trade: The Medieval Law Merchant, Private Judges, and the Champagne Fairs. *Economics and Politics* 1 (March): 1–23.

Milgrom, Paul and John Roberts. 1982. Predation, Reputation, and Entry Deterrence. *Journal of Economic Theory* 27 (2): 280–312.

Millar, Ronald. 1970. *Death of an Army: The Siege of Kut, 1915–1916*. Boston, MA: Houghton Mifflin.

Milner, Helen. 1991. The Assumption of Anarchy in International Relations Theory: A Critique. *Review of International Studies* 17 (1): 67–85.

Moore, Bob. 1996. "Axis Prisoners in Britain during the Second World War: A Comparative Study." In *Prisoners of War and their Captors in World War II*, eds. Bob Moore and Kent Fedorowich, 19–46. Washington, DC: Berg.

2010. "The Treatment of Prisoners of War in the Western European Theatre of War, 1939–45." In *Prisoners in War*, ed. Sibylle Scheipers, 111–125. New York: Oxford University Press.

Moore, Bob and Kent Fedorowich. 1996. *Prisoners of War and their Captors in World War II*. Washington, DC: Berg.

Moorehead, Caroline. 1998. *Dunant's Dream: War, Switzerland and the History of the Red Cross*. London: HarperCollins.

Morgenthau, Hans Joachim. 1978. *Politics among Nations: The Struggle for Power and Peace*. 5th ed. New York: Knopf.

Morrow, James D. 1994a. *Game Theory for Political Scientists*. Princeton, NJ: Princeton University Press.

1994b. Modeling the Forms of International Cooperation: Distribution Versus Information. *International Organization* 48 (3): 387–423.

2001. The Institutional Features of the Prisoners of War Treaties. *International Organization* 55 (4): 971–991.

2002. "International Conflict: Assessing the Democratic Peace and Offense-Defense Theory." In *Political Science: State of the Discipline*, eds. Ira Katznelson and Helen V. Milner, 172–196. New York: Norton.

Morrow, James D. and Hyeran Jo. 2006. Compliance with the Laws of War: Dataset and Coding Rules. *Conflict Management and Peace Science* 23 (Spring): 93–113.

Murray, Williamson. 1985. *Luftwaffe*. Baltimore, MD: Nautical & Aviation Pub. Co.

Nachbar, John H. 1997. Prediction, Optimization, and Learning in Repeated Games. *Econometrica* 65 (2): 275–309.

Neillands, Robin. 2001. *The Bomber War: Arthur Harris and the Allied Bomber Offensive, 1939–1945*. London: John Murray.

Newbolt, Henry John Sir. 1928. *Naval Operations, Vol. IV*. London: Longmans, Green and Co.

North, Douglass Cecil. 1990. *Institutions, Institutional Change, and Economic Performance*. New York: Cambridge University Press.

O'Neill, Barry. 1999. *Honor, Symbols, and War*. Ann Arbor, MI: University of Michigan Press.

Ober, Josiah. 1991. "Hoplites and Obstacles." In *Hoplites: The Classical Greek Battle Experience*, ed. Victor Davis Hanson, 173–196. London: Routledge.

1994. "Classical Greek Times." In *The Laws of War: Constraints on Warfare in the Western World*, eds. Michael Eliot Howard, George J. Andreopoulos and Mark R. Shulman, 12–26. New Haven, CT: Yale University Press.

Oren, Michael. 2002. *Six Days of War: June 1967 and the Making of the Modern Middle East*. New York: Oxford University Press.

Ousby, Ian. 2002. *The Road to Verdun: World War I's Most Momentous Battle and the Folly of Nationalism*. New York: Doubleday.

Overmans, Rudiger. 2005. "The Repatriation of Prisoners of War once Hostilities are Over: A Matter of Course?" In *Prisoners of War, Prisoners of Peace*, eds. Bob Moore and Barbara Hately-Broad, 11–22. New York: Berg.

2010. "The Treatment of Prisoners of War in the Eastern European Theatre of Operations, 1941–56." In *Prisoners in War*, ed. Sibylle Scheipers, 127–140. New York: Oxford University Press.

Overy, Richard J. 1998. *Russia's War*. London: Allen Lane.

Padfield, Peter. 1995. *War beneath the Sea: Submarine Conflict during World War II*. New York: John Wiley.

Panayi, Panikos. 1993. "An Intolerant Act by an Intolerant Society: The Internment of Germans in Britain during the First World War." In *The Internment of Aliens in Twentieth Century Britain*, eds. David Cesarani and Tony Kushner, 53–78. London: Frank Cass.

Parks, W. Hays. 1990. Air War and the Law of War. *Air Force Law Journal* 32: 1–221.

Piccigallo, Philip R. 1979. *The Japanese on Trial: Allied War Crimes Operations in the East, 1945–1951*. Austin, TX: University of Texas Press.

References

Polian, Pavel. 2005. "The Internment of Returning Soviet Prisoners of War after 1945." In Prisoners of War, Prisoners of Peace, ed. Bob Moore and Barbara Hately-Broad, 123–139. New York: Berg.
Polyviou, Polyvios G. 1980. Cyprus, Conflict and Negotiation, 1960–1980. London: Duckworth.
Pouliot, Vincent. 2008. The Logic of Practicality: A Theory of Practice of Security Communities. International Organization 62 (2): 257–288.
Powell, Robert. 1994. Anarchy in International Relations Theory: The Neorealist-Neoliberal Debate. International Organization 48 (2): 313–344.
1999. In the Shadow of Power: States and Strategies in International Politics. Princeton, NJ: Princeton University Press.
Price, Richard M. 1997. The Chemical Weapons Taboo. Ithaca, NY: Cornell University Press.
Priebe, Eckehart J. 1990. Thank You, Canada: From Messerschmitt Pilot to Canadian Citizen. West Vancouver, BC: Condor Publishing.
Rachamimov, Alon. 2002. POWs and the Great War: Captivity on the Eastern Front. Oxford: Berg.
Raleigh, Walter Alexander and Henry Albert Jones. 1922. The War in the Air: Being the Story of the Part Played in the Great War by the Royal Air Force. Oxford: The Clarendon Press.
Ranft, Brian. 1979. "Restraints on War at Sea before 1945." In Restraints on War: Studies in the Limitation of Armed Conflict, ed. Michael Howard, 39–56. Oxford: Oxford University Press.
Reus-Smit, Christian. 1999. The Moral Purpose of the State: Culture, Social Identity, and Institutional Rationality in International Relations. Princeton, NJ: Princeton University Press.
Richter, Donald C. 1992. Chemical Soldiers: British Gas Warfare in World War I. Lawrence: University Press of Kansas.
Risse, Thomas. 2000. "Let's Argue!": Communicative Action in World Politics. International Organization 54 (1): 1–39.
Roberts, Adam. 1994. The Laws of War in the 1990–91 Gulf Conflict. International Security 18 (3): 134–181.
Roberts, Adam and Richard Guelff, eds. 2000. Documents on the Laws of War. Oxford: Oxford University Press.
Robin, Ron Theodore. 1995. The Barbed-wire College: Reeducating German POWs in the United States during World War II. Princeton, NJ: Princeton University Press.
Robinson, Julian Perry and Jozef Goldblat. May 1984. "Chemical Warfare in the Iraq-Iran War 1980–1988," SIPRI Fact Sheet. http://www.iranchamber.com/history/articles/chemical_warfare_iran_iraq_war.php.
Rosendorff, B. Peter. 2005. Stability and Rigidity: Politics and Design of the WTO's Dispute Settlement Procedure. American Political Science Review 99 (3): 389–400.
Rossino, Alexander B. 2003. Hitler Strikes Poland: Blitzkrieg, Ideology, and Atrocity. Lawrence: University Press of Kansas.
Rubinstein, Ariel. 1982. Perfect Equilibrium in a Bargaining Model. Econometrica 50 (1): 97–110.

Ruggie, John Gerard. 1998. What Makes the World Hang Together? Neo-Utilitarianism and the Social Constructivist Challenge. *International Organization* 52 (4): 855–885.

Russell of Liverpool, Edward Frederick Langley Russell Baron. 1958. *The Knights of Bushido: The Shocking History of Japanese War Atrocities*. New York: Dutton.

Sanchirico, Chris William. 1996. A Probabilistic Model of Learning in Games. *Econometrica* 64 (6): 1375–1393.

Sbacchi, Alberto. 1997. *Legacy of Bitterness: Ethiopia and Fascist Italy, 1935–1941*. Lawrenceville, NJ: Red Sea Press.

Schauer, Frederick F. 1991. *Playing by the Rules: A Philosophical Examination of Rule-based Decision-making in Law and in Life*. New York: Oxford University Press.

Schelling, Thomas C. 1960. *The Strategy of Conflict*. Cambridge, MA: Harvard University Press.

1966. *Arms and Influence*. New Haven, CT: Yale University Press.

Schindler, John R. 2001. *Isonzo: The Forgotten Sacrifice of the Great War*. Westport, CT: Praeger.

Schotter, Andrew. 1981. *The Economic Theory of Social Institutions*. New York: Cambridge University Press.

Schrijvers, Peter. 1998. *The Crash of Ruin: American Combat Soldiers in Europe during World War II*. New York: New York University Press.

2010. *Bloody Pacific: American Soldiers at War with Japan*. New York: Palgrave Macmillan.

Schultz, Kenneth A. 2001. *Democracy and Coercive Diplomacy*. New York: Cambridge University Press.

Schultz, Kenneth A. and Barry Weingast. 2003. The Democratic Advantage: Institutional Foundations of Financial Power in International Competition. *International Organization* 57 (1): 3–42.

Seuss, Dr. 1961. *The Sneetches, and Other Stories*. New York: Random House.

Shapley, Lloyd S. 1964. "Some Topics in Two-Person Games." In *Advances in Game Theory*, eds. Melvin Drescher, Lloyd S. Shapley, and A. W. Tucker, 1–28. Princeton, NJ: Princeton University Press.

Shepsle, Kenneth A. 1986. "Institutional Equilibrium and Equilibrium Institutions." In *The Science of Politics*, ed. Herbert Weisberg, 51–82. New York: Agathon.

Sherry, Michael S. 1987. *The Rise of American Air Power: The Creation of Armageddon*. New Haven, CT: Yale University Press.

Showalter, Dennis E. 1991. *Tannenberg: Clash of Empires*. Hamden, CT: Archon Books.

Simmons, Beth A. 2002. Capacity, Commitment, and Compliance: International Institutions and Territorial Disputes. *Journal of Conflict Resolution* 46 (6): 829–856.

Singer, J. David. 1987. Reconstructing the Correlates of War Dataset on Material Capabilities of States, 1816–1985. *International Interactions* 14: 115–132.

Singer, J. David, Stuart Bremer, and John Stuckey. 1972. "Capability Distribution, Uncertainty, and Major Power War, 1820–1965." In *Peace, War, and Numbers*, ed. Bruce Russett, 19–48. Beverly Hills, CA: Sage.

Slaughter, Anne-Marie. 1995. International Law in a World of Liberal States. *European Journal of International Law* 6 (4): 503–538.

Slim, Hugo. 2007. *Killing Civilians: Method, Madness and Morality in War.* London: Hurst & Co.

Small, Melvin and J. David Singer. 1982. *Resort to Arms: International and Civil Wars, 1816–1980.* Beverly Hills, CA: Sage Publications.

Smith, Alastair. 1998a. Fighting Battles, Winning Wars. *Journal of Conflict Resolution* 42 (3): 301–320.

1998b. International Crises and Domestic Politics. *American Political Science Review* 92 (3): 623–638.

Spaight, J. M. 1911. *War Rights on Land.* London: Macmillan.

Speed, Richard B. 1990. *Prisoners, Diplomats, and the Great War: A Study in the Diplomacy of Captivity.* New York: Greenwood Press.

Spiers, Edward M. 1986. *Chemical Warfare.* Urbana: University of Illinois Press.

2010. *A History of Chemical and Biological Weapons.* London: Reaktion.

Springer, Paul J. 2010. *America's Captives: Treatment of POWs from the Revolutionary War to the War on Terror.* Lawrence: University Press of Kansas.

Stein, Arthur A. 1990. *Why Nations Cooperate: Circumstance and Choice in International Relations.* Ithaca, NY: Cornell University Press.

Stevenson, David. 2004. *Cataclysm: The First World War as Political Tragedy.* New York: Basic Books.

Stockholm International Peace Research Institute (SIPRI). 1971. *The Problem of Chemical and Biological Warfare: A Study of the Historical, Technical, Military, Legal and Political Aspects of CBW, and Possible Disarmament Measures.* Stockholm: Almqvist & Wiksell.

Stone, Norman. 1975. *The Eastern Front, 1914–1917.* London: Hodder and Stoughton.

Straus, Ulrich. 2003. *The Anguish of Surrender: Japanese POW's of World War II.* Seattle: University of Washington Press.

Streim, Alfred. 1997. "International Law and Soviet Prisoners of War." In *From Peace to War: Germany, Soviet Russia and the World, 1939–1941*, ed. Bernd Wegner, 293–308. Providence, RI: Berghahn Books.

Streit, Christian. 2000. "Soviet Prisoners of War in the Hands of the Wehrmacht." In *War of Extermination: The German Military in World War II, 1941–1944*, eds. Hannes Heer and Klaus Naumann, 80–91. New York: Berghahn Books.

Tannenwald, Nina. 1999. The Nuclear Taboo: The United States and the Normative Basis of Nuclear Non-Use. *International Organization* 53 (3): 433–468.

Terraine, John. 1989. *Business in Great Waters: The U-boat wars, 1916–1945.* London: Cooper.

Thelen, Kathleen Ann. 2004. *How Institutions Evolve: The Political Economy of Skills in Germany, Britain, the United States, and Japan.* New York: Cambridge University Press.

Thomas, Martin. 1996. "Captives of their Countrymen: Free French and Vichy French POWs in Africa and the Middle East, 1940–3." In *Prisoners of War and their Captors in World War II*, eds. Bob Moore and Kent Fedorowich, 87–118. Washington, DC: Berg.

Thompson, Mark. 2008. *The White War: Life and Death on the Italian Front 1915–1919.* New York: Basic Books.

Towle, Philip. 2000. "The Japanese Army and Prisoners of War." In *Japanese Prisoners of War*, eds. Philip Towle, Margaret Kosuge, and Yoichi Kibata, 1–16. London: Hambleton and London.

2010. "Japanese Culture and the Treatment of Prisoners of War in the Asian-Pacific War." In *Prisoners in War*, ed. Sibylle Scheipers, 141–153. New York: Oxford University Press.

Towle, Philip, Margaret Kosuge, and Yoichi Kibata, eds. 2000. *Japanese Prisoners of War*. London: Hambledon and London.

Trager, Robert F. and Dessislava P. Zagorcheva. 2005. Deterring Terrorism: It Can Be Done. *International Security* 30 (3): 87–123.

Trumpener, Ulrich. 1975. The Road to Ypres: The Beginnings of Gas Warfare in World War I. *Journal of Modern History* 47 (3): 460–480.

Tsebelis, George. 1990. *Nested Games: Rational Choice in Comparative Politics*. Berkeley: University of California Press.

Tuchman, Barbara Wertheim. 1966. *The Proud Tower: A Portrait of the World before the War, 1890–1914*. New York: Macmillan.

Tucker, Spencer. 2004. *The Second World War*. New York: Palgrave Macmillan.

Valentino, Benjamin, Paul Huth, and Dylan Balch-Lindsay. 2004. "Draining the Sea": Mass Killing and Guerrilla Warfare. *International Organization* 58 (2): 375–407.

Valentino, Benjamin A., Paul K. Huth, and Sarah Croco. 2006. Covenants without the Sword: International Law and the Protection of Civilians in Times of War. *World Politics* 58 (3): 339–377.

Van der Vat, Dan. 1988. *The Atlantic Campaign: The Great Struggle at Sea, 1939–1945*. London: Hodder & Stoughton.

Vance, Jonathan F. 1994. *Objects of Concern: Canadian Prisoners of War through the Twentieth Century*. Vancouver, BC: UBC Press.

1995. Men in Manacles: The Shackling of Prisoners of War, 1942–1943. *Journal of Military History* 59 (3): 483–504.

Vance, Jonathan F., ed. 2000. *Encyclopedia of Prisoners of War and Internment*. Santa Barbara, CA: Abc-Clio.

Voeten, Erik. 2001. Outside Options and the Logic of Security Council Action. *American Political Science Review* 95 (4): 845–858.

Vourkoutiotis, Vasilis. 2003. *Prisoners of War and the German High Command: The British and American Experience*. Houndsmills, Basingstoke, Hampshire: Palgrave Macmillan.

Wagner, R. Harrison. 2000. Bargaining and War. *American Journal of Political Science* 44 (3): 469–484.

Wallace, Geoffrey P. R. 2012. Welcome Guests, or Inescapable Victims? The Causes of Prisoner Abuse in War. *Journal of Conflict Resolution* 56(6):955–981.

Waltz, Kenneth Neal. 1979. *Theory of International Politics*. Reading, MA: Addison-Wesley.

Waterford, Van. 1994. *Prisoners of the Japanese in World War II: Statistical History, Personal Narratives, and Memorials Concerning POWs in Camps and on Hellships, Civilian Internees, Asian Slave Laborers, and Others Captured in the Pacific Theater*. Jefferson, NC: McFarland.

Watson, Alexander. 2008. *Enduring the Great War: Combat, Morale, and Collapse in the German and British Armies, 1914–1918*. Cambridge: Cambridge University Press.

Watt, Donald Cameron. 1979. "Restraints on War in the Air before 1945." In *Restraints on War: Studies in the Limitation of Armed Conflict*, ed. Michael Howard, 57–77. New York: Oxford University Press.

Wendt, Alexander. 1992. Anarchy Is What States Make of It: The Social Construction of Power Politics. *International Organization* 46 (2): 391–425.

——. 1999. *Social Theory of International Politics.* New York: Cambridge University Press.

——. 2001. Driving with the Rearview Mirror: On the Rational Science of Institutional Design. *International Organization* 55 (4): 1019–1049.

Werth, Alexander. 1964. *Russia at War, 1941–1945.* London: Barrie and Rockliff.

Williamson, Oliver E. 1985. *The Economic Institutions of Capitalism: Firms, Markets, Relational Contracting.* New York: Free Press.

Wilson, Peter H. 2010. "Prisoners in Early Modern European Warfare." In *Prisoners in War*, ed. Sibylle Scheipers, 39–56. New York: Oxford University Press.

Winter, Denis. 1978. *Death's Men: Soldiers of the Great War.* London: Allen Lane.

Wylie, Neville. 2010a. "The 1929 Prisoner of War Convention and the Building of the Inter-War Prisoner of War Regime." In *Prisoners in War*, ed. Sibylle Scheipers, 91–108. New York: Oxford University Press.

——. 2010b. *Barbed Wire Diplomacy: Britain, Germany, and the Politics of Prisoners of War, 1939–1945.* Oxford: Oxford University Press.

Yin, James, Young Shi, and Ron Dorfman. 1997. *The Rape of Nanking: An Undeniable History in Photographs.* expanded 2nd ed. Chicago, IL: Innovative Publishing Group.

Young, H. Peyton. 1998. *Individual Strategy and Social Structure: An Evolutionary Theory of Institutions.* Princeton, NJ: Princeton University Press.

Zetterling, Niklas and Anders Frankson. 2008. *The Korsun Pocket: The Encirclement and Breakout of a German Army in the East, 1944.* Havertown, PA: Casemate.

# Index

aerial bombing
  accounts for noncompliance by democracies,
    121, 131, 176
  clarification of coding of violations on, 154
  efforts to limit during interwar period, 251
  escalation of during World War II, 251–252
  Hague Conventions provisions on,
    247–248
  ideas on during the interwar period, 250
  inaccuracy at night, 252
  inaccuracy of and the problem of noise,
    248–249
  inaccuracy of during World War II, 253
  inaccuracy of strategic bombing, 249
  lack of clarity of law concerning during
    World War II, 251
  predictions of model about, 82
  strategic bombing of Germany during World
    War II, 252–253
  strategic bombing of Japan during World
    War II, 253–254
  summary of lack of restraint in World War
    II, 254
  V-weapons used by Germans for, 253
  in World War I, 249–250
Afghanistan war 2001, 301
appeals to universal values as mechanism of
    change in norms, 280
armistice
  clarification of coding of violations on, 155
  nonproportional hazards in survival
    analysis, 189
  predictions of model about, 84

*Athenia*
  sunk by submarine during World War II, 260
audience costs
  as mechanism for law and norms, 113
  as mechanism to enforce legal
    obligations, 114
Austria-Hungary
  blockade of by Great Britain and France
    during World War I, 257–258
  did not attack hospital ships during World
    War I, 259
  treatment of civilians during World War I,
    266–267
autocracy
  hold life in less regard as explanation for
    noncompliance, 114

Bari
  chemical weapons accident at, 245
Battle of the Sexes game
  definition of, 51
on the battlefield model
  best reply correspondences in, 92–94
  formal statement of, 90–94
  formal statement of equilibria, 90–91
  informal description of, 72–74
  informal description of equilibria in, 73–74
  proof of equilibria, 91
  strategic expectations in, 94
  strategic logic of, 91–92
Belgium
  German atrocities against civilians during
    World War I, 265–266

Keohane, Robert, 46
Kosovo war 1999, 301

law
  codifies norms, 55
  establishes common conjecture, 55
  as incomplete contract, 57
  induces strategic dynamics, 18
  versus flexibility of state decisions, 317
  versus norms, 274
Law Merchant game, 48
law of war
  bright lines in, 81–82
  can increase legitimacy of use of force, 32
  clarity of, 66
  combat model vs. criminal model, 305–306
  combatant as identity in, 31
  deliberate violations of, 63–64
  description of, 60–63
  differences across issues in compliance and
    reciprocity, 116
  history of, 61
  how different issues pose different
    challenges, 71
  how it addresses the three strategic
    problems, 71
  how they create restraint, 15–17
  how they restrict violence, 61–62
  hypotheses on compliance with, 86–88
  implications of model for specific
    issues, 82–86
  inadvertent violations, 68–69
  in the Middle Ages, 306
  noise in, 62
  obligations for soldiers, 63
  opportunistic defection from, 64–65
  perfidy, 69–70
  practical problem of noise, 67–68
  practical problems at the individual
    level, 67–70
  practical problems at the state level, 63–67
  as self-enforcing institution, 8
  self-interested interpretation of, 65–67
  specific issues in. (*see* aerial bombing;
    armistice; chemical and biological
    weapons; civilians: treatment of;
    cultural property: protection of;
    declaration of war; high seas, conduct
    on; prisoners of war (POWs); wounded,
    treatment of)
  strategic expectations produced by, 58
  strategic logic of, 59
  strategic logic of combat model, 307–309

strengths and weakness of with respect to
    terrorism, 311–312
  three strategic problems facing, 70–71
  violations by individuals, 68
law-bound states
  democracies, 114
legal clarity
  about aerial bombing in Hague
    Conventions, 247–248
  effect on compliance and reciprocity, 124
  effect on reciprocity in statistical
    analysis, 175
  effect on reciprocity in the dyad, 180
  how lack of contributed to spread of aerial
    bombing during World War II, 254
  lack of concerning aerial bombing during
    World War II, 251
  lack of opened space for self-interested
    interpretations, 275
legal clarity of violations
  coding for, 150
legal obligation. *See also* joint ratification
  influence on compliance and reciprocity, 113
  interaction with regime type in producing
    compliance, 131
  regime type and, 113
  two views of, 113
legal principles
  as way to deal with disagreements, 56
legitimacy
  definition of, 32
  of international law always in question, 320
  and power in world politics, 319–320
  rests on shared understanding, 32
Legro, Jeffrey
  critique of his argument about military
    culture, 270–271
  response to his argument about military
    culture on aerial bombing, 254–256
  summary of his argument about military
    culture, 270
Lieber Code
  for POWs, 296
lifeworld
  shared understanding of meaning, 32
*Llandovery Castle*
  sunk by Germany, 259
London Declaration 1909
  provisions for conduct on the high seas, 257
London Treaty for the Limitation and
    Reduction of Naval Armaments 1930
  tried to limit submarine warfare during the
    interwar period, 260

survival analysis
  of first violations, 136
  general description of technique, 186
  of responses to first violations, 138
survival analysis of first violations
  details of statistical analysis, 183–191
Sylvester McMonkey McBean, 49

take-it-or-leave-it bargaining game
  definition of, 27
temptation
  on specific issues, 82
temptation in on the battlefield model
  definition of, 72
terrorism, 309–314
  attacks between the criminal and combat
    models, 309
  criminal model and, 309–311
  judging which model to use, 313–314
  and legitimatization of violence, 314
  strengths and weakness of combat model
    for, 311–312
  third model for, 312–313
Thelen, Kathleen
  critique of *How Institutions Evolve*,
    291–293
Tit-for-Tat equilibrium of iterated Prisoners'
  Dilemma, 35
Tit-for-Tat equilibrium with Errors in Moves
  equilibrium
  inefficiency of, 42
Tit-for-Tat with Errors in Moves Equilibrium
  in iterated Prisoners' Dilemma, 41
Tokyo
  firebombing of, 254
total compliance
  definition of measure, 123
Treaty of Paris 1856
  provisions for conduct on the high
    seas, 256
treaty ratification. *See* ratification of treaties
treaty standards
  clearer than norms or customary law, 17
trials for war crimes
  after World War I, 267

UN Security Council
  military intervention and, 319
unified command
  used in measure of relative power, 162
unilateral obligation
  liabilities of for international law, 316–317

unilateral restraint by democracies
  effect of, 121
United Kingdom. *See* Great Britain
United States
  brutality of soldiers towards the Japanese,
    228–229
  conduct on the high seas by during World
    War II, 262
  did not ratify 1925 Geneva Protocol on
    CBW, 244
  did not ratify all provisions of Hague
    Conventions for conduct on the high
    seas, 257
  efforts to encourage enemy soldiers to
    surrender, 216
  entered World War I against Germany in
    part because of German submarine
    attacks, 259
  preparations for chemical warfare during
    World War II, 245
  public opinion on POWs, 210, 213
  reaction to British blockade of Germany
    during World War I, 257
  reasons for not using chemical weapons
    against Japan during World
    War II, 244
  role in negotiation of 1929 Geneva
    Convention on POWs, 297
  strategic bombing of Germany during World
    War II, 252–253
  strategic bombing of Japan during World
    War II, 253–254
  treatment of civilians during World War
    II, 269
  treatment of German POWs after World
    War II, 231
  treatment of Italian POWs after surrender in
    World War II, 232
  treatment of Japanese POWs held after
    World War II, 232
universalism of international law
  liabilities of, 315–316

Valentino, Benjamin
  critique of his argument about civilian
    victimization, 271–274
violations by individuals
  POW cases as hypothesis test of, 238
  scope for across issues, 127–128
von Ribbentrop, Joachim
  charged with encouraging the lynching of
    downed airmen, 212